BETHLEHEM CHURCH

AND ITS PASTOR;

OR,

A NARRATIVE OF THE INJURIOUS PROCEEDINGS

OF THE

REV. MESSRS. ALBERT BARNES AND H. W. [illegible]

IN RELATION TO THE PASTOR OF

THE PRESBYTERIAN CHURCH, BETHLEHEM, NEW JERSEY.

BY ROBERT W. LANDIS.

Hath God forgotten to be gracious? Hath he in anger shut up his tender mercies? And I said this in my infirmity: but I will remember the years of the right hand of the most High.—*Psalm* lxxvii. 9, 10.

PRINTED FOR THE AUTHOR.

1851.

ADVERTISEMENT.

I now lay before the reader, in a printed form, a work which, for more than a year, has been circulated in manuscript. I am advised still to withhold it from *publication*, in hope that the timely repentance of those whose injurious conduct it exposes, may yet render that truly painful but unretraceable step unnecessary. The reader may see on every page that it was prepared for publication: but as I have no personal resentments to gratify, and aim solely to benefit the church of God, and the transgressors themselves, I am not unwilling to indulge the hope (faint as it is) that this end may be secured by the course suggested. The work is therefore merely *printed*, with the view of distributing it amongst the parties interested, and of placing it in the hands of some judicious friends. I, myself, shall see that the Rev. Messrs. Barnes and Hunt are supplied with copies. I would state, however, that should any attempt be made to take advantage of this forbearance, or to inflict further injustice and injury upon the writer and his friends, the only alternative that will then remain will be immediately to publish the work, and scatter it, broad-cast, over the land.

He would also here take occasion to express his gratitude to those friends who have read the work in manuscript and have favored him with their valuable suggestions.

Robert W. Landis.

Hillsdale, N. Y., *September* 25, 1851.

CONTENTS.

PREFACE.

The object of this Tract is soon told. Some time since, an effort was made to destroy the character of a laborious and successful minister of Jesus Christ, by the adoption of measures which are herein succinctly delineated. That effort not only failed of accomplishing its aim, but was, with fearful power, rebounding upon its projectors, when a clergyman in Philadelphia stepped forward, and so employed both his influence and endeavors as in some degree to secure the result which had been sought by the projectors themselves. The reader's attention is earnestly solicited to the facts of the case, and may God guide him to that conclusion in relation thereto which is according to truth and righteousness.

Reputation, in the necessity of the case, is, and must be, dear to every man who desires to promote the glory of God and the welfare of his fellow-men. In certain circumstances it may be right to disregard the expressed sentiments and judgment of the world, for the world has not unfrequently decided erroneously in relation to the motives, acts and characters of men, and has acknowledged as much by subsequently reversing its decisions. The circumstances, therefore, which may warrant a disregard for the present judgment of our fellow-men, are those wherein duty to God requires us to adopt a course which they disapprove, or where they judge unfavorably of us from prejudice, or from an imperfect knowledge of facts. In such a case the individual, without regarding such erroneous judgments, may continue fearlessly in the same path of duty, and with confidence leave his motives and actions to the Providence of God, and to the decision of other times. But so far as man's reputation is in his own power and keeping, so far is he responsible for whatever influence it exerts. For example: when important facts in relation to an individual are falsified by his enemies, and consequently misunderstood by those who rely on their statements; and when this misapprehension exerts an unhappy influence in relation to himself and religion, I conceive that he is bound to furnish the means necessary to enable his fellow-men to understand the matter correctly; and that he is bound to do this at every sacrifice and at all hazards.* This course, however, is not necessary in cases which are at best but unimportant or trivial, and whose effect is only partial and temporary; for "he is indeed a poor warder of his fame who is ever on the watch to keep it spotless," and who is nervously anxious always to trace up and correct every trifling misapprehension in relation to himself. Such a course evinces, in either man or woman, no small degree of weakness; and no mind which is truly aiming at great and noble ends will descend to it. Purity of motive and intention will elevate the soul above such weakness, and in no trivial matter will it stoop "to prove its rights or prate its wrongs, or attempt to prove its worth to others."

The subject on which I thus come before my fellow-citizens is of high importance to myself and to the Church of God, and I believe with the fullest confidence that, as a member of their community, I shall be heard with all proper respect and attention. They will decide whether the occasion is too trivial to demand an effort like this, and whether an appeal based upon such grounds is worthy of being regarded. My enemies have already too long imposed upon mankind, and abused the credit which has been given to their insinuations and misstatements. What innocence can be so universally known, as not to suffer some stain from the unblushing calumnies of men who, under the garb of religion, conceal souls so utterly destitute of every vestige of it, as

*It is a well known maxim that *De non apparentibus, et non existentibus, eadem est ratio. The same conclusion is drawn in respect to things which do not appear, as in respect to those which do not exist.* Though, as an old writer remarks, "We are not *always* to conclude that a wise man is not hurt, because he doth not cry out and lament himself, like those of a childish and effeminate temper."

coolly to perpetrate a crime like slander? It is time that my own reputation, and that of my beloved but cruelly slandered and injured congregation and friends in Jersey, should be restored. And it is high time that in such matters Christian principle should begin to show itself in the conduct of those who profess to be actuated by it; and that the malignant traducer, when he whispers abroad that "*A person of honor*, who would not have his name mentioned, told some terrible things against Mr. So-and-so," should be instantly reminded that he is both a liar and a slanderer.* The whole matter, however, in all its relations, has been laid before a good God, and I am assured that his Providence will conduct it to such a consummation as shall redound most to his own glory, and the good of his blood-purchased church.

The injury done to myself and to religion, in the matter referred to, being so disproportionate to the *apparent* means by which it was effected, many, who knew the asserted facts in the case, have, with reason, wondered at the discrepancy. I apprehend that the attentive reader may, in the subjoined narrative, discover the real element or ingredient which has been mingled in my cup of sorrow, and which has produced fogs and clouds that nothing now can dissipate unless the thunderings and dissolving fires of truth. We shall then, I am persuaded, so far as our little portion of this great world is concerned, have a serene atmosphere. The lightning may strike and rive, but it will be those only who have madly continued to expose themselves to its power.

The reasons why I thus appeal to the Christian public may be briefly stated: they are,

1. Because I am under the necessity of meeting my enemies before the tribunal at which they have been secretly assailing me. They have, in every conceivable way, though by an underhand process, been operating to destroy me in the public estimation; and their reasons for this procedure are still in the dark. They have never adopted an open and frank course, so as to allow to me the opportunity of joining issue with them in their slanderous statements; but all the appliances in their power have secretly been brought to bear against me, especially in Philadelphia. I have been made to feel the effect of such a course, without being allowed the least opportunity to confront the individuals who were so destitute of all the principles of honor and integrity as to resort to it: for brethren, who ought to have known better, have, without further inquiry, received their sinister statements as true.

2. Because it is just and proper that individuals who act in this manner, should be compelled to give to their statements an open and tangible form and character.

3. Because it is desirable to ascertain whether an individual assailed, as I have been, by a spirit of envy or literary jealousy, and for whom the conventional rules of proceeding furnish no redress, has indeed any resource. It is desirable that this question should be thoroughly tested.

4. Because by this procedure of mine, no undue advantage is taken of the clergyman who is principally concerned in the matter. He himself has all along been secretly assailing me in the way and by the means brought partially to view in this narrative. I feel called upon, therefore, to ask for a reversion of the incorrect judgment which has thus improperly and to some extent been obtained. I have moreover informed this individual of my intention to make this appeal, for I scorned to take him unprepared. He is also at leisure; is accustomed to the use of the pen; and if his course of conduct can be defended, he doubtless can defend it: and if I have done him injustice, or misstated the case, or attempted to give a coloring to facts which they will not bear, he is well able to make it appear. Let him therefore have the opportunity to be fairly and fully and patiently heard before ultimate judgment is pronounced in the case. I am aware that this is asking for him the very reverse of what he wished to allow to me; but it is nevertheless, just and proper; and only what every honest man would desire in his own and in every case.

To the tribunal of the Christian public, therefore, I make my appeal. If my enemy is unwilling to meet me openly at this bar, which he has so long been endeavoring secretly to influence against me, I am indifferent as to what other course he may see proper to pursue. I have disdained all attempts to strike a blow covertly or so as to evade its responsibility. It will however, be in vain for him to attempt by further art or management, or by civil processes either *in propria persona*, or by representatives in Jersey, to prevent this matter from undergoing a thorough investigation. No lie is endowed with the attribute of immortality: and it is the purpose neither of myself

* Or, as the honest Capuchin has it, "*Mentiris impudentissime.*" See Pascal's Letters, Let. 15.

nor of my friends, who are acquainted with this matter, to allow it to evaporate in a silly personal controversy, or false issues. *The facts of this narrative must be fairly and fully met.* My own statements throughout are clear and definite. And I trust that the public will not permit my adversary with impunity to resort to equivocations, anonymous insinuations and what not: and that they will not permit themselves to be at all influenced by vague indefinite denials, or charges of *coloring* the facts herein recorded. Conscious guilt will ever seek by some such course to avoid a fair and open issue; but truth and candor disdain it. If the facts herein stated be falsely colored, therefore, let them be presented in their true light, (for nothing could then be easier) that so a full and fair and direct issue may at once be joined. And if they are correctly stated, then let justice be done to the suffering church of the Redeemer, and also to the guilty cause of all her sorrows.

This history was prepared soon after the occurrences took place which it describes. Its publication was delayed unavoidably, for reasons which need not be here specified, but which will be developed in the course of the concluding part of the narrative. But as I seek not so much to regain the good opinion of those who have, without inquiry or sufficient evidence, treated me as guilty, as to do essential service to the church of God by calling attention to those principles of the gospel which in this age are so grievously overlooked by many in their treatment of persons who are accused, I have in no wise been anxious to anticipate the provisions of Providence for laying it before the world. In fact I know not but that I should have continued to withhold it had I not perceived still in the individual principally referred to, an unabating determination to ride me to death on the cruel and heartless calumnies which are here exposed; and that with many they were successful beyond my expectation. Religion was thus injured through my silence and forbearance; and I felt that it would be but little short of moral suicide to myself, and treason to the cause of God, to continue to withhold a true statement of the matter.

During my severe trials I never solicited either the sympathy or assistance of any one, and yet the Lord has raised me up a multitude of faithful and devoted friends, who, notwithstanding all that cunning and malignity could effect to alienate them from me, have continued steadfast. There are those who, like shadows, will adhere to you while you walk in sunshine, but who, like them, will also forsake you so soon as you depart out of it, and will even seek to unite their own obscuring influence to that of the shade you enter. There are others who can decide with certainty that you are guilty of an alleged offence, if only Mr. So-and-so asserts it; "for he can have no improper feelings to gratify by such a statement." On such grounds, not a few professed friends have deserted me, claiming to be influenced by either the direct or indirect statements of an individual whom *they* presumed to be candid and unbiassed, but who in reality is the very man that from the most disreputable motives was seeking my ruin. This fact will probably furnish a useful lesson to such persons. And it may not be amiss to hint to those who, on such grounds, have been so ready and willing to treat a Christian brother thus, that there are others in this great world besides themselves; and that there is still, perhaps, another generation or two to come after the one which is now upon the stage, a generation or two by which their own conduct will be reviewed and tried, and the question soberly settled, whether such a course is exactly conformable to the precepts of Him whose servants they profess to be; and that there is also another tribunal at which this matter is to be reviewed by Him who said, "Inasmuch as ye have done it unto one of the least of these my brethren, ye have done it unto me." But for myself I really have not thought it worth an effort to regain the professed friendship of persons who could thus sacrifice it as they have done, upon a mere baseless inference. And knowing that sooner or later God would disappoint my enemies, and raise me out of all my sorrows, I was in no wise displeased to have such *friendships* brought to such a termination. Let it be final as regards the present life.

I mean not, however, to employ this language offensively, but merely as importing that *friendships thus severed* never can be perfectly renewed in this world. While they lasted they were very dear and delightful to my heart; and I supposed them to be based upon Christian principle, and that they would be regulated by the laws of Christ's house. Had these brethren treated me as I should have treated them (if our cases were reversed), and as I have always treated any reputedly erring brother, they would not have *inferred* that any unfavorable representation of myself *must* be fair and unbiassed, until they had had the opportunity of *knowing* at least something more of the matter as relating both to the accuser and accused; and until they had also had the opportunity for hearing my own statement; and this they would have directly sought for. And more especially ought they to have done this, since they saw that my name was still upon their ecclesiastical records, evincing me to be in as good and regular standing as they are, even in the church itself. This would have been doing to me as they (in a case similar to mine) would wish to have others do to them, and in this way alone is there the least possibility for the slandered to have justice shown him at the hands of brethren. But instead of this they have *first*, willingly listened to the representations emanating directly or indirectly from Mr. Barnes. *Secondly*, They have allowed me no opportunity for confronting him, or of disproving these representations; and *finally*, they have *inferred* that his representations *must be true and unbiassed;* and upon the strength of this most false and injurious inference they have ever since treated me, not as a brother, or even as a stranger; but "as a heathen man and a publican." In this manner their influence has gone to support my enemies in their efforts to ruin and destroy me. I have not complained of this, and I shall not. The matter is between those brethren and that God whose I am, and to whom they are responsible for the use which they voluntarily make of their influence. I shall, however, not have suffered in vain, if these things only result in calling the church of Christ away from all such worldly policy to the proper observance of the rules which He has ordained.

Hillsdale, New York, May 25, 1850.

ERRATA.

For reasons which need not be here mentioned the author was unable to revise the proofs, and in consequence a few errata have been printed.

Page 25, line 40, for *I* read *and.*
" 27, line 1, for *strictness* read *strictures.*
" 30, line 1, for *voted down* read *not seconded.*
" 36, *note*, line 3, for *disposed* read *disproved.*
" 38, line 1, for *serving* read *saving.*
" 39, line 9, after *and* read *as I am informed.*
" 46, line 15, for *observations* read *asseverations.*
" 56, line 9, for *late* read *later.*
" " line 11, for *Morristown* read *Norristown.*
" 74, *note*, line 11 from bottom, for *there* read *then.*
" 85, line 25 from bottom, for *efforts* read *effort.*
" " line 23–24 from bottom, for *deservedly* read *decidedly.*
" 94, line 15, for *bold* read *bald.*
" 102, line 5, for *who* read *he.*
" " line 10, after *permitted* read *to retain.*
" 106, line 13, after *then* read *I.*
" 117, line 14 from bottom, for *case* read *request.*
" 127, line 25 from bottom, for *this* read *their.*
" 139, line 15 from bottom, for *statements* read *abatements.*
" 161, line 28, for *point* read *present.*
" 184, line 12, for *examples* read *example.*
" 195, line 15, for *even* read *ever.*
" 197, line 2 from bottom, for *on* read *up.*
" 201, line 17 from bottom, for *causeless* read *ceaseless.*
" 202, line 25, for *them* read *themselves.*

BETHLEHEM CHURCH AND ITS PASTOR.

PART I.

THE CASE STATED.

CHAPTER I.

INTRODUCTORY AND HISTORICAL.

Many events connected with the recent history of the Presbyterian Church of Bethlehem, New Jersey, have excited a considerable degree of interest in the public mind, and I enter upon the task of narrating them at the earnest solicitation of multitudes, who, like myself, entertain the hope that the history thus furnished will be of signal usefulness (at least to the Church of God) for many years to come. Such, too, is my earnest and heart-felt prayer. But I cannot present a full and satisfactory view of the subject without referring to the antecedent history of the church. This shall be done, however, with as much brevity as the necessity of the case will allow.

The Bethlehem Church was founded about A.D. 1730; and the pulpit was for a number of years furnished with supplies by Presbytery. At length a call was made out for the services of the Rev. James M'Crea, (father of Miss Jane M'Crea, who was butchered by the savages belonging to Burgoyne's army;) but though he consented to supply the pulpit in part, for several years, he ultimately refused to settle as pastor. Finally the Rev. Thomas Lewis, a graduate of Yale, was applied to, who accepted the call; and in October, 1747, was installed as pastor over the Bethlehem Church and the two associate churches of Kingwood and Alexandria (sometimes called Upper Bethlehem). In 1761 he was succeeded by the Rev. John Hanna, who continued the faithful and unwearied pastor of the charge during a period of forty years.

Dr. Hanna, Mr. Lewis, and their predecessors, who supplied this charge with the ministrations of the gospel, were all thoroughly Presbyterian, both in church polity and doctrine. Every member of the congregation, as far as practicable, was made acquainted, not only with the Bible, as such, but with its system of doctrines as presented in the symbols of the Church. The various benevolent operations, in the promotion of which the American Presbyterian Church was then engaged, received the decided countenance and support of both pastor and people: while the children and youth of the charge were regularly instructed in the Westminster catechisms.

Such continued to be the state of things till in 1801, when Dr. Hanna died in charge. His removal was greatly lamented by his people; for though, as a disciplinarian he was rigid and stern, he was nevertheless most kind-hearted and self-sacrificing as a man and a friend. All the people of his charge believed him to be honestly desirous of doing them good, and regarded him as a faithful ambassador of God. His memory is still fragrant, and he is embalmed in the hearts of all who recollect him.

It was about eight or ten years previous to Dr. Hanna's death, that a tall young man, poor, but rather of prepossessing appearance, stopped at the residence of one of the trustees of the congregation, (Colonel Charles Stewart, of Washington's military staff,) and announced himself to be "a Methodist circuit-rider;" he stated also that his views of theology had undergone a radical change, and that, though he wished to enter the ministry in the Presbyterian church, he had not the requisite funds to complete his education. Col. Stewart brought the matter before the board of trustees, (of which General Maxwell, of revolutionary celebrity, was a member,) and also introduced the person to Dr. Hanna. Funds were accordingly raised, and the individual referred to, (being then about twenty-seven years of age,) was supported for a year or two in his studies; after which he was licensed by Presbytery to preach the gospel; whereupon (as he himself informed me,) he added to his paternal cognomen the name of *Whitfield*, making it Holloway *Whitfield* Hunt. Being of rather a popular address, he was, on the death of Dr. Hanna, finally selected to be his successor.

It might appear invidious were I to dilate upon the points of contrast between Dr. Hanna and this his successor. Mr. Hunt, however, continued pastor about as long as Dr. Hanna had done, though during that period the character of the charge underwent so utter a change that it ultimately ceased to be regarded as Presbyterian. Bethlehem church was split into factions, one of which separated from the rest, and erected the Presbyterian church in Clinton; while the remaining portion became extensively incorporated with the Unitarians. Kingwood church separated itself wholly from its associate sister churches, peremptorily refusing to continue any longer under his watch and care; while the church at Alexandria (now called Mount Pleasant,) became so utterly extinct, as regards ecclesiastical organization and efficiency, that the Unitarians had controlling possession of the ground. In fact, when their views became popular in that region, (which was in 1828 to 1830 inclusive,) Mr. Hunt advised his people to unite with them, "as they would then help to pay the salary." However strange this may now appear, it is nevertheless a well known fact. The venerable John Bloom, elder of the church, remonstrated against this procedure, but in vain. To Mr. Hunt's own mind the argument for this union had all the force of a mathematical demonstration: connected as it was with the fact that for a number of years the salary had been moving on at a very halting pace, like the tail of a wounded snake. The tail end of it had, since Dr. Hanna's death, become entangled with some thorny immovable obstacle in such a way that the folds of the Gordian knot itself were perfectly plain in comparison: and the gold of the Unitarians seemed to possess all the virtues and edge of Alexander's sword.

It affords me no pleasure to find myself under the necessity of narrating facts of such a nature. I relate, however, those only which are necessary in order to enable the reader to form an accurate judgment in relation to the whole subject which is to be brought before him; and I am entirely willing to abide by the decision of the candid on the question whether any unnecessary facts of this nature are brought forward.

In 1837-8, Mr. Hunt having abandoned and denounced the standards of the Presbyterian church, and committed many other irregularities, was arraigned on several charges before the Newton Presbytery; and amongst other things, falsehood of a grave import was said to have been established against him.* But while Presbytery was about to suspend or depose him from the gospel ministry, he with great dexterity slipped the ecclesiastical noose from over his head and renounced their jurisdiction. The churches of Bethlehem and Alexandria then became independent, and so continued for little more than a year: at the end of which period the people insisted so strongly upon being connected with some Presbytery, that Mr. Hunt, whose obvious intention was "to live and die Rector of Bray," was compelled to acquiesce. He accordingly made application to several Presbyteries to be received, but was refused. At length, in the fall of 1839, he with the churches of his charge, applied to be received into fellowship with the Third Presbytery of Philadelphia. The Presbytery being desirous to save the churches if possible, deliberated upon the matter for some time: but finally hesitated to receive them, on account of the superadded encumbrance of Mr. Hunt. One member of the body, (Rev. Mr. Barnes,) openly declared during the deliberation, that he could have no confidence in the integrity of Mr. Hunt: from whom he had lately received a *double* letter, which he (Mr. Hunt,) had superscribed "*single*" on the outside. The question of reception was however finally postponed.

The application was renewed by Mr. Hunt in April, 1840, at the meeting of Presbytery in Philadelphia. He had had a meeting of both congregations, and brought along with him a number of his most influential friends as delegates. But just before the application was formally renewed, and while Mr. Hunt and his delegates were all present, a church in the interior of Pennsylvania had applied to be taken into connection with the Presbytery: and whose application was promptly refused, on the ground that there were several "liquor sellers" in good and regular standing in its communion. These men stood high in the community, and came forward expressing themselves willing to furnish any pledge or security which Presbytery might require, that they would abandon their business utterly by the following autumn; provided the church was now admitted. All was, however, of no avail; the application was promptly and (I believe) unanimously rejected. After witnessing this decided action of Presbytery, Mr. Hunt and his delegates (four besides himself) came forward and renewed their request to be received; and not only were they in general decidedly anti-temperance in their views, but one of the number, (Peter Sigler,) was himself a distiller of "apple whisky" on a large scale; while Mr. Hunt him-

* See *Letter of Newton Presbytery*, in *Hunterdon Gazette*, Feb. 28, 1838.

self was in the habit of annually turning the produce of his very large orchards into whisky. He does so still. These facts were, of course, then unknown to Presbytery.

From the apparently open and frank manner in which this application was now renewed by Mr. Hunt, after the pointed refusal of the delegates aforesaid, it was of course rationally inferred that there were no distillers nor liquor sellers in communion with the churches which he and his friends represented. Hence the question was not even propounded to them, if I recollect rightly; at all events it was not done in my hearing. But as several members of the Presbytery had heard of various aberrations of Mr. Hunt—it was unanimously concluded to propound to him the following queries, to each of which he was required to give an affirmative answer in writing.

"1. Do you believe the doctrine of personal election, and that God from all eternity elected some of mankind to everlasting life?

"2. That in perfect consistency with this, God has endued man with liberty of will, so that it is neither forced to good, nor to evil, and that if men perish it is because they choose death?

"3. Do you approve of the various benevolent operations of the day, viz., Sabbath-schools, Tract, Missionary, Education, and Temperance societies; and do you purpose to render your aid in furthering these objects, and by your preaching testify your deep interest in thus furthering the spread of the Gospel and its purifying influences?*

"4. Do you heartily approve of revivals of religion, and the diffusion of their hallowed influences in promoting the personal holiness of the people of God, and calling sinners into the fold of Christ?"

Mr. Hunt then gave his assent to the questions propounded by the constitution of the church. (*See Form of Government*, chap. xv. sec. 12.) After which he and the churches were received under the care of Presbytery.

It is not improper to remark in this connection that only two years previous to this time, the Presbytery of Newton, in their pastoral letter to the churches of Bethlehem and Alexandria, (between whom and Mr. Hunt they had just dissolved the pastoral relation,) employ the following language: "And now we beseech you to look around and see where practical religion, where the friends of *temperance*, *of prayer-meetings*, *of Bible societies*, and missionary efforts are?—we ask where? How many prayer-meetings, and temperance societies, &c., do exist under the *fostering* influence of your late Pastor? Is there one?" *There was not one.*

But to continue the history. I was moderator of the Presbytery when Mr. Hunt first made his application to be received; and being known as such by the delegates, was earnestly requested to hold a protracted meeting at Bethlehem church in June following. I assented; and went over at the time appointed, and on the third day of the meeting† a great awakening commenced. The results of the meeting are

* The reader is requested to notice this pledge particularly, and to bear it in mind.

† I was there nearly four days, during which time, I preached eleven sermons, and made six other addresses: the consequence of which imprudence was a severe attack of illness.

mentioned by Mr. Hunt in a letter to me, dated Jan. 3, 1842, (and written at the request of the people to urge me to become pastor of those churches, as they had insisted on his resigning the charge.) He says: "One evidence that God, in his providence, calls you to this field, is the rich blessing of your labors while with us. It exceeded any thing witnessed by the old pastor during his ministry; and between 50 and 75 that were brought into the church by your instrumentality continue faithful to our Divine Master." There were 72 who were regarded as thus faithful. The letters written to me by Mr. Hunt and the Bethlehem congregation induced me at last to leave Allentown, Pa., and enter upon that field; after earnestly seeking the direction of the Great Head of the church. But I must here pause in the narrative, in order to bring up to this period the rest of the history.

When in 1802 or 1803 Mr. Hunt undertook the charge of these churches, he, like most ministers of the gospel, was poor; and had nothing to depend upon for support except his salary. He, however, rented a farm, and soon increased his pecuniary resources, and then by teaching the rudiments of an English education he at length accumulated considerable money: so that when I became acquainted with him he was able not only to live upon his income, but annually to put out money on interest.

During Mr. Hunt's ministry, Presbyterianism, as has been mentioned above, went down rapidly, until there was scarcely a single copy of our doctrinal symbols to be found in either of the congregations. The people, when I came among them, were terrified at the bare idea of having the book introduced into their midst; and one prominent and active member of the Bethlehem church assured me that he would quite as willingly introduce into his family Tom Paine's Age of Reason as the Presbyterian Confession of Faith. He had imbibed his notions respecting the book from the constant denunciations of it by Mr. Hunt.

Mr. Hunt professed also to regard the Westminster catechism as "getting out of date," and soon laid it entirely aside; but not wishing to be without a catechism, he wrote one himself, which he substituted in lieu of the other; and it was accordingly committed to memory and recited on Sabbaths by the children and youth of his charge.* The following extracts from the *second* and improved edition of it, will, by giving an idea of its character and contents, evince how well adapted it is to supersede that of the Westminster Divines. It contains 178 questions with the answers, besides 50 others, which are introductory.

"*Q.* 5. Was the whole universe created at the same time? *A.* I suppose not: but only the solar system.

"*Q.* 16. Where was Paradise situated? *A.* In Asia.

"*Q.* 24. Where did the ark rest? *A.* On a mountain in Armenia, Ararat, in Asia.

"*Q.* 40. Who is the first conqueror mentioned in profane history? *A.* Ninus.

"*Q.* 58. What was the probable design of the pyramids?

* In order, I suppose, to give the Third Presbytery an idea of the depth and versatility of his powers, Mr. Hunt, when he applied to be admitted, (April, 1840,) actually brought a pile of these catechisms and distributed them among its members. The extracts given above are made from a copy which he himself presented to me.

"*Q*. 59. From whence did Greece receive her learning?
"*Q*. 60. Was Athens built at this period? *A*. Yes.
"*Q*. 61. By whom? *A*. Cecrops.
"*Q*. 77. How do you account for Samson's catching three hundred foxes?
"*Q*. 84. Who wrote Judges and Ruth?
"*Q*. 104. What was the occasion of the hatred of the Jews to the Samaritans? *A*. Their opposition to the second temple.
"*Q*. 111. What does Daniel intend by the Ram? *A*. Darius.
"*Q*. 112. Who is the he-goat spoken of by Daniel?
"*Q*. 116. Who are we to understand by the Little Horn which came up afterwards?
"*Q*. 120. What time was the Alexandrian Library furnished?
"*Q*. 121. What became of this Library? *A*. Burnt by accident.
"*Q*. 122. When was the Septuagint translation made?
"*Q*. 128. When did Pompey take Jerusalem?
"*Q*. 134. When did Xerxes invade Greece?
"*Q*. 136. Mention some of the most learned men of this period? *A*. Xenophon, Plato, Aristotle, Demosthenes, Diogenes, Julius Cæsar, Cicero, Sallust, and Virgil.
"*Q*. 139. When was Jerusalem destroyed? *A*. In 63, by the Romans, &c.
"*Q*. 141. Did any heresies arise at this time? *A*. Yes: Simon Magus, A.D. 34, lived at Samaria, and founded many heresies, and after him, Cerinthus; at this time the notion of the Æons was introduced. The Gnostics took their rise from Simon Magus and Cerinthus.
"*Q*. 142. What were the doctrines of the Gnostics?
"*Q*. 153. Did the Pope rise gradually?
"*Q*. 162. Who were the promoters of the Reformation? *A*. John Wickliffe, John Huss, Martin Luther, Jerome, Melancthon, &c.
"*Q*. 163. When did the Crusades begin? *A*. A.D. 1096.
"*Q*. 164. When was printing invented?
"*Q*. 166. How came the Kings of England to have the title of Defender of the Faith?
"*Q*. 168. Mention the names of the Kings and Queens that have reigned since Henry 8th in England?
"*Q*. 172. What religious wars have taken place since the reformation, called persecution by some? *A*. In Germany, Bohemia, Holland, Spain, France, Ireland, England, &c.
"*Q*. 173. What was the state of the Protestants in France in the time of Louis 14th?
"*Q*. 174. In what language was the Old Testament written? *A*. Mostly in Hebrew, the rest in Chaldaic.
"*Q*. 175. In what language was the New Testament written? *A*. Principally in Greek, except Matthew and the Hebrews.
"*Q*. 176. When was the New Testament divided *into lines*?
"*Q*. 177. When were verses introduced? *A*. 1551.
"*Q*. 178. What version of the New Testament is considered the most ancient? *A*. The Latin."

Thus endeth the "*Ecclesiastical and Historical Catechism for Children and Youth. By Holloway W. Hunt, A.M., Minister of the Gospel, Bethlehem, New Jersey; Second Edition. Printed by George Sherman, Trenton*, 1831." The author designed that it should supersede the Westminster Catechism, and in the churches of Bethlehem and Alexandria, it was as regularly recited to Mr. Hunt by the children on the Sabbath, as the Westminster had been previously: And not a few of the members of these churches have assured me that in their recitations to Mr. Hunt, on the Sabbath, they have gone regularly through this wretched tissue of absurdity and incredible ignorance.

Having become acquainted with Mr. Hunt amid the stirring scenes of a great awakening, in the midst of which his own soul seemed aroused, I supposed him to be a good old man; who, though unlettered, had the interests of the Redeemer's kingdom at heart. When I accepted the invitation therefore to supply the pulpits of the charge, I was prepared to put myself under his guidance, and actually did consult him, on all occasions, in reference to what was best to promote the cause of the Redeemer within our bounds, until such consultation, as the reader will see, was utterly out of the question.

CHAPTER II.

THE HISTORY CONTINUED FROM APRIL, 1842, UNTIL SEPTEMBER, 1847.

In April 1842, I removed with my family from Allentown, Pa., to the congregations aforesaid, and at once commenced the arduous labors which there devolved upon me. I had always been an earnest supporter of those benevolent institutions which are specified in the foregoing questions propounded to Mr. Hunt at Presbytery; as also an unyielding advocate of the theological system presented in our Confession of Faith. But upon my consenting to supply the pulpits of the charge, a scene opened up before me, the features of which I shall now proceed to describe.

As I was on the eve of commencing to preach at the Mount Pleasant (or Alexandria) church, Mr. Hunt came to me and begged earnestly that I in my sermons would "say nothing on the subject of the Divinity of Christ, as the people there *would not stand it to have that doctrine preached*." He likewise informed me that "in the Bethlehem Church, nothing must be said about the doctrine of the Trinity." To this state of degradation had the once active, efficient, and intelligent charge of the venerable Dr. John Hanna deteriorated under the ministry of his successor.

The Lord's Supper was celebrated twice annually, in each of these churches. But on my first Communion Sabbath, at Bethlehem, I found in the little grove in which the church stood, *a sutler's table*, at which fruit, cakes, drink, &c., were being sold amid the frivolity and boisterous mirth usual at a militia training. I at once stated the fact to Mr. Hunt, supposing that he must of course be ignorant of its existence, and promptly insisted on the removal of the table. He, however, objected to its being disturbed. I then brought the matter before the Elders, but neither were they willing to move in it, until at my request Mr. Joseph Boss took the matter in hand, and the debasing spectacle was never after witnessed in the grove.

Then also in visiting the people of my charge, I was greatly disappointed and grieved to find amongst them more whisky distilleries than I had ever before come in contact with. I kept silence, however, for it was then useless to complain; but I could not help feeling that Presbytery had been cruelly imposed upon. I ascertained also that of all the objects which Mr. Hunt had, at Presbytery, pledged himself to advocate, not one had as yet been brought before them by him, though two years had already elapsed. In fact, the mass of the people of the congregations had not the remotest conception of the pledges which had thus been given on their behalf. Nor was this all; but on one occasion when expressing to Mr. Sigler, a noted and extensive distiller, my views of the nature of his business, and reminding him of his promise to Presbytery, (he was one of the delegates who accompanied Mr. Hunt on that occasion,) he remarked that the very next autumn after they had been thus received by the Presbytery, and in the midst of the forementioned revival, which continued several months, Mr. Hunt had sent all his apples to the distillery. Upon inquiry, I found this to be even so; and Mr. Hunt attempted to justify the procedure of thus manufacturing the produce of his orchards into whisky.* I was truly sick at heart to find into what a state of things I had been unconsciously betrayed; but upon reconsidering the whole matter, I viewed it as the design of Providence that I should go on here and do the work of my Divine Master. I therefore gave myself to prayer, and with renewed zeal prosecuted the work of my ministry.

A few months after I had thus commenced my labors, a temperance meeting was appointed to be held at Lower Milford, on the Delaware. Upon this Mr. Hunt called upon me and requested that I would not attend the meeting, as my doing so would make a disturbance amongst my people. I informed him in reply that I should not attend it; but that my only reason for not doing so was a prior and important engagement on the evening of that meeting. I soon ascertained, however, that scarcely any of my people had ever heard a temperance lecture, or had any idea (except the most absurd) of the nature and objects of the temperance reform. But regarding myself as accountable to God for the discharge of my duty, I endeavored to be prudent, though firm and faithful, in the discharge of it. Calling to mind also the example of our blessed Redeemer, who, when referring to the unpreparedness of his disciples to receive his instructions in their full extent, said, "I have many things to say unto you, but ye cannot bear them now," (John 16: 12,) I endeavored to prepare my people for the reception of the truth without unnecessarily awakening their prejudices. For some months I said nothing *directly asserting* the Godhead of Christ, or the doctrine of the Trinity (though in all my preaching I presented and illustrated such principles as irresistibly *inferred* these truths), or of the temperance cause, and other benevolent associations.

* A clerical brother, who was present at my trial in Bethlehem, and to whose perusal I had submitted this work in MS., adds the following note to the above remark: "At the trial Mr. Hunt acknowledged before the Presbytery that he had *seven* or *ten* barrels of whisky made out of the apples of his orchard two or three years before; and that he did so because he did not like to see the apples wasted." This was Mr. Hunt's usual plea in self-defence.

The first formal difference which arose between Mr. Hunt and myself, occurred in consequence of introducing "a covenant" into the form of receiving members into the church. Our Synod, a little while before, had urged this matter upon the churches, and had prepared and recommended a "form of admission." Mr. Hunt, however, strongly opposed me herein, for he had required no pledge whatever of those who desired to be admitted. Hence Unitarians, and the whole tribe of, I know not what, were baptized into nominal Presbyterianism. The point was one, however, which I refused to yield, and the church accordingly adopted the measure.

A second difficulty arose from my receiving into the pulpit the agent of the American Bible Society, to present to my people the claims of that institution. He was a worthy man (his name has escaped me), but on entering the house he was so grossly insulted as to the object of his mission by a prominent member of the church, that he burst into tears. I however insisted on his being heard, and followed his address with an earnest recommendation of the object. A collection was then taken amounting to between four and five dollars, three of which I myself gave. This occurrence took place in the summer of 1842.

Another difficulty arose from the determination of a majority of the session to discipline a member of the church, who, although he had united with a Unitarian Society, and had received its baptism by immersion, still persisted that he was a member also of the Bethlehem church. Mr. Hunt had quietly permitted such abuses; but in Dec. 1842, and after a great revival in the church, many members complained of this conduct of the Unitarian, and some refused to sit with him at the communion table. Mr. Hunt labored to "stave off" the crisis as long as possible; but it finally arrived. The man, a Mr. William Waggoner, presented to the session a communication in which he bitterly complained that he should be thus dealt with, while "others holding similar sentiments remain in the communion without censure," and which concluded with his renunciation of the jurisdiction of the session. This procedure, though I conducted it with all possible kindness, injured me with many prominent members of the church and congregation, who were known to be favorable to Unitarianism.

In the mean time, however, the attendance on my ministry had greatly increased,* and in the autumn of the first year the Lord poured out his spirit on the congregations in a wonderful manner, so that in the course of that year two hundred and fifteen were, on examination, received into the communion of the Bethlehem church, and upwards of one hundred into that of Alexandria. I was very particular and pointed in the examination of these candidates (for the churches needed a thorough renovation,) and in general required that every head of a family who presented himself for admission, should commence family prayer, and that the young men should hold prayer meetings and assist us in establishing and conducting Sabbath-schools.

I now felt that duty required of me to be more plain in my references

* The reader must pardon these instances of apparent egotism; I would gladly avoid them if possible, but cannot in duty to myself and to the subject.

to the subjects which Mr. Hunt had, on entering the Presbytery, so solemnly pledged himself as Pastor of the churches to support; and accordingly I labored to familiarize the minds of my people with the doctrines of grace, and preached on temperance and on the duty of sustaining the missionary cause, and other benevolent enterprises. My course herein was supported by the generality of the new members, but bitterly opposed by Mr. Hunt and his friends. His influence was not small, as any one can perceive from a moment's reflection on the fact that he was wealthy, and held mortgages on the property of a great many persons in the region. Over these in general he had great influence. But now he formally begun to impair my influence with the people. An instance or two may illustrate.

He took an early opportunity to call upon an Old School brother, the Rev. David X. Junkin,* who resided a few miles distant, and with whom I had been at swords' points, in consequence of having successfully defended the Rev. Albert Barnes against his brother, the Rev. Dr. Junkin. Mr. Junkin strongly sympathized with his brother in this controversy, and, of course, his feelings were, to some extent, hostile to me. Mr. Hunt knowing this fact, and supposing that such hostility must operate upon Mr. Junkin's manly and generous nature, as it would upon himself, called on him, and made me the subject of a long conversation. He then returned home and reported through the congregations that Mr. Junkin had accused me of the most appalling ignorance; and of other things calculated to impair my influence with the people. In an interview which I subsequently had with Mr. Junkin, he promptly and most decidedly denied the truth of the statement, and said to me, "I saw that Mr. Hunt's aim in calling on me was to find out something against you, by means of which he might lessen you in the estimation of your people, supposing me to be *personally* hostile to you, and I was therefore on my guard."

Soon after this the Rev. E. R. Fairchild (since D.D.), Secretary of the Home Missionary Society, paid me a visit, and, with my cordial approbation, presented the claims of that institution to my people. He collected between $20 and $30. Hereupon Mr. Hunt proceeded to calculate how much Mr. Fairchild's salary for each Sabbath amounted to, and circulated amongst the congregation that their contribution did but little more than defray his expenses for visiting them; and I, of course, came in for a full share of hard thoughts, for thus introducing a man "to eat out their substance." The effect of this artful story, upon a people who knew but little of such matters, was exceedingly pernicious, and, for several years, operated more or less against the agents who visited us from benevolent societies.

Not far from the time of this occurrence I attended a "Harvest Home" at Milford, and delivered a lecture upon temperance. This produced a very great excitement, and a number of my congregation left me entire-

* Since D.D. To avoid unnecessary confusion, I shall herein speak of my brethren not according to their *present* literary titles, but according to those which they bore at the time of the events with which they are associated in this history.

ly.* Mr. Hunt, however, a short time after this meeting, sold eight or ten barrels of his whisky.

During the first two years of this my ministry, the congregations had so increased in number, that Alexandria (which was almost extinct as a church when I went there,) erected a beautiful house of worship and *paid for it* without any foreign assistance,—and also a smaller one at a place called Little York, within the bounds of that congregation. The church of Bethlehem also found it necessary to enlarge their own house by an addition of twenty feet to one end. In its incipient state Mr. Hunt violently opposed the proposition for this enlargement; but it was carried by a nearly unanimous vote.

The grounds of this opposition will be in the general sufficiently obvious to the reflecting mind, perhaps, without a very particular specification: and if such a course be pardonable at all, or capable of extenuation, may it not be in such a case as the present, where an old preacher beheld his charge more than doubled in number, during the first two years subsequently to his resigning it? His *reasons* however, for he was obliged to state some, must, with all the allowance that can thus be made, be regarded as peculiar. One, which he urged in private, was, that when the two churches of the charge separated, (as they obviously soon must do, for each was now abundantly able to support a pastor) he felt himself sufficiently able to supply the pulpit of Bethlehem. A second reason, and one urged by him at the meeting of the congregation when it assembled to consider the subject, was, that, as the house was too much thronged on the Sabbath, to admit any more persons, those who could not find room ought to go and worship at the surrounding churches where there was plenty of room. A third reason, and one urged from the pulpit in my absence, was that "Mr. Landis is too great a preacher to be willing to settle permanently here, and that when he leaves Bethlehem the congregation will dwindle again to its original size." Hence of course, the house should not be enlarged.

Mr. Hunt, notwithstanding he boasted of being very wealthy, began by this time to feel a diminution in his finances, arising from the non-reception of a salary to which he had been so long accustomed. He cast about therefore to ascertain some remedy for "the consumption of the purse," and finally concluded to become a candidate for Congress. His real friends were grieved at this procedure, and endeavored to dissuade him from the step, but he was encouraged therein by a multitude of thoughtless persons, who regarded it only in the light of a pecuniary advantage. He attended political meetings and made speeches; and such was the state of society that his name was very near being placed upon the ticket. Having failed in this, he next endeavored to obtain a seat in the state legislature; and never have I seen him look so young and "spruce," or drive so rapidly, as when he passed my house (where he stopped a moment) to attend a political caucus meeting at Flemington, where the candidate was to be nominated. After some crossing of

*The Rev. Mr. Warren, Temperance Agent for the State, in his published report of this meeting, makes a remark in relation to this address which may perhaps develop one reason for the animosity which it excited. After giving a brief outline of the lecture, he adds: "Much was expected from this discourse, and *much was realized.*"

swords with another aspirant (which made abundant sport for the papers,) he was laid upon the shelf. And here ended the last act of his political life.

Being thus frustrated in his plans to obtain an increase of income, (though at this time he boasted of being worth from $50,000 to $75,000,) he appeared to settle down in the determination that I must in some way be induced to vacate the Bethlehem pulpit. The first two years of my ministry were now drawing to a close (though I was still but a stated supply,) and each congregation was able of itself to sustain the ordinances of religion. At the close of this period each church made out "a call" for me to settle as its pastor, offering the same salary ($600 annually) which I had been receiving from the united charge. Mr. Hunt manifested great opposition to my settling at Bethlehem, in the bounds of which he resided, though he was strongly in favor of my accepting the invitation from Alexandria: and when both invitations were being made out for my services, he wrote me a cruelly insulting letter to dissuade me from accepting the Bethlehem call, and pretending that some of the people agreed with him in the opposition. But when the question was soon after taken in the presence of nearly the whole congregation, it was perfectly unanimous. In Alexandria also, the call was unanimous, with the exception of two brethren who opposed it on the score of my temperance views.

Had I consulted my personal interest or ease, or my private inclinations, I should at once have selected Alexandria as the field of my labors. This I said to some of my friends at the time. The salary was as large and more punctually remitted, (because better arrangements now existed there for this purpose than at Bethlehem,) the people were as kind and intelligent, and their society was not cursed with that vein of base ore extending through the whole valley from Bethlehem nearly to Belvidere, as is known to all who are acquainted with the region, and from which even during the American Revolution, the worst and most unprincipled tories were manufactured by wholesale. Moreover the location, to say the least, was equally pleasant, and the pastoral labor but half as great as that which must devolve upon me at Bethlehem. It was likewise out of the neighborhood of the operations of my predecessor; the fact of whose residence within the limits of the Bethlehem congregation formed the great obstacle to my concluding at once to settle there. The nature of this difficulty, after what has been already stated, need not be expatiated upon. I however, calling to mind the words of Nehemiah (Shall such a man as I flee ?), finally concluded to remain at Bethlehem, because the field was larger, and the labor more arduous; and because many of the most intelligent and pious of the members assured me, that if I should now leave the church open to the manœuvering and management of Mr. Hunt, there was reason to apprehend that it would soon become divided into parties and scattered to the winds. And from what I had already witnessed I had little doubt that the foundation of these fears was real. These considerations appeared to me to be conclusive that God designed me to labor in this field: and to this hour I rejoice that such was my determination.

The Sabbath preceding the day on which the call was to be formally made out, I, agreeably to previous notice, and in the presence of a crowded house, declared my views frankly and fully, (stating too the course which I intended to pursue,) in relation to all the points upon which difficulty might thereafter be apprehended; and added that I felt it my duty to make these things thus known to them, in order that they might fully understand what they had to depend upon, should they conclude to extend to me, and I conclude to accept, an invitation to become their Pastor. After briefly stating my theological views, which are the reverse of Mr. Hunt's in relation to the doctrines of grace, I expressed in exalted terms the view which I entertained of our incomparable doctrinal symbols. I then presented my views of the importance of sustaining the temperance reform, and the various benevolent institutions of the day; expressed also my inveterate hostility to slavery, and insisted on the importance of restoring catechetical instruction throughout the whole congregation, by means of the Westminster catechism; and on the duty also of restoring and enforcing ecclesiastical discipline. I urged the congregation to consider too, that objections to me on any or all of these grounds would be too late after I became pastor (if I should become so), and that they would then appear with a very ill grace after the declarations made by me to-day directly in view of the vote which they were to give on the morrow. So stood the matter, and on the following day, a congregation assembled, far more numerous than had ever before come together in Bethlehem for the transaction of business. If any opposition to me did really exist, it was overawed, except in the case of Mr. Hunt. He, to be prepared for any result, came with *a speech against* me (which he partly delivered), and with a *call* regularly drawn up *for* me, and which he produced immediately after the vote was taken. That vote, as already stated, was perfectly unanimous; and on witnessing it he became so agitated as to be scarcely able, on account of the tremor, to read the call which he then produced.

The principles which I had, in the discourse above referred to, announced my intention of continuing to advocate, were at this time unpopular through that region. They were all *new* to the generation then on the stage. God, however, enabled me to labor with zeal and success, and soon afterwards blessed the church with another great revival of religion. I had strength imparted to me to render assistance to my brethren of other denominations; in which labors God made me the instrument of the conversion of many souls.* It is surely my privilege, in this connection, to refer to these seals of the Lord on my ministry.

In addition to these labors, I lectured much on the subject of temperance throughout the county of Hunterdon. The moral aspect of things imperiously demanded it; and during the winter of 1846–7, I lectured more frequently in the county on that subject, than all the clergymen therein put together: and nearly all of them were temperance men. It was chiefly by the invitation of these my brethren that I did so. Nor was there a hard field, nor a place in which it was difficult to introduce the subject, to which I was not urged to come, in order to lecture. To

* For example; in the church at Northampton, Pa., 200 were hopefully converted: in the Lutheran church, near Easton, N. J., 120: in the church at German Valley, N. J., upwards of 60: in Bridgeton, N. J., a large number, &c., &c.

all such places I went accordingly. Tremendous was the opposition which I encountered in some of them, where the reign of Bacchus had previously never been disturbed. In one place (Quakertown) I was "pelted" with addled eggs; and in others (Rum Corner, for instance) I was repeatedly threatened with personal violence: and in most places calumniated almost beyond belief. But knowing these things to be but the last resource of cowardice and crime, I paid no attention to them: and without returning railing for railing, (as even my bitterest opposers confess,) went calmly onward in the discharge of my duty.

My efforts in this cause, and in inculcating the principles of practical benevolence, were greatly blessed amongst my own people. I taught them the great principles of the temperance reform; and a very large proportion of them, so soon as they understood the true nature of that enterprise, gave it not only their countenance but cordial support. A single fact may serve to illustrate also the success bestowed by God upon my efforts to inculcate the duty of beneficence. During the year which terminated in August, 1847, my congregation, besides raising $100, to pay a small debt on their house, raised and paid over the sum of $521, in aid of the various benevolent operations of the day: an amount ten times larger than their aggregate contributions of such a nature, during the whole of my predecessor's ministry. Other facts and illustrations, connected with these matters, will come up more properly hereafter.

In the midst of a population that had ever regarded the manufacture, sale, and use of alcoholic liquors (as a beverage) as morally right; and who had been pre-eminently trained to selfishness, and to regard the acquisition of wealth as the chief end of man in this world; these efforts, and efforts to promote kindred interests, could not be made without encountering stern opposition, nor without promoting a considerable degree of dissatisfaction with the instrument of such reforms. To enter fully into a delineation of the manner in which my predecessor endeavored to take advantage of such hostile feelings, and thus to circumvent me in every effort of the kind, would be as painful to my own feelings as it would be to those of the truly Christian reader. But these efforts are known to the community in which they occurred; and do not, unless indirectly, bear upon the point before us: and hence a few instances, in addition to those already furnished, must suffice. I am assured, too, that Mr. Hunt, with the Judgment Bar of God so immediately before him, will not venture to deny that (whatever were his motives,) he did everything that a man in his circumstances could do, to resist me herein, and to impair my usefulness. In the course of nature, he must soon pass away to his last account; and this matter must meet him THEN, for I have laid it all before Him who is to be our Judge. May God grant that through the infinite mercy of Redeeming Love, we may both be prepared for the scenes that will then transpire!

In addition to the forementioned efforts of Mr. Hunt to frustrate my endeavors to awaken my people to the duty of imparting of their property to assist the sacred cause of missions and other benevolent enterprises, he proceeded as follows. In order to neutralize the effect of my own example herein, he circulated the idea, that I set the example of subscribing largely to these institutions, *merely for effect*, in order to induce others to subscribe; but did not pay my own subscription. Then, when this cruel slander was put down, he told the people that I knew not the value of money, and therefore gave it away so freely.* Then, when the claims of divine truth in relation to the duty of beneficence came to be somewhat extensively and practically recognized by the church and congregation, he appeared to be really alarmed for the consequences, and seemed to be afraid that all the money was "going out of the county;" and one day, (having previously boasted of his intention to some of his friends,) called at my house to "set me right" on the subject. I happened to be at home; and the usual preliminary remarks being gone through, he thus proceeded: "I have called upon you, Mr. Landis, to say that which I am aware will displease you, and perhaps make you a little angry. The course you pursue in relation to what you call 'the duty of contribution' produces great dissatisfaction amongst your hearers. *You* have never *toiled* for your money; and have always had as much as you want; and hence you know not its value, and part with it so easily. We *have* toiled for ours, and have obtained it by long and patient labor; and you must not think to put your hand into our pockets and take it whenever you please. I am aware that these remarks will make you angry; but I felt it my duty to tell you these things." Such were his ideas, and I think the very words he used.

I had no difficulty (and neither will any competent reader have) to see the design of all this. But without noticing the insulting nature of his insinuations, I immediately replied as follows: "Your remarks, Father Hunt, have not at all angered me; but on the contrary, I am truly glad that you have called upon me and introduced this subject. I hope you will calmly and kindly listen to what I have to say in relation to it. As to money, it is not much that I have to give; and I never have had the abundance of it of which you speak. It is, however, because I *do know* its value, that I put it to the use to which you refer, and of which you so much disapprove. As to getting my money *easily*, how can you say so? I rise earlier than you, and sit up later. I labor harder, I study more, and preach oftener than you ever did while Pastor: and my income is beyond comparison smaller than that which you even now annually receive. Father Hunt! I believe the declaration of our blessed Redeemer, that 'It is more blessed to give than to receive'; and I try to act in accordance with that belief. DO YOU BELIEVE HIS DECLARATION? If you do, why are you so constantly opposing me in my efforts to inculcate this truth? If you *do not* believe it, you ought at once openly to say so. It is because I believe it, that I am willing to intrust my little savings into his hands; and wish also to induce my people to do the same. And do not be displeased with me when I tell you that I have found you to be the greatest obstacle in the way of my

* There was, however, nothing extraordinary about this asserted liberality of mine. For obvious reasons, it appeared remarkable to Mr. Hunt and the people (I was obliged to "*head*" the subscription papers), but my conscience is very far from acquitting me of having done my whole duty there in this matter of beneficence. I might have given much more.

endeavors to impress upon the minds of my people the teachings of Christ on this subject."

Before I had quite concluded, the poor old man began to weep; and drawing out his pocket-book, which was well lined with bank-bills, he reached me a dollar, saying, "Here, Brother L.; you took up a collection for missions the other day, please to add this to it." And this was all he said in reply. I hoped that the impression would be permanently salutary. But after this event, he made it a point never to be present at church when there was reason to believe that a collection would be taken for aiding any benevolent enterprise.

Then too Mr. Hunt considerably lessened my means of doing good by adopting a procedure for monopolizing the marriage perquisites in the congregation, to which I as Pastor was of course fairly entitled. In his letters to me at Allentown, he had particularly specified this source of income as considerable; and as furnishing an additional inducement for me to undertake the charge: and his constant boast was, and still is, that during his forty years' ministry, these perquisites, with the interest, have amounted to $10,000. But after my removal to Jersey, Mr. Hunt perpetually went to the families of my charge, as any prospect of a marriage would arise amongst them, and would converse in the following style: "The old pastor has been amongst you for a long time; but his life is now drawing to a close. You will see him, my children, but a little while longer. (*Here he would cry.*) You are all my children, (and, turning to the youth of the family he would add,) I married your grandparents, and your parents: I may live to marry you, but" &c. This course he pursued as long as it was available; and thereby actually obtained a very large portion (about two-thirds, for a considerable time,) of those perquisites. Some of my people remonstrated with him, but it was unavailing. The conclusion of this begging farce was, however, supremely ludicrous. For the people reasonably supposing that as his affection for them, since he resigned his charge, had become so great and disinterested, he would take a melancholy pleasure in sympathizing with them amid life's keener sorrows, and in mingling his tears with the tears of his "children" at the funeral of their dear departed ones, always made it a point on such occasions to invite him to be present.* But on one or another pretext he almost always declined. And at last he published from the pulpit a notice to the following effect: "Through the infirmities of age, in consequence of which I feel the changes of weather very sensibly, I am under the painful necessity, from this time forward, to decline invitations to attend funerals. These causes have often compelled me to disappoint you; and it is better hereafter to have the matter perfectly understood. Your present efficient pastor is fully competent to the discharge of all such duties." Now this certainly appears to be very reasonable; and but one thing prevented its appearing so to the people of my charge; to wit, every man and woman in the whole county knew that neither distance, nor change of weather, nor cold, nor wet,

* The custom of charging for such services, which is, I believe, still prevalent in some places, even in the Presbyterian Church, ceased in these congregations a short time before my removal thither. I have always refused such fees.

nor snow, nor sleet, nor hail, nor wind, nor the infirmities of age, ever prevented Mr. Hunt from accepting an invitation to a wedding, or from fulfilling his appointment to be there. It was only in the discharge of this duty that he seemed to regard "the present efficient pastor" as in need of any assistance. That part of my income therefore to which I regarded the poor and destitute as pre-eminently entitled, was thus considerably curtailed for a long time after my settlement in this charge.*

In justice to myself it will be necessary also here to illustrate briefly the methods by which Mr. Hunt endeavored to promote any supposed cause of dissatisfaction with me amongst my people. In my efforts to restore the exercise of ecclesiastical discipline (a step well calculated to produce dissatisfaction in a community where discipline had been so long neglected), Mr. Hunt was always the rallying point for the disaffected. I state simply a notorious *fact.* I offer no explanation of it: nor would I wish to intimate that Mr. Hunt was actuated herein by personal hostility to me. On hearing the statement of the offender, he *may* have concluded that it was right thus to counsel and advise him. But however the fact may be explained, Mr. Hunt stood always ready to advise any and every offender how to proceed so as to give me the greatest possible difficulty in the administration of discipline.

Then too in my efforts to introduce the Confession of Faith amongst the people, I found him laboring in every possible way to hinder my success; though he, when admitted into our Presbytery, had subscribed fully his adherence to that symbol. He also visited my people for this purpose; and in my absence (and once too when I was present) denounced the Confession publicly in the church; and said that its introduction would distract and divide the church, &c. He likewise repeatedly accused me of being an antinomian or fatalist in disguise. These facts need no comment to evince their bearing on the subject.

My anti-slavery views likewise furnished him with a plausible pretext for promoting dissatisfaction. It was at a time when such views were exceedingly unpopular in that region; and Mr. Hunt with much art availed himself of the occasion thus afforded. All these points, however, I firmly insisted on, though I made neither of them a "hobby;" but merely sought in my ministrations to give to each the same relative degree of importance with which I found it invested in the Holy Scriptures.

These facts, and multitudes of others that can be specified, develop, as the reader has doubtless observed, the real ground of Mr. Hunt's oppo-

* The following anecdote, exhibiting the worldly disposition of Mr. Hunt (and by consequence the grounds of his enmity to benevolent enterprises and their supporters) may suffice instead of a dozen illustrations. Its author, the Rev. Albert Barnes, has so repeatedly stated it in the presence of numbers of people, that it has long become public property. In April, 1844, Presbytery met at Mount Pleasant to settle a pastor over that church; and once during the meeting, Mr. Barnes, for some reason, went all the way home with Mr. Hunt and spent the night with him. The topics, however, upon which Mr. Hunt delighted most to converse were money and the accumulation of property, and Mr. Barnes came away (as he expressed it) thoroughly disgusted with his worldliness; and said, "Mr. Hunt is the most worldly-minded man I *ever* knew. I do not say *minister* but *man*." The reader will please keep in mind this remark and the visit, for they have other bearings besides those which are obvious in their present connection.

sition to me, no less than the peculiar element in the minds of a considerable proportion of the community, upon which his efforts were based. In the general sense that element was covetousness, or a love of pecuniary gain; to which, in his own case, was superadded a high degree of jealousy in consequence of the influence I had acquired through the blessing which God had bestowed upon my poor labors. There was also in the minds of many, a great and growing dissatisfaction arising from the "new" doctrines and practice inculcated; and from the pointed manner in which many things heretofore regarded as "allowable follies," were exposed and condemned. Among these, as before remarked, were the manufacture, sale, and use of alcoholic liquors, *as a beverage;* and also the pernicious practice of Sabbath visitation, which was indulged without restraint by the great mass of professors of religion. A stranger can form no adequate conception of the moral and intellectual degradation of a large class of the community through this district and the valley running north of it. They seem to have no conception of the import of the terms *moral principle and moral obligation.* A large nest of counterfeiters* has been there from time immemorial, practicing with impunity their schemes. Once in a while one would be detected, but methods were always found by which to evade the ultimate penalty of the law. Atheism too in its most horrid form appeared openly. And its connection with that dreadful tragedy of May 1, 1843, called "*the Warren Murder*," is known well to the people there.† One Dr. Sicarius, who frequently attended Bethlehem Church, though a member of another church some miles distant, used *to rise from the communion table*, and go into the grove to trade horses on the Sabbath. Just before September, in 1847, this man became my inveterate enemy, because, soon after he had in a "horse-deal," at Quakertown, cheated a poor man entirely out of his beast, he happened to be at Bethlehem Church, and supposed that some pointed remarks made on the subject of honesty, were by me directed against that cruel transaction. His head dropped, as though a rifle bullet had pierced his heart, and I could not but notice his apparent confusion. At that time, however, I knew nothing of the "deal" referred to. But this man so soon as the rumor was raised against me in 1847, at once assumed the lead of the crusade under Mr. Hunt; and in the transactions hereinafter described, has done more efficient service in the work of injuring me, and the cause of religion through this rumor, than any other individual *in Jersey*. He made the accusations which

* A worthy divine, Mr. M'Nair, who had been settled in a church north of me, got into some difficulty with his people, and the matter came before Presbytery. He had as he told me, five or six witnesses of unimpeachable and excellent character, who swore directly and positively as to the point in his favor; but his enemies being determined to carry their point, procured without difficulty five or six persons who swore just as positively *to the contrary*. Soon after the rumor (which is the occasion of this work) started, he called on me, and after mentioning the above, and remarking on the character of that vein of base ore which runs through society in that whole valley, said, "You will find, my brother, that your greatest difficulty in this matter will arise from false swearing. And that there are those here who are determined at all hazards to put religion down."

† One individual who was concerned in that tragedy, offered a daughter of his $500 if she would name her infant son, "Jesus Christ." He lived north of a place then called *Sodom*, but now Clarksville.

were raised against me, the ostensible reason for thus gratifying his malevolent feelings; and has thus secured to himself, and perhaps to his family, (as sure as there is a God who has said Vengeance is mine, I will repay,) an inheritance of Divine wrath and heart-breaking anguish.

The last *public* effort, (previous to August, 1847,) which Mr. Hunt made for the purpose of inducing my dismissal from Bethlehem, was in October, 1845. I was about leaving home, to attend the meeting of Synod at Lewistown, Del., when he came forward and volunteered to preach for me on the Sabbath, which should intervene during my absence. I assented to his proposal, and he preached on the text, "Thy kingdom come." During the sermon he remarked to the congregation, that "if they were at all dissatisfied with their Pastor, they could easily have him removed." And upon descending from the pulpit he attempted to enter into conversation with the Elders respecting the best method by which this could be effected. They declined to converse with him, however, on the subject; and one of them, (Mr. Jacob S. Johnson,) rebuked him with great severity. Upon my return, the congregation sent me an earnest request never to ask him to preach in my absence again; stating that they would decidedly prefer to hold a prayer-meeting, or even to have the house closed. I did not ask him to preach afterwards; though I always invited him to accompany me into the pulpit, until he uniformly refused to do so.

It will be easily perceived how well calculated were remarks of such a nature as these of Mr. Hunt to foster and strengthen dissatisfaction in the congregation where it might already exist, in an incipient state. I attempted to excuse them to the people, however, by stating that he was doubtless in his dotage; but to this it was promptly replied, "You will change your opinion on that subject, if you should have any dealings with him of a pecuniary nature."

There is still another point to which it is proper to refer before concluding this chapter. The reader may well suppose that such success, as by the blessing of God had attended my poor labors, was naturally calculated to call into exercise the spirit of denominational rivalry. There was an Old School Presbyterian Church in the neighborhood, (comprising with others, a number of excellent brethren, who had separated from Bethlehem Church during Mr. Hunt's ministry,) and the unhappy spirit which agitated and ultimately rent our American Zion, had not yet been fully exorcised in the region where I labored. There were likewise other denominations in the vicinity; but no congregation could in numbers compare with that of Bethlehem. I never have been a *sectarian*. I have my own cherished and deliberately formed views of doctrine and duty, and they are known to be Calvinistic,* and these views

* It may be proper to mention here an illustrative anecdote. Being urged by an Old School clergyman some twenty miles north of me to preach a few days to his people, I consented; and the Lord poured out His Spirit abundantly upon the congregation. A member of the church, a very worthy and good man, was present; who on account of his difficulty in receiving the doctrines of the Confession of Faith, had come to the conclusion to join the Methodists. But before our series of meetings had concluded, he went to his Pastor and said, "I have been so greatly perplexed by the doctrines of the Confession, that I was just about leaving you in order to unite with the Methodists. I am glad that I did not do so, for the preaching of Mr. L. has con-

I have ever pointedly promulged. It was the exhibition of what are called "The Doctrines of Grace," without any attempt at philosophical refinement, which God so honored with his abundant blessing amongst my people, and in the other congregations referred to above. Divested of mere theological technicalities, these doctrines find ready admission into every heart which has been touched by the saving influence of the Spirit of God. I labored, therefore, as earnestly and cheerfully in other denominations as in my own charge. But still the spirit of *Sect*, in my vicinity, was grieved at the prosperity of my churches; and its partisans evinced a readiness to favor any "hue and cry," that might be raised against me, and which promised to impair my usefulness.

CHAPTER III.

THE ORIGIN AND NATURE OF THE RUMOR.

I NOW enter upon a detail of the particulars of a plot which was devised to crush me, and which being favored by a singular combination of adverse influences has succeeded in producing results which must have brought hopeless ruin upon me, had not the goodness and faithfulness of a covenant God continually interposed to shield me from the machinations of my enemies.

Though from the reckless falsehood and perjury which have been resorted to for the purpose of making out a case against me, I should on principles of strict veracity be justified in pronouncing the accusation in its origin and statement to be one great lie, and nothing but a lie, yet I scorn to take even a seeming advantage of my calumniators. They are entitled to whatever advantage I may have given them, and they may have it. Truly they need it, for there is a tremendous reckoning before them, and already in prospect. With all their efforts, they have, according to their own voluntary confession, failed to prove anything even in the shape of crime against me, although they have ransacked the country for evidence, goaded to madness by the necessity they felt of doing something to sustain themselves after they had taken their first step in starting the rumor, and also by the fact that at the very outset I promptly challenged them to make good their base insinuations by the testimony of any female who would say before me that I ever had in any way by action, word, or look attempted to lead her into sin. And yet, after all their efforts, as will fully appear hereafter, God would not permit their chief witness (or more properly *victim*,) to do otherwise than freely and fully to exculpate me, not only from crime, but from even attempting or designing it: which she did in the presence of hundreds of

vinced me that these doctrines are and must be true. They are the very truths which, instead of comforting sinners in their impenitence, (as I once thought they would,) make them feel their guilt and need of a Savior." His Pastor, deeply affected, called me to them, and repeated to me the above in his presence.

people. Her statement in this respect was true: and God, to cover the conspiracy with confusion, thus brought out the expression of it. Here then I might rest the whole matter of this accusation, and proceed with the other events of the history, but I shall pursue no such worldly policy.

Those who are well acquainted with me know that I have been during the most of my life, a close student, and that perhaps there is no person living who is more subject to what has been called "a flux and reflux of the animal spirits," than myself. Prone to a melancholy of the most sombre tinge, and then to a sudden reaction of the spirits, approximating to levity, I find myself often totally unfit, from these causes, to mingle in society. An almost irresistible propensity to make sport has been the source of many sorrows to me even from a child; and it is the disposition against which, even in childhood, I used most fervently to implore the Divine assistance. But in spite of myself, (and I speak thus neither to excuse nor extenuate, but simply to explain,) this disposition would often obtain an ascendency over me upon leaving my study to mingle in youthful society at a wedding or on some other festive occasion.* Thus, through a sinful thoughtlessness, I prepared the way for my enemies to insinuate suspicions against me. *Hinc illæ lachrymæ!* Often have I called to mind, in this connection, the striking and beautiful remark made by Octavius Cæsar to Alexander and Aristobulus, (the sons of Herod the Great) who had been accused of a conspiracy to dethrone their father. The case was investigated before the emperor, and they were pronounced innocent; whereupon, and with much tenderness, he remarked to them, that though he "rejoiced to find they were entirely innocent of the crime for which they had been so greatly calumniated, yet they were to blame so far as this, that they had not so demeaned themselves towards their father, as *to prevent the very grounds of that suspicion*, which had been spread abroad concerning them." Amid such abundant blessings of God upon my poor instrumentality: blessings which called for the exercise of the greatest watchfulness and most devout gratitude, and which demanded of me the most perfect consecration of heart, soul, life and all to His service; it is a matter of perfect astonishment and grief to me to think that I, even for a moment, lost sight of the high character of the Ambassador of Christ, to mingle in the vanities and follies of the world. How many reasons, too, had I for sleepless prudence, environed as I was by so many hostile influences ready to take advantage of the least asserted indiscretion on my part, and thus through me to inflict a wound on the blood-bought Church of Immanuel! Oh, it crushes my heart to think that under such circumstances, I, a minister of Jesus, could trifle, and joke, and jest: and I have therefore not repined at a single stroke with which the Lord, in just chastisement, has visited me, from whatever instrument it has come; and though

* It was a custom observed by the venerable Dr. Hanna, (Mr. Hunt's immediate predecessor,) in his pastoral visitations, to salute the female members of every family with a kiss. Mr. Hunt followed the same practice, but perhaps not so extensively except on wedding occasions. Nor did he regard it as improper to salute with a kiss those women whom he had ever married. These foolish usages ceased during my ministry, though at the commencement, and for several years, I had, against my better judgment, conformed on some occasions to the custom.

utterly undeserved on my part, so far as the accusations of my enemies are concerned. And if the sufferings and sorrows I have endured shall but have the effect to awaken any of my brethren in the ministry to a higher degree of watchfulness in their intercourse with the world, one end which our covenant God has had in view in thus afflicting me will doubtless have been accomplished.

Amongst the numerous grounds of dissatisfaction with me, (hinted at in the preceding chapters) in consequence of my efforts to promote various unpopular enterprises, one thing and another had been from time to time pitched upon by my enemies as the basis for an attempt to overthrow my influence with the community, and thus either hinder or impair the result of my labors. A most malignant effort of this kind was made in reference to my introducing the Confession of Faith and new Hymn Book amongst the people; but it is not of sufficient importance to the main issue, to admit of being here dwelt upon. Other and more determined efforts were, however, made in consequence of my unceasing labors in promoting the cause of temperance, as already intimated: and as these have a direct relation to the origin of the RUMOR, I shall here be somewhat specific.

The last of these attempts (previous to August, 1847,) was made in the autumn and winter of 1846–7. The Rev. Thomas P. Hunt, (a well-known advocate of the temperance reform,) came into the region in November, 1846, and delivered several lectures near Rum Corner, in Clinton, where I had been lecturing previously; and I not only stood at his side and seconded his efforts while he was upon the ground, but after he was gone followed up the strong impression which his discourses had made upon the public. On November 30, I lectured on the same subject to an immense audience in my own church: and proved the liquor-seller to be guilty of all the crimes which are perpetrated by his victim, the poor inebriate. On December 3, I lectured again near Rum Corner, taking for my text the words, "*Not this man, but Barabbas;*" and a few days after, at the temperance convention at Flemington; and so on through the winter. But while the Rev. T. P. Hunt and I were laboring as aforesaid, at Clinton, the liquor-sellers raised the most abominable falsehoods concerning him: and also reported that I had purchased and used great quantities of brandy: all of which they pretended to be able to prove. We of course paid no attention to these things, but went on with our work. My last sermon (the one referred to above,) near Rum Corner, however, so enraged the liquor-sellers that two of them waited on Dr. Manners, a lawyer residing in the neighborhood, and endeavored to have me indicted for a libel. They were however dismissed by that learned and accomplished advocate, rather more promptly than comported with the idea they had formed of their own dignity. And so soon as I had heard of this movement of their fraternity, I gave public notice at a lecture which I delivered on the same subject and in the same place. a few evenings afterwards, that if they did not conduct with more propriety, I should immediately get up a petition to revoke their licenses. The proposal was received by the audience with delight. It presented to the liquor-sellers also a view which they had never contemplated; and they were at once awed into silence, and compelled to smother their rage; and one of them, a Mr. Bonnel, sent me a frank and handsome apology for the course he had taken.

So stood matters, when an attempt on my part a few months afterwards, to restore the exercise of church discipline, furnished these men with an occasion for their final assault upon me, and which a wise and holy God for reasons yet to be fully developed, has permitted to be more successful. This assault, and the fact of its being by a clergyman in Philadelphia followed up to all the injurious results that were attainable by means of it, is the occasion of the present work. So that here I must go more fully into detail.

The case of discipline was the following. A young woman with whom (together with her father's family,) I had been on the most intimate terms from her childhood, was ascertained to have been guilty of ante-nuptial fornication. Subsequent events developed occurrences also in relation to this guilt which were of a most shocking character; some of which we shall be compelled to refer to hereafter. The marriage, however, was hastened (though the cause which hastened it did not publicly transpire until some months afterwards,) and her parents and the family all were of course justly offended at the occurrence which required such a procedure.

The Session having been trained under Mr. Hunt, were all exceedingly averse to the exercise of church discipline; for during the latter part of his ministry, for many years, the reins had been getting more and more slack in this particular, and finally seemed to be utterly abandoned: and from the exegesis which he gave of that much abused passage, 1 Cor. 7: 36, the elders supposed that such intercourse between affianced individuals, though impolitic, was not really criminal.* Consequently they took no notice whatever, of the offence of the young woman referred to; until I finally brought the case before them, on the ground of general rumor, and peremptorily insisted that some action should be taken in respect to it. After a good deal of demurring and hesitation, however, they finally voted that the offenders (both of whom were members of the church,) should be waited on. The question then arose as to the appointment of a committee for this purpose: *Sed quum jam inter mures quæreretur qui feli tintinnabulum annecteret, nemo repertus est.* All were willing that a committee should be appointed, but not one was willing to serve upon it: and each one on being named positively and pointedly refused. I then volunteered, provided that one of them would accompany me: but here, too, the fears of these timid but well-meaning men got the better of the claims of duty, and they each one peremptorily refused. The only alternative, then, was for me to attend to the matter, or suffer it to rest as it was. I did not hesitate; and to this hour I bless God that I did not. But when subsequent occurrences evinced how sinful and injudicious was this refusal on the part of my Session, bitterly indeed did they one and all deplore the course which their timidity had induced them to pursue. And

* This exegesis arrived at the conclusion, (though *how* or by what means, I never have been able to ascertain) that a promise of marriage if subsequently fulfilled, justified ante-nuptial intercourse. And one venerable elder of Bethlehem openly averred to me that persons who acted thus "were only following the advice of the Apostle."

one of their number, the venerable Asher Smith, being soon after called to die, expressed to me and to others on his death-bed the deep and continual anguish of his soul for his refusal to accompany me in the discharge of that most painful but imperative duty. But this anguish came too late, for my enemies had already done their work.

Soon after this resolution to wait upon Mr. and Mrs. Vanderbelt had passed the Session, and I found that no one would accompany me, I called at their residence, and had an interview with them both. They professed to be penitent, and wished to avoid if possible the exposure and pain of a public trial. I had consulted with the Rev. Dr. Kirkpatrick (of Ringoes, N. J.,) on the case, and found that his views coincided with my own: and in accordance with these views, I now stated that if they would lay before the Session a written acknowledgment of their sin, I thought such an exposure might be avoided. They wished to consider the matter: and after prayer with them I promised to call again to receive their answer.

I called again in the course of a week or two: but the young woman being alone, I did not tarry (or "did not go in," to use the expression which she subsequently deposed under oath,); but appointed a day during the following week for another call; a day on which her husband, she said, would certainly be at home. I accordingly called at the time appointed, taking with me a written form of submission to session, such as I had been advising them to employ. It was on the afternoon of the day (Thursday) preceding the commencement of the services preparatory to our communion. She, of course, understood the object of the visit, and invited me into the parlor, which was upon the second floor, stating that her husband was not at home. I informed her that my stay must be very short, as I had three other families to visit that afternoon; and it was already about two o'clock. This she also admitted under oath; and along with her servant-girl further deposed before Presbytery, that our stay in the parlor was not over fifteen minutes.

I had now no alternative left but to proceed with the case, or allow them to approach the communion table unrebuked, *after* it was known that the Session had formally commenced to take action on the subject: for it was impossible for me to call again before the Sabbath. I inquired of her when her husband would be at home. She replied "not before evening"; but assured me that he left word for me, promising to adopt any course that his wife would agree to in the matter.

This young woman, when scarcely out of her childhood, had been brought into the church under my ministry, and had always been as free and familiar with me, as if I had been her father. I had hitherto reciprocated her confidence and treated her as a child: and during this interview I spoke to her of the great sin she had committed against God, his church, and her own family. She confessed it; and came across the room, stood at my side, and putting her head on my shoulder, wept bitterly, and entreated that I would not make her and her husband a public example. I stated to her that while the crime was not so great as it perhaps would have been, had no engagement for marriage existed, that still it was a crime, and of such a nature as to require the prompt and energetic action of Session. I stated also that if she and her husband would send to the Session a letter such as I had previously mentioned, confessing their guilt, and promising to submit to whatever sentence might be pronounced, I would save them from the exposure she dreaded. She requested to have a copy of the form of such an act of confession and submission; and I copied for her the one I had with me; telling her that if she and her husband adopted and signed it, the Session would probably suspend them for a time; but that the sentence would soon be removed, if they conducted themselves so as to render it proper and advisable. She seemed much affected by the neglect with which many of her former friends treated her now, and I said what I could to cheer her; and told her that though she and her husband had done very wickedly, I trusted that they had sought and obtained the forgiveness of God; and that though others treated her with neglect, I never had (for she complained that I had but very seldom called upon them), and never would; for I regarded her still as my own dear child. At the conclusion of the interview I had prayer with her, (as she subsequently deposed, and also that she knelt down at a chair a yard or two distant from mine,) and as I was retiring she requested me to bring my wife to visit them soon, as they expected ere long to remove to New York: and in conclusion promised, that she and her husband would copy and sign the paper I had left with them, and send it to the meeting of Session on the following Saturday.

I look upon the whole of this interview as unjustifiable and imprudent in the extreme; and I have been mortified and humbled every time it has occurred to mind. Though I have never, for one instant, entertained towards this young woman such a feeling as my enemies have represented me as wishing to indulge on this occasion, nor done what they pretend, I shall not attempt to extenuate the glaring indiscretion exhibited by me on the occasion: for under the circumstances I ought not to have gone with her alone, however intimate and familiar I had previously been. I did not make the obvious distinction between the familiarity which friendship may warrant, and that which only the nearest relationship by blood may justify: though God knows I felt towards the poor transgressor the affection of a parent for a child, and could not refrain from weeping during the interview. The attempt to cheer her under such circumstances, by any such considerations, was wrong: at least I should never do it again. And I feel that without any regard to former intimacy, I ought to have performed my mission (since I was thoughtless enough to enter the room with her alone,) as the ambassador of God; I have left the matter, with its result, to his Providence: and the remembrance of my folly herein has done more to prostrate me before God, and to weaken my hands in any effort to exculpate myself from the accusations of my enemies, than all the wretched falsehoods which they have concocted. Nor have I ever objected to the sufferings which I have been called to undergo, in consequence of this indiscretion: but I do object that the base and cowardly passion of envy and literary jealousy should seize upon such an occurrence, in order to justify its malevolence. I had no suspicion when I called, that the poor young creature was so corrupt as subsequent disclosures evinced, or I should have cut off my right arm ere I should have consented to such an interview.

I ought to have remarked that the door of the parlor by which we entered, was not closed, as she and her servant both testify; and that there was also another family with six children living in the house, who occupied the room opposite the parlor, and the one under that below stairs.

On the following day (Friday) our preparatory services commenced at the church; and on Saturday the woman and her husband sent by the servant girl (who also was a member of the church,) a transcript of the forementioned paper signed by them both. I laid it before the session, who agreed to take such order thereon as I had suggested to the woman herself: and an answer, stating this, was written and given to the girl; who, on her return from the meeting, immediately delivered it to them, as she and the woman both subsequently testified. This same girl attended divine service at my church a number of times afterwards (as she admitted on oath), which I here mention for reasons which will appear presently.

Thus stood the matter: and I was felicitating myself on the happy establishment of this precedent for the restoration of discipline; when lo! on the Sabbath following they appeared at church, and actually communed. Discipline had been so much neglected, that upon second thought they came to the conclusion to resist its restoration in their case. The elders noticed their conduct: but not wishing to produce a disturbance they were permitted to commune by those who distributed the elements. And for the six following Sabbaths this young woman and her husband attended public worship at Bethlehem with their usual regularity; and also the servant girl, (who changed her place of residence,) and a female, a Miss Sweezey, who boarded with them; and who will appear again in the course of this narrative.

During the latter part of August following, I and my family left home for a week or two, on an excursion for recreation—and before our return, a scheme had been concocted by Mr. Hunt and the liquor-sellers at Rum Corner (near which the aforesaid family resided), and other places, to break down my influence; taking for its basis the above-named private interview with the woman. It was said that when alone with her I committed an assault and attempted to violate her person. Such was the rumor and its origin: the attempt to confirm and carry it out will be detailed in the course of this history.

CHAPTER IV.

DEVELOPMENT OF THE PLOT.

Such was the origin of this scheme to destroy my influence. A woman and her husband are disciplined for a disgraceful crime. When that discipline begins to be felt through the merciless strictness that the would-be-virtuous are ever so prone to indulge in, she, knowing that through me the case had been brought up for adjudication, gives vent to her feelings in scurrilous abuse: and being prompted therein by my enemies, and not supposing that she would be held responsible, says everything that malice and ingenuity could suggest for the purpose of vindicating herself, and presenting me in an unfavorable attitude. The enemies of the gospel of Christ who had long desired an opportunity to impair the effect which was being produced by my labors in the community, finding that I had indeed laid myself open to an assault by the injudicious interview aforesaid, seize upon the statements of this woman, and encourage her to add to them the most revolting accusations. She is at first (without exciting her suspicions as to the object) required to repeat these assertions until the statement, and its additions and improvements, are what my enemies wish them to be; and then a noted counterfeiter and liquor-seller offers her husband $200 with which to prosecute me in reference to the matter. Her husband then, by the advice of Mr. Hunt, insists upon her making oath to the truth of her declarations. This she pointedly refuses to do; and says that she has never had the least idea of deposing to the truth of what she had said. He insists upon it, however, and threatens to leave her unless she complies with his demand. Thus is the affidavit obtained; and the facts above stated are known to the whole community, and their truth undisputed.

When this rumored charge was started and understood, it appeared so absurd when viewed in connection with the delay of the woman and her husband to make such a shocking outrage known; and as connected with the fact also that subsequent to the asserted outrage itself, she and her husband, and her servant, had attended for weeks upon my ministry, that it was treated by the public with the most contemptuous disregard. I was however absent from home, and ere my return some of the aforesaid adverse influences had every desirable opportunity to concentrate their energies in giving plausibility to the plot, and to furnish it with their countenance and support.

The liquor-sellers at Rum Corner were the first to take the matter publicly in hand; and one of them volunteered to the woman's husband $200 to aid him in prosecuting me.* All this occurred previous to my return. After I had returned, however, their movements were more cautious and secret; and it was several days before I heard that such a report was in circulation. I reached home on Saturday, August 28th, and on Tuesday the 31st, on my return from a funeral, Mr. William Emery first mentioned to me the subject. The proceedings of my enemies, as subsequently ascertained, were as follows:

Two of the party had formally gone to Mr. Hunt for counsel in the matter, and the course he advised them to pursue may be learned from the following statement, made by himself when unexpectedly called upon by me to testify before Presbytery: "*I advised him* (the father of

* This was the individual who had taken the lead a few months before in the efforts made by the liquor-sellers to have me indicted for a libel, for denouncing the liquor-traffic.

the young woman) *to collect a number of the prominent opponents of Mr. Landis to meet at a time—no time fixed—at Esquire Boss', a most central place, and from the number that should there assemble select a committee and send them to Mr. Landis with a request to give them notice in writing that he would apply to the next* (meeting of) *Presbytery to have the pastoral relation dissolved between him and the congregation of Bethlehem.*" After naming some of these "prominent opponents" who "for a long time had desired to get rid of their pastor," and among whom were G. Conover the father of my accuser, J. Exten said to be a Unitarian, P. Sigler the distiller, D. Carhart who not long before had violated his temperance pledge, and others of the same class, Mr. Hunt continued his testimony as follows: "I wrote a paper, very short, to these opponents of Mr. L., giving advice how they might get rid of our pastor in a constitutional way." The reader may comment for himself upon these astounding disclosures, and will be at no loss to determine what would now have been the fate of such a plot thus exposed before Presbytery, had not one prominent individual in that body determined to make it subservient to my ruin.

Mr. Hunt was very unwilling to be called upon to testify, and resisted as long as he could. But though *he* would not state the fact, it was proved that he not only gave to these enemies of mine a letter of instructions, but appointed by name the committee which was to carry out his wishes, and advised them to proceed and take the woman's affidavit without notifying me at all. This committee consisted of a man known to be very hostile to me, and of another who is a distiller on a large scale, another a liquor-seller, and the other two (making five in all) were near relatives of my accuser; Mr. Hunt evidently supposing that enmity, and relationship, and love of gain, must operate herein to produce the result which he desired. A few days after this I met him at the church, and asked him why it was that he used me in this manner; upon which he promptly denied the charge *in toto*. But two gentlemen who were standing near and overheard the conversation, hereupon stepped up and said, "You did, Mr. Hunt, for we saw your letter." He then turned about in great confusion, and Dr. Sicarius (a relative) who was near, and saw the procedure, came up and took him away. At Presbytery also, being unexpectedly called on to state what part he had taken in the matter, he, as the reader has seen, freely admitted the truth of all which he had thus previously denied.

It was on a Tuesday afternoon, as stated above, that I was first informed of the matter. On Wednesday, which was September 1st, the congregation met to pay their pew-rents. The subject of the rumor was introduced, and I at once proposed to meet the woman in the presence of her parents, and of the elders of the church. To this proposition, however, my enemies would not accede; and through Mr. Hunt's influence and counsel the "prominent opponents" of mine insisted on proceeding to take the woman's affidavit. And they did so, coolly informing me that I could not be present; and they were also assured that no human agency could prevent their accomplishment of this most villanous piece of iniquity. After the informal selection of a committee by themselves for this purpose, without even allowing me a choice therein, (for the meeting was not organized,) the congregation was invited to meet again on Saturday the 4th instant, to learn the result.

In the interval the committee, without in the least apprising me, proceeded to the residence of my accuser to take her affidavit. She wept much, and said, "I do not want to swear to the truth of what I have been saying." Her father was also present, and objected to her being required to depose to the truth of her statements. Her husband, however, became angry and told her that unless she swore to their truth he would leave her. She finally consented, and the committee was eight hours (from 3 o'clock until 11, P.M.) with her, before they succeeded in obtaining her statement, occupying but two pages, loosely written, of ordinary sized paper. The committee, and a lawyer (employed by them) and a magistrate, were with her, and a foul-mouthed scurrilous female by name of C. Sweezey was permitted to be present all the time, *and not only to correct her statements, but even to dictate to her*, while the woman herself was, time after time, permitted to leave the room and consult her husband and friends in relation to what she should depose. Then, in order to conclude the business consistently, by the advice of one member of the committee, (Mr. Exten the Unitarian,) a copy of her affidavit was left with the woman, who was thus secured against the danger of subsequent contradiction. The committee frankly acknowledged these facts, and their undisputed and indisputable truth was known to the Rev. Albert Barnes. But who has heard either him or any of his satellites give the least hint thereof in their representations concerning me? Let those brethren, who, relying on his veracity, have, from this source, received and propagated the most injurious impressions respecting a brother now, in the light of this single truth, think upon what they have been doing. They have unwarrantably and without troubling themselves to inquire into the facts sufficiently to justify such a procedure, *inferred* that he could have no sinister aim in endeavoring to blast my reputation, and that consequently I was guilty. And thus *upon such grounds* they have aided him in the attainment of his aims in prostrating my family, injuring the cause of religion, and in cutting off many of my opportunities for doing good. But though my plans for promoting God's glory and the good of men have thus been frustrated, I have felt throughout that God has other and better plans to be accomplished even through the frustration of mine. Blessed be His name! Thus then was this affidavit obtained. And it is proper to state also, that with the exception of Mr. Exten, all the committee, and the magistrate himself, (whom Mr. Hunt named as one of my strongest opponents,) left the house declaring their firm and full conviction that the whole story was a tissue of falsehood; a conviction which they still retain.

On Sept. 4th, the congregation met. During the interval since the 1st inst. Mr. Hunt had been riding through the congregation, doing what he could to arouse the people against me. Hence the meeting was very large, consisting both of men and women. When it was organized Mr. Hunt made four speeches to persuade the congregation to hear the affidavit which he himself had read. The committee, however, reported that it was not a proper document to read before a promiscuous audience. Mr. Hunt, however, insisted that it should be read; but his motion was voted down. A motion was then made by Asher Housel, Esq., that, inasmuch as the congregation had heard only a vile rumor against its pastor, and had heard nothing from him on the other side, though it was now about to take a vote touching the matter, the pastor should have an opportunity of speaking to the point touching the rumors which had been circulated against him. Mr. Hunt opposed this motion strongly, both speaking and voting against it; but it was carried. I then addressed the congregation, (amongst whom were the bitterest enemies I had in Jersey, being counterfeiters, distillers, liquor-sellers from Rum Corner, Mr. Hunt, and his relative, Sicarius, from a place named Sodom.) I addressed the congregation about twenty minutes, and, on the question being put by the chairman, "Shall our pastor now continue his ministrations amongst us?" one tremendous AYE burst from the multitude; and when the question was reversed, there was not a soul to be found amongst my guilt-stricken accusers who ventured to vote in the negative. Even Mr. Hunt was overawed. In my statement I gave the whole history of the case of discipline, with the unwillingness of the elders either to act therein or to accompany me, as well as my own indiscretion in going alone.* The subject-matter of the affidavit will be considered when we speak of the trial before Presbytery.

I have no wish to anticipate, by remarks of my own, the reflections of the reader on the facts of this history, nor would the limits to which I must confine myself permit me were I so disposed; but what serious mind can contemplate the foregoing without asking why Mr. Hunt and my other enemies should be so anxious to prepossess the public against me, if they themselves truly believed this evil report? Why all this indecent haste? Does it not betray on their part a consciousness that the whole movement was merely the result of a combination to secure a sinister aim? Does it not also betray an apprehension that a fair and impartial investigation would roll back the infamous accusation upon themselves by discovering the true origin and design of the plot? Why should there be such anxiety to pledge the poor woman and commit her beyond the hope of repentance by securing her deposition? Whence could this all have proceeded, unless from fear that the compunctious visitings of remorse might (if not held in check by an apprehension of the doom which the law allots to perjury,) break in and lead her to confess the truth, and explain how and by whom she had been induced to utter what she did? Mr. Hunt knew beforehand of her own and her father's unwillingness that she should swear to the truth of it; and feared that if he failed to secure her affidavit at the outset, and during the excitement which the story had aroused, it would not be secured at all. And does all this look like a sober and deliberate conviction that wrong had been done by me, which wrong ought to be impartially tried and righted to her and to her family, and to the cause of religion and good morals?—or does it all appear like a determination to take advantage of a preconcerted scheme to remove me from the church by destroying my

* On the Monday following I wrote to the Moderator of Presbytery, stating the rumor, and requesting him to call a meeting of that body as soon as possible to investigate the matter. Mr. Barnes however at once opposed this request, and I was advised therefore to let the matter lie over till the regular meeting of Presbytery.

character? The facts are before the reader, and let every upright mind judge for itself.

Such then is the origin, and such the foundation, of an accusation upon which a clergyman in Philadelphia has taken occasion to acquit himself of an immense debt of gratitude which he owed me, by seeking, in every conceivable way, to destroy my reputation, and utterly to close up all my avenues of usefulness as a laborer in our blessed Master's vineyard; and whose inuendoes other clergymen—professed expounders of the laws of Christ—have not scrupled to repeat, again and again, to my serious injury, and in sections of the land where God was still abundantly blessing my labors to his church, and to multitudes of my fellow-men. Oh why is it! why should it be that, even amongst brethren, it so often happens that so soon as some vile disparaging rumor is started against one whose labors God has distinguished by his blessing, the godlike virtue of charity falls asleep, or rather dies in the heart as though it had never been! Will God permit such things to pass unreproved and unvisited? Time and the judgment seat of Christ will soon determine.

CHAPTER V.

EFFORTS TO SUSTAIN THE PLOT—ORGANIZATION OF THE ADVERSE INFLUENCES ALREADY REFERRED TO.

THE incipient movements therefore of this conspiracy to destroy me, were made at Rum Corner, the place where Mr. Hunt occasionally sold the whisky produce of his orchards, and near which my accuser and her husband resided. Hence it was at first treated with contempt by the moral part of the community. But when at length other individuals, who, besides the liquor-venders, had been operating against me, (deeming that something could be made of the plot to effect their purposes,) stepped in and took it out of the hands of these men, it began to assume an important aspect. And rarely indeed has Satan been served amongst men (as the reader will see) by a more active and energetic agency than was now brought into the field by Mr. Hunt and Dr. Sicarius.*

The husband of my accuser had borne a very indifferent character previous to his reception into the church; but he came into it during a revival, and it was hoped and believed that he had reformed. After his ante-nuptial sin was discovered, he frequently absented himself from the church and was in constant association with the depraved creatures who hung around Rum Corner. The character also of the other conspirators (though he was more properly their victim,) is a fair subject of remark,

* This individual, who had practiced medicine many years without a diploma, was called "*Doctor*" by courtesy. His son-in-law, a clergyman, can explain his *sobriquet* by a *forcible* illustration.

so far as facts are concerned, which no one will dispute who is acquainted with the parties. A man who promised $200 to my accuser's husband, had been indicted for circulating a large quantity of counterfeit money, and it cost him a considerable sum of good money and not a little difficulty to avoid the penitentiary. A second had been arrested for similar practices, and, I believe, imprisoned. A third had been heavily fined for selling the meat of a cow which had died without the aid of the butcher's knife. A fourth had a narrow escape from arrest for purchasing and putting in circulation a considerable sum of counterfeit bank bills.* Another, a distiller, was notorious for his amours. Another, who was peculiarly bitter, had seduced his wife's sister. And a third, equally clamorous and denunciatory, had been in New York about two years before, and while there became syphilitic, and, on his return home, communicated the disease to his wife. The occurrence made considerable noise in the neighborhood. But, instead of any further detail of particulars, I will here quote the remark made to a neighboring clergyman (who was endeavoring to make capital out of the effort to destroy me,) by Mr. William C. Young, a worthy and excellent man, who had, all his life, resided in the neighborhood: "Who are these accusers of Mr. Landis?" said he. "You can find no one who even professes to believe this report, who was not his avowed opposer before it was started. And who are those that abuse and vilify him the most? I know them all; and know that there is not a notorious adulterer, or seducer, or fornicator, in the whole region, who is not amongst them. Yes, sir, and men who are known to have not restrained the gratification of their lusts to persons of their own color." There is no denying the truth of this statement, and it may furnish an idea as to what kind of material constituted no small part of a community amongst which I was laboring to build up the kingdom of Christ. I need scarcely remark that but few of these men attended my ministry except occasionally, and that they hated me because I told them the truth. But to return from this digression.

These Rum Corner men and their pot companions proceeded as far as they were able against me; but their characters being known, it may be supposed that such advocacy only injured the plot with the respectable part of the community. The cause of their hatred to me was likewise known. I had often lectured on temperance in their vicinity, and only eight months previously they had endeavored to indict me for a libel. On failing to do this, one of them rode even to Allentown, Pa., and visited the low "grog-shops" and oyster-cellars to see if something

* When Rev. T. P. Hunt and myself were lecturing near Rum Corner on temperance (as above stated), he established the fact that "liquor-selling was worse than counterfeiting." The day following one of the liquor-sellers there was standing at his door swearing and abusing Mr. H. and myself in a most scurrilous manner; and seeing an old acquaintance passing by, he hailed him and said, "What do you think? them d——d fellows say that selling rum is worse than counterfeiting." The man stopped, and looking at him a moment, gravely replied: "Well, Jake, *you* ought to know whether this be so, for you have practiced *both*." To this poor Jake made no reply whatever, being utterly dumb-founded. Jake was one of the prime-movers in the plot to destroy me, and yet, as facts have proved, was not too low a tool for envy and literary jealousy to employ in gratifying its insatiable desires.

could not there be hatched up against me. As my labors there had also met with great success, I expected that he would scarcely come away empty-handed. But on his return, one of his friends accosting him by name, said, "Well, Jake, what did you find against the Dominie?" To which he replied, "Why, to be honest, I could not learn anything to his disadvantage." The efforts of these men and of my accuser, therefore, did me no real injury. But now, as the report was dying a natural death, *Mr. Hunt all at once seemed to acquire new spirits in the crusade*, and Dr. Sicarius also, who now stepped forward to galvanize the expiring falsehood, hoping to restore it to life and vigor again.

The reason why my accuser's story was thus rapidly passing into oblivion, was not however wholly attributable to the fact that the conspiracy was known to have originated at Rum Corner. This of course had its effect; but in addition thereto many things came to light, upon a little cool reflection, which tended greatly to facilitate its exit. For example: one prominent enemy of mine, a distiller, had (only a few months before this plot was developed), avowed his intention of compelling me to leave Bethlehem either before or during the autumn of that year. He resided not far from the place where, as before remarked, I had been pelted with addled eggs for lecturing on temperance; and where such horrid oaths and threats of personal violence were uttered against me, that some of my people apprehending that I would be really murdered if I went there again (for the "rummies" there made a great display of fire-arms, tar-barrels, &c.), entreated me not to fulfill my next appointment to lecture there on a subject so obnoxious. I did fulfill it, however, and delivered without interruption a lecture of nearly two hours in length, to the utter amazement of those cowardly "rowdies." And the only thing that this distiller and his anti-temperance friends could accomplish in return was to vote me into the office of "Pound Keeper" at the next election. A little reflection soon brought many such things to the minds of the people. There were other occurrences which made considerable impression; an example or two of which must suffice. My accuser's father sympathized with the opposition to the temperance reform. And there was also a man, who, shortly after I went to Bethlehem, appropriated to his own use a large part of the funds of the church. I discovered his knavery; and the matter, on being investigated, was proved against him so strongly that he was obliged to refund. But he was ashamed to be seen at church afterwards; and being of a revengeful spirit, was glad of any opportunity to injure either the pastor or trustees of the church. As he was thus opposed to me, Mr. Hunt showed him a good deal of favor; in return for which he also went over to Allentown, soon after my accuser's affidavit was taken, to ascertain for Mr. Hunt whether anything could there be learned to my disparagement. Now in the summer of 1847, and of course not more than two or three months before the development of the conspiracy, this man's wife informed Mrs. Sarah Headen (a lady of high respectability, and a member of the Old School Presbyterian Church at Clinton, New Jersey), that Mr. Conover and old Mr. Hunt "intended to compel Mr. Landis to leave Bethlehem next fall." Mrs. Headen paid no particular attention to the remark at the time; but when, two or three months afterwards, the abovenamed report was raised against me by this man's daughter, and Mrs. Headen seeing that the affidavit was so much insisted on by Mr. Hunt, the remark returned to her recollection and she promptly made it known. Such is the naked fact; I have not been able to penetrate the darkness which is behind it. The light of eternity, however, will soon develop it all.

Then further, the husband of my accuser, at the meeting on Sept. 4th, said to me that he hoped I would not resort to law in the matter. He was pale and appeared to be very much terrified. He had told Messrs. Gronigal and Deats, of Clinton, that he did "not intend to expose Mr. Landis, but to make him pay well for it;" and his previous character being known, this remark was, and I think properly, understood to mean that he wished to make a little money out of me in the way of "false pretences." He had committed himself too in various other ways, as, for example, by saying to Mr. Stiger that he "did not believe that anything criminal or even improper had passed between his wife and Mr. Landis."* He had made other and similar admissions, before Dr. Sicarius formally took the matter in hand; after which he became reserved and cautious. The knowledge that the story had been got up for sinister purposes, together with the recollection that he had made such admissions, therefore induced him thus to come over and speak to me. I replied to him that I did not design to go to law unless it was necessary. He replied that he did not think there was any occasion for it. To this I answered that there would be none if his wife would plainly retract what she had asserted concerning me.

On Monday, August 30th (and before I had heard anything of the plot), I spent most of the afternoon in Clinton and called on a number of families. As I was expecting that this man and his wife would remove to New York in a few days, I went to their residence beyond Rum Corner to bid them adieu. She was not present, but I had some close conversation with him on the subject of personal religion, urging him not to neglect the Sabbath-school, or prayer-meeting, or the public service of the Sanctuary. He conversed with me freely and kindly, and promised to act in accordance with my suggestions. A day or two afterwards, and soon after the story of the woman was detailed to me, it was rumored by my enemies that when I called upon him on Monday, he was much exasperated and treated me very harshly. Hence during the aforesaid interview with him at the church (on Sept. 4th), I asked him in the presence of several gentlemen whether he had given countenance to such a rumor. In answer to my question he promptly replied, "I never said that I treated you harshly. I treated you at that interview as politely and kindly as I ever did in my life." This he uttered with much vehemence, as is still remembered by Messrs. Asa M'Pherson and Asher S. Housel, Esq., who were standing near. And now, reader, can you conceive that if this man truly believed the report—nay, if he had not known it to be false, he would thus have treated me? I hold the thing to be an utter impossibility. It is contrary to the very

* All these points and many others equally impressive were shut out from Presbytery at the trial, as the reader will hereafter see, by the perverse ingenuity of one unhappy man who evidently had forgotten Is. 50:11.

nature of things. But the poor man was the dupe of an artful scheme, of whose hellish depths he then had no idea.

A while after the meeting on Sept. 4th, the whole story in our vicinity was fast hastening to the land of forgetfulness, and the public were settling down in the conviction that the affair was but a wretched conspiracy to compel me to leave my charge. At this juncture, however, a new actor was brought upon the stage,—the servant girl of my accuser. She had been received into the church during a revival, though against the wishes of many; for her character had been extremely abandoned, and in the neighborhood where she was reared (a short distance south of the place called Sodom), the bare idea of believing her word in any matter wherein she has the least inducement to conceal the truth, is treated with cool contempt. This is notorious through the region. And when it is remembered that respectable and unimpeachable witnesses testify that she was detected in the act of stealing corn from a neighbor's corn-crib; and had been discovered in the very act of getting into bed to a man; that she openly avowed herself to be *enciente* by Mr. Abram Banghart; and a hundred other things equally enormous; the reader will be able to decide as to what the extremity of Mr. Hunt and Dr. Sicarius must have been at this stage of the business, when it was found to be necessary to solicit the favor and patronage of such a female. Yet this is not the worst feature in their case; for, when the report of my accuser first started against me,* many persons knowing that this girl had resided with her in the beginning of July, at once inquired of her whether she knew anything of the matter: to whom she uniformly declared, that though she had been up stairs, and looked into the room (as the door stood partly open) and saw both the young woman and myself, she saw nothing whatever that was improper. These things she had said to numerous and unimpeachable witnesses (as will be more fully remarked upon in Part II.), but as she was known to be the only person in the accuser's part of the house while I was there, and as the affidavit was now sadly in need of support, this poor girl must be in some way induced to come forward to confirm its statements; and this would answer an important purpose where her character was unknown. Dr. Sicarius, who needs but the pen of a Burns to be rendered immortal as a practitioner, is a physician for whom she always professed a remarkable partiality, though for reasons not to be here named, a fact which I should not mention, did it not afford *the* clue to the full ascendency which was now obtained over her, and by which she was induced, in defiance of her previous statements, to patronize the respectable association who so anxiously entreated her favors, and nearly *one month after the date of my accuser's affidavit*, this girl was taken before a Squire Case (who resided not far from Rum Corner), and sworn. Her statement will also be considered in Part II.

Previous to this, great efforts had been made to continue the excitement by the invention of a mass of as bold and bare-faced falsehoods concerning me, as could be easily imagined. They were however imme-

* This, as above remarked, was in the latter part of August, before which time this girl had gone to serve in one or two other families.

diately followed up by my people and their falsity proved; which, of course, always produced a reaction in my favor.* Hence this second extra-judicial oath; of the taking of which I had not even heard, until some days after it was obtained; so that in the taking of both of these affidavits I was not permitted to be present either in person or by representative: those very honorable personages justly deeming that they could transact the business quite as much to their satisfaction in my absence, as if I were present; nor was the procedure without its appropriate climax. For when I sent a friend (Mr. John R. Emery,) with a note to this worthy justice, politely requesting him to furnish me with a copy of the affidavit (which he was in the habit of reading to all who wished to hear it), he refused promptly, with a flourish of language and ideas, which to appreciate fully, would require a better knowledge than I yet possess of the dialect and idioms of Rum Corner. Nor could I procure a copy of this document until after my trial in Presbytery had commenced. To offer any comment on such ludicrous baseness and iniquity, were absurd.

By this time Mr. Hunt and Dr. Sicarius found that they had laid themselves open to a civil prosecution of a very grave character. Mr. Hunt's own son informed him, that if I were disposed to do so I could take from him his very farm: and some of my friends had injudiciously threatened as much. Hence these men regarded my triumph as their own destruction; and everything that cunning and malevolence, superadded to wealth, could effect, was now brought to bear to insure their own safety by my overthrow; and had it not been for this view which they took of the subject, I believe that their efforts would have ended here. But Messrs. Hunt and Sicarius had gone so far that wading fully over seemed to them less perilous than going back: especially as Mr. Barnes (as will be seen hereafter) had already begun to favor the efforts of these men, in such a manner as assured them of his support. Why he should do so is for him, and not me to explain. The reader will however find my own view of the matter in Part II. of this narrative.

CHAPTER VI.

USES MADE OF THE PLOT.—CONCENTRATION OF THE ADVERSE INFLUENCES.

When it was at length perceived by my enemies therefore, that there was a fair prospect of powerful assistance from abroad; and that it

* There were some five or six of these falsehoods in all, every one of which wa "manufactured out of whole cloth." They were however, in a little while so satisfactorily disposed and fastened upon my enemies, that they never afterwards in that region ventured to refer to them. Yet these tales were by a hoary-headed infidel taken to Philadelphia, and told as matters of fact: and from his mouth they were directly repeated to Dr. P., a clergyman, and a mere *pes felinus* of Mr. Barnes, though professing a sincere friendship for me. *And he, without knowing anything further on the subject, favored the whole mass at once with his full endorsement.* What think you of this, reader? I immediately called him to account for it; but what earthly resource could I have under an assault like this?

adroitly managed the plot could be so employed as materially to impair and perhaps wholly to destroy my influence, Messrs. Hunt and Sicarius became more busy than ever. All latent prejudices against me were called forth; and all the hostile influences were soon concentrated in the effort to accomplish my removal from Bethlehem. But every laborious and faithful minister of Christ can, from the foregoing history, and his own experience, readily appreciate the nature, extent and weight of such influences as were now brought to bear for this purpose.

At this juncture the wealthiest man in the congregation informed me through a friend, that *if I would cease to preach on temperance, and admit into the pulpit no more agents for benevolent operations, and say nothing more against slavery*, he would at once espouse my cause against the vile efforts that were being made to destroy me:* for with the exceptions which he thus named he professed to be extremely partial to my ministrations. I knew the extent of Mr. Vansyckel's influence, which even over Mr. Hunt was next to absolute; and that with him for my advocate, the conspiracy of my enemies in Jersey would have been overawed. I promptly replied to the message, however, *that nothing should induce me to entertain any such proposal.* This gentleman thenceforth became my enemy, and entirely fell in with the schemes of my opposers.

And now was the hour in which all that were hostile felt that they could with impunity denounce the man whose uncompromising promulgation of the gospel had given them offence. I had been stern in my rebukes of wickedness: and Sabbath visitation; and this and other methods of desecrating that holy day, had found no favor, though connived at by my predecessor. I had required that the sutler's tables should be removed from the grove on the sacramental Sabbath; and had restored church discipline; and had separated the church for the most part from Unitarianism, and the ungodly practices of worldly policy; and had denounced slavery, and intemperance, and the traffic in intoxicating drinks; and the gospel, I truly believe, was faithfully proclaimed. The enmity of the human heart had been aroused at the fearless promulgation of the truth of God; and the enmity of Satan also, in consequence of the eminent success which had, through the Divine blessing, crowned my poor labors. And now all the deadly hostility which such things were calculated to arouse in such a community, and which had been slumbering like a pent-up volcano, was concentrated; and the moment that Hell thus gave the signal, all its fury burst upon me. Sectarian jealousy likewise mingled therein, and justified and gave impulse to the whole. Professional envy also raised its croaking voice. And now was seen the form of an aged man,—a professed minister of Jesus, riding upon the whirlwind and directing the storm against a brother who had given his

* Though some who knew what I had to contend with in this charge, have expressed surprise that I did not resign it previous to 1847, seeing that such constant and determined efforts were made to ruin me, yet I never have for a single moment regretted that I disregarded such policy. Through the grace of God, I have never learned to hesitate between the alternative of deserting a post which He had plainly assigned to me, and that of being sacrificed. God designs to effect some great good by means of what I have been there called to suffer. And all efforts in that community to crush me would have been unavailing, had it not been for that external influence of which I shall particularly speak in Part II. of this Narrative.

whole soul and energy to the work of glorifying God and serving men. It was such a storm, directed by the aged Caiaphas, that led to the judicial murder of Him who said to his disciples "In the world *ye* shall have tribulation: but be of good cheer; I have overcome the world."

Mr. Hunt, in the latter part of September, wrote the letter to Mr. Barnes, which will be found in its proper connection in Part II. I being ignorant of any correspondence between these gentlemen, did on September 6th, write to Dr. Converse (moderator of Presbytery), requesting that the charge against me should be investigated with as little delay as possible. This letter was written on September 6th; and contains the following passage. "The object of this letter is to request an *immediate investigation* by Presbytery, of the charge. Do not, oh do not delay the matter. Let a commission be appointed to come up and examine into the matter, and report the facts to Presbytery; or else call a *pro re nata* meeting." A few days afterwards, and in reply to Dr. C.'s answer, I wrote again on the same subject; and from this letter the subjoined extracts may be in place.

"God will, I believe, bring me out of this trial, refined as silver. Certain it is, that if he enables me to exculpate myself from the accusation, it will give me still greater power in wielding the sword of the Spirit. And, if not, I trust, I shall be able through grace to show that I can suffer his righteous will, as well as labor to perform it.

"The excitement has subsided greatly; and the confidence of my people is still unimpaired. I have labored to work on in the vineyard; and the community immediately around me (who have become acquainted with the facts,) already take my part with a decision and earnestness, for which I feel truly grateful to God. They view the whole as an infamous scheme to crush me, for what I have been endeavoring tc do for morality and religion. I leave the matter with my people, and have taken no active part in it."——"As to the charge of ever having attempted to violate this woman, I say, that *if I ever attempted, or designed to make such attempt, or desired to do so, then may all to whose adjudication the case may come, decide it against me: may I be an outcast from society; may my name be execrated and execrable amongst men; and may this sentence be registered in heaven as a prayer against me.*"

The reader may be able to judge from these passages, whether I interposed any delay in coming at once to a trial; or whether I was inclined to ask any favor of friend or foe, either in or out of Presbytery. But Mr. Barnes, of whose aims I and my brethren had then no conception, (and whose influence in Presbytery was very commanding, in consequence of his position in the church,) at once opposed the motion for a speedy investigation; and to accommodate his unyielding disposition, though he stood, I believe, entirely alone in his views, the brethren in Philadelphia, who belonged to the Presbytery, concluded to advise me to defer the investigation, until the regular meeting of the body in October. It was then, (as the reader will see,) by the management of Mr. Barnes, postponed until after the middle of November. So that I, with my church and family, was left in this suffering condition for nearly three months (as Mr. Hunt advises in his letter to Mr. Barnes. See Part II.), till time should be allowed my enemies to concentrate all their powers, in order to have me indicted at the county court. But the particulars of this whole transaction will be given hereafter.

Messrs. Hunt and Sicarius having thus secured the depositions of my accuser and her servant, and considering their own liabilities in case of a failure to make out the charge, as well as my own disadvantage on the score of witnesses in relation to the alleged fact, advised Mr. Conover to take his daughter before the grand jury in November. He did so. The jury, however, regarding the wretched tale in its true light as both absurd and contradictory, treated it with derision, and, by a decided majority, refused to find a bill. They were, however, remanded back and directed to find a bill. Through the influence of one man named Hofman,* they were then induced by a majority of one to find a bill against me *for simple assault and battery*, in consequence of which I was bound over in a trifling sum to appear and answer at the court in February.

On November 16th, the Presbytery met at Bethlehem to investigate the case; the particulars of which meeting will come up more appropriately for consideration in Part II. It is sufficient to remark here, however, that when I had entered upon my defence, and before I had examined many of my most important witnesses, the prosecution came forward, and through Mr. Barnes, asked permission of me to withdraw the suit; professing truly to relent for the course they had pursued against me. Mr. Hunt also, shedding an abundance of tears, asked my forgiveness publicly three several times. They promised also to take the suit out of court, on condition that I would permit them now to withdraw it from the Presbytery. I assented; for I had no personal resentments to gratify. The father and the husband of my accuser then came forward in the presence of the Presbytery and congregation, and shook hands with me. My accuser had, during her examination, repeatedly and most unequivocally acquitted me not only of crime, but even of intending it, or any harm whatever. This was obviously the workings of conscience; and was the only thing that the poor little creature now could do, by means of which she could even hope to repair the cruel injuries I and my church and family had suffered from her lawless tongue. The testimony of her servant was found so grossly contradictory that no one regarded it, and her character was shown to be what it truly is. Thus was the matter adjusted, and settled; and Presbytery returned home.

I then proceeded with my pastoral labors, and did what I could to heal the wound which had been given to the church and religion. The presbyterial document, however, which Mr. Barnes had drawn up, purporting to state the merits of the case,† (and which the Presbytery had, without time for due deliberation, adopted late on a Saturday evening,

* This individual, a neighbor of mine, soon after our great revival at Bethlehem, had evinced much uneasiness at the unrivalled prosperity of my charge, and from the first rising of this rumor against me, had greedily seized upon it for the purpose of impairing my influence. But how striking are the retributions of Providence! Not long after this occurrence, and many months before I left Bethlehem, rumors incomparably worse than this against me started in his own church against its pastor, (the Rev. Mr. Van A—, a laborious, self-denying, and excellent divine,) which not only compelled him to leave, but rent the church itself into fragments. In fact, about this time Hell seemed determined to recover possession of that whole region, by destroying every faithful minister therein, *for not one such escaped unscathed.*

† This paper will be given in its proper connection hereafter.

after being wearied out by a tedious session,) in the course of several weeks was sent to the parties. It is just such a document as is calculated hopelessly to destroy a man's character, by conveying the impression that the author of it deems him guilty of the charge, and yet wishes to screen him from justice; and on receiving it my enemies were consequently assured that it could thus be urged with very great effect against me. Messrs. Hunt and Sicarius obtained copies of it, and took great pains to make this impression, (and the reputation of Presbytery was made to suffer along with myself in consequence;) and endeavored to persuade the father and husband of my accuser to violate their pledge to me to take the suit out of court. But being without any real or apparent reason to justify so shameful an act, the following incident was seized upon for the purpose.

The day of the Annual Thanksgiving, (appointed by the State,) occurred soon after the adjournment of Presbytery. The usual congregation attended at Bethlehem, I myself officiating on the occasion; but at the conclusion of the services, Asher S. Housel, Esq., President of the Board of Trustees, at the request of the ladies, gave notice to the congregation that "after the gentlemen had retired, the ladies present would hold a meeting." The gentlemen of course retired, with the exception of the president, whom the ladies requested to remain in order to furnish what counsel might be needed in respect to the proper forms of conducting the proposed business. At this meeting a series of resolutions was unanimously adopted, of which the three following are the last:*

"*Resolved*, That we do not believe that any female of truth or purity of character, has ever accused Mr. Landis of taking improper liberties, and that the base slanders circulated to ruin and destroy him, originated with 'the Father of Lies;' who, like other great Inventors, has lost much of his reputation by the very ingenious improvements recently made upon him.

"*Resolved*, That as the insults (*i.e.* to the ladies of the congregation,) were publicly given by Mr. Hunt, we feel it due to our wounded feelings, that an apology equally public be made to the daughters of the church: as we are resolved to be 'first pure, then peaceable.'

"*Resolved*, That a copy of these resolutions be sent to Mr. Hunt; and that Mr. Landis shall not be made acquainted with them until carried into effect."

Mr. Hunt in his testimony before Presbytery (forgetting the language of his letter to Mr. Barnes) had truly said that "all the women go for Landis." They did, with scarce an exception: and these resolves express the conviction and feelings of as large and reputable and intelligent a body of ladies towards their Pastor, as can be easily found in any church in the country. I had heard that they contemplated holding such a meeting, and did my utmost to dissuade them from it. But let the reader here contemplate this unadvised and spontaneous expression of the feelings of the ladies of my charge, in the face, too, of all the cruel and malignant efforts which had been made to destroy me. I immediately foretold what use my enemies would endeavor to make of

* The whole paper will be given hereafter. It contains some references to Mr. Barnes's course, which, to be understood, will require more extended remarks than can here be made without indulging in too much of a digression. Their proper place is in Part II.

these proceedings; though I now believe the ladies were right in calling the meeting.

This procedure, as before remarked, afforded Mr. Hunt and Dr. Sicarius an apparent reason for the violation of the pledge to enter a *nolle prosequi*. They ridiculously charged me with having "got up" the meeting, and asserted that by so doing I had become the aggressor; *though neither I nor any of my family had anything whatever to do with it:* and being now doubly sure of the co-operation of Mr. Barnes (and this they made no secret of), they recommenced their persecution to compel me to resign my charge. They had, near the close of December, received their copy of Mr. Barnes' paper, and on the evening of Jan. 15, 1848, held a meeting at the residence of Daniel Carhart, and adopted a paper calling on me to resign my charge, under the threat that should I refuse to do so, the suit should not be taken out of court. This paper was brought to me by a committee appointed for the purpose; and was by me immediately laid before the officers of the congregation: hereupon a meeting of the congregation was called on Jan. 27th, and the paper laid before them. The meeting was a very large one, and a series of resolutions was unanimously adopted, of which it is necessary in the present connection to give only the following:

"*Resolved*, That our Pastor be respectfully requested to return as an answer to the resolutions passed at the meeting at Mr. Carhart's, the following statement as the unanimous sense of this meeting; to wit: That we recommend to him to continue as he has heretofore done, to abide by the late decision of Presbytery; and that we purpose to do so ourselves; and hereby pledge ourselves to sustain him in doing so. And that we earnestly recommend to every member of the church and congregation to abide by it likewise; assured that in the end this will prove to be the best for all concerned."

A copy of this resolution was forwarded in reply to the committee who had waited on me; whereupon my enemies immediately resolved that the promised *nolle prosequi* should not be entered, and accordingly before the session of our County Court for February occurred, my counsel, Alexander Wurts, Esq., apprised me that the suit would come on. I made this known to my brethren of the Presbytery: and had it not been for the counter influence of Mr. Barnes (who could himself with a single word have stayed the prosecution, see Part II.), very decisive measures would have been adopted in relation to the matter.

As the time drew near, I prepared for the trial by subpœnaing my witnesses respecting the character of the servant girl. Dr. Sicarius, to whom Mr. Hunt and the rest of my enemies had now assigned the lead in this business, was so amazed at my coolness and determined preparation (for I had summoned his own wife as a witness), that he became too sick to attend court, and sent word to the State's Attorney to have the case postponed. My friends were on the ground, and we were ready, with the exception of a lawyer* whom I had employed at the de-

* This man accepted my fee, and it was a large one; and let me continue in hopes of his attendance until the very day before court. He then, to be "*faithful to his client*," and yet prevent my securing other efficient aid, wrote me a letter, stating that he did not think he could attend, though on that day he did attend to a less important cause in another court. This letter, too, he sent not to my post-office address, to

sire of my own excellent counsel, Mr. Wurts. Still we said to the prosecution, Go on with your case! I procured another lawyer, *pro forma*, (for the opposition had two,) a man by the name of Clark, a mere "Jack of the pinch"; not considering the risk I ran by intrusting any part of the case to such inferior and miserably incompetent advocacy, and my enemies knew him much better than I did, and I learned too late for my own interest that they were delighted that I had employed him. He was a reformed inebriate, and had become a professor of religion. This was about all I knew of him, until experience favored me with her instructions. He had sent me word by a member of my church (Captain Moses Hoyt), that if I would accept of his service, he would undertake my cause free of all charge. This, coming from him, ought to have excited my suspicions. But as I had not the remotest idea of employing him, I let the matter pass with a slight acknowledgment. When, however, the other lawyer did not appear, and Mr. Wurts thought that I ought to have another, I went to this Clark, and accepted of his proffered services, and paid him $10. He apologized for receiving the money, because of his previous offer; and justified himself by saying that "his acceptance of it would enable him to tell my enemies that he had received my money." Had I not been in the anxious state and hurry of such an hour, expecting the trial to be called at any moment, such a remark would at once have opened my eyes to the real character of the man. I had no time to think of it till afterwards, and then it was too late.*

My counsel, Mr. Wurts, who in sound scholarship and legal ability, has no superior at the New Jersey Bar, had frankly assured me that as the case stood, my enemies had such an advantage that there was not the least prospect of my acquittal if it came to a trial: and he wished me to consider whether there was no method by which the matter could be peaceably adjusted. I knew that my disadvantages were such, especially since the use which had been made of Mr. Barnes' paper, and that no hope remained for me from a trial, unless God should in some way confound the unhappy creatures who had been suborned against me. I may have mistaken my duty here; for in January (1848) I was offered an excellent field of labor with more than twice the salary which I was receiving at Bethlehem; and the offer was urged upon my acceptance by two eminent divines, who were also members of the Presbytery. Yet I refused it; though my enemies, also, by means of a committee, urged me to accept the call, stating, that if I would do so (as they merely wished me to leave Bethlehem) they would immediately cause a *nolle prosequi* to be entered. These considerations however did not influence me. I refused the call; and refused to have any further intercourse with the prosecution, who had so basely violated

which he had previously directed, but to another office several miles distant. My enemies dreaded his attendance; *and they were wealthy*. But *Time* is the great Discoverer.

* He made one short speech on the trial, and did not ask a question of any of the witnesses. And for this service, and in defiance of his promise and apology, he then charged me $20 additional. Whether he made anything else out of the case, I know not; but I felt that I was justly punished for permitting such a character to be in any way connected with my cause.

the sacred pledge given me at Presbytery: and to either of these alternatives, I preferred a third, *viz.*, to be tried and cast.

The prosecution thinking, I suppose, to intimidate me by the mere paraphernalia of the court, had themselves made but little preparation for the trial; for, when the case was called, the court was kept waiting for half an hour (to which his Honor the presiding Judge very courteously consented) until some arrangement should be made by these men for postponing it. One of them (P. Sigler, the distiller) came to my friends who were in court, and said, "For God's sake let this matter be put off." They replied, "If the case is to be tried, now is the time, for we are ready." A consultation was held in a corner of the room, in which my enemies offered to pay me a year's salary in advance; or to allow me to remain a year or eighteen months, or even longer, as Pastor of the church, and also to enter a *nolle prosequi* at once, if I would only set a time in which to resign my charge. This was promptly refused. They then gave my friends a solemn assurance that if I would permit the case to be now deferred it should never be called up again. To this no objection was made. I was not present at the conference, and regretted when it was too late, that my friends had accepted the mere word of such men, instead of insisting that a *nolle prosequi* should be at once entered. But they did not think of this. The question then arose, how to get the matter deferred, as I was present and ready for trial. This, however, was soon arranged by the prosecution and Clark (my late employed lawyer), who went forward and stated that as one of my counsel had disappointed me by his non-attendance and was said to be sick, it was deemed desirable to have the case postponed. I was indignant at the shameful falsehood; but he stated to me in his defence that this plea was the only one on which the case could be arrested: and then, as both my friends and enemies knew the truth of the matter, and the postponement was regarded as final, I did not consider the subject as of much importance.

The reader must judge what ought to be thought of the impanneling of the jury; for never before was such a "Falstaff's regiment" of jurors packed together; and even my enemies when they came to look upon them were ashamed of the pannel. Unitarians, Infidels, Rumsellers, and Rumdrinkers, and my avowed enemies, were there, and even one man who expected to be prosecuted by me for a libel touching this very case. In the whole pannel there was not, with an exception or two, an individual who was friendly to me or to the cause of temperance. But my enemies boasted of having abundant means at their disposal.

I now proceeded as usual with my pastoral labors. My evening lectures were as largely attended as ever; while the attendance on the Sabbath services was large, and on the increase; the reports against me had become stale, and were discredited. We elected several new elders, and also welcomed an agent for a benevolent enterprise, the claims of which had not before been presented to the congregation, and gave him a handsome collection.* Nothing further was said of the trial, by my

* This gentleman was the Rev. John Patton, agent for the Education Society. He was sincerely delighted to witness the prosperous state of the Church. But his inter-

opposers, except that it had been abandoned. My accuser and her husband had removed to New York, and asserted that they never would appear again at court. And so the matter rested, and ceased even to be a subject of conversation. We were lulled into perfect security. I made no preparation for the trial; summoned no witnesses. But just before the opening of the court in May, I received word, that the promised *nolle prosequi* had not been entered, and that the case would proceed. To secure the attendance of my fore-cited witnesses was now impossible, (some of them living forty miles apart,) and my trial was appointed to be the first.* And soon finding that my enemies had laid their plans to take me thus by surprise, I committed myself and the case to God, and prepared for the result. My accuser and her servant had availed themselves of the opportunity to compose the contradictions in their previous testimony, before Presbytery; several persons had been found who were ready to swear that they knew the servant, but *knew* no harm of her; the testimony impeaching her character as notorious and infamous, was refused; and I was cast. Not one particle of new evidence against me was in any form elicited; and though a statement was sworn to which involves a physical impossibility, the judge took no notice whatever of it in charging the jury.

I shall close this section with a brief notice of one or two additional efforts made by my enemies to secure this result of the trial.

I had no personal acquaintance with Mr. Randolph, the presiding judge; but it had been whispered that at the November and February terms of the court, he had evinced a disposition, from what he knew of such cases, and of the parties, to view the whole matter in its true light. Before the May term, however, Mr. Porpoise, a young lawyer of Flemington,† was procured to lay before his Honor, at his private room in the hotel, an attested copy of Mr. Barnes's minute in my case. The perusal of that paper made upon Judge Randolph's mind the only impression that it can make upon any candid and upright mind, who calmly weighs its language, and is unacquainted with the facts in the case; and during the trial, he twice in an excited manner referred to that apparent effort to screen a guilty brother from justice. The document, (being attested,) had obviously more effect upon his mind, (and I see not how it could be otherwise,) than the statements of the witnesses, and even the opposing counsel had it circulating in court, though they did not attempt to introduce it into the trial. Other artful efforts were made to influence his Honor; for example: All the seats at the

esting account of it to the brethren in Philadelphia, did me no good with one individual there, who saw that I should have no difficulty to triumph over the efforts *hitherto made* to prostrate me. But see Part II.

* In the hurry thus occasioned I could only send messages to a few witnesses. One of the number, who was of great importance to me, resided near the place called Sodom. His name, if I now recollect rightly, is Honnis. He is a reliable man, and had promised me to attend without fail. But while he was making preparation to do so, Dr. Sicarius, to whom there was a mortgage due on his property, heard of it; and immediately called and assured him that if he went near the court, the mortgage should be instantly demanded. He could not without sacrificing his property pay so large a sum; and so was intimidated.

† The act is notorious; and I will not pollute these pages with the *real* name of this ature.

table of the hotel (where he always puts up during court,) had been secured by my most malignant enemies; who, during meals, would make it a point to speak of me in a very disparaging manner, as though they were uttering the public sentiment. The judge did not appear to see through this scheme; or even to suspect that there was design in such conduct. By these remarks I mean not to speak disparagingly of Judge Randolph. A man must be more than mortal to avoid being influenced, at least in some degree, by such artful proceedings. And though many have censured the course which he pursued, they were not so fully aware as I was, of all the facts appertaining thereto.

To be compelled to defend one's self against such proceedings, and such characters as were associated in this conspiracy, is indeed humiliating. And even a victory over men who would deliberately resort to such villany, cannot be contemplated without such a sense of degradation, as might almost tempt a worldly-minded man to hang himself; for he might apprehend that such a triumph would imply on his part a capability of meeting them on their own ground; an imputation that would be worse than death to any upright and honorable mind.

CHAPTER VII.

RESULTS OF THE PRECEDING EFFORTS.

The effect of this trial, so far as injury to myself and to the cause of religion was concerned, was slight compared with what it would have been under almost any other circumstances. I had committed myself to the care of a faithful and covenant God, and he remembered His promise; and afforded to His unworthy servant, His constant and sustaining presence. To this I attribute also the endearing kindness of many beloved friends, who, while others forsook and neglected me, adhered closely to me and my family amid all our sorrows. Amongst the people of my charge also, were a large number of as true and kind friends as ever man could expect to have in this world; for they made my interests entirely their own. The same kind Providence of God also signally frustrated the scheme of my enemies, even when they thought their work was complete. The verdict against me had no effect upon my people, for they understood the whole case, and treated the efforts of my enemies at court with no attention whatever. Then too the atrocious breach of faith on the part of the prosecution was known to the public, and had its effect; as also the fact that they had got old Bolivar, (who had become syphilitic in New York,) and E. Cooley, and other like characters, to depose that the testimony of my accuser and her girl was the same in court that it had been in Presbytery; when every person who heard it, knew that their testimony in court contradicted what they had previously delivered.* Their endeavor to spring a mine upon

* We could not introduce their previous depositions into court, as the witnesses in Presbytery were not sworn by a magistrate.

me, or to take me by surprise; and their wretched manœuvring as described in the conclusion of Chapter VI., were also extensively known—and my enemies in Jersey, therefore, gained but little, while they lost much by this whole precedure; and only aroused anew the sympathies of my people on my behalf, who now declared their intention of taking higher ground than ever in sustaining me.

A fact or two may serve also to show the state of the public mind on the subject. Notwithstanding all the efforts of my enemies to create a public sentiment in favor of their proceedings, the trial convinced many who were previously prejudiced against me, on account of the rumor, that the whole was but a base conspiracy to effect my destruction. The editors of the two political papers in the county also attended the trial. I had little or no personal acquaintance with either of them; but so fully were they convinced of the same truth, upon hearing the most silly observations of the witnesses, that they pointedly refused to mention the trial in their papers, though earnestly requested to do so by my enemies, and though it was their constant custom to publish an abstract of the proceedings of the court. Nor could any threats of a withdrawal of patronage, or promises of an increase of it, induce them to depart from this their determination. They acted uninfluenced, save by their own convictions of duty to a fellow-citizen, whom they believed to have been most basely slandered. Had they complied with the solicitations of my enemies, and only made mention of the trial, the injurious effect upon myself would have been incalculable. Other papers regarding it as coming from head-quarters, would have copied the statement, and the way would have thus been prepared to disseminate through the Union any representation which my enemies might have chosen to make of the matter. A scurrilous pettifogger, the Quilp of the Trenton bar, was then hired to prepare a report for a paper published, I believe, in that city. But no respectable print noticed it, though an effort was made by my theological opponents at the west to employ it to my disadvantage. I have never seen it however—no copy having been sent either to me or to my people, and my enemies were too chary of theirs to loan me one. I shall ever hold in high honor Messrs. George C. Seymour and Henry A. Buffington, the editors of the county papers, for the noble stand which they took in this matter, directly against their own pecuniary interests.

Here then this malignant effort of my enemies in Jersey would have ended, *and ended forever*, so far as injury to myself or to religion was concerned, had it not been for another influence which all along had been at work secretly, and which now, as we shall see, excited and encouraged a spirit of dissatisfaction amongst a few weak-minded men in the church and congregation, and so harassed me and my family that I was at length compelled to resign my charge. To trace and develop this influence is the design of our SECOND PART.

The results of this whole procedure, as they affected many of my enemies, were however peculiarly striking, and I will close the present chapter by referring to a few of them. Seldom has an individual, by a given course of conduct, been so utterly prostrated in the estimation of the community, and so utterly forsaken by all, as Mr. Hunt, in consequence of the part which he took in this affair; and most bitterly does he complain that he is left without a friend. How could it be otherwise? After persecuting me in the cruel manner recorded above, he came forth publicly and repeatedly, and with tears entreated my forgiveness, professing deeply to relent for the course he had pursued. He then, in the manner stated above, re-commenced his iniquitous course, and encouraged my enemies to refuse to enter the promised *nolle prosequi.* Yet he has my full forgiveness, and I pray God that he may obtain mercy and that "his hoar head may go down to the grave in peace." Another case was that of a hoary-headed infidel, who lived some fifteen miles off, but many of whose Unitarian and infidel relatives were connected with the Bethlehem congregation when I took charge of it. This man (for my father's sake, with whom he was associated as an officer in the war of 1812—I will spare his name), in order to oblige his friends, collected, by means of a physician, those five or six shameless falsehoods to which on a former page I have referred, and repeated them in the store of a friend of mine in Philadelphia. My friend (John Price Wetherill,) who is a man of deservedly high influence in the political world, was not present, and knew nothing of this iniquitous conduct, till some time after. However, this old sinner had been there, and during my trial at court he came and publicly told it at Flemington, that Mr. Wetherill (whose character is well known there and highly respected,) had said to him that I was "a bad fellow." This falsehood was so timed as to put it out of my power to contradict it, until it had produced its full effect, and it had great influence from the use that was there made of it. The trial had, however, scarcely ended, before the horrors of remorse seized the hoary miscreant, and from fear of the justly apprehended results, his relatives were under the necessity of taking him abroad, and watching him for a long time. His remorse, however, was not repentance; but let him not forget the dread tribunal of God. A clergyman, too, a Mr. W., who took an active part against me, hoping thereby to gain over to his own congregation some of the members of mine, was soon after, and apparently "without hand," broken down among his own people, (many of whom had little sympathy for me, they being strongly sectarian,) and so utterly abandoned by them that, long before I left Bethlehem, he was compelled to give up his charge, in which it was said, and I believe truly, that he had no friends left. It is painful for me to record such facts, but I cannot think otherwise than that duty requires it at my hand. The above-mentioned physician also, who had played a similar game, sunk at once from a very extensive and lucrative practice, and was compelled to sell out and leave the country. The last news I heard of him was, that he was driving an ox team in the streets of one of the cities of California for a livelihood. The servant girl (my accuser's witness), after her affidavit before Squire Case, joined the Methodist church in Clinton. But soon after my trial at court, she and another opposer of mine were expelled therefrom for the acknowledged crime of living together in habitual fornication. It was simply on this girl's testimony that I was cast at court. After the trial at Presbytery, Dr. Sicarius, who had testified on oath that he never knew "*much harm*" of this creature, said to her, "Now, Ann, we have had a great deal of trouble to patch up your character; see that you live hereafter different from what you have done." The caution, however, had no lasting influence. My enemies betray a greal deal of anxiety respecting this poor girl, for she is able to reveal the whole plot, at least in its origin. Hence the feverish anxiety with which Dr. Sicarius came all the way down to Clinton to attend her, after the trial, when she was taken sick and thought herself dying. It was rumored that she wished to make a confession; but the Doctor was scarce ever from her side. Hence, too, although she has been thus disgracefully expelled from the church, for an acknowledged crime of the most degrading nature, and though she can find employment in no respectable family, Mr. Conover became her patron, took her home to his young and rising family, and had her constantly ride with them in his carriage to church. I take it, however, that God and conscience will render all such precautions unavailing. Vanderbelt himself became a perfect sot and outcast, and left his wife and children to the tender mercies of the world. Once since the trial, when I was on a visit to my people at Bethlehem, I unexpectedly met this poor young man at the White House (the terminus of the Easton and Somerville Railroad). He, on seeing me, became deadly pale, and, going up to the bar, called for and drank off a large draught of raw brandy. I then thought and said that I feared he would become a drunkard. Squire Case, who had utterly sold himself to Mr. Hunt to work wickedness, and who used to bring the affidavits of Mrs. Vanderbelt and Ann to the grove of Bethlehem church on the Sabbath, and read them aloud while the people were assembling for worship, soon after had his own spirit crushed by discovering that his own daughter (a young woman of 24 or 25 years of age) had been having illicit intercourse with a married man in his employ. He would not believe her criminal until the offspring of their guilt was ushered into the world. It almost broke his heart, and he, for a while, became raving distracted. The retribution was so striking, however, that even many of my enemies could not but acknowledge it, and no one showed him any sympathy. I saw him in this condition, and was pained to find that, instead of receiving any pity, he was the subject of universal derision. I omit to mention other instances of the manifest retributive justice of Heaven, though there are numbers of others no less striking that could be named. God's work in this matter is, however, still in progress. Arm after arm that was raised against me has thus been shivered, and not one shall escape without being made to know that they who thus touch the servants of God touch the apple of his eye. Ps. 27: 2, 3, and Is. 54: 14–17. Let my zealous persecutors who still continue in their impenitence, think of this before it is too late. Many a man has sought a cardinal's cap who has both deserved and obtained one much less desirable, and under which, however crooked he may previously have been, he has been rendered perpendicularly straight through all coming time. Haman's example ought not to be forgotten.

PART II.

WHEREIN IS POINTED OUT THE COURSE PURSUED BY THE REV. ALBERT BARNES IN RELATION TO THIS CONSPIRACY; TOGETHER WITH THE ELEMENT WHICH WAS THUS BROUGHT INTO THE CASE, AND THE RESULT OF ITS OPERATION.

CHAPTER I.

INTRODUCTORY AND EXPLANATORY.

To any man whose life's purpose is to promote the glory of God and the good of our fellow-men, it would be no trivial matter to be drawn aside from his work to contend for character against the wily efforts of an individual who had no right whatever to place him in a position demanding it. Such events have, however, occurred in the life of better men than myself; but there can be no question as to how a crisis of this kind should be met. The silence of an accused man is regarded as almost equivalent to the flight of a soldier from the field. Then, too, in the case before us, it will not be questioned that other interests, besides those which are merely personal to myself, are involved; interests which are of the highest concernment to the purity and well-being of the Redeemer's kingdom, so far at least as the Presbyterian branch of it is concerned; and these interests concern not merely individuals, they extend much farther. Principles are involved which concern the very soul itself of the religion of Christ. Hence, it cannot be doubted, that if facts are as this narrative represents them to be, they are the property of the public. I believe that Mr. Barnes cannot successfully controvert the truthfulness of a single fact herein alleged as such, whatever explanation he may attempt to put upon them. Yet, it is but just and righteous that he should have *a fair and full opportunity* to be heard on the subject before any decision is pronounced affecting his interests. My own mind is fully made up on the subject, for I have afforded him such opportunity. And I freely admit that I cannot survey the matters of this history without feeling that the individual principally concerned in securing the results which they develop, has really forfeited all claim to be treated with any more consideration than if he had imbrued his hands in my blood. Still, I have no disposition to do him injustice. And if I know the feelings of my own heart in relation to Mr. Barnes, I can, while I say, *nec timeo te*, truly add, *nec odi, nec sperno*. I cannot forget that he is my fellow-man, and like me, a candidate for eternal happiness or woe, nor that we soon are to receive according to the deeds done in the body.

The operations of the human mind, notwithstanding all that has been said and written on the subject, are but little understood; and all attempts thoroughly to analyze the minds of others by referring to our own mental exercises, must be involved in some degree of uncertainty, from the fact that the state of the heart furnishes the only clue to the real operations of the intellect. Hence the diversity which is found to exist in the views of men in reference to some action, the motive of which is not fully apparent. Where the feelings of the man who expresses an opinion thereupon, are prompted by a candid and kind disposition, the views entertained and expressed are the reverse of what they are found to be in cases where, for example, jealousy or wounded pride, or a spirit of rivalry and love of pre eminence predominates.

Why Mr. Barnes, from the very commencement of the aforesaid rumor, and months before it was in any way investigated, was induced to take so decided and prominent a part against me, is not for me to determine, but for the reader. On the nature of such conduct I have expressed my views without reserve. But I claim not to judge for others. I no more believe that a man can have just and pure motives for such an act than that he may have such motives for the perpetration of any other iniquity. To say that an individual may *honestly* believe a vile rumor of a Christian brother (and consequently regard and treat him as guilty) without the least evidence of its truth, and before that brother has had the remotest opportunity for defence, is to say that a man may be honest in the perpetration of an atrocious wickedness, and to justify the Jesuits in the omission of calumny from their catalogue of crimes.

At the commencement of this affair, I had a reputation as a scholar, a Christian, and a minister of Christ, which I should have been loth to exchange for that of Mr. Barnes, were his even "thrice doubled." The obscuring influence which calumny has brought to settle partially over it, can produce but a temporary effect, however hard my enemies may labor to render it permanent. But, in reviewing the causes which produced the injury, it will be necessary to go somewhat into detail. That Mr. Barnes has been most zealously and prominently concerned in producing this effect will be questioned by no one, not even by himself. And, therefore, while I inquire into this procedure, and attempt to trace the effect to its cause, I mean not to forestal the judgment of the reader. Let it be supposed, if possible, that Mr. Barnes' course has been upright and honorable throughout. I am willing, *for the sake of the argument*, to suppose it to have been so; and on this supposition nothing can be easier than his task in rejoinder. He is now at leisure, so far as writing commentaries on the Bible is concerned; his noble-hearted congregation will stand by and sustain him at all hazards until he proves himself to be unworthy of their confidence, and his position and influence furnish every facility that a man could desire in such a case, though they can afford him no shield or protection, if his course, *and in such a matter as is here referred to*, be unworthy of a Christian and a man. Let the reader, therefore, while he sacredly guards his heart from the incursions of prejudice, and against all hasty judgment in the case, give his serious attention to the statements which follow.

It will be remembered by many, that in the very heat of that unfortunate controversy which (in 1830–1838) agitated and ultimately divided the Presbyterian church, I came forward prominently in defence of Mr. Barnes. This may be gathered even from the wretchedly mutilated account which has been published of his trial at York, Pa., in 1835. I never, however, either adopted or endorsed his theological views, but merely took the ground that they were not fundamentally erroneous, and might safely be tolerated within our bounds. More than a year after his suspension from the ministry, and while he was regarded with much suspicion by no small part of the Christian world, he, in the course of our ordinary correspondence, encouraged me to appear still more prominently in his defence; and in a letter dated July 12, 1837, speaking of a proposed treatise by me, he says, "This would have a *permanent* value; besides doing more than almost anything else to put an end to the spirit of bigotry and illiberality which now culminates in our distracted church. I do not know of any man that is so well qualified for this as you are; and in this I think you would do valuable service to the cause of truth." In another letter, dated August 23, he says, in relation to the same subject, "It would do *vast good* to bring out the views of the fathers of the Reformation on the subject of Justification, and I hope you will do it. I do not know any one better fitted for it than you are, and I think your time would be well bestowed in doing it."

The treatise here referred to, which cost me much labor (as any person by a glance can perceive), may be found in the *American Biblical Repository* for April, July and October of 1838. Its success in soothing the angry elements that were then at war in our church, was on all hands acknowledged to be very great; and whether justly or not, it was declared to have settled the *doctrinal* dispute, by satisfactorily determining the question that the views advanced by Mr. Barnes, and for the avowal of which he had been suspended, might without injury to the church be tolerated within her borders. The result of this publication was however peculiarly unhappy on myself, as it at once alienated from me the most of those of my brethren with whom I have ever sympathized in my doctrinal views (for I never have entertained the peculiar sentiments attributed to Mr. Barnes), and in their estimation, I, along with my *protégé*, underwent the imputation of heresy.

These essays also gave me a prominence before the religious public which I had not sought, and which, from its effect, was by no means agreeable to me. I love retirement; and am not ambitious of the honors of a theological disputant. But they operated likewise in another way, and very unpleasantly. The public remarked that Mr. Barnes, with all his claims to literature, had been for six or eight years defending himself against the charge of heresy, and had written extensively on the subject, and that yet in no part of his writings or speeches did he evince the least acquaintance whatever with the numerous and important authorities which I have so triumphantly adduced on the subject. I had thought of this before committing my work to the press, and requested the then editor of the *Repository* (Dr. Peters) to publish it anonymously, and in fact (as it was against the rule ordinarily observed in that work) *insisted* on his doing so. He did not, however, grant my request; and I received, along with the *Repository* containing my first essay, the letter containing his reasons for the refusal. I could do nothing therefore to relieve Mr. Barnes from his predicament. But when he attempted (as he did, again and again, and once even in my own study) to relieve himself by insinuating that I "had made my extracts containing the sentiments of the Reformers from some old and forgotten volume of controversy," instead of their being the result of my own reading, I denied it with indignation, for it was shamefully false. I had, moreover, never even seen such a volume. It was also an implication of dishonesty on my part, involving a mean plagiarism which Mr. Barnes had not the least external reason for attributing to me. And hence, some time afterwards, I took occasion, in a letter addressed to Dr. Junkin, and published in the *Philadelphia Observer*, to remark that if any person doubted the fairness of these my extracts, he was at liberty to consult the originals in my library. Such was the first and most direct return for the benefits I thus conferred upon Mr. Barnes, and for the injuries I thereby brought upon myself. Could I help recalling to mind the lines of old Cowley:

> "But in this thankless world, the giver
> Is envied oft by the receiver;
> 'Tis now the cheap and frugal fashion
> Rather to hide than own the obligation:
> Nay, 'tis much worse than so;
> It now an artifice does grow
> Wrongs and injuries to do
> Lest men should think we owe."

The idiosyncrasies of men—of all men, so far as they do not lead to injurious and sinful results, are to be looked upon with forbearance; and every honest man can find in his own heart enough of frailty to plead that the failings of his brother, so far as they are of the character above described, should be thus regarded. A beautiful writer of our own times has remarked, that "He who will turn away a friend for one fault is a stranger to the best feelings of the human heart: who has not erred at least once in his life? If that fault were not overlooked, to what depth of infamy would not thousands have descended? We know not the peculiar and pressing temptations to which another may be exposed. He may have fought manfully against the sin, and still kept the secret in his bosom. At last he has been overcome. In a moment he yielded. He has mourned over it in secret, and has repented in dust and ashes. Shall we forsake him? Earth and Heaven, Justice and Humanity, Philosophy and Religion, cry out, Forgive him! He who will not forgive him must be at heart a demon. Truly the love of God is not in him."

The application of all this is sufficiently obvious, and in my own case, I felt that much allowance ought to be made for Mr. Barnes, cruel and unkind as had been his return for the obligations which I had so freely conferred upon him; and I therefore kept the matter within my own bosom, and determined to let it die there. But after it was thus disposed of, I soon found him acting as though he thought that I had at his expense obtained an eclat of which I ought without ceremony to be deprived. I had seen him helplessly struggling with the surge in no shallow frith; and leaping therein to his rescue, soon placed him ashore on a bank so high that neither waves nor tide could reach it; and from which he could in perfect security smile at the storm. Greatly was I applauded by some of the spectators, and greatly censured by others. The plaudits were not however grateful to Mr. Barnes, for he deemed them plaudits at his own expense. And scarcely was he yet dry, before, (reaching over his shoulder) he drew an arrow from his quiver, and, dipping its point into a mixture prepared and sold by one Diotrephes, shot it directly at my heart. It struck where he aimed; but the briny river up which the waves and tide had been driving him, had so relaxed the nerve of his bow that the arrow penetrated only the skin. I, as above stated, seized hold of it and threw it away;—but had scarcely done so, ere another and another came, some hitting and others missing, till I was at a loss what to do. I did not, however, return the warfare, and continued to indulge the hope that my forbearance would ere long be appreciated, and induce him to cease from efforts so unbecoming and unprovoked.

But to drop the metaphor. Mr. Barnes continued still to act as though he viewed me as somehow or other standing in his way. I can mention numbers of occurrences, each of which, as it seems to me, can admit of no other solution,* but shall content myself with only a single additional one which, while it will enable me to correct some misrepresentations, will be, with the one already stated, sufficient for the purpose of introducing our subject. And if I go back a few years, for these instances, the necessity which exists for tracing Mr. Barnes' course from its commencement will justify me in so doing. Nor will he be disposed to complain of the procedure; for (as the reader will see) he, in receiving and acting upon the slanderous statements of my enemies concerning me, suffered himself to be influenced in no way whatever, by any regard to the constitutional limitation of time.

In the early part of my ministry (*anno* 1835,) I accepted an invitation to labor in the church and congregation at Lower Providence, Pa. The church was near its last gasp, and for some time had had no pastor. In fact it was already so completely lost sight of by Presbytery, as to be seldom supplied as a vacancy. There had been something of an awakening there in 1834, under the preaching of a licentiate of the German Reformed Church, and some few members were added, who established a prayer-meeting. The field was a hard one, and my salary small; but in the course of the three years of my ministry there, the Lord poured out his Spirit several times; and the church became greatly strengthened by its accessions. Catechetical instruction was revived, and prayer-meetings and weekly lectures held. The Confession of Faith also, of which there was scarce a single copy to be found in the congregation, became

* I ought not perhaps to omit the one connected with the rabid assault upon me by that scurrilous Jesuit, Dr. P. E. Moriarty of Philadelphia, in 1840: but my limits at present do not permit it.

deservedly popular again; and of which I purchased and distributed sixty copies soon after our first revival.

These things were not, however, accomplished without encountering much stern opposition. Many of the old members opposed revivals, and prayer-meetings, the exercise of church discipline, the monthly concert of prayer for missions, &c., &c. But the revivals, and the presence of the Spirit of God, greatly overawed opposition. Still it continued, and finally appeared in the form of a refusal of those members to pay their stipulated portion of my salary. This, however, and all their other movements failed of effecting anything of moment; for the church soon became large and flourishing, and in the division of our denomination in 1838 united with the part called "New School;" though this was done on constitutional grounds, and not from any sympathy for the theological speculations of such men as Messrs. Hunt and Barnes. It continued in this prosperous state; and in April, 1839, I accepted a unanimous call to the Pastorate of the English Presbyterian Church of Allentown, Pa.

But in October, 1839, when Presbytery met at Norristown, Pa., a man who was notorious for his Sabbath-breaking and profanity, and who had also brought a Unitarian minister into the congregation and sustained his preaching, and was also a bitter opposer of the temperance reform, came to Presbytery, and during recess got Mr. Barnes and Mr. Grant together, and had a long interview with them. He was an utter stranger to Mr. Barnes, and, I think, to Mr. Grant also.* I had not the remotest idea of what were the nature and object of this interview, and during the whole of it happened to be near at hand, in conversation with several members of Presbytery. When however the recess had expired, I was, as may be supposed, utterly astounded to find Mr. Barnes get up and bring against me by name a series of accusations respecting the transfer of the Providence church to the New School; and assert, on the authority of the man above-mentioned (who, in the mean time, had disappeared), that I did it by a manœuvre of the most contemptible kind. He had listened to these slanderous statements, and yet never breathed a word to me on the subject, though I was in sight, and within a few yards of him all the time. Instead of saying to the man, let us now hear Mr. Landis' statement on the subject, he, on the mere word of a stranger, of whose character he was utterly ignorant, arose and publicly made his scurrilous statements concerning me.† I own that my feelings

* I believe that a clergyman by name of Haight introduced this man and a companion or two to Messrs. Grant and Barnes.

† About six or eight days previous to this meeting of Presbytery, a lady of the highest respectability, (and one of "the upper ten thousand," though I believe a truly pious woman,) who was intimate with my family, stated in the course of conversation that a large portion of Mr. Barnes' church had became very much excited on the subject of his too great intimacy with a young lady of his congregation. I permitted her to finish the statement, and then with strong emphasis remarked, "Madam, why do you repeat such contemptible slander? I know Brother Barnes well; and I believe the story to be a miserable lie got up by the Devil to injure him. You ought never on the ground of mere rumor to repeat a matter thus derogatory to any one, and so injurious to the cause of religion." The warmth and point of my remarks offended my

were aroused at so gross a breach of decorum and propriety; and had I taken time to reflect, I should have proceeded differently, and so as to have taught him a lesson on constitutional order at least, which he would not have soon forgotten; but I instantly arose, and with vehemence pronounced the statement to be both slanderous and false; and added, "I therefore throw it back upon the brother who has thus ventured to assail me." Mr. Barnes made not one word of reply; and neither apologized, nor attempted to explain or justify his course. Presbytery, however, concluded to examine into the grounds of the alleged grievance; and as Mr. Barnes had introduced the subject, he was, with Mr. Grant, named as a committee on the business; every upright mind of course expecting after what had passed, that he would decline the appointment. He however displayed so little acquaintance with the human heart,—with its liability to be perverted, where prejudice, interest, or passion is concerned,—that he at once consented to act, and really did act in the business.* He was, of course, chairman of the committee; and thus effected the resignation of several elders who (on a written application to me, signed by a large number of the members of the church, to call a meeting for such a purpose) had been constitutionally elected and ordained. He did likewise a number of other things in which my reputation as a Presbyterian was concerned: and neither he nor Mr. Grant made any inquiry of me in relation to a single point connected with the whole business: nor even notified me as to the time when they proposed to meet as a committee to examine the subject. The business was all "done up" by them, and their report adopted during my unavoidable absence from Presbytery. The charge, however, which Mr. Barnes had so unkindly brought against me, though investigated by this committee in my absence, was found to be wholly unsupported and false; and yet he made not the least public or private apology or retraction. The act (electing the elders) which on his recommendation was thus reversed, was the only thing that saved the church from distraction and ruin: and its absolute necessity as well as utility, I could with perfect ease demonstrate. I knew that Mr. Barnes had been greatly imposed upon by the man whose statements he had repeated; but as he had been so willingly duped, and evinced a disposition to believe unfavorable reports of a brother, and would not deign to ask me for an

friend so much, that for a long time afterwards I forfeited her good-will. She had no personal acquaintance with Mr. Barnes.

I might therefore at once have returned Mr. B.'s treatment effectually, and in kind; and it still affords me no little pleasure to reflect that I did not do so.

* Judge Sewall, of Massachusetts, who died in 1760, went one day into a hatters' shop, in order to purchase a pair of second-hand brushes for cleaning his shoes. The master of the shop presented him with a couple. "What is your price?" asked the Judge. "If they answer your purpose," said the hatter, "you may have them and welcome." The Judge, upon hearing this, laid them down, and bowing, was leaving the shop; upon which the hatter said to him, "Pray, sir, has not your honor forgotten the principal object of your visit?" "By no means," answered the Judge; "if you please to set a price, I am ready to purchase; but ever since it has fallen to my lot to occupy a seat on the bench, I have studiously avoided receiving to the value of a single copper, lest at some future period of my life, it might have some kind of influence in determining my judgment." Mr. Barnes had obviously no such fear. Hence *he* could *conscientiously* sit as judge in so grave a matter as that above referred to.

explanation of anything relating to the matter, or even to notify me that I might be present at the meeting of the committee, neither the church nor myself had any resource but quietly to submit. But the deed was done, and a most ambitious record placed upon the minutes of Presbytery. But, as I may say, the ink with which that record had been written was scarcely dry, when, (as I had foretold to several brethren,) the man by whose statements Mr. Barnes had thus been influenced, violated his promise in a most offensive and insulting manner, (as may be learned also from a late record of Presbytery,) and the church split asunder: Mr. Haight and a portion going to the Old School, and the rest remaining *in statu quo*. And now on the turnpike above Morristown may be seen two small houses of worship, about a mile apart, one on each side of the road. They are the houses built by the two parties into which this once flourishing and efficient church is now divided; neither of them able to maintain a pastor. Mr. Barnes, therefore, by thus "taking up a reproach against his neighbor," and by acting as a judge in circumstances in which conscientious jurists have ever refused to act, has, in that neighborhood, achieved an immortality which may safely be expected to outlast the remembrance of any work he has ever published.

No one can be more distressed than I am at the necessity which com pels me to make the disclosures contained in this volume. Had the matter concerned myself alone, I should have left it wholly with God, and have kept silence. But it does not affect my reputation only. The cause of Christ is still suffering, and great wrath has come upon the church with which Mr. Barnes and I are connected. I have wished and sought to lead him to repentance; but in vain. Hence I take the only course that is left to one circumstanced as I am. Let God and the Christian public now judge between us.

Cuncta prius tentata: sed immedicabile vulnus
Ense recidendum, ne pars sincera trahatur.

CHAPTER II.

MR. BARNES' COURSE IN RELATION TO THE ORIGIN AND SPREAD OF THE RUMOR.

In Part I. I have briefly presented the history of the churches of Bethlehem and Alexandria from the time of my connection with them until September, 1847; and have given also a view of the adverse influences with which, during that period, I was environed. Mr. Barnes was well acquainted with the history of those churches through that period: but the blessing with which God favored my labors, did not appear to produce that unfeigned pleasure in his mind which it should have done. God greatly honored an humble instrument, and the spirit and policy of the world (against which good men are not always sufficiently on their guard), was thereby annoyed. The assertion was openly made (though I do not know that Mr. Barnes did more than silently encourage it), that the great awakening in 1842 was only the result of the labors of my predecessor. It was, of course, not for me to say a word on such a subject. The fact, however, is mentioned as an illustration of a disposition which has since been operating almost to the utter ruin of constitutional Presbyterianism in and about Philadelphia. Mr. Barnes had been a "revival preacher," and his labors were once blessed. No revival had now attended him for years, and it was not uniformly as grateful to him as it should have been, to see my humble efforts blessed so extensively. But this is poor human nature: I do not speak of it with harshness; let the man who is without human weakness do so. However, whatever had been asserted attributing to my predecessor the success which attended my labors, was effectually and forever silenced by the aforesaid indignant remark made by Mr. Barnes after spending a night with him: "Mr. Hunt is the most worldly-minded *man* I ever met with. I do not say *minister* but *man*." Whether he would have made and repeated such a remark had he foreseen its practical bearing, is left for the reader to determine. In his best moments I believe that he would.

Few persons when they give the reins to prejudice ever design to proceed to the extent to which they almost always are inevitably brought. But the experiment is dangerous; for this is pre-eminently a matter in which the *first step* is the only difficult one. When the first step is thus taken against another, it involves the necessity of a second step, in order to secure the advantages already supposed to be gained: and this procedure at length involves a third step, and then a fourth, and so on, until, in the estimation of the aggressor, it becomes as perilous to wade back again, as to go entirely over; and this last alternative, though it invariably involves the ruin or the deep repentance of the individual himself, is too often chosen. *Felix quem faciunt aliena pericula cautum.*

Such have been, a thousand times, the thoughts of my mind as I have observed, step by step, the course which Mr. Barnes has been pursuing in relation to myself. Other members of Presbytery noticed it, but no one of that whole body was faithful enough to that poor brother's soul to give him a proper admonition on the subject. His conduct was explained as an idiosyncrasy, and as evincing no evil design: and thus deed after deed was perpetrated by him, and the same salvo applied: for as no one was willing to become an object of his displeasure, this opiate was suffered to lull the conscience into a fatal slumber, from which, however, it *must* awake. Those brethren are good men, and they know that I sincerely love them; but God having seen that they needed more than a mere precept to stimulate them to duty, has permitted them to furnish for themselves an example of the consequences of neglecting it, which must prove effectual in their case through the remainder of life.

I never suspected Mr. Barnes of coolly designing at the outset to destroy me. I do not suspect him of designing at first to do a tithe of what he has done in the matter. But the results are now accomplished, and both God and man will hold him responsible for them, unless in some way he shall succeed to justify a course which has been attended and followed by such fearful consequences.

In Part I. I stated that when this cruel rumor arose, I wrote to the Moderator of Presbytery, requesting that that judicatory should be speedily convened in order to investigate the charge. There was a strong disposition at once to favor my request, but Mr. Barnes so opposed the measure, advising, too, that the subject should lie over till the stated meeting of Presbytery, that the brethren acquiesced, and united in requesting me to permit it to lie over till then. I yielded. But then at that meeting Mr. Barnes urged again that the case should be postponed until the latter part of November; all of which, though against the expressed wishes of every other member who took part in the discussion, was at length acceded to in compliance with his wishes. He professed also to find evidence of "artfulness" in my aforesaid letters to the Moderator. However, after some manœuvring between him and Mr. Hunt, which I never could fully explore, (and the cunning old man had not failed, when Mr. Barnes was at his house, to notice the nature of his feelings towards me,) Mr. Hunt wrote, under cover to Mr. Barnes, the following letter "To the Fourth Presbytery of Philadelphia." I give it *verbatim et literatim;* and shall append a few notes to the margin.

"BELOVED BRETHREN: As the former pastor of Bethlehem church for forty years, although painful, consider it a duty to give the outlines of the deep affliction and division of our church. Mr. Landis has labored among us with great popularity and apparent usefulness for the first four years. Last summer and in September common fame injured his moral character, and measures were taken, a committee of five were sent to take the affidavit of Mrs. Vanderbelt, the daughter of Mr. Garret Conover and granddaughter of the aged widow Stiger, one of the most pious and respectable of my acquaintance; her nephew the honorable Jacob Miller is in the Senate of the United States. They are a very numerous and highly respectable families, and by intermarriages hold a strong influence in our church.* When the affidavit came to light by the dispersion of copies—which affidavit I send you a copy as delivered to me, that you may all judge for yourselves.

"At present there are but four ruling elders, one on a sick bed. At a considerable numerous week day meeting Mr. Landis refused to have the affidavit read. But spent about half an hour in nullifying it.† The former pastor and all the

* The object of this amplifying process is sufficiently plain: and it is doubted whether Senator Miller knows that he has such relations in the world as Mr. Conover and family. This "old and most pious lady" came into Presbytery during my trial, to testify against me. She refused to answer any questions, but handed in a piece of writing, saying that "*the Lord had appeared to her, and commanded her to hand in this writing, and to answer no questions whatever.*" And hence she refused to answer a single query. She died some months afterwards: and though the county papers publish the deaths of all; no one, not even Mr. Hunt, was found to prepare a single line giving notice that she had died. I mention these facts merely as a commentary on the ridiculous exaggerations of Mr. Hunt.

† No such "refusal" to have the affidavit read was in any way expressed by me; for I had no such authority as is here pretended. The Committee reported that it was too filthy a document to be read in a promiscuous assembly, and the house thereupon refused to hear it. I submitted entirely to the decision of the meeting. The object of this untruth of Mr. Hunt's is clearly apparent, however.

elders then present, namely, Mr. Fritz and Daniel Carhart, then went to Mr. Landis and said we advise you to say you will ask leave of Presbytery to resign your charge of Bethlehem church: we believe your usefulness is done and finished among us.*

"Mr. Landis refused, and said he would call on Presbytery and meet common fame,† and Mr. Conover the father of Mrs. Vanderbelt undertakes to defend common fame, and according to our church government ought to have able counsel assigned, See chapter 4th, item 21st, and his counsel to put up at his house and sit by him. Then a clear field and fair play—and no suppressing of testimony for or against—or our people will be entirely dissatisfied. If you ask as to the strength of parties can only give an opinion. In building the first stone church 40 by 50 feet that those who believe it best for Mr. [Landis] to leave us gave at least two thirds of the money, and one of said families six hundred dollars.‡ Now we would say although the money is a small matter—to be turned out of our church and cut off from the privileges of our church a sore grievance—for we cannot in conscience receive the Lord's Supper when he administers it. But if the Presbytery should leave him saddled on us, some will go to the Old School, some to the Methodists, and some we fear turn Infidels!! You will say party spirit runs high—yes, as strong as whig and tory in the revolutionary war!! Our peace and unity is gone. The only prospect is for Mr. Landis to leave, and we get a minister who has had no part in our division. We who live on the spot have made up our minds from our intercourse with each other, and if the Presbytery, Synod and General Assembly should pronounce him the right sort of a man—and say hold on, it would be what Paul calls sounding brass and tinkling symbol—to a large and respectable portion of Bethlehem church,—vide 1 Timothy 3d chapter. A Bishop that is a pastor must be blameless, the husband of one wife, sober, of good behavior—of good report, &c.

"But if the Presbytery should think him yet fit to preach and that he will reform, and make in substance the following decision we shall make no demur.§ On mature deliberation we dissolve the pastoral relation between the Rev. Robert W. Landis and church and congregation of Bethlehem, New Jersey, and declare said church vacant—and appoint the Rev. Mr. Landis to supply said church three successive Sabbaths, (and use his influence with all in public sermons and private conversation to restore the peace and unity of the congregation according to his ordination vows,) and then retire peaceably to some other church of the vineyard of Christ—and we are led to hope and pray that you will do so from our ordina-

* This also is utterly untrue. For, 1. the two elders above named were not "all the elders then present." Mr. Johnson attended and took part in the proceedings of the whole meeting. 2. I had no interview with Mr. H. and the two elders *after* the meeting, as Mr. H. says, to give color to his misrepresentations. 3. *Before* the meeting, Mr. H. brought these elders to me, but neither of them uttered a syllable in support of what he really did say, but did speak decidedly against his procedure. 4. All that Mr. Hunt did say at this interview, was "Mr. Landis, you had better go away." I sternly rebuked him, and he left me in a towering passion.

† This is a most shameful violation of truth. The words "*common fame*" were not uttered by Mr. Hunt in my hearing; and I never in any way consented to take such a position as he represents me as expressing a willingness to take. The old man wished to escape from the responsibility of being regarded as my accuser: and took this course to accomplish his purposes.

‡ This was Mr. Hunt's own family. The $600 was made up of a contribution by Mr. H's second wife, (who was wealthy,) and of the hopeless "odds and ends" of his "back salary;" which had been accumulating for about thirty years: and which, as it could not be collected, at least easily, he *generously* bestowed upon the church.

§ The reader will please to bestow particular notice upon what it is that Mr. H. here promises for himself and friends, not to "*demur*" at; and he cannot fail to discover the real object of this vile conspiracy against me.

tion vows, to study the peace the unity and purity of the church.* All is gone in our opinion if he remains,—we ought to love the peace and unity of the church better than any minister. Can you leave us the cant ridicule of the surrounding churches and infidels? We put ourselves under your guardian care and protection, and you will not leave us to mourn over lost privileges and our church to dwindle away. The world is large; let Mr. Landis try some other part to labor in. He would do best we think as a missionary.† If he continues, we believe the salary after Presbytery will not be paid,‡ and in time the house and grove sold for arrears of salary, and the debt on the new addition to the church building, which some of us thought not necessary, therefore not paid for yet.

Mr. Conover has fears that Presbytery will be appointed only among those families who advocate Mr. Landis, and that Elder Carhart, and the ex-pastor, and Mr. Conover, and others, will not be favored with their share of the members of Presbytery.§

It was not our wish to have Mr. Landis and our holy religion exposed to a public trial on common fame, and we are disposed to think Mr. Landis will call our advice, to leave us in peace, the best he has received. We do not believe that the overt act of the breach of the seventh commandment can be proved. But yet so many circumstances leading to suspicion, bearing on the same point, that with many all confidence is gone, and they would not trust him as an inmate in their families.‖ I do not wish to spread evil reports, and would prefer that all the members, not neglecting Mr. Landis, read this letter, and not judge in full of its contents, till after they know the testimony to be offered as well as we think we do. It has been the general subject of conversation in our congregation for weeks; and even husband and wife, parents and children, come to different conclusions. Our hearts bleed on this subject. God grant light, truth and righteousness may prevail, which is the prayer of your aged, feeble brother in Christ,

HOLLOWAY W. HUNT, Sen.

On the sheet of paper containing Mr. Hunt's copy of this affidavit, he wrote the following: "It is out of my power not to believe the above affidavit to be true.—H. W. Hunt." Mr. H. was a member of Presbytery, and expected to sit in judgment on the case which he thus decides before he had heard it. How true is Prov. 18:13. The only other instance of this cruel injustice in Presbytery, was, as the reader will see more fully presently, that of the Rev. Mr. Barnes.

* This then was all that Mr. Hunt and my enemies sought at the outset to accomplish—*simply my removal.* They took not the ground that crime had been perpetrated, which ought to be punished, but were perfectly willing that I should go and labor elsewhere. In the light of this fact alone, the reader may discover the dreadful nature of that element which Mr. Barnes introduced into the case.

† The reader must decide for himself whether this remark evinces the *high opinion* which Mr. Hunt entertains of the requisite qualifications of a missionary; or the *low opinion* entertained by him of the truth of the infamous charges which he sought to establish against me.

‡ The justice of this apprehension (which Mr. Hunt here expressed only to convey the impression that a respectable portion of the congregation believed these reports against me,) may be judged from the fact, that after the propagation of this rumor I remained pastor of the church during a year and a half; and that during that period my salary was as punctually paid as it ever had been before. Every farthing was promptly paid to me; and would still have been had I remained longer.

§ It was this remark which gave Mr. Barnes a plausible reason for pursuing that course which enabled him (during the meeting of Presbytery at Bethlehem, for the investigation of the charges against me) to secure his "going home with *Father* Hunt," as will be shown in its proper place hereafter.

‖ The reader will have abundant data hereafter, by which to judge of the utter falsehood of this scandalous asseveration.

On the same sheet he writes thus:

"And as Mr. Landis intends to attend next Presbytery, and defend himself with great tact and art, I believed it to be my duty to let you have glimps of our great affliction, before I am called on to give an account of my stewardship to our divine *Savior*. You will have the prayers of the pious in Bethlehem church, to direct and guide your measures to deliver us from what now grieves us, and to deliver us from the likeness of the ex-Bishop, Dr. Onderdonk, of New York.

"HOLLOWAY WHITFIELD HUNT, SEN."

He likewise requests Presbytery still to delay the trial. His object in this was to have the matter deferred, 1, until my enemies should have full time to concentrate their powers against me; 2, until the grand jury should have an opportunity to find a bill against me; and 3, until, on the approach of winter, the roads being broken up, and the travelling difficult and wearisome, there might be but a small attendance of the members of Presbytery. In view of these facts, however, which were brought before the Presbytery, in October, Mr. Barnes directly moved, without stating any reason for it, that the trial should be postponed, (agreeably to the wishes of Mr. Hunt,) until late in November. Dr. Gilbert and others had urged that it might proceed immediately, or with as little delay as possible. But when Mr. Barnes arose and made the motion (immediately after my explaining the reasons why Mr. Hunt wished the delay), though no formal vote was taken upon it, no one cared about opposing him directly, and so it passed by silent consent. But to return.

This libellous production was superscribed, not to the Moderator of Presbytery, but "To the Rev. Albert Barnes," and I think that Mr. Brainerd's name was also added. It was dated Sept. 24, 1847. It obviously, however, was not *precisely* the thing which Mr. Barnes either expected or desired: and hence, instead of handing it over to the Moderator (or destroying it, as every upright mind surely would have done*), he actually retained it in his possession until about October 12th, and spent most of the interval in riding about the country adjacent to Philadelphia, on horseback, carrying the letter with him. And the first knowledge that the Moderator, Dr. Converse, had of the existence of such a document was when, just before the meeting of Presbytery, he found it lying upon the desk in his printing office, all soiled and worn, and bearing the marks of having been frequently and thoroughly used. After making this deposit of it, Mr. Barnes again started out on his riding excursion, and on the day of the meeting of Presbytery (Oct. 15th), he, in

* How much suffering and grief of heart to others, and anguish of repentance to himself, might Mr. Barnes have spared, by simply acting agreeably to the following rules by a late celebrated writer:

"LISTENING TO EVIL REPORT.

"The longer I live, the more I feel the importance of adhering to the rule which I have laid down for myself in relation to such matters:

"1. To hear as little as possible of whatever is to the prejudice of others.

"2. To believe nothing of the kind till I am absolutely forced to it.

"3. Never drink into the spirit of one who circulates an evil report.

"4. Always to moderate as far as I can the unkindness which is expressed toward others.

"5. Always to believe that if the other side were heard, a very different account would be given of the matter."

company with Mr. Brainerd, arrived at a hotel, near the church at Marple (Delaware Co., Pa.), the place of meeting, where he took up his quarters during the sessions of Presbytery.

CHAPTER III.

FURTHER PARTICULARS: THE COURSE PURSUED BY MR. BARNES WHEN THE CASE FIRST CAME UP BEFORE PRESBYTERY.

THE object of these historical sketches is to illustrate the statement, that Mr. Barnes introduced an element into the case, the operation of which has unnecessarily injured me and the cause of religion through me. The entire bearing, therefore, of what is offered in these primary chapters, cannot be so fully perceived by the reader as it can when he becomes thoroughly acquainted with the case. Nothing superfluous is introduced, though from the fear of rendering my book unreadable, by reason of its bulk, I am compelled to confine myself to limits which exclude a mass of important facts and illustrations bearing on the same subject.

Soon after Mr. Barnes and Dr. Brainerd reached Marple, I and my elder arrived and stopped at the same hotel. Those brethren appeared as friendly towards us as usual. But as I knew that Mr. Barnes had been speaking with much freedom on the subject of the rumor against me, I, in the course of conversation with him, twice, and in the most distinct and direct manner, adverted to the subject, for the express purpose of affording to him an opportunity of conversing with myself respecting it, if he thought proper. Each time, however, that it was thus mentioned, his conversation at once ceased, and he preserved a profound silence until some other topic was introduced. He had carried the letter of Mr. Hunt for a long time, and had viewed it over and over again and ascertained all the uses which could be made of it against me; had freely discussed its statements, and professed to be influenced in no small degree by them. He had professed also to find artfulness in my letters to the Moderator requesting that a meeting of the Presbytery should be called to investigate the charges. He was the only member of that body who was thus influenced; and Dr. Brainerd himself, who had been so much with him, still dissented from his views, and did not hesitate, when the subject was introduced before Presbytery, by the reading of Mr. Hunt's letter, to declare that the whole matter "had every appearance of being a mere got-up affair for the purpose of injuring the brother who was thus accused."* Mr. Barnes had come to Presbytery prepared to take *some* action in the matter. He had, through Mr. Hunt's correspondence, made himself thoroughly familiar with most

* Dr. Brainerd and I had had no intercourse whatever, either direct or indirect, touching the matter.

that had been said against me; and now before he commenced acting he had a full opportunity of conversing with his calumniated brother,—an opportunity too for the most direct and pointed inquiry, inasmuch as I, myself, in conversation with him, had directly adverted to the subject. This, of course, would have justified the utmost point and frankness on his part. Had he not manifested so much interest in becoming acquainted with the accusation, I should not have felt justified in even wishing to converse with him in relation to the matter, as he was so soon to sit upon it in judgment; but since he had evinced this interest, and a high degree of willingness to believe Mr. Hunt's statements, why should he not have embraced the opportunity so freely afforded of examining into the points with which his mind might be laboring? Why was this? It was not an indisposedness to converse on the subject, for no one in Philadelphia had been so busy as he in relation to it, or had conversed upon it more, if we, perhaps, except Dr. Parker. The other members of Presbytery, including Dr. Parker, when opportunity presented, manifested no such reserve; and why should Mr. Barnes? He surely will not pretend to say that he had lost confidence in me, for he had had as yet no opportunity to examine into the truth or falseness of the statements of my accuser;* and the very last letter which I had received from him, and only a few days before (Oct. 6th), commenced in this very affectionate style: "*My dear brother Landis.*" The letter had no relation or reference to the rumor against me, and is the only one in a correspondence with him of nearly twenty years that begins in this affectionate manner. The emphatic addition after "*brother*" is, however, added to this, as though he sought in a kind and gentle, though incidental, manner to lead me to feel that my affliction had only increased his love for me. Whatever else, therefore, might have been the reason why he refused to converse with me on this subject, while he so freely received and discussed the statements of Mr. Hunt, it could not have arisen from any want of confidence in me, or from any diminution of *affectionate* regard. Mr. Barnes can say why it is, unless, perchance, it should prove to be one of those incidents which have "escaped his memory."

However, in the light of this, and so many other facts, all evincing a

* What a prodigious difference some persons make between *meum* and *tuum!* The fable of the farmer going to the lawyer with the information that his bull had gored the lawyer's ox, may find many applications in our day. Mr. Barnes, when on trial at York, in October, 1835 (during which I, at a great sacrifice, stood at his side), thus expressed his indignation when he thought that Mr. Winchester had prejudged *his* case: "I wish this remembered, because it may be my duty, hereafter, to object to his retaining his seat as a judge, in a cause which, according to his own declaration, he had *prejudged before he heard it.*"—Trial, p. 18. *Heu! quantum mutatus ab illo Hectore.* Mr. Barnes has Dr. Barrow's works, and in sermon seventeen might have read the following passages: "And in reason, *before exact trial and cognizance, to meddle with the fame and interest of another, is evidently a practice full of iniquity*, such as no man can allow in his own case, or brook being used towards himself, without judging himself to be extremely abused by such reporters. The matter should be clear, notorious, and palpable, before we admit a disadvantageous conceit into our head, a distasteful resentment into our heart, a harsh word into our mouth about him." "He that breweth lies may have more wit and skill; but the broacher showeth the like malice and wickedness. In this there is no great difference between the great Devil that frameth scandalous reports, and the little Imps that run about and disperse them." Nothing can be more true and just. *Verbum sapienti*, &c.

like disposition, surely I may ask why he should treat me thus? He still professed to be my friend, and why then should he evince this readiness to hear and be influenced by an evil report before it was at all in any way investigated? Lord Bacon has said, that "a man who hath no virtue in himself, ever envieth virtue in others; for men's minds will either feed upon their own good, or upon other's evil; and he who wanteth the one will prey upon the other; and whoso is out of hope to attain another's virtue, will seek to come at even hand by depressing another's fortune." But I could not then, without doing violence to my own mind, attribute such a motive to a Christian brother, or suppose for a moment that I could be in possession of anything that he could envy. And as I attributed his preceding conduct towards me (as above narrated) to idiosyncrasy, and sought to palliate and excuse it both to my own mind and to others, so I attributed also this his conduct respecting the letter and his strange refusal to converse with me. But now, in the light which his subsequent acts have cast upon this transaction, the question returns: Why should he, and at such a time, when I was enduring anguish worse than a hundred deaths, thus at the very outset bring to bear against me the whole weight of his influence? Is not this the very "PRACTICE FULL OF INIQUITY" described by Dr. Barrow? I had never, to my knowledge, injured Mr. Barnes, but had always been his firm friend, in the best sense of that word. It is true, I never did esteem his "Commentaries" as other than the merest *rudes indigestaque moles* (a view entertained of them by, I believe, every thorough biblical scholar in the land, who is at all conversant with them), and I believe he knew it; though of this I am not fully certain. But he does know that I always spoke of them kindly in my writings, and gave them all the praise that they deserve. But this surely could not have induced a Christian minister to pursue such a course as this. Could it be, then, because in the faithful discharge of my duty to the cause of God and of truth, I had, in my then recent work on the Resurrection, controverted and pointedly exposed a few of his innumerable shallow and erroneous expositions of Scripture?* I certainly had a right to do so, when such exposition was pleaded in justification of absurd and soul-ruining errors. Was it because I was, just at this time, preparing a labored essay on the penal nature of Christ's sufferings, in which I had exposed the wholesale fallacies and illogical reasonings of the school of Drs. Beman and Jenkyn, and Mr. Barnes?† Could it be that he was permitting such or

* See especially pp. 140–152, 270, 279, of my Reply to Professor Bush on the Resurrection.

† For many years it was Mr. Barnes' invariable custom to ask me, whenever we were together, "What are you now writing?" In April, 1847 (a few months before this effort of Mr. Hunt to injure me), he and Brother Adair remained at my house for several days, as the Presbytery was in session at Bethlehem; and while there he made the usual inquiry. I replied that I was preparing the essay above mentioned, and with all frankness showed it to him. After he had become acquainted with its contents he said, with a tone expressive of a feeling of deep dissatisfaction, "Do you intend to *publish* that?" I replied, "Certainly I do!" He said no more, but relapsed into a moody silence. God knows whether this could have in any wise influenced him to adopt the course which has resulted in crushing my spirit, and in the breaking up of my church and family.

similar considerations to influence his conduct? I do not know, and am desirous that Mr. Barnes himself should explain why he pursued against his brother "a practice so full of iniquity."

Finally, however, Presbytery was convened and the case introduced. The letter of Mr. Hunt was read, and a committee appointed to consider and report thereon. This report was not satisfactory to Mr. Barnes and to several others, I believe. Hence, in order if possible to meet his wishes, another committee was chosen, of which he was a member. He made a show of unwillingness to serve, and did not arise from his seat (though the rest of the committee had already retired) until I suggested to the Moderator (Dr. Fairchild) the propriety of also placing the elder from Bethlehem on the committee, as there appeared to be a difficulty in coming to a conclusion, and the members might wish to consult with him. Immediately on my making this remark, Mr. Barnes arose and said, with much warmth, "You had better appoint half the Presbytery at once!" and started with unusual haste to join the committee. The Moderator remarked, however, that my suggestion was proper, and the elder (J. S. Johnson) was appointed accordingly.

Mr. Barnes was *chairman* of this new committee, (so desirous was Presbytery that their views and his should, if possible, coincide,) but their report, as drawn up and presented by him, gave still less satisfaction than the former. I took no part in the discussion of the subject, during this whole session, but left these preliminary steps in the hands of my brethren. The points, however, on which they could not agree, were chiefly these: *whether Mr. Hunt, on account of the letter aforesaid, ought not to be regarded as my prosecutor? and whether Presbytery should meet at Bethlehem to investigate the case, or appoint a commission to ascertain and report the facts?* During the discussion of this last point, Mr. Barnes, perceiving that the general voice was for the appointment of a commission, arose and made a remark which certainly imports a great deal in respect to the purity of his aims or the contrary. It is this: "By the appointment of a commission and their action in the case, a stain will be left on Brother Landis' character which he will never be able to remove. But if the matter be investigated by Presbytery, there is no danger of this." He meant, of course, that there was no danger of this on the supposition that the accusation could not be substantiated. On his expressing his preference so decidedly in this matter, Presbytery agreed at once to meet at Bethlehem, instead of appointing a commission.

Although Mr. Barnes (and he knew it perfectly well) possessed an almost unlimited influence with the members of Presbytery, yet thus far *he stood entirely alone* in professing to be influenced by the statements of Mr. Hunt's letter, and the cruel unkindness with which he had been pursuing me, was not approved by any of his brethren, except the author of that letter. They saw his course and deplored it; but he knew that they were very unwilling to provoke his prejudice or resentment by intimating, publicly, that his proceedings were improper and wicked. They could not then believe that his motives were, what his subsequent acts have proved them to be, and hoped that no evil would arise from the course he was pursuing. Being men of peace, and inclined to pursue

5

their way without contention, if possible, it was perfectly natural that they should not wish to thwart him when it could be avoided. He as yet took no open ground against me, but continued his professions of friendship and affection, and thus their suspicions were not awakened. He saw all this, and now, when Presbytery was not in session, he sought to take advantage of such a state of things, and to bring his influence so to bear as to secure the adoption of the course which he, from the first (when riding about with Mr. Hunt's letter), evidently designed to pursue. At length, however (the evening after the first session), there was some loud talking between him and several other members. I was not present, having retired a few yards from the place where they were standing. But at the close of the conference, Dr. Fairchild (and I hope he will, under the circumstances, pardon the mention of a private conversation) came to me, under considerable excitement, and said, with much feeling, and, I believe, with tears—"My dear brother, you can have no fairness shown you in this matter. *Were I in your place, I would wash my hands of the Presbytery and leave it!*" The last sentence he uttered with vehement indignation. To his earnest and kindly-intended remark, however, I only replied: "No! I shall do no such thing; God will take care of me."

Mr. Barnes had been employing his influence (though I then knew not to what extent), in the same manner when with his brethren, for now almost six weeks, and yet such was the result. With all his efforts he could not alienate them from me, though, unfortunately, he succeeded in too greatly intimidating them from acting according to their fullest convictions of duty. This fact proves them to be but men, and is not mentioned for the purpose of casting any unkind reflection upon them. I know not a nobler set of men on earth, than those who composed the majority of that body; and if their "thinking no evil," and "hoping all things" from a member, who occupied so prominent a position in their body, led them to yield to what they deemed his superior judgment, and so to some extent to depart from their own convictions of duty—"let him who is without sin first cast a stone at them." I mourn that they did so; I know I should not have done it in their case, (perhaps because I had a more just appreciation than they had of Mr. Barnes' real talents and attainments,) but I know also how to make allowance for it. If they deem it unkind in me to refer to this matter, I shall be deeply grieved, but my convictions of duty in the matter will remain unaltered. Mr. Barnes had, moreover, four weeks in which to operate, and correspond with Mr. Hunt, and the rest of my enemies, and how he employed this interval may perhaps be learned from the sequel. But it would not be wonderful if such a disposition, with such an influence, and ever at work to secure its aim, should, in the lapse of nearly three months, succeed in inducing even good men to regard me with suspicion, and incline them to view "trifles light as air," as "confirmation strong" of the suspicions which he had so artfully thrown out against me.

CHAPTER IV.

THE SAME SUBJECT CONTINUED.

At the conclusion of the session at Marple, the business being unfinished, Presbytery adjourned to meet during the following week in the lecture-room of the Fifth Church in Philadelphia. Mr. Barnes was uncommonly careful to be present at every meeting, and the unprecedented and most tedious delays that occurred in coming to a conclusion in the business arose chiefly, and, I believe, *entirely*, from a disposition which all the brethren naturally felt to meet with the concurrence of the views of so prominent a member of their body. The points referred to in our last chapter were still unsettled, and, on the morning of the second day of this adjourned meeting, I endeavored, in a brief speech, to shed what light I could upon the matter, and remarked to the following effect:

"There are two points before us upon which I wish to say a word, after which I shall no further occupy the time of Presbytery. My character is very closely connected with your proceedings, and, of course, I must feel a great interest in them; yet I have not the least desire to dictate, but only wish to suggest a few thoughts in a very few remarks, and then I shall acquiesce in any decision to which you may arrive. I have, from the first, made it my constant prayer to God, that you might be guided in this matter so as to do what will be most for His glory! for His ways are inscrutable and far above ours. I sometimes think that He designs that I should serve as an example, to show how to *suffer* the will of God, where He sees proper to permit Satan's efforts to destroy his people by false accusations, and He has made me willing, and even desirous, that, if this be His design concerning me, He would thus employ me for the purpose of glorifying His name. He has wonderfully supported me under this trial thus far, and, though I am unfortunately one of the most sensitive of mortals, He has enabled me to be joyful in the midst of the most terrible and soul-crushing trial of my life—a trial for which, if I had had a choice, I solemnly protest, I would gladly have exchanged martyrdom at the stake.

"The two points before us are, 1. What is the best method of bringing the subject before us; and 2. Shall the charge be investigated by a commission or by Presbytery?

"As to Brother Barnes' paper which brings me forth as demanding an investigation, let it be considered that when this application was made by me, I had not the remotest idea that Mr. Hunt had sent to Presbytery a paper accusing me. Had I known this, I should have made no such application.* This is wholly lost sight of in that paper. It also states that in consequence of that accusation (of Mr. Hunt's), the slanderous reports have been extended to my disadvantage. Now, this is not so at home; for there, it has died a natural death already; and had not the affidavit been taken, I should not have thought it worth while to give you any further trouble respecting it.

"As to the position of Mr. Hunt in the matter, I state frankly that I do not believe he *designed* to become my prosecutor; and if there is any unfairness or injustice in regarding him as such, I should oppose it as strongly as any person here. If my cause cannot be defended without taking an undue and unjust

* The application here referred to was not made till October 15th. As my earlier *requests* had been set aside through Mr. Barnes' influence, I now, with my session, made a direct application in the proper form.

advantage of any one, I shall look upon it as an evidence that God designs me to suffer. I believe that old man is *the* guilty one in the sight of God—that is, that there would have been none of this had it not been for the course which he has pursued. I do not think he originated the slander; but when he had heard thereof, it was he who took the measures to embody the wretched story in the form of an affidavit. This, you will have all the proof of that you can desire. I believe that he cruelly wished to destroy me, or drive me away. I, moreover, am fully convinced that it is not the design of any one to appear as my prosecutor; but they wish to throw me upon the necessity of proving my innocence. I am assured also, that if Mr. Hunt can be regarded as my prosecutor, he will bring forward all these persons to sustain him—and he is the only man living who can do it—and thus you can fully learn all that is now said against me, together with the alleged proof on which it rests; but still, if he is not the prosecutor by a fair construction of the principles of our constitution, I hope he will not be dealt with unfairly, in order to secure me, at his expense, an advantage in my defence, to which I am certainly entitled in such a case.

"One of the brethren (Mr. Brainerd) remarked, in favor of appointing a commission, that if Presbytery should meet at Bethlehem, it would only be to listen to a few severe retorts from Mr. Hunt and myself. So far, however, as I am concerned, this is a mistake. During all this severe affliction, I have been enabled to regard Mr. Hunt and the rest of my persecutors, without any indulged feelings of resentment. I believe that no one has ever heard me even refer to them with feelings of anger. I have never felt so sad in view of their spiritual state, nor prayed so much and so fervently for their salvation, as I have done since they have made this attempt to destroy me; and you will find, that I shall not employ any such language as denunciation, through the whole course of this investigation. I shall aim only to elicit facts by testimony. I *may* offer a few remarks on the evidence; but if severe reproof is to be administered to my persecutors, it will not be administered by me. If it were the case of any other brother of the Presbytery, I should probably act differently; but I am not a proper judge in my own case. When the testimony is therefore elicited, I shall submit the case, and leave it and myself entirely at your disposal; I shall submit to your decision. I know you honor God and his truth too well to spare me if such things can be proved against me; for it is better that ten thousand such as I should perish, than that one particle of his truth or glory should be compromised. And I know, too, that if you find me innocent, you will be at no loss how to proceed, nor hesitate to say so, and to stand by me with your influence.

"When the trial is over, I shall submit to your decision; and if you condemn me, I shall not carry up my case by appeal, nor trouble our judicatories further with it;* neither will I carry my congregation with me, in opposition to such a decision, though I could easily do it, but shall feel it my duty to submit, and wait till God shall bring to light my innocence of this charge. I have no fortune, nor rich relations to fall back upon. What I inherited from my father, I gave to my widowed mother; and with the exception of purchasing a library, I have never even laid up fifty dollars in the world; my principles do not admit of it, while there are so many others more needy than I. So that, though I know not what I can do for a maintenance for myself and family, I shall yet, if you find me guilty, calmly lay aside my work, and get my people to acquiesce in your decision. God, who heareth the young ravens when they cry, will take care of me. He will, in his own best time, roll away my reproach, though the whole world should now believe me guilty. He may wish me to serve as an example to this generation, how his holy will should be suffered in a case of the

* Such was my full determination; but the announcement of it at this stage was injudicious, especially after what I had already witnessed of the disposition and manœuvring of Mr. Barnes.

severest affliction. Shall I repine then? No; I truly and from my heart rejoice in this evidence that he has not forsaken me, but designs, through me, in some way to promote his glory. I have even ceased longer to feel anxious about the effects of such a vile rumor on the minds of the enemies of religion, for I am assured that it is my precious privilege to cast this anxiety (which at first troubled me more than all things else) entirely upon him who careth for me.

"At our former meeting, I avoided mentioning particulars; but in order to assist you in coming to a result of some kind, I will here state a few, the truth of which will, I think, be found to be unquestionable, when you come to investigate the case.

"1. Mr. Hunt appointed the committee to take the affidavit of my accuser, before I had ever heard the first word of the rumor against me; and great efforts were made to keep the whole matter carefully concealed from me until the affidavit had been taken. In a letter of instruction to this committee, he directed them to take the affidavit; and that after it was taken, to advise me immediately to leave Bethlehem.

"2. This committee being composed chiefly of noted opposers of mine, and near relations of my accuser, several of them (two at least) refused to serve. A second committee was therefore appointed, who took the affidavit. As I had no choice in the selection of the first committee, neither had I in this; nor was I permitted to be present when the affidavit was taken.

"3. It is not true that I ever forbade the affidavit to be read to the congregation; I never even requested that it might not be read, and only remarked, that I did not think the filthy thing ought to be read before a promiscuous audience. Mr. Hunt himself made no less than four speeches to the congregation, insisting that it should be read, and finally, he moved that it be read, but not a soul in the whole congregation would second the motion.

"4. It is painful to be obliged to give so direct a contradiction to the statements of that old clergyman, but the truth and my reputation require it. And I therefore remark further, that it is not true that there was any such interview between the elders, myself and Mr. Hunt, as he has represented in his letter.*

"5. A copy of the woman's affidavit was left with her, from which my enemies have made copies, and sent them all over the country.

"6. When the voice of the community pronounced upon the story, and declared it to be ridiculously false, my enemies obtained a girl to swear that she saw take place the thing that is charged upon me. I had not the least notice that she was to be sworn; and as soon as I learned that her oath had been taken, I sent to the magistrate a polite note by a friend, requesting a copy, but he absolutely refused to grant it. Now, this same magistrate has repeatedly brought this same affidavit, together with a copy of the one made by my accuser, to the Bethlehem church on Sabbath days, and read them aloud in the grove, to the congregation as they were assembling. He makes a practice, too, to read them to all who call upon him, and to every one who desires to hear them.

"7. My accuser, though she *talked* very freely against me, was very unwilling to depose to the truth of what she said. The committee were with her from 3 o'clock P.M., until 11, before they obtained the affidavit. She wept, and told the committee that she would not have sworn, had she not been *compelled* to do so.

"8. There has been a great reaction in my favor, in consequence of these proceedings, wherever the facts have transpired; and I believe that not one of my

* The discussions in Presbytery respecting Mr. Hunt's letter rendered it necessary for me to notice these falsehoods; for the course which Mr. Barnes pursued was to bring out the statements of that letter against me as facts, and yet deny me the privilege of holding him who made them responsible as my accuser.

people, that is, the praying and contributing part of them, has lost confidence in me.

"These things are so. But now, when through the unfair and wicked proceedings of my enemies, a *fama clamosa* has been created, they wish to deny me the right and advantage of having a prosecutor. Neither the woman herself, nor her husband, nor her father, is willing to appear as such. But if Mr. Hunt has truly taken this position, and should, in consequence, be required to meet its responsibilities, he will bring everything forward that can be said against me; and nothing will be omitted by him to sustain the charge. All I wish is fair play. And I am persuaded if Mr. Hunt finds that he has involved himself, he will do all this; and he is the only man in the country who is able to do it. And thus you will be enabled to decide intelligently from all the facts in the case.

"As to the second point, whether Presbytery had better meet at Bethlehem, or send there a commission to ascertain and report the facts in the case, I would merely say, that, if the commission can meet in the church, and try the case, and act as the Presbytery and for it, and the matter all be transacted openly, I and my people will be satisfied. But if they cannot do this, it will be infinitely better that Presbytery should there convene; and I urge upon the brethren to call a meeting for this purpose as soon as possible. The object of Mr. Hunt, in wishing the meeting delayed until late in next month, is sufficiently obvious. But I trust he will be disappointed, and that you will meet as soon as possible; and that we shall have a large number of the members of this Judicatory in attendance."

This address made at least *some* impression upon the Presbytery. But immediately as I concluded, and even before I could resume my seat, Mr. Barnes (who had listened to every word of it with very great attention) hastily rose, and said: "I am opposed to meeting there on this business until the middle of next month;" and having said this, and without giving the shadow of a reason for the delay, or adding another word, he sat down. He knew that the court was to convene before that period, and that my enemies designed (unless the Presbytery should, in the mean time, meet, and try the case, and acquit me,) at that court to find a bill against me, if possible; he knew, also, that the roads by that time (for I had stated the fact to Presbytery in his presence) would, in all probability, be so broken up, and the travelling, in consequence, be so difficult, that there would be really no reasonable hope of a full attendance of the members of Presbytery. He knew, too, that, with the single exception of himself, the feelings of *every presbyter there* were with me in regard to the importance of a speedy meeting. But as they did not attach a *primary* importance to the matter, he felt that they would not oppose his wishes when thus decidedly expressed. What, then, was his object in urging this delay? Let him explain it. The case had been already delayed about six weeks from the time of my first application, all of which time, as Mr. Barnes knew, I and my church and family were left at the mercy of a set of as malignant and unprincipled men as ever assassinated human character. Why, then, should he thus, without explaining the reason, ask for a month longer? Such delay is excusable where it may be difficult to convene an ecclesiastical judicatory; or where witnesses are absent; or the parties unprepared for trial: but thus, without a reason (except to accommodate his own wishes, or those of Mr. Hunt), and for week after week, to refuse to relieve the suffering interests of the Redeemer's church, is a procedure, so far as

I know, without a parallel or precedent in Protestant Christendom; and is unaccountable on principles of either humanity, religion, or equity.

The question had now been brought up again, whether Mr. Hunt was not in equity bound to sustain the position of my prosecutor, inasmuch as he had in his letter not only alleged charges against me, but professed his full belief in their truth, and consequently that I was criminal. The question was taken twice: the second time by rising. *And every member of Presbytery, both clerical and lay, voted that Mr. Hunt was, properly and in fact, my prosecutor—except this self-same Rev. Albert Barnes.* He voted *in the negative.* I am not disputing his right to vote agreeably to his convictions, but merely stating a fact. And now, at length, when a member of Presbytery (Mr. Conkling) arose, and begged of Mr. Barnes to assent to the resolution, so that the vote might appear on the records as unanimous, he refused, without stating any reason whatever.* To comment on such conduct, with the preceding facts in view, would, indeed, be a work of supererogation. But why was it that Messrs. Barnes and Hunt thus agreed to withhold from me the right of having a responsible prosecutor, and sought to subject me to the disadvantages of meeting common fame? "Can two walk together, except they be agreed?" And is this an illustration of what Mr. Barnes meant by his expressed desire that "no spot might be left on the character of *Brother* Landis? Can I doubt that it is an illustration of his *real* meaning? *Credat Judæus Apella: non ego.* The members of Presbytery likewise (as the reader will see) ultimately yielded, and let Mr. Barnes take the lead in this matter, also: regarding him with that deference which men usually pay to those superior geniuses who will exact it of them.

Thus the matter ended for the present; and Mr. Hunt received from Presbytery a notification to collect and present such testimony as he deemed necessary to sustain his statements. The following is a copy of the whole minute:

"The committee on the papers of the Rev. H. W. Hunt, Sen., and Rev. Robert Landis, and the Session of Bethlehem Church, made the following report, which was adopted, to wit:

"*Whereas*, The Rev. H. W. Hunt, Sen., a member of this Presbytery, has sent to this meeting a paper containing the deposition of a woman before a civil magistrate, affecting injuriously the character of Rev. Robert Landis, one of our members, and avowed his belief of its truth; and

"*Whereas*, It appears from the accompanying statement of Rev. H. W. Hunt, Sen., that the character of Rev. Robert W. Landis, and the cause of religion, are suffering from the injurious reports in circulation: *and whereas further*, Rev. Robert W. Landis and his Session have asked an investigation of these injurious reports, therefore,

"1st. *Resolved*, That this Presbytery meet at the Church of Bethlehem, on

* When the matter came up subsequently in Presbytery, at Bethlehem, Mr. Hunt, being thus sustained by the influence of Mr. Barnes, positively refused to submit to the decision which recognized him as prosecutor. His refusal excited much indignation in all the members of Presbytery (except Mr. Barnes), and some of them proposed at once to adjourn, and return home. I opposed the adjournment, however; and ultimately, the old man, after consulting with Mr. Barnes, procured the girl's father to act as prosecutor. The results of this whole procedure will be noticed hereafter.

Tuesday, 16th of November, at 3 o'clock, P.M., to take up and investigate the whole subject.

"2d. *Resolved*, That the Rev. H. W. Hunt, Sen., be notified to collect and present such testimony as he deems necessary to sustain his statements contained in his letter to this Presbytery, in regard to the Rev. Robert W. Landis, and essential to a full and impartial examination.

"3d. *Resolved*, That the Rev. H. W. Hunt, Sen., and Rev. Robert W. Landis, be furnished with copies of this document, by the Stated Clerk of Presbytery.

By order of Presbytery,

"ROB'T ADAIR, *Stated Clerk*."

Appended to Mr. Hunt's copy, was likewise the following postscript:

"You will regard the foregoing document as the notice referred to in Resolution 2d of the foregoing.—R. A."

I now wished to have some competent brother assigned me as counsel; but was informed by several excellent brethren (among whom were Rev. Messrs. Fairchild and Adair), that this matter had been thought of, and that a legal gentleman of great learning and acuteness had been secured, to whom the case had been stated, and who had given them his assurance that he would attend. I felt and expressed great gratification at the prospect of having a man of that character engaged in ferreting out the case; and on inquiry, learned that he was an elder of Mr. Barnes' church, by name of Samuel H. Perkins. I then had no acquaintance with this eminent and excellent barrister; and felt serious misgivings upon learning that his attendance must, after all, greatly, if not altogether, depend upon Mr. Barnes, as his Pastor. But my brethren had taken Mr. Hunt's letter to him, and assured me that he *was* the man, and that there could be no doubt whatever of his being present—that he was willing to come, and fully expected to do so, inasmuch as the members of Presbytery desired and requested it. Here the interview ended, and I returned home.

CHAPTER V.

THE MEETING OF PRESBYTERY IN BETHLEHEM.

ON my return from the meeting of the Presbytery in Philadelphia, I brought with me the forequoted copy of the minute designed for Mr. Hunt, and immediately sent it to him. He also was desirous of allowing me as little advantage as possible for defending myself; and accordingly waited until the *seventh of November* before he replied to me, though he knew that Presbytery was to meet on the 16th of that month. The following is a copy of his letter:

"Reverend Sir: Your communication of the 23d of October is received, and in answer observe, You are the prosecutor of common fame* by inviting the Presbytery to come and investigate the subject. Mr. Conover and Mr. Vanderbelt will defend general rumor by their counsel to be yet appointed, when they enter on business, according to our discipline, 4th chapter, on actual process. See also general rules number 41. But in cases of process on the ground of general rumor where there is, of course, no particular accuser.

"By order of Presbytery, I have cited the following persons as witnesses in defence of general rumor, namely, the widow of the late Judge Stiger, Mary Catherine Stiger,† and her granddaughter Catharine Vanderbelt, and her hired girl Sarah Ann Seals, Catherine Sweezey, Benjamin Chew Bird, Morris Rodenbough, Doctor Thomas E. Hunt,‡ and Judge Peter Sigler.§

"With ardent prayers to the Lord Jesus Christ that the trial may be fair without cringing on either side, and open doors for public inspection, and that the issue may be according to truth, light and righteousness,

HOLLOWAY WHITFIELD HUNT, Senior."

This letter was dated Oct. 30th, and had the subjoined postscript:

"Rev. Mr. Landis,—At the ensuing sessions of our Presbytery from the 16th, say to the 18th or 19th of November, the days will be very short and the evenings long; time will not permit of going from one to three miles to dine. Permit me to recommend that we meet each morning at 9 o'clock, and continue in session till 4 P.M., with a recess at noon a few minutes to eat some cakes and apples furnished by our good ladies, and at four o'clock all repair to their quarters for dinner, and again to business at church at 6 o'clock, and continue during the pleasure of Presbytery, when our carriages will attend to bring them to their lodgings.

"Let the first evening, if you choose, be occupied by a sermon from a brother located near the church. From age have not ventured out evenings for some years.‖ But health and weather favoring, will be with you from nine in the morning till four in the afternoon. You know the eyes of God, of the church, friends and foes, will be on us.

"Let all be done without partiality. Receive in your house and among your especial advocates only half the Presbytery, the other among your opponents. Let Mr. Conover have his counsel, Elder Daniel Carhart two members, H. W.

* In the published proceedings connected with Mr. Hunt's withdrawal from the Newton Presbytery, he charges that judicatory with "appointing a committee of investigation at the mere suggestion of *that lying herald, common fame*." Mr. Barnes' extreme sensitiveness on the same subject may be seen in his "Defence" against Dr. Junkin, pp. 94-100. Yet these are the self-same men who sought to subject me to the mercy of the same lying gossip. "But," said the lawyer, "it alters the case prodigiously if it was my bull that gored your ox." It is really humiliating to witness, in a human being, such utter absence of every attribute of manliness.

† This is the person who came into Presbytery with a piece of writing as her deposition, but refused to answer any questions touching the matter, "because," says she, "the Lord appeared to me and told me to give you the paper, but to answer no questions." Such were the extremities to which Mr. Hunt and my enemies *in Jersey* felt themselves reduced.

‡ A mere child, *still in leading strings*, grandson of Mr. Hunt.

§ They call all mere magistrates in Jersey "Judges." This man was one of the lowest of the low distillers, and still is. Some wag in the Legislature, knowing his illiteracy, and in order to have a little fun, procured and sent to him a Justice's commission, but having never learned to write, he could not act under it, but he was always afterwards saluted as "*Judge*." Were not the matter so serious, one could not help laughing at Mr. Hunt's powers of amplification.

‖ This was said merely to give some color of reason to his refusal to act as prosecutor, for he *did attend* the Presbytery every evening during the trial, nor did he ever make any objection to attend weddings on evenings.

Hunt two, Judge Sigler two. If less than twelve* we will be content with our dividend, if more, give us our share, and we beg of you to rule us no longer by arbitrary power. H. W. Hunt, Senior."

Such, then, was the notice which I received from my accuser. Not a charge was specified, nor had I any means of ascertaining what these witnesses designed to testify, except in the case of the young woman, whose affidavit had been first taken. Our constitution requires that an accused person should be furnished, not only with the names of witnesses, but with a fair and full copy of the charges made against him, and that this should be furnished at least ten days before the trial. Supposing that Mr. Hunt would comply with the requisition of Presbytery in this matter, I had consented to waive my right to the ten days after the first assembling of the judicatory, in order that Presbytery might not be under the necessity of taking so long a journey again. Though it is doubtful whether they would have done so, for it was plainly intimated that, if the trial were not concluded at this meeting of Presbytery, the subsequent sessions must be held in Philadelphia; and it being my wish to have it in the presence of my people, I had adopted this step for the accommodation of all, but at what a sacrifice will be seen presently.

The distance from Philadelphia to the Bethlehem church is a little over fifty miles, and there being no direct line of stages by which Presbytery could arrive in a single day, I proposed that the members should proceed from the city directly to Flemington (eight miles south of Bethlehem), at which place I engaged to meet them with carriages.† I accordingly went down at the time appointed, but, upon meeting with the brethren, learned that the promised and expected counsel (Mr. Perkins) *would not be present.* What my feelings were the reader may imagine. It was now too late to select other counsel from amongst the lawyers who are elders of our churches, and thus was the plot thickening which threatened my beloved church, myself, and my family with ruin. Mr. Barnes, instead of taking measures to secure the attendance of Mr. Perkins, who had promised to attend, (that is if his pastor desired it, and if nothing beyond his control occurred to prevent his doing so, and nothing of the kind did occur,) and who knew that no other counsel could then be employed with anything like equal advantages, and who knew also

* This remark may show what Mr. Hunt's expectations were in respect to what might be the attendance of the members of Presbytery, if the meeting should be delayed until late in the season. Our Presbytery then numbered (including the lay delegates) forty-five members and one foreign missionary. Mr. Hunt calculated correctly that by delaying the meeting, about one-fourth of the members, and perhaps less, would attend; and he knew the great influence there wielded by Mr. Barnes. *Three* elders only were present besides those from Bethlehem and Alexandria, and *seven* ministers besides Mr. Hunt and myself, to wit: Messrs. Barnes, Brainerd, Fairchild, Ramsey, Adair, M. L. R. P. Thompson and Cornelius S. Conkling.

† Mr. Barnes, however, preferred to take the journey on horseback, and Mr. Brainerd accompanied him. But when he arrived within three or four miles of my house, where he had partaken of many a meal, and professed to be always happy to stay, he paused and took some refreshment at a wretched little rum-hole, near the place where I had been recently pelted with addled eggs for lecturing on temperance; and where there was every facility for hearing, without particular inquiry, all the misrepresentations of my worst enemies concerning me.

that Mr. Perkins, nor no other gentleman, could push himself forward to secure such an appointment, had brought with him an inexperienced youth who seldom or never before had attended Presbytery as a delegate!

The case to be examined into was one in which a man of Mr. Perkins' learning and signal ability is of more worth, in order to develop the real truth and ferret out falsehood, wherever it may exist, than fifty clergymen. His experience in investigating cases at law, affords him advantages which are derivable from no other source. And notwithstanding all the influence which Mr. Barnes, as his pastor, may be supposed to have over him, I fervently rejoiced at the prospect of having the case thus thoroughly investigated. But none of the brethren of Presbytery had any other expectations than that Mr. Perkins would attend, until Mr. Barnes had chosen his delegate* a little while before they left the city for Bethlehem. Mr. Barnes not only *could* have brought him, had he so desired, but he knew that I, and a number of the other members of Presbytery, had based our calculations on his being present. And why, then, did he not bring him? or, at least, why did he not state to his session that Presbytery expected him, and that an accused brother had fully calculated on his attendance, and that it was of great importance to have the case thoroughly sifted? And why did he not, in consequence thereof, urge them to appoint him? I should have done all this in the case of Mr. Barnes, or of any other brother; and why did he not do it in mine? Is this a commentary upon his remark, already referred to, expressing an anxiety that *Brother* Landis might have all the advantages that were proper and just in order to clear himself from the imputations against him? And does not this act chime in with the whole of his preceding course?

The brethren arrived at Flemington on the evening of Monday, Nov. 15th, and, on the following day, at 3 o'clock P.M., Presbytery was to convene. On that day a number of them dined with me and my family, and, while we were yet at table, Mr. Barnes and Dr. Brainerd arrived at my house and sat down with us to dine. Brother Brainerd was frank and communicative as usual, and ate heartily. Mr. Barnes was unusually reserved (even for him) and scarcely ate a mouthful. Whether this arose from his having eaten heartily at the miserable little tavern above referred to, or from the thoughts now present to his mind, I cannot say. He was in a house and with a family, wherein he had spent many a pleasant hour, and, as he now was looking upon the kind-hearted woman, who was ministering to him at table, and expressing solicitude because he appeared not to enjoy his meal,† could it be that he was struggling with compunction for having, with such appalling determination, sought the ruin of her husband, and of herself, through him, and

*This language, though not *in form* agreeable to that of the constitution of our church, is yet accurate; for where no routine is established as to the order of attendance, and circumstances do not render it inexpedient, the pastor's wishes have a controlling influence in the selection of a delegate, especially in such circumstances as those of the case before us.

† I had not as yet made Mrs. Landis acquainted with the course he had pursued towards me.

that merely to gratify the basest passion of the human heart? But poor dear wife! her sorrows were not long. A few months more of this relentless hostility to me, were all that were now necessary to rock her bleeding and broken heart to the soothing slumbers of the grave.

As Mr. Hunt, in his letter aforesaid, had requested that the members of Presbytery might be equally distributed amongst the parties, the stated clerk was directed to give me notice that they were not to be distributed amongst *the parties* at all. This notification (which, if not suggested by Mr. Barnes, as I believe it was, had at least his concurrence,) the clerk gave me on his arrival at Flemington. But so soon as Presbytery convened, and before Mr. Hunt had had the least time or opportunity to commit himself to act as my prosecutor, Mr. Barnes went directly to him, and, after a moment's conversation, (for men of great genius, it is said, can as easily discover each other's plans and character as Free Masons can,) arose and said: "Moderator! I am going to put up with *Father* Hunt." The members had not yet been distributed, and this was said in view of such distribution. But how sweetly, at this time, must the cognomen of "*father*," bestowed by so prominent a clergyman, have sounded to that old man and to the rest of my enemies, whose spirits had begun to quail at the bare idea of the approaching investigation! And further, while Mr. Barnes made this remark, which sounds as though it were addressed to the Moderator, *he looked directly at me*, and not at the Moderator at all, whose seat was in a different direction. But then what does this announcement portend when viewed in connection with the preceding notice given me by the stated clerk? Was that notice designed, on the part of Mr. Barnes, to prevent Mr. Hunt from being supplied with his quantum of members of Presbytery, that so the place might be occupied by himself without the uncomfortable contiguity of some other member, whose presence might interfere with the full completion of his plans? He had also, as the reader will see, provided against that contingency, by securing the attendance of one from whom he had no such apprehensions. But dropping this for the present, I ask why was this announcement thus publicly made? Who ever dreamed before of giving a public notice, through the Moderator to Presbytery, and to a whole congregation, where he was going *to lodge!* unless, indeed, he had some covert design in it? He, however, and in this soothing manner, became the guest of this cruel, hard-hearted old man, who, as Mr. Barnes knew, had been for years doing all he could to break down my influence, and who, for months, had been collecting and circulating all the slanders that my enemies had fabricated against me. And thus, with the feelings which the preceding facts display, and when expecting soon to act as one of my judges in a case in which were involved all my dearest interests on earth, he voluntarily assumes not only the direction of that case, so far as it was under Mr. Hunt's control, but also seizes the opportunity to hear (after evincing such a disposition to be influenced by) all that falsehood and malignity could suggest against a calumniated brother.*

* *Mr. Barnes did not only listen to those slanders, but during the trial made use of them in a covert manner, against me.* Many proofs of this can be given, besides what the reader will find in the subsequent narrative.

But before Mr. Barnes left Philadelphia to attend this meeting of Presbytery, I believe he had resolved upon this whole plan of procedure: and if so, who can think of it without blushing for human nature! All my reasons for this belief cannot be here given; but I will submit a single one to the reader, and rest the whole question upon that. It is the following. Mr. Thomas P. Sparhawk, the elder of Mr. Barnes (and a truly excellent and accomplished young man), came to Flemington with the other members of Presbytery, as aforesaid; and as soon as he was presented to me he said "It is my wish, Mr. Landis, that you would appoint me to be with the family with whom Mr. Barnes may put up during the sessions of Presbytery." I assented of course; for no distribution had as yet been made of the members. But so important, from some cause or other, did Mr. Sparhawk deem this arrangement, that on the next day when we met at the church he reminded me of it, and repeated the request. And as Mr. Barnes had *just then* made the public announcement of his intention to put up with "*Father* Hunt," Mr. Sparhawk of course was assigned to the same location. Now Mr. Sparhawk could have had not the remotest idea of Mr. Barnes' designs against me, much less the least sympathy with them: for he is a man and a gentleman in the truest and best sense of those terms. He moreover could have had no preference of his own as to where he should remain; for he was not a child; and assumed the responsibility of attending this Presbytery, not as a parrot, to repeat what might be said to him, but as a Christian, with a sincere desire to do his duty, and to benefit the cause of truth and righteousness as occasion might serve. In making this request therefore, he merely sought to comply with the wishes of his Pastor, *expressed to him of course before he left Philadelphia.* Can the reader draw any other conclusion? I think not. And if this be the proper and fair inference, *it is not the only one that is deducible.* There are others which are obvious to any mind, and not to be here expressed in words. The fact, if it stood alone, might indeed prove nothing; but as associated with all the circumstances with which it is connected, it truly becomes "a deed without a name."

But why did Mr. Barnes desire an arrangement of this kind? Was it from fear that there might be some other guest assigned to Mr. Hunt, whose presence might operate more as a restraint in carrying out the plans he had devised? Or whose views, should Mr. Hunt consult them, might not accord with those of Mr. Barnes? The youth and modesty of Mr. Sparhawk precluded the probability of his being consulted; and hence no such risk was incurred by his being there. But could it be a holy, upright, honorable design which demanded all this manœuvring and secrecy? No, reader, *no!* Mr. Barnes however was now the guest of Mr. Hunt, *and at once entered closely into conversation with him*, and whether Mr. Hunt's subsequent action was in whole or in part suggested by Mr. Barnes, the reader will have the opportunity of deciding from the facts and illustrations which shall be presented.

However, Presbytery at length convened, and commenced business. The decision requiring Mr. Hunt to act as my prosecutor was read, upon which he at once arose, and in the most decided and peremptory manner refused to sustain that position. All the Presbytery except Mr. Barnes manifested great indignation at this procedure. Mr. Brainerd made an eloquent and touching appeal to the old man, and to the audience, explaining the whole matter, and showing that Mr. Hunt did really occupy this position, and ought therefore as a man and a Christian to be willing to assume its responsibility. He was followed by Messrs. Fairchild and Adair, and I think by Dr. Gilbert, in the most pointed and impressive strain; but all was of no avail with Mr. Hunt, for he was sustained in this refusal by the influence of Mr. Barnes. But finally a motion was made to adjourn *sine die;* and the motion if at once put would, I believe, have been carried. I however opposed it, and earnestly besought my brethren not to adopt a course like that. But before the house took action in the premises, Mr. Hunt (who still continued sitting near Mr. Barnes) arose and went to Mr. Conover, and after a moment's conversation said, "Moderator, Mr. Conover will act as prosecutor; and I move that Mr. Barnes be appointed as his counsel." The alternative was therefore either to have no trial, or to allow Mr. Hunt to escape from the responsibility into which he had brought himself. Hence he was permitted to escape; and I was thus left not only deprived of my counsel, but also under the necessity of changing the whole of my argument (going to show the motives which obviously actuated my prosecutor) upon a moment's notice, and with my mind in a distracted state: and thus, solely through the manœuvring of Mr. Barnes, lost all the advantages of a pre-arrangement of the topics based upon the intended form of the prosecution. Under the circumstances, however, what could I do but submit?

When the motion was made to appoint Mr. Barnes as the counsel of Mr. Conover, I at once arose and seconded it, and urged it upon Mr. Barnes; for now for the first time the preceding facts flashed a strange light upon my spirit which brought the conviction that he was really operating with a view to break me down:* and I now of course preferred that he should be brought to act openly and tangibly. I stated too as a reason for my urging the appointment upon the acceptance of Mr. Barnes, that I wished Mr. Conover to have the best counsel that Presbytery could supply. But whether Mr. Barnes' suspicions were excited by my remarks, I know not. He, however, declined the appointment, and accompanied his refusal with the remark that "every one knew the high esteem which he entertained for his brother Landis; and that he was unwilling to take a position which might seem inconsistent therewith." At this juncture a member of Presbytery, Mr. Thompson, (who must excuse me for mentioning it,) leaned over and whispered to me, that "from the disposition which Mr. Barnes had hitherto manifested in relation to the matter, it would be injudicious to urge this appointment upon him, as in that case it would not be strange if he threw his whole influence into the scale against me." This however only increased my desire to have him appointed. I forbore however to insist upon it; and Mr. Hunt and his son, *Parvus Iulus, sed qui sequitur patremque passibus*

* I had resisted this conviction as long as possible; but when it could no longer be resisted, it really did more to crush my spirit and break my heart, and drive sleep from me, than all other things connected with this cruel persecution. God only knows what anguish it produced in my soul.

æquis, were assigned as counsel for the prosecution; and the Rev. David X. Junkin of Newton Presbytery (an able and efficient presbyter) was, at my request assigned as counsel for myself: for the number of ministers in attendance was quite too small to admit of its being broken in upon, if such a thing could be avoided. By this time the whole afternoon was consumed, and Mr. Adair had been appointed to preach in the evening. And as the whole aspect of my case had thus been unexpectedly changed, and as I had waived my right to the ten days, and could not of course cite my witnesses in the regular form; and had only that day learned what the charges against me were, I, amongst the notices given that evening, named the names of a number of persons whom I desired to attend punctually the meetings of Presbytery; stating that I should probably want them as witnesses, and that time did not permit me to issue regular and formal citations. This was of course all that I could do under the circumstances.

On the following morning the trial formally commenced; and the first step in order was, to appoint a committee to prepare and present in due form from the affidavits and prosecutor the charges preferred against me. Mr. Barnes obviously expected to be appointed to this office, and that expectation had a controlling influence upon Presbytery, *for he actually was appointed as this committee.** The conscientious reader will ask with amazement, *What! did he serve?* Yes, *he did serve!* And with all the feelings which dictated his preceding course, he not only, and without offering any excuse or objection, permitted the appointment, but at once entered upon the office. He went out, and consulted with the prosecutor and witnesses, and thus matured and presented the charges, which might through life affect the character and prospects of a minister of Christ! All the circumstances considered, I have never known any human conduct equal to this.

After an absence of perhaps half an hour, he returned with the specifications in form. As I then had no difficulty to recollect them, and they were lying on the table before me during the trial, I did not think of procuring a copy; and must therefore state them from memory. The *substance* as here given, is, however, entirely accurate, and the language as nearly as I can recollect is that employed by Mr. Barnes. The charges were

1. Improper conduct towards my accuser at a "giving-visit," several years before.

2. Improper and lascivious conduct at some cherry trees on her father's farm, about a year and a half previous.

3. Attempting to violate, or seduce her at her house on July 1.

To confirm this last charge, her servant-girl was brought as a witness: and old Mrs. Stiger, the grandmother, was designed in some unknown way to substantiate charge 2d: and Catherine Sweezey to confirm in like manner the three charges.

* It was a committee of one. But how strange that Mr. Thompson, and the other excellent brethren, should have consented to yield in this, and in a score of other instances, to the wishes of Mr. Barnes, after they had so clearly ascertained what was his real disposition towards me! It illustrates, however, the nature of the influence which he possessed in that body.

4. The fourth charge was of foolish conduct at another "giving-visit," two or three years before. Two witnesses were named for this, Benjamin Bird and Thomas Hunt.

5. The fifth was of unministerial conduct at a wedding, some four or five years previous. The witness for this was a poor silly creature, named Nathan Wyckoff.

6. The sixth was something connected with Allentown. It was called "*serious charges*" by Mr. Barnes: but he did not name either the accusation or witnesses; and I do not to this day know what it was. It was said to have occurred some six or eight years before.

Mr. Barnes was proceeding to name some other charge, but the Moderator called him to order.

Such was the paper presented by this ecclesiastic; and of the last two charges I had not heard a word previous to his report.

Before I proceed with the case, however, it will be proper here to offer a few remarks, in order to give the reader a correct idea of how the whole matter stood at this juncture.

It will be remembered that my enemies (as Mr. Barnes perfectly well knew) had had the whole period from about the middle of August to the middle of November to concoct, digest and mature all they designed to say or do in support of this their last and greatest effort to destroy me. Mr. Barnes knew likewise that there were leagued against me in this matter any number of drunkards, liquor-sellers, and distillers; and might have known, (and I believe that I mentioned the fact publicly in his hearing,) that many of the originators of the conspiracy were counterfeiters, and those who circulated counterfeit money. He further knew that these men had sent not only to Allentown, Pa., long before, but even all the distance to Jeffersonville* in order to ascertain whether matter of accusation could be thence brought against me: and moreover, that only about *eight* days before Presbytery met, Mr. Hunt had sent me the names of the witnesses without mentioning a word of the charges themselves: and now though Mr. Barnes knew all this, he at once fell in and co-operated with Mr. Hunt in the following-named effort to make unexpectedly a strong impression against me in a most unfair and inhuman manner.

The case was as follows. Mr. Hunt, upon a close scrutiny into the charge of my accuser, had found that nothing could be fairly made of it: for her story was contradictory, and absurd, and wholly discredited by all who had not been previously prejudiced against me; the affidavit of the servant-girl was also at direct variance with it, in a way that could leave upon no mind any reasonable doubt that the whole story was a fabrication. And though Mr. Hunt, as above-stated, had ransacked the country, nothing further could be produced against me. Hence, and in a way which he thought I could not successfully rebut, he

* I have often wondered how they were induced to send to Jeffersonville. The reader has already seen the course which Mr. Barnes pursued in relation to my church there and its results: but no one at Bethlehem had known anything of the occurrence. Whether this movement was suggested by Mr. Barnes in his correspondence with Mr. Hunt, I leave him to say. While I wish not to suspect him wrongfully, I have ever been puzzled to account for it on any other supposition.

sought to make a strong impression against me, in the minds of my co-presbyters and of the public; and with this view prepares a paper with some names upon it (*although a considerable proportion of those whose names were thus employed knew nothing thereof, until the fact was afterwards made known to them,*) and at this juncture had it presented to Mr. Barnes, as a catalogue of witnesses who were ready to substantiate against me other accusations; and then, as Mr. Barnes was looking over the paper, several persons came forward and pretended to be ready to deliver their testimony. Such was the shallow artifice contrived for this occasion by at least Mr. Hunt, and to which, without ceremony, Mr. Barnes acceded.

And now, admitting for the sake of the argument, that Mr. Barnes really knew nothing of the manner in which the three charges of my accuser had been concocted, we may well ask whether this last case is one in which an upright mind ought to have felt any difficulty as to the question of duty? Such a mind, if only acquainted with the fact that the prosecution had had three months in which to collect and mature their charges, and that one month had elapsed since they were notified by Presbytery to do so, would instantly have reminded those persons that their contemplated course was a violation not only of the gospel and of the constitution, but also of all manliness and moral principle. But how did Mr. Barnes act? Why, he at once received all their new accusations and pretended witnesses, and actually brought them into Presbytery, and stated that many persons had come to him wishing to testify against me; and then proceeded to report their silly stuff and to hand over their names as witnesses!* I was astounded at such scandalous conduct; and arose and asked the Moderator (Dr. Fairchild,) whether such proceedings were to be tolerated? He appeared to be as much surprised as I was, and immediately called Mr. Barnes to order. By this time, however, he had reported two new charges, (the 5th and 6th above-named,) which, of course, left me the alternative of remaining under their odium, or of meeting them thus at once, and without any time for preparation. I chose the latter; but now believe that I was wrong in furnishing any such precedent. But oh, what a proof have we here of the sincerity of Mr. Barnes' expressed desire that "no spot might remain upon the character of *Brother* Landis"!

As the prosecution, from very shame, subsequently dropped these charges, it is in place here to consider them, and Mr. Barnes' conduct in relation thereto. Our large house of worship, in which Presbytery had convened, was crowded with people anxious to hear the report of the committee. And Mr. Barnes, after specifying the accusations and witnesses relating to the charges made by Mrs. Vanderbelt, remarked that an accusation had also been brought against me of improper conduct at a wedding (it is the fifth of the charges aforesaid), some four or five years before. It was to the effect, that, after having had a solemn conversation with the people who were assembled, I turned to a young lady, and

* Is it any wonder that this ecclesiastic was so willing to dispense with the attendance of so eminent a barrister as Samuel H. Perkins? No such unheard-of outrage as the above could have been perpetrated, or even attempted, had that gentleman been in attendance.

addressed her in a trifling, foolish manner, asking her something about her lover. "And," adds Mr. Barnes, "the person who told me this says, that he never mentioned it to any one but his own wife, until a week or so ago. He seems to be a respectable man." By these remarks, Mr. Barnes designed, among other things, to justify himself for bringing in this charge, on the pretence that it had "recently become flagrant," and therefore ought to be noticed at this time. But further, this man was an utter stranger to Mr. Barnes, who knew not whether he was "respectable," or the veriest knave in existence. Why, then, should he thus publicly, at such a time, and under such circumstances, append his own signature to recommend a charge brought against a brother by an entire stranger? If the charge must be brought, was it not enough to say, simply, that the individual had mentioned thus or so? But why attempt to give the silly charge his sanction in the presence of this immense audience, and to recommend, at my expense, the character of a witness known to be a low-minded, illiterate, and bigoted member of another denomination, who disliked my doctrine, and repined at the success which attended my ministry? However, when the inquiry came to be made on the subject, it appeared, on the testimony of the witness himself, that this alleged impropriety had occurred in the presence of a score of people; and the pretence that it had recently become known by the revelation of this "*respectable man*," was so preposterous, that both Presbytery and the congregation could not refrain from one general burst of laughter. But so keen was Mr. Barnes to find matter of accusation against me, that he failed to see this absurdity, though it was, as the reader can see, involved in the very words in which he stated the charge.

The other one of these new accusations, and upon which (without specifying it, except in the most vague terms,) Mr. Barnes spoke in a manner equally well calculated to make an unfavorable impression, was in relation to some occurrence said to have taken place at Allentown, Pa., some six or eight years before. What this alleged impropriety was, I never, to this day, have been able to learn, though I have often made the inquiry. Mr. Barnes *specified* nothing, but merely said that "*there were serious charges from that quarter*." What name to bestow upon an act like this, I do not know; for my feelings, in view of the dastardly outrage, can find no expression in language. He did it, also, openly, in the presence of the large audience there collected; and this was the first moment in which I had even the remotest idea that a charge was to be preferred against me from thence. I knew that efforts had been made to get up something, as Mr. Hunt had sent his grandson and another individual thither, who had gone to the low oyster-cellars and grog-shops, to learn what could be said against me; Mr. Hunt had not even referred to the matter in his letter to me: and I, knowing that their success could never prove equal to the extremity which demanded the effort, had treated the whole thing with derision and deserved contempt. However, when the matter was now introduced by Mr. Barnes, I, as above stated, suffered the charge to lie; and through the singular Providence of God, I happened to have then available, an abundance of evidence, which would at once have put my accusers to hopeless shame and silence.

And when the prosecution subsequently adverted to the fact, that a charge stood against me, of improper conduct in Allentown, and endeavored to employ that fact to my prejudice without descending to the proof, I immediately arose and said: "Moderator, I wish Presbytery to notice this assertion of the prosecution; for should this charge be now thus passed over, I shall, in my defence, claim the right to disabuse the public mind in relation to what has been asserted respecting it." Upon this, Mr. Barnes, who was the only member that objected to my doing so, arose and said: "Oh, no, Moderator; I hope that matter will not be gone into!" This was all he said; and it was said in the tone of one who feels that his expressed wishes are to be respected. But, in the name of candor, if the matter was not to be gone into, why did he bring in the charge at all? And why did he sit still, and hear the prosecution employing against me the fact, that it had been brought in? Why did he suffer it to lie, in this form at least, until, from the confident tones of my voice, he perceived that nothing could be gained by investigating it? If he "*hoped* that that matter would not be gone into," why did he not express that *hope* when the prosecution were employing the charge to make an impression against me? Surely he was *very* anxious that no spot might rest upon the character of "*Brother* Landis."

But further, what was now demanded of Mr. Barnes, as a man, both in equity and righteousness, after the course which he had pursued in relation to this charge? He had produced it, and suffered it to remain uncontradicted; and now, if he "hoped" it would not be gone into, why not tell the reason? He said not one word to the effect that he thought the rumor absurd or false, (though he afterwards did say so in private, at the residence of a member of my church,) and, therefore, not worth "going into;" or whether he thought there was enough without it; or whether Presbytery could not stay to examine it; or to give any reason whatever. And then, he had introduced the subject when the house was crowded, and now, when the audience had greatly diminished, he offers this unexplained remark; leaving *me* thus under the odium of an accusation so presented, and leaving his own conduct in relation to its withdrawal, subject to any construction whatever. I do not *say* that Mr. Barnes was unwilling to have me clear myself from this imputation. It *may* be that, upon considering it further, he found the evidence of its being a shallow, got-up affair to be irresistible. But if such were the fact, why was he not man enough to say it, especially, as he had, in the presence of hundreds of people, asserted that "there were serious charges from that quarter?"

The conduct here remarked upon, however it may be explained, and to whatever motive it may be ascribed, is sufficiently revolting, let it occur at any time, or under *any* circumstances. But in what light it ought to be regarded, occurring under the circumstances in which it did transpire, is more than I can pretend to determine. Who can conceive what an hour of anguish was this for a minister of Christ, and for his church and family! What *human* heart is there who could so far forget itself as to wish to take advantage even of an enemy at such an hour! The bare remembrance that such a sufferer is a partaker of our nature would be sufficient, one would think, to fill the heart of even his sternest foe with compassion and sympathy. But Mr. Barnes took these advantages of a brother, who, in order to have the slanders against him fully investigated, and to afford the Presbytery every facility for such investigation, had, at the greatest inconvenience and sacrifice, waived his right to the ten days; a brother, too, who had been cruelly disappointed by the failure of his counsel, and in the whole form of the prosecution, and in a matter in which were involved his own and his family's dearest interests for life; and that suffering man, too, a Christian and minister of Jesus Christ, and one whom Mr. Barnes was still bound to regard as an innocent and calumniated brother. Do such facts need to be dwelt upon? When Mr. Barnes was prosecuted and suspended from the ministry, I stood faithfully at his side; and on my shield received many a javelin that had been aimed at his heart. I never, in any way, reminded him of the service I did him; but the battle of the Granicus was scarcely closed, ere he snatched a javelin, and plunged it into my side. I lavished my affection and sympathy upon him, when he was in distress, and had need of it; and never, even in thought, looked for a return: but when I was called to undergo an infinitely severer storm, he remorselessly tears away, so far as he could do, every kindly shelter, and leaves me all exposed to the pitiless blast.

Perhaps I cannot bring this chapter to a more appropriate conclusion, than by quoting the following passage from Seneca: "Not to return one good office for another is inhuman; but to return evil for good is diabolical. There are too many even of this sort, who, the more they owe, the more they hate. There is nothing more dangerous than to oblige those people; for when they are conscious of not paying the debt, they wish the creditor out of the way. It is a mortal hatred which arises from the shame of an abused benefit. When they are on the asking side, what a deal of cringing and profession appear! '*Well, I shall never forget this favor; it will be an eternal obligation to me.*' But within awhile, the note is changed, and we hear no more words of it, until by little and little, it is all quite forgotten. So long as they stand in need of a benefit, nothing is dearer to them, nor anything cheaper when they have received it; and yet a man may as well refuse to deliver up without a suit, a sum of money that is left him in trust, as not to return a good office without asking." "The principal causes of ingratitude are pride, self-conceit, avarice, envy, &c. It is a familiar exclamation: '*True, he did this or that for me, but it came so late, and it was so little, I might as well have been without it; if he had not given it to me, he must have given it to somebody else; it was nothing out of his pocket.*' Some pretend that they want power to make a competent return; and you will find in others an unprincipled baseness that makes a man ashamed of requiting an obligation, because it is a confession that he has received one." See Seneca *de Beneficiis*. Socrates also remarked that, "It is a noble thing to make ingrates." A strange expression at first glance, but one that will well bear scrutiny.

CHAPTER VI.

FURTHER PARTICULARS.

THE depravity and deceitfulness of the human heart are perhaps never more strikingly exhibited, than in the efforts made by an individual (who is pursuing some improper course) to conceal from the scrutiny of conscience, the real motives by which he is actuated. Since my trial, Mr. Barnes has avowed that, "so far as he knew, the motives which actuated him in what he did were pure and upright." *Quod volumus facile credimus.* Motives are often complex; and where an asseveration respecting them involves a clear moral impossibility, (as the above does; for how can a man have *pure and upright motives for pursuing "a course full of iniquity"?*) the question as to the motives which really induced a given course of conduct, constitutes a legitimate subject for inquiry.

I have always felt much sympathy for Mr. Barnes, on account of the peculiar position which he was called to occupy. Called in early life to exchange a pleasant country location for a laborious city charge, and with but a moderate share of talents, and a mind by no means thoroughly furnished, to be required to minister to a people who had been under the pastoral care of some of the ablest divines which our country has produced, it is too little to say that he did well; he performed his part to admiration, and we all felt proud of him. His efforts to supply a commentary on the Gospels for Sabbath-schools was likewise deservedly popular, and brought him both fame and fortune, so that he needed nothing but a sound and thorough persecution, in order to become, in the eyes of many, a great man. This at length came, and with no halting pace, or scantiness of measure. The interests of himself, and of his people, were so completely involved with our own, from the shape which the prosecution assumed, that even had we felt disposed to abandon Mr. Barnes, (of which there was no inclination, however,) we could not have done it. We therefore defended him; and as he became, for the time being, on account of his position, our Magnus Apollo, we bestowed upon him the quantum of praise usual in such cases, and eulogized him *etiam ad astra.* We professed to be men of sense, and I suppose most of us were; but had we been the most arrant fools in existence, our efforts to shout and hurra louder than our opposers, and to exalt our hero far above theirs, were enough to turn the head of a far stronger-minded man than Mr. Barnes. The excitement of controversy, than which nothing is more trying to the virtue even of a wise man, betrayed both parties into indiscretions, which have at length alienated brethren, and left the church much to deplore. The effect upon Mr. Barnes was what it might have been upon any man; he did not consider the producing causes of the praise that was lavished upon him, and of the interest attached to his then position, and so lost the modest estimate which he had previously formed of himself, and began to fancy that he was at least something more than he had supposed. And since then, the prominent weakness in his character has been an intolerant ambition to be regarded as the chief man in point of ability in any and everything in which, for the time being, he might be engaged. These remarks are not invidious, but are offered as the only rational solution of the phenomena of Mr. Barnes' course in relation to myself. Many strikingly confirmatory illustrations may be adduced of their truth, and the indulgence of this disposition has, I believe, involved him so seriously in the matter now under consideration.

I have, in a former chapter, briefly alluded to this subject; and I may here add, in connection with what is there stated, that he and I simultaneously, and by the same publishers, issued a work of equal dimensions and price, on topics of Biblical and historical criticism. His work presented an able discussion of the question of Slavery, and mine, a modest view of the doctrine of the Resurrection. His work, however, fell deadborn from the press; while mine, on the contrary, became popular, and was regarded as a standard work on the subject of which it treats. It was, perhaps, however peculiarly unfortunate for me that in July and August of 1847, a number of very flattering notices of my book appeared in the Philadelphia *Christian Observer*, to wit:

The Princeton Review says: "We regard this as a very valuable book. It consists of two parts. Both parts evince learning, research and ability. An amount of pertinent material is here presented, which the student of the Bible will find of real value. To say that Mr. Landis has refuted Professor Bush, would be saying very little. In refuting Professor Bush, he has presented arguments of permanent value in defence of the truth."

The Christian Observer says: "This work has been very favorably commended to the public from the most respectable sources," &c.

The Philadelphia Presbyterian says: "Mr. Landis has addressed himself to his work with intelligence and zeal, and perhaps it is a fault of his book that he follows his antagonist with too much minuteness, that he may not have an inch of ground to stand upon. A building may be demolished without going so thoroughly to work, as not to leave one stone standing upon another."

The New York Evangelist says: "Prof. Bush's recent assault upon the cherished doctrine of the Resurrection was the occasion of this volume, to which it is a formal, and we hardly need to say, at least to those who know the author, a most successful reply."

This and much more was republished in the Observer, and many other very favorable notices of my work were continually appearing, while Mr. Barnes' little book, which he had taken the precaution to stereotype in order to meet the expected demand, was treated with silent neglect, no one scarcely looking into it. Then, I had given the copyright of my work to the Home Missionary Society. Mr. Barnes, I believe, never had done such a thing, notwithstanding all the works he had published. Could it be then that motives drawn from such considerations were now influencing him to take the part he did against me? No other presbyter except Mr. Hunt manifested any such interest or zeal in the matter. Were those brethren therefore indifferent to the interests of morals and religion, while Messrs. Hunt and Barnes were simply doing their duty?*

* Well has Burke, with that singular insight into human nature, for which he was so justly celebrated, remarked that "Wisdom is not the most severe corrector of folly. They are the rival follies which wage the unrelenting war; and make so cruel a use of their advantages."

or were Messrs. Hunt and Barnes actuated by motives which did not influence the other members of Presbytery? Mr. Barnes, of course, had *some* motives, and what were they? What was it that induced him to take the course he did throughout this whole business? Why has he continued to follow me up to the crushing of my heart and impairing of my usefulness, to the distraction of my beloved charge, and to all those other fatal results which have been consequent upon the course which he now pursued? Time will determine this matter. But I believe that Mr. Barnes will never find rest for his soul until he frankly discloses his motives herein; and also why, even before any opportunity of defence was afforded me, he thus at once threw the whole weight of his influence into the scale with those wicked and debased characters, distillers, counterfeiters and what not, who had for years been endeavoring to destroy my character.

Whatever were his motives however, the conduct of Mr. Barnes in the foregoing particulars, (and in others which cannot be dwelt upon without extending this history to too great a length,) broke my spirit and crushed my heart far more than all the combined efforts of my enemies previously. He could not help seeing this. How he was affected by the consideration will be shown hereafter.

Here perhaps some one may be inclined to say, Why did you permit these things? But let such a one consider with what complete management and subtlety everything referred to was performed by Mr. Barnes, so as to accomplish its intended aim, without his incurring the responsibility of the act. I did once, on a flagrant instance of misconduct in the matter, call him to account, as the reader will see; but his remarks in self-defence evinced, that before he entered upon the act, he had well considered how he should retreat from its consequences. There are (so to speak) powerful moral essences so subtle as to defy all efforts to confine or secure them by any conventional rules of human conduct or intercourse, and when it is necessary to secure them, other powers and processes must be resorted to. So it was in the case before us, and any formal attempt at this stage of the business, to call Mr. Barnes to account, could have accomplished nothing, and could have operated in no way to change the feelings of his heart towards me, though such an effort on my part must have tended to induce him to try to gain his ends, whatever they were, by means still more subtle if possible.*

There were some circumstances which occurred about that time, the influence of which could not but be peculiarly unfavorable to any one against whom suspicion had been at all awakened by such accusations as those under which I was suffering, and of which (as may be seen even from Mr. Hunt's letter to Mr. Barnes,) my enemies failed not to take

* I cannot but remark here, however, that a perception of the fact that Mr. Barnes was from some sinister motive operating to injure my character, and for this purpose even stooping to encourage the wretched individuals aforesaid, convinced me that God has some strange work in hand in connection with this procedure, though what it is, I durst not even imagine. The voice of his Providence seemed to say to me "Be still, and know that I am God!" The reflection that He would guide the matter to some blessed result, and the assurance that He would in the mean time take care of me, and of the dearest interests of his church, was a source of joyful consolation not to be expressed in human language. Time will make all things plain.

every advantage. Two clergymen of high standing in another denomination, and one in our own, had been but recently set aside on charges of immorality, and such a state of feeling had been produced that a clergyman circumstanced as I was, with an artful old man directing the efforts against him, and keeping up the storm by all the means in his power, could scarcely without the direct interposition of Providence expect to pass unscathed. *Ad calamitatem quilibet rumor valet*; any rumor is proof against the unfortunate, says the proverb, and truly I found it so. Such were the circumstances too, of which Mr. Barnes now took advantage. The fact of his being determined to view everything in the most unfavorable light, not only encouraged the misrepresentations of my enemies, but cast suspicion upon me in consequence of the freedom of the intercourse which existed between me and my people, and in which, as remarked on a former page, my predecessors freely indulged. He manifested a disposition to give the worst possible construction to all my words and actions, and appeared to evince a determination which was perfectly appalling, that whether guilty or innocent, I should fall. After the reader has perused the whole of this narrative, I shall be perfectly content to abide by his decision whether this language is at all too strong.

One might have reasonably expected that after the service which I had rendered Mr. Barnes in his hour of need, he would have been anxious to show himself among the first to appear on my behalf, at least until a thorough investigation of the subject had developed undoubted evidence of my guilt, and that until then he would have endeavored, if necessary, to suggest and present the most favorable aspect of the whole matter. Friendship itself would have demanded this,* irrespective of the claims of gratitude. Such would have been (nay, such was) my course in relation to Mr. Barnes. But instead of this, he at the very outset became my determined opposer, advised the delay of the trial for many weeks, without one assignable reason, favored Mr. Hunt's cruel assault, suggested suspicions against me, brow-beat those who spoke kindly for me, chilled the affections which my brethren exhibited on my behalf, and all this before one particle of evidence had been elicited against me by an impartial investigation. An additional fact or two will close this chapter.

While the Presbytery were yet considering what course should be pursued in relation to the trial, and had arrived at no final determination, Mr. Barnes, who was sitting near Mr. Hunt and at considerable distance from the Moderator, arose, and, looking directly at me, called out as follows: "Moderator! I understand that a bill has been found against Mr. Landis by the grand jury." He did not state what kind of a bill it was, whether for murder, or robbery, or simple assault and battery. As to *the fact itself*, however, he knew it before, and knew also that not only all the Presbytery were aware of it, but likewise the whole community, though many had not yet learned what was the na-

* "The duties that are owing to a friend," says a beautiful writer, "are integrity, love, counsel, assistance, and care for his reputation. It is not intimacy and frequency of conversation that makes a friend, but a disinterested observance of these duties."

ture of the bill. The fact moreover was in no way connected with anything that the Presbytery were doing at the time, nor with anything that he had himself been saying. It was the only remark that he did make, and immediately after uttering it, he sat down. No motion was offered by him, and nothing further said in relation to the subject. I however arose and explained that the bill did not sustain in reality the allegations of my enemies, it being for simple assault and battery, and read to the Presbytery the indictment, of which I happened to have a copy. No one said anything further on the subject, and here the matter ended. But *the very next day*, and after the case had been gone into, Mr. Barnes arose, and *in precisely the same manner employed the same words.* Now he knew that this matter had nothing to do with the business then before Presbytery. A bill altogether *ex parte* had been found, but there had been no investigation of the facts. What then was his design in this strange and uncalled-for procedure? Could it be to sink my spirits more, and thus incapacitate me for defending myself? This would be a horrible supposition, and ought not to be entertained without the best of reasons; for the malignity of a fiend could not transcend such an act. I refer the matter to Mr. Barnes for explanation.

The reader will remember also that Mr. Hunt's refusal to give me a copy of the charges, and to act as my prosecutor, threw me into a great disadvantage, and that having no time to cite witnesses, I notified by name a number of persons, on the first evening, and requested them to attend the trial as regularly as possible. This was all that I could do in such a case, as every person can see. And when thus thrown into a disadvantage, and one to which I agreed to subject myself in order to avoid subjecting my brethren of the Presbytery to the inconvenient necessity of assembling again; and in order, too, that the trial might be in the presence of my people; all seemed to feel that I had sacrificed much for their accommodation. But Mr. Barnes, from some cause, was greatly annoyed at the preparation, which, notwithstanding all these disadvantages, I had been able to make; and he evinced it frequently. He knew the confusion into which the case must become necessarily involved in consequence of the refusal of Mr. Hunt to act as prosecutor; and that no time could now be taken by me to prepare to meet such an emergency by any re-arrangement of the argument, and yet in the course of some desultory remarks he repeatedly went out of his way to fling a sarcasm at "*Mr. Landis' thirty witnesses*," as he called them. There is a way of doing such a thing, of which it is difficult to convey an impression, and which precludes the possibility of your expressing dissatisfaction therewith, without incurring the suspicion of being over-sensitive. Had he made and repeated the remark in a pleasant jesting manner (though this would have been improper on such an occasion), it would have passed unnoticed. But the remark could not have tended in a greater degree to render persons unwilling from fear of ridicule and sarcasm to appear upon the witnesses' stand, if it had proceeded from deep-seated malignity. Many of the witnesses were retiring, unassuming persons, who dreaded to be questioned in the presence of a large congregation: and Mr. Barnes knew, that as no regular citations had been served upon them, they might, from apprehension of ridicule, absent themselves without any fear of incurring censure for so doing. No other member of Presbytery indulged in any such impertinences; and why should he, the very last person who should have been guilty of treating me thus, have pursued such a course? He may answer this question also; for I am at a loss to account for such conduct upon any just or honorable principle.

CHAPTER VII.

THE TRIAL.

I HAVE remarked that Mr. Barnes was willing to be appointed and to act as the committee to make out and report the accusations which my enemies had been laying to my charge. How such a thing came to occur, after the disposition towards me which his previous conduct had developed, may well seem strange. But these acts had not been sufficiently reflected upon by Presbytery; and then, whenever suspicion had been awakened, he would lull it by speaking of me kindly *in private*, even while all his public acts were of the character above-described. Then further, he obviously expected to be appointed to this office. And as every man of prominent influence in a deliberative body is always attended upon by some obsequious flunkey; so there was a man here found who nominated him as that committee; and as no one opposed the motion, he at once entered upon the office.

When I became Pastor of Bethlehem church (in April, 1844,) Mr. Barnes, and I believe by my request, preached my installation sermon. He was at that time perfectly aware of the prodigious difficulties with which, for the two preceding years, I had been obliged to contend: and at the time of my trial he was equally aware of all the opposition which had beset my pathway, from the first of my going into this field of labor. He, moreover, had long been acquainted with the character of old Mr. Hunt; and had repeatedly declared him to be the most worldly-minded man, without exception, that he ever knew: and in 1840, when this old clergyman had applied for admission into Presbytery, Mr. Barnes objected directly to his reception, on the score of falsehood and dishonesty; as already remarked above: and up to the period of the effort made against me in August and September, 1847, nothing had transpired which in any way modified these views of Mr. Barnes in respect to Mr. Hunt, except by operating so as to deepen his impression of their entire accuracy.

Now, since Mr. Barnes did so readily consent to act as the committee aforesaid, it seems to me that these facts, with a multitude of others that could be named, and which were well known to him, ought, at least, to have been referred to in the report which he presented. In connection with the charges he should have said that "We are all aware that Mr. Landis has had great and peculiar difficulties in the discharge of his duty; and at every step of the way. In considering the charge of his accusers, therefore, we should not proceed as though no sinister reason could exist for the effort now made against him; and as though there was no sinister aim connected with this prosecution. I do not decide that there *are* such aims in the case. Nor do I wish you, on my representation, to proceed as if the matter were certain: but you will bear in mind that the affidavit, itself, on which this whole charge is based, was got up not only in a most strange and suspicious manner by an extra-judicial oath, but in a style which is utterly at war with everything like justice, propriety, or decency. In the *first* place, the woman herself had been suspended from the communion for ante-nuptial fornication, the consequences of which crime she would have escaped, so far as relates to church discipline, had not Mr. Landis peremptorily insisted that the Session should take some action on the subject. She likewise admits her own criminality in the matter, and attempts neither to excuse nor to palliate it. And it should be considered, also, that this woman, her husband, and servant-girl all attended Mr. Landis' ministry for many weeks after this alleged impropriety, though they all profess to have known of it within at least two days of its occurrence. Then, further; the committee who took her affidavit were selected, without allowing to Mr. Landis any voice in their appointment: and they never notified him as to the time when the affidavit was to be taken, or even consented to his being present on the occasion. Nor should it be forgotten that this young woman, who had evinced great willingness to speak unfavorably of her pastor, was yet very *unwilling to depose* to the truth of what she had said. She wept, and begged that she might not be required to give it the sanction of an oath. And though her deposition, written in large hand, would not occupy more than two pages of ordinary sized writing-paper, she was full eight hours in delivering it, and often went from the room during that time, in order to consult with her friends as to what she should depose: while another female who remained in the room with her during the whole time of the delivery of her deposition, was permitted not only to suggest to her what to say, but even to correct what she had said. It should be remembered, also, that on September 1, in the presence of this church and congregation, Mr. Landis proposed to meet her and her parents, along with the Session of the church, in order to inquire into the matter that she had been circulating, and to see whether she would repeat the same in his presence: the proposal, however, was not acceded to by the individuals who have accused him. And thus this affidavit has been got up, while he was denied the right of being present, or of putting a single question, either in person or by representative. I need not remind you how such unheard-of proceedings would be regarded in any competent civil court; where no witness is permitted to open his lips against an accused person, without being subjected to the severest scrutiny as to his motives, means of knowledge, his own previous character, and the degree of credit which may be attached to what he swears. Thus cautiously does the law guard that most sacred possession of man—character: and how these principles have been outraged, according even to the admission of the prosecution itself, in the matter before us, you will have full opportunity to decide for yourselves. For these reasons, together with a multitude of others that could be named, the committee therefore would recommend that Mr. Landis in defending himself should have full liberty to go into this whole matter, without restriction: and that the members of this judicatory should be careful not to sustain in any way the impression which at least some of his accusers have attempted to make; to wit: that a woman of unstained reputation has, without any apparently sinister motive, accused this brother of immorality."

Now, reader, all this is true, and what Mr. Barnes *may* not have known of it, he could easily have ascertained by a very few questions propounded even to the prosecution themselves. Is not some such course as the above, therefore, the course which he, on every principle of religion, and honor, and common honesty, was bound to pursue? Such is precisely the course, which, if our positions had been reversed, Mr. Barnes would have expected me to pursue; and why then should he not have pursued it in relation to me? What reason under heaven could he have for acting otherwise? Can any person be so arrant a trifler, as to pretend that a man's motives could be *pure* and upright, for conduct like this? And if his motives were not pure, what was it that induced him to treat me thus? And in the presentation of his report to lose sight altogether of these considerations; leaving it to be inferred by those who might never learn any better, that no sinister feelings or aims operated to induce my enemies to get up this wicked charge?

One item of his course on the occasion has already been given, in relation to new charges, and "*respectable*" witnesses: others could be mentioned, but it is unnecessary to go into further particulars. He presented the whole matter of accusation, without referring to a solitary one of the foregoing considerations, which would have made a favorable impression for me. He could have introduced them constitutionally; but did not in any way refer to the subject: while, on the contrary, he went out of his way to introduce in a very unlawful and heartless manner, matter that was calculated to injure me irreparably, if its statements were believed. Matter too, which I was thus forced to meet at once, without being allowed any time for obtaining rebutting testimony; or as the only alternative, I must remain under the odium of the accusations. I determined however to introduce all these particulars into my defence; but Mr. Barnes urged upon the brethren of Presbytery to advise me not to speak in my own defence: and then in order to influence me directly, he so contrived matters, that the prosecution should waive the right of speaking. And thus it has occurred that neither Presbytery nor the Public has ever heard my defence, solely through the contrivance of the Rev. A. Barnes.*

* In a case somewhat resembling mine, and which occurred in the Synod of N. Y. and Pa., in May 1763, Mr. Ewing, a venerated pastor of the First Church of Philadelphia, and of course a predecessor of Mr. Barnes, brought before that body and had recorded on their minutes a protest of which the following is an abstract.

"1. Because, whether Margaret McCleland first informed the mother or not, it is certain she joined the other young woman in the report; and they only are the raisers and propagators of that shocking defamation. But, by the late judgment, a person de-

On the morning of the second day, the trial commenced in due form, the Moderator admonishing the members of Presbytery that they were now entering on judicial business. Mr. Hunt calculating on the effect of his laudation of his witnesses introduced first "Mary Catherine Stiger, wife of the late *Judge* Stiger, and grandmother of Mrs. Vanderbelt." She was brought forward for the purpose of confirming in some way charge 2d. And the object of this odd procedure of introducing a witness to confirm a statement before that statement had been made by its author to the court, was simply this;—that her *great piety and respectability* (See Mr. Hunt's letter to Mr. Barnes) might at the very outset make an impression upon Presbytery favorable to the cause of my accuser. Well, she was sworn in due form, and Presbytery, having prepared their paper to take notes, began to question her. Her reply was as follows: "I have brought a paper (holding it up in her hand), containing what I have to offer on the subject. The Lord has appeared to me and told me to hand this to the Presbytery; but to answer no questions." And upon the strength of this *revelation* she refused to answer a single question touching the matter. It is needless to say that the Moderator promptly ordered her to be removed from the witnesses' chair.

As the *defence* was not thoroughly gone into, in consequence of the withdrawal of the prosecution, as will be shown hereafter, I shall offer a few remarks upon the character and testimony of these witnesses, in the order of their presentation.

serving to suffer as a vile defamer and a slanderer, may save herself by swearing that the person defamed is guilty.

"2. Because it is contrary to the express word of God in many places, concerning the number and qualifications of witnesses.

"3. Because the admission of such single or interested evidences is contrary to the judgment of our best divines. It is against the law of nature and the sacred rights of mankind, in the judgment of all our moralists; and contrary to the laws and customs of all civilized nations. So the admission of such evidences is contrary to the reason and common sense of mankind and dishonorable to this body.

"4. Because civil courts require witnesses to swear that they are disinterested in the issue of the cause. And our church rules also require that witnesses swear themselves free of bribery, malice, and party counsel before they are admitted to bear testimony, which Margaret McCleland cannot safely do, and therefore should not be admitted.

"5. Because the Gospel requires, that, in case of private offence, the offender shall be dealt with privately, then before witnesses, and lastly before the church, if the former fails. Now if a person, in opposition to our Saviour's directions, spreads horrid defamations and scandal, without either speaking to the person offending, or relating it to a proper judicature at first, such a person cannot be accounted afterwards simply an informer, but a gross defamer, be the matter true or false, and therefore unworthy to bear testimony either in their own case or any other, until he or she reforms; and this appears to be the present case.

"Therefore, I cannot but protest against such a procedure whenever it happens, for the exoneration of mine own conscience, and declare that I think it would be criminal in me to pay any regard or submission to any sentence that may hereafter be passed, by any of our judicatures, upon such evidence as has been herein specified.

"John Ewing."

Mr. Ewing was in no way *personally* interested in this case. And now let the reader compare the course of Mr. Barnes with that of this illustrious divine, and then decide which is in accordance with the gospel of Christ. They both have not the same origin. One is of that wisdom which is from above, and the other, of that which is from beneath. This will surely be doubted by no one.

The whole paper of Mr. Ewing may be found in the published minutes, pp. 326, 327.

The reader may easily imagine to what extremities a cunning old man like Mr. Hunt must have felt himself reduced, when he found it necessary to favor such a wretched farrago of nonsense, and bring forth a poor old woman to swear that the Lord had directed her to pursue such a course. As the paper which she offered was a deposition, I had the curiosity to procure a copy of it from the justice who administered the oath. In it she states that her granddaughter, at the time referred to, at *my* request, went into the field, a short distance from the house, to show me in what direction her father was at work, and that, on account of evil reports then in circulation about me, she (Mrs. S.) felt very anxious about the child, who soon after *returned alone* as a frightened person, and said that my conduct to her had been scandalous, and had pained her to the heart. It is not to be wondered at that the poor old creature was unwilling to answer the questions which she well knew would have been propounded to her respecting this bold and infamous fabrication; for ever since that same period, (July 3d, 1846,) as well as some time before it, she had, at her own request, occupied with my family my pew in church, because it was nearer to the pulpit than her own. She attended regularly every Sabbath, with perhaps one exception, (as she herself incidentally acknowledged,) until Sept. 1847, and *invariably* waited to speak with me after service, and always expressed, on such occasions, and in the presence of a crowd of people, her high and affectionate regard for me as a faithful servant of Christ, calling me her son, &c. &c. Not only this, but in May, 1847 (ten months after this asserted immorality), and at her own and this granddaughter's repeated request, I and Mrs. Landis spent an afternoon with her at Mr. and Mrs. Vanderbelt's (my accuser), in the most social manner, and took tea with them—and they, *in view of our coming*, had invited a number of their relatives, who also attended. In June of that same year, and only about two months before the hatching up of this last plot, she had spoken of me in terms of the most exalted respect and affection to Rev. Mr. Snowden, agent of the American Protestant Society; and not only this, but in no way whatever, previous to Sept. 1847, had she made the most distant allusion to any such transaction. And then to crown the climax she had, on June 7th, 1847, sent me to New Hope, Pa., in her stead, to visit and comfort her dying daughter, Mrs. Lambert, an excellent and devoted Christian. I went down and she (Mrs. S.) spoke with much gratification of my having done so. These facts were also all known to the public, and hence the apprehension which required the *revelation* aforesaid. This poor old creature must be thus sacrificed in character, and perhaps in soul, in order to get her sanction to the fabrications of my enemies. She died a year or so afterwards, and, if she died in her sin, her blood will be required at their hand.

The next witness was Mrs. V. herself, who stated and affirmed the truth of the first three charges aforesaid. Previous to her affidavit of Sept. 2d, she had been telling to the low and degraded characters about Rum Corner, whatever she supposed would make an unfavorable impression of me, because I had insisted on her being disciplined; and when she was, against her own earnest entreaty, compelled to repeat it on oath before the committee, or confess herself to be a liar and slanderer, she preferred to re-affirm what she had stated to those persons, and thus stereotyped a mass of as vulgar and filthy expressions as I suppose Rum Corner itself could produce.

Her *first* charge was, that in 1843 or 1844, at a "giving visit," I had taken her into my study, and, after placing the lamp in the hall, seated her upon my knee. Her counsel asked her whether I kissed her, or took any other liberty with her? to which she gave a prompt and decided answer in the negative.

Her *second* charge was of lascivious conversation and conduct at "some cherry trees, which stand," says she, "in sight of my father's house."

Before entering upon her *third* count, we shall briefly consider these two, that the subject may not become involved or confused in the mind of the reader. And as the *third* is regarded as the most important of all the charges, it would be better to consider it separately.

No other testimony was brought to sustain the first accusation. In the defence, however, it was so thoroughly demolished by the witnesses who came forward, that I believe my enemies have never referred to it since.

The satisfactory manner in which this count was set aside, seemed really to chagrin Mr. Barnes. I will mention a single fact, in illustration, which may serve to evince the spirit of this ecclesiastic, during a trial upon the results of which he knew that my all, for this world, was staked.

In repelling the accusation, I introduced as witness an intelligent young lady (Miss Catherine Race, a first cousin of Mrs. V.), who had no expectation of being called upon until the clerk mentioned her name. I had just learned that she was in the house, and being reminded too that she also had attended the "giving visit," I requested her, so soon as she had taken the witnesses' stand, to state, to the best of her recollection, all that transpired during that "visit." Her testimony was full and conclusive, and wholly subversive of that of my accuser. But while she was stating particulars in reply to some cross-questioning, Mr. Barnes very improperly and impertinently said to her: "Well, what did you say occurred there *during the frolic?*" Now there had not been one word said respecting a frolic, or anything of that description. The remark was wholly gratuitous, and the reader must judge whether its obvious design was not to confuse or brow-beat the witness—a thing which Mr. Barnes' commanding position at that time enabled him to do with more effect than any other member of Presbytery. To this coarseness of the questioner, the young lady, however, with promptness and dignity replied, "I said nothing, sir, respecting a frolic. There was nothing of the kind in the house during the evening." I then arose, and, through the Moderator, asked Mr. Barnes what he meant by thus annoying me and my witnesses?. and reminded him also (for how could I help it?) of the very different treatment which he had received, at my hand, when undergoing his trial (at the Synod of York, Pa., in 1835). He stammered out a lame and childish apology, and seemed to fear that he had incautiously betrayed the true state of his feelings towards me.* When

* It is astonishing that Presbytery suffered such shameless conduct to pass without

he made this grossly indelicate remark, the church was filled with spectators, many of them, as he knew, my enemies, and ready to seize upon anything that could be construed to my disadvantage. And yet, with no call or reason for doing so, he threw out the contemptible insinuation, at a time when he saw that I was too ill in body, and too much crushed in spirit, to resent the indignity as it ought to have been resented. This, his continued course of conduct, was now also already producing its effect upon my able and efficient counsel, inducing him, by degrees, to lose confidence in the goodness of my cause, and ultimately to leave me, for a very insufficient reason (to visit a sick person), and go home in the very midst of my trial. Mr. Junkin is a member of an Old School Presbytery, and one of the noblest-hearted men I have ever known. But how could he help supposing that, when Mr. Barnes, my most prominent co-presbyter, evinced such desire and zeal to have me destroyed, there must be some sufficient, though undeveloped, reason for it?

The spirit and conduct of Mr. Barnes, as exhibited by these facts and illustrations, was uniform throughout the whole proceedings of the trial; and sincerely glad would I be to be able to specify even a single instance, which might be regarded as exhibiting a contrary feeling. And though, throughout the whole, he took a far more active part than any other presbyter, yet he never brought into prominence, as the other members did, those aspects of my case which were favorable. Nor did he, in any way, attempt to rebuke or expose the many unlawful and base advantages which the prosecution was perpetually endeavoring to take against me. But I must proceed to remark upon the *second* charge.

The shallow trick of the prosecution to palm upon Presbytery a new revelation through old Mrs. Stiger, in support of this accusation, need not be further dwelt upon, and no other witness was called by them to sustain the count. But providentially, I was enabled to meet it most satisfactorily; for immediately, as Mrs. V.'s affidavit on September 2d became known, two women, Mrs. Jones and Miss Rosan Pickel (who was up to that period a confidential friend and adviser of Mrs. V.,) came forward and declared, that so far as its statements concerned this charge, they were contrary to fact. For the sake of effect, the monstrous lie had been fabricated, that though the young woman and I went out together to the cherry trees, she yet returned home alone, in a state of much excitement. Now Miss Pickel was at the house when we went out, and heard Mrs. V. say to me, "I will go and show you, Mr. Landis, where father is at work;" and after a short absence, she saw us return together, and enter the house together, where we and old Mrs. Stiger remained in cheerful conversation for some moments before I went away.* She also declared, that in the field adjoining the cherry trees, there were laboring men at work.

rebuke. It can only be accounted for in some way analogous to that of Cervantes respecting his hero: "He had the property of awakening, within those who associated with him, the same madness by which he himself was actuated." So did it seem to be, to some extent, with those who implicitly confided in the purity and integrity of Mr. Barnes. No one could suspect a good or honest man of being actuated by such motives, and hence he was thus enabled to take advantage of the confidence which was reposed in his assumed integrity and honesty of purpose. I can give no other explanation of the matter. Perhaps my brethren can.

* I found Mr. Conover (whom I had called to see) to be quite too far from the

The statement of Mrs. Jones covered the whole remaining ground, and was to this effect: that when I and Mrs. V. reached the little hill on which the cherry trees stand, she (Mrs. Jones) was at one of the trees, picking cherries, in company with two of her children, and that we were in her sight during the time we were there, and that she could distinctly hear portions of our conversation; and that there were men laboring in the adjoining field. She further says, that her daughter came over to the place where we stood, and remained, and went back with us to the house; and moreover, that she (Mrs. Jones) was in a position to see any impropriety that might have occurred on the part of either of us, and saw none; and that her daughter neither saw nor heard any; and further, that she (Mrs. Jones) preceded us in going back to the house, and yet arrived but a moment or two before us, and saw us both walk up leisurely, and enter the house together, in pleasant and familiar conversation. These women, though decidedly against their interest, came forward voluntarily, and made these declarations, (intending, too, if necessary, to depose to them,) so soon as they were acquainted with my accuser's affidavit. Of Mrs. Jones, I had no knowledge whatever, having never been at her house; nor had I any recollection of her and her children's presence at the time referred to, and I could account for these circumstances, only on the principle that the hand of my Faithful and Covenant God was extended for my protection.

It may well be supposed that when these counter-statements of Mrs. Jones and Miss Pickel transpired, so soon after the affidavit had been given, my enemies were taken hugely by surprise, for the veracity of their chief witness was at once gone, and they, by advising that the affidavit should be taken, had overshot the mark, and put it out of her power to save herself from merited infamy. Mrs. Jones was a tenant of Mrs. V.'s father, and every inducement that could be devised was repeatedly tried, to lead her to retract or modify her statement, but in vain; she reaffirmed it with more and more decision, the further she reflected upon it, by recalling all the circumstances to mind, and reaffirmed it too, notwithstanding the expressed threat, that if she persisted in it, her privileges as a tenant should be curtailed, she and her family deprived of the work which afforded them a livelihood, and be expelled from their home in the spring.* Then, when all means of intimidation had failed, a plot was formed between the Conover family and a brother of Mrs. Jones to prevent her, if necessary by force, from attending the Presbytery. I sent after her twice during the trial, but each time, so soon as it was known that she was sent for, this brother jumped into a carriage which had very swift horses provided for the occasion by Mr. Conover's brother, and outrode my messengers, so as to reach the house before them. These facts, let it be remembered, were all stated publicly to Presbytery, and Mr. Barnes' subsequent action was in full view of them. Mrs. Jones still declared to the messengers her purpose to testify to the truth of what she had said, but

house to allow of my calling on him that afternoon. He was in a remote part of the farm, which contains between five and six hundred acres. The cherries being ripe, I stopped long enough to partake of them, Mrs. V. waiting for me when she learned that I would not go to her father.

* This threat was to the letter barbarously executed.

was unable to overcome the brutal force brought to prevent her attendance at Presbytery. I then proceeded to have a commission appointed to wait upon her and obtain her testimony, but at this juncture my calumniators came forward, and volunteered, if I would permit them, to withdraw the prosecution, as will be narrated in Chapter VIII.

Similar means were likewise resorted to in order to hinder the attendance of Miss Pickel, and just before the trial Mr. Conover found some *very important* business for her in the "Barrens," a number of miles from the church, but the withdrawal of the prosecution rendered it needless to examine any more of my witnesses; they can, however, still be consulted, and Miss Pickel's testimony is very important on other points besides the one now before us.

As to the testimony of the chief witness herself, I must add a word before proceeding to the next count.

This young woman, who owed me no malice or ill will in the world until I disciplined her, but was always, until that period, affectionately attached to me, as much so as if I had been her parent, was made the victim of my enemies, in their efforts to strike me down. In answer to the questions put to her *by the prosecution*, she said, "I have been connected with Bethlehem church about five years. Mr. Landis occasionally paid pastoral visits to my father's family, and always conversed and prayed with them when they were together, but never paid me but one visit, and was then accompanied by his wife. I never, so far as I remember, had any conversation with Mr. Landis when alone, but once, and that was in July, 1846, on Thursday before the Communion." This was at the cherry trees. She deposed, also, that her grandmother, old Mrs. Stiger, *had requested her to go and show me where her father was at work.* Also, that she herself made no outcry when the alleged liberty was taken with her at the "cherry row;" that she united with me in all the conversation that was had on that occasion, and also, that Mrs. Jones was at the trees when we went there, and that "she could have seen Mr. Landis and me at the time referred to, if she had looked," and that when we returned from the cherry trees, Mrs. Jones was at Mr. Conover's. These particulars do not require to be dwelt upon.

She deposed, also, that the very next day, she informed a Catherine Sweezey of all that had occurred on this occasion. This Miss S., though a Methodist in sentiment, and a scurrilous defamer of our Confession of Faith, was a member of the Bethlehem church, and yet, after this period, not only continued her constant attendance on my ministry, and communed regularly with the church, but on several occasions subsequent to the disclosure of the criminal intercourse of Mr. and Mrs. Vanderbelt, spoke to me very impertinently, and censured me for not calling to see them, saying that, "though other friends forsook Mrs. V., she did not think her pastor would treat her so, to whom she looked for counsel and consolation." Other particulars connected both with this count and the third will be considered hereafter.

At the time of this walk to the "row of cherry trees," I had not, of course, the remotest idea of her having had illicit intercourse with Vanderbelt. I had married them only about three weeks before, (June 13th,) but had no suspicion that the marriage was hastened; it had been, however, and she was much denounced by her family, and Vanderbelt was ordered to take her away as soon as possible. She and her brothers and sisters (they were but children when I went to Bethlehem) were always peculiar favorites of mine, and never could I call at Mr. Conover's without having the whole eight of the children around me, and hanging on my chair, clambering upon my knees, and what not; and in truth, I was very strongly attached to them all; nor can I describe the anguish I felt when her ante-nuptial fornication was made known. I remembered the freeness and familiarity of my manner towards her and all of them, and though they could not possibly have suspected that I had any improper or impure design, I feared that I might unconsciously have too much encouraged an intimacy which resulted in this most distressing manner. She never said that this was so, but such were my agonizing reflections. Subsequent disclosures, however, evinced that Vanderbelt had employed the most contemptible and brutish means to obtain his beastly object.

I do not recollect the conversation at the cherry trees; but, as I had always treated her as a child, and felt like a parent towards her, and had just given her away in marriage, I have no doubt that I did converse with her on the nature of the new obligations which she had assumed—but which conversation, her mind, being corrupted by her intercourse with Vanderbelt, not only distorted, but subsequently seized upon and exaggerated, with the view of palliating her own and V.'s guilt. And when, on Sept. 2d, 1847, she was requested to recollect everything that might be construed so as to sustain the last accusation of my enemies, she was reminded, by C. Sweezey, of these her former misrepresentations, and without having time to consider the consistency of the story, swore to their truth. In her testimony, also, she declared that, after her removal to the neighborhood of Rum Corner, I did not visit her for a long time (and in court she complained that I had not called upon her for many months after the birth of her child), which may have been true: though I think that I did call once, and found the family all absent. But this apparent neglect was not owing to disinclination, but to the other numerous and pressing duties of one of the largest pastoral charges in New Jersey. However, her repeated and pressing invitations to me to call and see her—invitations repeated whenever we met, and for more than a year after this alleged immorality, surely is more than sufficient to discredit the story, even without the overwhelming weight of the testimony of Miss Pickel and Mrs. Jones.

The *third* count is the alleged occurrence at her house, near Rum Corner; and which (both before the Grand Jury and the Presbytery), she deposed, took place on July 1st, 1847. At court, however, she swore that the date was July 8th.

As this was the charge upon which, by the testimony of her servant, I was cast at court, I have referred to it somewhat particularly in Part I. In the depositions before Presbytery, there were irreconcilable contradictions between the statements of herself and servant (upon which, however, it is unnecessary to expatiate); but the interval from November to May afforded them ample time, with the assistance of their counsel, to compose their contradictions and make out the worst possible case.*

* Although I sat directly opposite to and in full view of the witnesses in court, Mrs.

Hence, in respect to this charge, the reader shall be favored with the advantage of having the matured version of it as presented at court. I and my counsel both took down all the evidence; and, in brief, it was as follows:

"Mr. Landis called once at my house with his wife, and spent the afternoon. This was the only time he ever stayed. My child was then four months old. On the Saturday previous to July 8th (1847), he called; but as my husband was not at home, he did not stay, but said he would call again next week. He stopped not more than three minutes, and did not more than sit down. I was alone, for my girl was gone out; and Mrs. Wyckoff, who had called on me, was just leaving as he came. He said that he wanted to see me and my husband together on church business. He said he would call the following week, when my husband would be at home. In the early part of that week, we removed to the house near the church in Clinton. I and my husband had subjected ourselves to the censure of the church. I suppose they thought so. Another family (Mr. Mattison, and his wife, and six children,) lived in this house with us; and the front door and stairway were common to both families. Mr. Landis called again on July 8th. I was down stairs in the sitting-room when he came in; and a servant girl, Sarah Ann Seals, was there also. He said he was in a hurry, and wanted to see me a little while alone. I had but one room down stairs and two above; so I took him up stairs, because I knew what his business was. He sat down under the north window of the room; I sat down near the fire-place, on the other side of the room. Then he read a piece of writing, and wished me to come to him to see if I could read it. I went to him and read it. I had not more than read it, when he pulled me around on his knees, and enough of my dress came up to pull me astride of his lap. He put his arms around me, and drew me up to him. I told him to let me go, and he told me not to be afraid, he won't break through. Then he let me go; and I started to go down stairs, and he jumped up, and caught me in his arms, and held me over the bed, and said, 'How easy!' I then told him to let me go, and he let me go. I then started to go down stairs, and he said, 'Stop; let us have prayer first.' I stopped, and had prayer; we both fell upon our knees. He made a very short prayer. Then we went down stairs. He did not remain any time; not over a minute or two. He told the hired girl that she should not think hard of his having prayer up stairs, because the child was so troublesome.

"He left a paper for me and my husband to copy off. We copied and signed it, and sent it back to the Session, for them to see. He requested that Mr. Vanderbelt should bring the paper to church next day; but I told Mr. L. that Mr. V. would be engaged that day, and that I would send it by Ann Seals. I did send it by her. The door of the room was not shut; and when Mr. L. and I went out of it, I did not notice that it was any wider open than when we went in. I did not weep that day, nor feel cross at any one. I stood on the side of Mr. L. toward the bed. He set me astride of his knees. This was all he did: and he offered no violence; nor tried to hold me at all after I told him to let me go. When I told him to let me go, I guess I did not speak any louder than common; and did not make any outcry, so as to be heard through the house. I

V. never once, during the delivery of her testimony, looked me in the face. It had been arranged, however, that her father should sit near her, and yet have his face directly in her view. And every question propounded by my counsel (Mr. Wurts) remained unanswered by her until she had first looked at him, in order to see, I suppose, whether his nose, or chin, or forehead stood in need of scratching—for he seemed to have caught a kind of flying erysipelas. It attracted much attention; but what right has a judge to forbid a man to put his fingers to his face? During her examination at Presbytery, too, Mr. C. also sat at her side, and suggested to Mr. Hunt so loudly the questions to be put to her, with his remarks thereon, that she knew just what to say. I ordered him to be removed, and in great wrath he went away; and after that, her testimony was much more hesitating.

made no objection to uniting with him in prayer after this thing took place. I and my husband went next Sabbath to the church, and communed. Mr. Landis officiated as minister on the occasion. I spoke to Mr. L. on communion Sabbath; but do not recollect asking him to come and visit us. He called at my house after this. My husband saw him; and Mr. L. said that as he was in the place, he thought he would stop. Mr. L. and I (on July 8th) were not up stairs more than ten minutes, or fifteen at the longest. There was no time that I was on his lap; not more than a minute. Mr. L. sent back an answer in writing from the Session, by Ann Seals."

At Presbytery, she also said that "she was afraid to accompany Mr. L. up stairs, from fear that he would offer her violence," because of what took place at the cherry trees; and, also, that "Mr. Landis never proposed, in any way or shape, to have any connection with me, beyond what I have stated." And also that, "she did not think he meant any harm by what he did." This she also told the committee (at least in the hearing of three members of it, Charles Carhart, Wesley Bird, and William Emery) who took her affidavit in September, 1847.

Such is the most improved version of the story. And in addition to this, Mrs. V. said that Ann Seals saw the outrage; and that she (Mrs. V.) told it the next day (Friday) to C. Sweezey; and that Ann Seals told it to Vanderbelt on Saturday. And yet this Ann Seals attended the preparatory services on both Friday and Saturday (on Sabbath she was required to stay at home to take care of the child). And on Sabbath, Mr. and Mrs. Vanderbelt, and this same Miss Sweezey, attended church and communed: and the whole of them, with Ann, as multitudes could testify, continued to attend for many weeks afterwards.

Such are my accuser's statements and admissions in relation to this charge. And, although Ann Seals, Catherine Sweezey, and Mr. and Mrs. Vanderbelt all knew of these asserted facts within two days of their alleged occurrence, yet the subject remained *in statu quo* for nearly two months, and all unknown to everybody save Vanderbelt and these tattling gossips. Upon such a story did the villanous conspirators succeed in having me cast at the county court; and upon the same has Mr. Barnes seized (how can I help saying it?) with the gusto of a vampire; and by means of which he has pursued me almost to the grave! I do not believe, however, that he was vicious enough to perform all this without remorse: but he had not virtue enough to resist the temptation to destroy a supposed rival. But let us return to the point now under review.

In Part I. I have given my sentiments respecting this very injudicious interview. I never attempted to defend its propriety, though I then supposed that it was called for by the necessity of the case. Many in the church, and many jealous sectaries out of it, were greatly offended by the scandal which Mr. and Mrs. V. had brought upon religion; and yet not a soul would enter a complaint, so as to enable me to bring the matter before Session. The elders would do nothing in the thing, but talk about it, and postpone its consideration, till common fame at length compelled them to allow me to introduce it; nor would a single soul of them consent to accompany me, though I urged it upon them in every possible way. I was at a loss to know what to do in such a case. My elders ought to have been at once suspended, and another Session elected. But this is easier said than done. The alternative of overlooking the case, and suffering the matter thus to die, I was determined never to submit to. So the only remaining one was chosen. I went myself, unattended, and performed the duty. I called *twice* before July 8th, as I have stated in Part I., Chap. III. On the first call, I saw them both; but the business was not concluded, for I could make nothing out of Vanderbelt; and who wished me to show him such an "act of submission" as I recommended. So I called again. He was not at home, and I did not go in, but deferred the business till the following week, at which time, Mrs. V. said, he would doubtless be at home. I therefore called on July 8th, the time specified: he was not in. So the case, with all its power of evil, must be deferred, and the offenders still permitted their standing, and commune, or I must attend to it at once. I did not hesitate; and the sad result will, I trust, be useful to my brethren in the ministry, and to elders of churches, for years to come.*

On this charge I was tried at court; and it is astonishing that as Mrs. V. and her girl explained it, in their answers to the cross-questioning, both judge and jury did not see that it involved as complete a physical impossibility as would the assertion that I had attempted to murder her by throwing at her a rock weighing fifty tons. But it is needless for me to go into this point, as the case does not require it. The matter was at once perceived by many at court; and had the Judge explained to the jury the difference between evidence and testimony; and adverted to that fact, there cannot be even a doubt as to what the verdict would have been. But he simply informed them that "they must decide according to testimony." According to which, if these same witnesses had testified that I had hurled at the head of one of them a stone of fifty tons' weight, I would of course have been brought in guilty. The jury were simple-hearted, honest men, and did as the judge directed them.

The main object of this part of the work, however, is to lay before the reader the facts as they came before Presbytery; that so, in view of what was there presented, the public may form an idea of the power and extent of that malignant influence, which, having seized upon these ac-

* The counsel of my accuser asserted at court, that I, "for the purpose of being alone with this woman, had *pretended* to have church business with her;" and this was thought to be an excellent version of the matter. So much so, that Mr. and Mrs. V. even deny that they were ever disciplined. This is hardly worthy of remark. Still I may be permitted to say, that in the application which the Session made to Presbytery, in Oct., 1847, and signed by Elders Fritz, Johnson, and Daniel Carhart, is the following passage: "A young woman, whom, together with her husband, *we had suspended from the communion of the Lord's Supper, for the sin of fornication before marriage*, deposed, on the 3d of September last, that our Pastor, at an interview which he had with her on July 8th, did," &c. &c.

With equal effrontery, Mrs. V. now denies, also, that she ever attended Bethlehem church after the communion, though many persons distinctly remember seeing her there until near the close of August. One case is too remarkable to be omitted. A lady from New York, paid a visit to a relative of hers at Bethlehem. She remained over the Sabbath, and attended church, and sat in the pew directly behind that which was occupied by the Vanderbelts. On that day, Mrs. V. for the first time appeared in a new and fashionable article of dress, which excited some attention. The lady-visitor, who sat directly behind her, noticed a large *louse* crawling over the article referred to, and was thoughtless enough to make it the subject of conversation; which produced some silly laughter at Mrs. Vanderbelt's expense. When the rumor was subsequently raised against me, this whole matter was at once recalled to mind. It was easy for the lady and her friends to fix the time of her visit, which was in August, and, I think, near the middle of the month.

cusations for a pretext, would now close up against me all the avenues to usefulness, and destroy me utterly if possible.

But before I proceed to a further consideration of the statements of this witness, it is in place to offer here a single remark on the course pursued by Mr. Barnes in relation thereto. After he had propounded to her a considerable number of questions, all of which she readily answered, he in conclusion proposed the two following: "Do you think that Mr. Landis had any evil intention or designed you any harm, by what you have charged him with doing?" She replied promptly, "No, sir; I do not think he did." Mr. Barnes then asked her in a most solemn and impressive manner, "Has Mr. Landis at any other time or place, or in any other way, besides what you have now mentioned, treated you in any improper manner?" She, with the same promptness, replied, "No, sir."

Mr. Barnes may, and probably did think it proper to propound such queries under the circumstances; and if the reader can here discover anything like kindness, and a disposition to do justly by me, let Mr. B. have full credit on that account.* I will not say that the questions were really improper, (for I was sincerely glad when he put them,) but the last one does not strike my mind as being at all fair, and what a question ought to be at such a time. The young woman, notwithstanding the promptings of my enemies, and the long time which had already been allowed to her, had brought nothing else against me. But suppose that she had been as artful as Mr. Hunt, for instance, and had answered this last question by saying, "*Yes, sir!*" Presbytery would not *then* have permitted her to disclose any such new charge, and thus I should have been brought under an increased suspicion without any remedy. I conceive, therefore, that Mr. Barnes had no right thus to

* Since writing the above, I have been able to call to mind two other instances, which, perhaps, ought to bear a favorable construction in respect to Mr. Barnes. I introduce them not only under a sense of duty, but with unfeigned pleasure, (though they are all that have come to my knowledge,) and should sincerely rejoice if they can furnish a possible clue by which he can be saved from the imputations which the multitude of opposing facts seem irresistibly to suggest against him: for my object is not to injure Mr. Barnes, but to show that the course which he pursued has injured me unnecessarily, and the cause of religion through me. I state simply *what* he did: the *why* and the *wherefore* I refer to himself.

The first of these instances, then, is this: When Mrs. V. was being examined, Mr. Barnes brought out from herself and *prominently* the fact, that I, *by her own choice*, had married her, though Mr. Hunt was in the neighborhood. This, if I recollect rightly, was also brought out by him, *in direct view of her assertion that I had treated her as is stated in charge 1st.* This fact seems inconsistent with a settled and deliberate purpose, on the part of Mr. Barnes, to destroy me.

The Rev. C. Conkling also informed me that he heard Mr. Barnes, when conversing in private, express his decided disbelief of the cherry tree story; and that along with Thompson, Gilbert and the other brethren, (when they were discussing it,) he declared it to be false and impossible; and suggested a motive which had probably induced Mrs. V. to get up the story. I did not learn what the suggested motive was.

Now if this be so, and I do not doubt Mr. Conkling's statement, Mr. Barnes' course of conduct may be susceptible of some explanation. When I compare these instances, however, with his course as exhibited in the narrative, I cannot but think that they were only the strugglings of a retreating virtue against a prejudice, which, by indulgence, had become dominant. But perhaps they were not. Therefore let Mr. Barnes' explanation be heard and regarded with all possible candor:—with that charity which "rejoices not in iniquity; but rejoices in the truth."

place in the hands of my accuser, the power of inflicting upon me such an injury. No other member of Presbytery propounded such questions.

As to the story itself of Mrs. V., I do not believe that a woman can be found in America who could believe it. She represents herself, in the first place, as being *afraid* to go alone with me because of my previous treatment of her at the "row of cherry trees." This fear, then, of course put her on her guard and rendered her cautious. And yet, without resistance or outcry, she suffers herself to be treated in this shockingly indecent and brutal manner, by the person whom she feared. To say nothing of the perfect fatuity and madness of the man who, at midday, with the door of the room open, and a half dozen of children running about the house, would attempt such an act, it is impossible that a female thus outraged and offended should have stopped an instant to weigh motives or look at consequences. Nature itself would have governed her conduct, and, overcoming every restraint, she would at once have given up to merited punishment and infamy the scoundrel who had thus ventured to insult her. And yet, after all this, she unites with him in prayer; and makes an arrangement about copying and sending to the Session the "Act of Submission," for a crime not perhaps half so great as that which she declares on oath to have been perpetrated by this man against her! There are many other equally forcible considerations, which the mind of any competent reader will suggest by reflection on the subject: but I must dismiss this witness after referring to a fact or two.

Mr. and Mrs. V. assert that they did not understand that the letter sent by the Session in answer to their "Act of Submission," announced a censure which amounted to suspension from the Lord's Supper: and that hence they communed on the following Sabbath. I think I can clearly *prove* this not to be so however; but it is not of much importance, and I have no wish to dispute it. Still, I cannot see how this at all relieves the matter. Mrs. V. and Ann and Miss Sweezey all report that the insult was known *before* Sabbath; and why, then, did they commune at all, and receive the ordinance at the hands of such a man? The *truth* of the matter has here at last found egress in spite of all their efforts to conceal it: for there is but one inference that can be deduced from such a fact: to wit; that at the time referred to there was no such story in existence, and consequently it was subsequently manufactured by my enemies: a conclusion singularly corroborated by the fact that so little impression was made upon her mind by this asserted outrage at the time of its occurrence, that two different periods were assigned by her as the date of its occurrence. Before the Grand Jury, and at Presbytery, she deposed that it occurred on July 1st. But when I disproved this by establishing an *alibi*, she swore at the court that it took place on July 8th.

Thus this wretched and wicked tale, first fabricated by idle gossiping amongst individuals of the most degraded and scandalous character, and with whom, after her disreputable marriage, poor Mrs. V. was led to associate; a story to the truth of which she was compelled against her will to depose, or to become infamous as a liar; a story which she was eight hours in stating to the committee, (with whom I was not permitted to be present,) and during the relation of which another female slanderer and most notorious liar was permitted to be present, and not only to prompt her, but repeatedly to correct her statements; a story to which her subsequent attendance on my ministry for six weeks gave the most direct contradiction; was through the influence and management of a single ecclesiastic made the occasion to justify the most cruel, barbarous, and heartless treatment ever experienced in Protestant Christendom at the hands of a professed disciple of Christ. Did I not now thoroughly understand the mental and moral organization of Mr. Barnes, I should actually despair of my kind, every time that this matter reverts to memory.

I ought not to omit the fact, that, late in the evening during which Mrs. V.'s affidavit was taken, a gentleman of the highest respectability, (Captain Moses Hoyt,) who thought the committee still in session, went to the house of Mr. Vanderbelt for the purpose of ascertaining from them the purport of her statement. The committee, however, had retired. But before he ascertained this, his attention was arrested by a loud altercation between a man and woman in the house; and he distinctly heard the man say, "Why didn't you swear in that way?" She replied with temper: and while the altercation continued, Capt. Hoyt ascertained that the committee had left. He retired immediately, not deeming it honorable to listen to the dispute. Such is the simple fact, to the truth of which he was prepared to testify. But before the time of the meeting of Presbytery, he was required to go to sea: he, however, took the precaution to state the fact to several gentlemen, whom he authorized to mention it in his name. And during the meeting of Presbytery, Mr. Barnes, I am sure, was informed of it; for he spent an evening at the residence of Capt. Hoyt.

The next witness in support of this count was Ann Seals. In Part I. I have already given some little insight into her character. In her extra-judicial oath before Esquire Case, she deposed that she came up stairs to hear me read the paper (which I had brought with me) to Mrs. Vanderbelt, and that the door being a little open, she looked in and saw the occurrence take place which is described by Mrs. V. This located the occurrence in the *south* end of the room, while Mrs. V. swore that it took place in the *north* end. Here, then, was a case which involved serious danger to the parties themselves, for one or the other, if not both, was, on their own statements, liable to an indictment for perjury. To escape this consequence, the matter was, by the assistance of counsel, improved upon previous to the meeting of Presbytery, before which Ann testified, that the door being a little open, she opened it wide enough to get her head in, and look around it to the north end of the room, and thus saw the occurrence. A commission was, at my request, sent by Presbytery to examine the room, and they made Ann repeat the asserted movement, and it was found, on measurement, that the door required to be opened fourteen inches, in order to enable her to do so. It was ascertained, too, that the door on being opened, creaks on its hinges about nineteen times out of twenty. She deposed, too, that the door being thus opened, she looked around it, and saw my face and the face of Mrs. V. both looking in the direction of the door, (the room being, perhaps, from twelve to fifteen feet square,) and that she kept her head in the room, looking at us all the time, for about ten or fifteen minutes, and saw the whole of the transaction, so as to be able to describe it minutely, even to the fact that Mrs. V.'s clothing was not, during the attempt, raised above her ankles.

Her oath before Esquire Case was as follows, in the squire's style and orthography:

"On Thursday before the Communion in July, 1847, Mr. L. came to Mr. Vanderbelt's, and Mr. L. asked Miss V. to go in another room, he wanted to read a paper to her, and they then went up in the parlor, and after a little I went up in the entry to hear what Mr. Landis was reading, and the room door being a little open, I saw Mr. L. pull Miss V. on his lap astrad, and drew her up to him, and then Miss V. said to Mr. L., let me go, and Mr. L. said to her, don't be afraid, he won't brake through, and he then let loose of her, and Miss V. came towards the door, and then went down stairs; and further, deponent sath not."*

At court, (and also at Presbytery,) she deposed as follows:

"Mr. Landis asked if Mr. V. was at home. He then said, now, Catherine, we'll go into another room, and see if you can read that paper. Mrs. V. started up stairs, and Mr. L. went after. After they were gone a short time, I went up to hear if Mrs. V. could read the paper. The door of the room in which they were was on a small crack. I did not stand longer than two minutes, and then, as I heard nothing, I thought I'd look in; and I took the back of my hand, and opened the door, and looked in, and saw Mr. L. sitting down, and Mrs. V. beside him; *Mr. L. took Mrs. V. on his knee, and then turned her around, and pulled her astraddle of his lap*, and she said, Mr. L., let me go; and he said, you need not be afraid, I'll not break through. Mrs. V. then stepped towards the door, and I thought she was coming down, and I went away."

Such was the fabrication which was found necessary, in order to support the first step in these proceedings. In Mrs. V.'s deposition before Presbytery, she stated distinctly, that when the asserted outrage was perpetrated, she was standing at my right side, and that I was sitting between the bed and herself. Ann Seals swore just as roundly, and still repeated it a half dozen times, re-affirming it on every question, that Mrs. V. stood between the bed and myself, on my left side, on the side next the church, and in every form, (for the questions were thus varied, in order to allow her opportunity to reflect,) but she swore just as positively as Mr. Vanderbelt had done, and was just as decided in regard to the positions.

When the rumor first started, this poor girl, (who was not then living at Vanderbelt's,) being asked in relation to the matter, frankly stated, (to Mrs. Nancy Fields, and Miss Elizabeth Seevers, and others,) in reply to the questions propounded to her on the subject, that her curiosity had led her to go up stairs to listen to the contents of the paper, and that the door being a little open, she saw Mrs. V. standing at my side, and that I was looking upon a paper, and that Mrs. V. was weeping, and had her hand resting on my shoulder, but that she saw no harm, and never in her life saw or knew any harm of me. This statement was true, for the copy of the *Act of Submission* which I had taken with me was written in characters which no one but myself could read; and after reading it to Mrs. V., and she expressing herself satisfied, and willing to sign and send it to the Session, she procured me a sheet of

* This affidavit was taken on September 25th, 1847, and Mrs. Vanderbelt's, on the 2d

paper, and I sat down at the table at the south end of the room, (and which could be seen from the door, if it were at all open,) and copied it off with my pencil, in a large round hand, Mrs. Vanderbelt looking over me in the mean time, to see that no word was left written obscurely. Ann, doubtless, saw us in this position, and told no other story about the matter, until more than three weeks after Mrs. V.'s affidavit had been taken; a sufficient inducement of some kind was then offered to her, and thus *the case* was regarded as made out, and the testimony of the chief witness supported.

It would be an insult to the reader's mind, to suppose it necessary to dwell upon a story like this—that this girl should have come to the door, and hearing no noise, should open it at least fourteen inches, and see the parties with their faces towards the door, in broad daylight, and should keep her head in the room all the time, without once withdrawing it, (as she deposed in Presbytery,) and yet that in the profound silence which reigned in the room, neither the creaking of the door, nor the opening of it, nor the protrusion of her head, nor its remaining in that position, should have attracted the notice of the parties, when they could have seen it by a mere glance of the eye. Such is her story, and if any person can believe it, I am perfectly willing that he should do so.

The father of this girl was much displeased when he heard that she had been regarded as qualified to testify as a witness, (though he himself is, in the dialect of his neighborhood, one of the veriest "*Ripstavers*" alive,) and told Mr. Conrad Honnis that her word could not be relied on. But that she, who had been detected in the act of stealing corn from a neighbor's corn-crib, and who had been driven out of a room in her attempt to get into bed to a man, and who had also declared herself to be *enciente* by an individual, (and I am informed *made oath to that effect*, though I do not assert it positively,) which turned out to be false, all of which with any number of other things equally disreputable could have been easily proved at court, or anywhere else, (but the Judge and lawyers would not admit these things, regarding them as not to the point,) should be *according to law* a proper witness in a case involving the fair and unblemished reputation of a man, argues an imperfection in the administration of justice which ought not to be suffered to exist in this country. In Part I. I have remarked that she continued her adulterous practices, and that in June, 1849, she, and a paramour of hers, with whom she had been for months living in the practice of this bestial sin, were, on their own acknowledgment of it, expelled from the communion of the Methodist Church.*

The next witness was Catherine Sweezey, one of the most scurrilous and foul-mouthed creatures alive. She had been very free in speaking against me, but on being now questioned under oath declared that she had never known anything to my disadvantage, upon which the prosecution withdrew her in double-quick time.

The *next charge* was for improper conduct at a "giving visit" some two or three years before. Two witnesses had been cited, a young man

* In her testimony before Presbytery, Ann mentioned that she had recently had a trance, in which she had received sundry revelations, (which however I have now forgotten,) and that this had made her truly religious, and led her to join the Methodist Church, and that until that time she had never known anything about religion.

by the name of Bird, and Mr. Hunt's grandson. The former was first called; who declared that he saw me sit on a lady's lap; but on being cross-questioned by Dr. Brainerd, could not say that I touched her lap when appearing to sit upon it. He admitted too that there was a large number of persons in the same room at the time. He became greatly confused, and perspired prodigiously after contradicting himself so preposterously as to set the whole congregation in a roar of laughter, and immediately as he left the witnesses' stand, the prosecution arose in great haste and said, "Mr. Moderator, we withdraw the remaining charges and witnesses." Mr. Hunt had by this time become dreadfully sick of the case.

In regard to young Mr. Bird, however, I ought to say that a short time previous to the starting of Mrs. V.'s rumor against me, he had been sternly reproved by me during public service for indecent behavior in church. He would not attend church until some time after this, and then very irregularly. He spoke rather freely and angrily against me, and what he had thus passionately spoken was subsequently seized upon by the prosecution, and he was required to reaffirm it. Hence his confusion and their shame. The other witness on this charge (Thomas Hunt) was a poor weak-minded overgrown child, who had said that he had seen all that Mr. Bird saw. And he doubtless did. But when Mr. Bird came to describe what he had seen, his story was so preposterous and contradictory, that the prosecution considered it safest to let it rest on its own internal evidence. Thus ended the matter, and as it was late in the evening, Presbytery adjourned.

On the following morning I commenced the defence. Mr. Hunt was the first witness whom I called. The substance of his testimony is given in Part I. He was very unwilling to come, and having no time to concoct a story (for he had not the remotest suspicion that I designed to call upon him), he at once "let the cat out of the bag," and acknowledged the existence of long standing efforts to get me to leave Bethlehem. Mr. Barnes seemed as much astounded at my audacity in calling up the old man, as Mr. H. himself, but said nothing.* The other members of Presbytery were however greatly delighted and amused. When the old man was asked why he did not, when he was first informed of this charge against me, go and call upon me, as Christ and our constitution require in such cases, he replied, "Why, *to tell the truth*," [as though this was by no means his usual custom,] "I was afraid of him; he is a large strong man, and could whip half a dozen such men as me."

The next witness was his son, who was acting with him in the prosecution. He had no idea either of being called upon. By his testimony I established an alibi, showing that during the whole day sworn to by Mrs. V. (July 1,) I was in his company, he having rode with me in my carriage from the celebration of the centennial anniversary of Princeton College.

* In fact neither Mr. Hunt's admission of making and selling rum, nor of his long standing enmity to me, and to the cause of evangelical religion, produced any repugnance to that old transgressor in the bosom of this ecclesiastical writer on "*The Traffic in Ardent Spirits.*" On the contrary the discovery of a mutual spirit of enmity to myself seemed to induce a mutual charity and oblivion of everything that might otherwise have been a ground of difference, and to operate as a substantial and permanent cement of their friendship. *Multi famam; pauci conscientiam verentur.*

Efforts were now made to keep away my witnesses, so that I was obliged to take them as they could be obtained. I announced this nefarious procedure to Presbytery, but Mr. Barnes received it with his usual placidity, and said not a word. While Mrs. Jones was being sent for, I produced in evidence the previous affidavits of the witnesses against me, and pointed out their inconsistency with the present testimony of the prosecution, and also a letter or two of Mr. Hunt to myself, evincing that several years before he had been laboring to effect my removal from Bethlehem. Commissions also were sent to Mrs. George Taylor, and Mrs. Ellen Lanning, whose testimony along with that of Miss Elizabeth Seevers and Mrs. Nancy Fields utterly destroyed the statement of Ann Seals. Mr. Wm. Emery also established the genuineness of Mr. Hunt's letter of instruction to the committee who took Mrs. V.'s affidavit. Mr. Asa McPherson testified also that on Sept. 4th, when the congregation met to consider the rumor against me, he saw and heard me call Mr. Vanderbelt to me; and that he (Mr. McPherson) stood near me at the time, and saw Mr. V. come to me, and heard me ask him whether he had been reporting that he had treated me rudely on the previous Monday; and heard Mr. V. say that he had never in his life treated me more politely, and that he had never said anything to the contrary; and that during this interview (at the church,) Mr. V.'s appearance was not that of a man who felt offended or disgusted with another, but that he evinced a disposition to oblige me in any way possible. I had now sent twice for Mrs. Jones; and a commission was about being appointed to take the testimony, when my accusers came forward and asked leave of me to withdraw the prosecution, as will be stated in the following chapter. I regret, however, that I consented to this before all my witnesses had been fully heard.* The counsel for the prosecution also asked permission of me to introduce some witnesses for Ann Seals' character, if any could be found who felt that they could say anything that might prevent her being given up to hopeless infamy, and thus deprived of the means of a livelihood; I assented to this, and that any who could say aught for the poor creature might do it. But in the whole region not one female could be found for their purpose, and only two males, Mr. A. A. Hunt (Mr. Hunt's son), and D. Carhart, both of whose reputations themselves are sadly in need of bolstering.

* The following ought still to have been examined:

1. *As to Mrs. V.'s character and habits:* Washington Leigh and Peter Stryker.
2. *Those who saw her and her husband at church after Communion Sabbath:* Mrs. Sarah Hoyt, Miss Mary Wilson, Harbert I. Rodenbough, and Ralph G. Ely.
3. *As to the statements of Mrs. V. respecting the cherry trees:* Mrs. Jones and Miss Rosan Pickel.
4. *As to Ann Seals' character:* Mrs. Jacob Henry, Miss Hannah Chandler, Abram V. Creger, Abram Banghart, James Hardy and wife, Capt. George Taylor, and Elisha Probasco. The respectability and unimpeachable integrity of these witnesses will be questioned by no one.

CHAPTER VIII.

THE WITHDRAWAL OF THE PROSECUTION.

When the defence was entered upon, as described above, it soon became apparent that the prosecution could not be sustained: and in consequence thereof Mr. Hunt and his family were greatly alarmed on account of the libellous letter which he had written to Mr. Barnes, and which at his own request had been laid before Presbytery. His own testimony had convicted both himself and the chief actors in the prosecution, of a long-standing conspiracy of the most malignant type, against me; and contained also the admission that he had grossly violated the rules prescribed by Christ and laid down in our constitution, in respect to alleged offences; and the important admission also that all the ladies of the congregation still adhered to me faithfully, notwithstanding the unceasing efforts which had been made to impair their confidence in my character.

Such disclosures, and many others of similar import, developed by the examination of witnesses on the defence, were calculated, as the reader may well suppose, to make a deep impression on every reflecting mind. And it was further manifest that the testimony on the part of the prosecution, being both contradictory, and invalidated by the defence; and having so dark a shade thrown over it by Mr. Hunt's confession; could operate only against themselves. Hence the tide was setting in against my prosecutors; and had the case gone on fairly, there can be but little doubt that Mr. Hunt would have been deposed from the ministry. He now therefore became extremely anxious to escape from the position into which he had brought himself; and Mr. Barnes, who was still his guest, here stepped in, and took the lead in the business, as we shall proceed to show.

As above remarked, the prosecution came forward, and expressed an earnest wish that I would permit them to withdraw their charges. On the morning of the last day of the trial (Saturday), and before Presbytery proceeded to business, the matter was introduced to me by Mr. Barnes, who called me aside, and spoke as follows (Let the reader mark every word): "That Mr. Hunt had been talking with him on the subject, and wished the matter would now stop. They (the prosecutors) were now willing to withdraw the prosecution if I would allow them to do so. That Mr. Hunt had said that he had not slept all night, and appeared as though he had been weeping: and had said to him (*i.e.* to Mr. Barnes) that he relented for the course which he had pursued towards me; that I was greatly beloved by the congregation; and that he ought to have been a peace-maker, instead of adopting the course which he had pursued. And that he wished him (Mr. Barnes) to see me, in order to learn whether there was the same conciliatory spirit on my part. That Mr. Hunt also said that his family pride was wounded from thinking that I had slighted him or treated him with neglect, in not counselling with him respecting the affairs of the congregation. And that as I had frankly admitted that I was sorry for having given any occasion for reproach, if I would allow Presbytery to administer a caution or admonition to me in the matter, peace would be restored, and that he believed all parties would be satisfied; and the suit also should be taken out of court; whereas if we were to go into pleadings and disputes, the breach would only be made wider than ever." To this (which, I then little suspected, had been moved by Mr. Barnes) I replied as follows: "That I was willing to refer the matter to my brethren in Presbytery; and was not anxious to press it any further: but was willing, if the brethren should think it best, to allow the prosecution to withdraw their suit. That as to slighting Mr. Hunt, I never had done it; but uniformly made it a point to invite him into the pulpit; and had always consulted him in relation to the affairs of the church, until I found that he invariably and strenuously opposed my efforts to restore Presbyterian order and doctrine; and to promote the cause of temperance; Sabbath-schools; catechetical instruction; and efforts to promote a spirit of beneficence in the congregation. And that since I learned the use which my enemies had made of my kissing my people, (though Mr. Hunt had used that mode of salutation far more than I had done,) I had always felt and expressed deep regret that I had thus given the enemy cause to blaspheme: and should be glad to have Presbytery, for the honor of religion, caution or reprove me; for it was better that I should suffer than that religion should." Such is a correct statement of Mr. Barnes' remarks on this occasion; and of my rejoinder: and when I closed my remarks he immediately withdrew.

The prosecution was therefore now withdrawn, as we have shown in Part I. And the nature of this withdrawal may be learned fully from the following letter of the Moderator, Dr. Fairchild, addressed to myself, (though as the reader will see, designed to be used if necessary,) on Dec. 15, 1847, after the prosecution had resolved to violate their pledge to myself and the Presbytery. Mr. Conover had written to the stated clerk for a copy of the testimony; and his request came up twice, at the adjourned meetings of Presbytery: but Mr. Barnes was, I believe, and am sure, the only member, at least of those who attended the trial, that was in favor of complying with the request. The iniquity of this whole procedure, the reader will see at a glance, when he remembers that in consequence of the prosecution coming formally forward, late on Saturday, (for the matter though suggested early by Mr. Barnes to myself, was not acted upon at once,) and proposing to withdraw their charges, while I was in the process of examining witnesses, the most important part of my testimony had not been elicited. Yet these very honorable personages desired to have that part of the testimony on the defence, which had been taken, exhibited as *all* that could be offered by me. Dr. Fairchild writes as follows, and the italics and capitals are his own.

"As to the course which I fear Mr. Conover is pursuing from the letters he has sent us (that is, sent our clerk, Rev. Mr. Adair,) I wish to express my deep regret: and I wish to say to him kindly and fraternally, that he much mistakes when he says he proved to the Presbytery the things which he charged upon his pastor. *He by no means sustained his charges as they were made:* and if the court had pursued its way and examined the testimony as usual in *judicial* cases, he and all others would have had little ground to say that they proved what they set out to do. They would have seen that they had made a failure to come up to what I now understand him to affirm in his letters. I hope that he will abide by the *settlement* as agreed to at the close of the meeting of Presbytery. It was understood that there should be a *cessation of controversy, a forgetting and for-*

giving, mutually; and a seeking of the happiness of the whole church. It was affirmed that such should be the effect of the settlement agreed to—*the civil suit should be withdrawn, and all should be peace.* Now I hope Mr. Conover will not stir more in this matter. Let him be advised that we look for an abiding by the settlement made: and such a course will be best for all parties all round. It will not do to stir up this matter and say what *was done* in the Presbytery, when the matter was *not* brought to *a close in a judicial way before Presbytery;* but was taken out of Presbytery BY THE REQUEST OF THE PROSECUTION, in order to be *settled amicably* by *agreement.* It was like two men who differ about book accounts, and get into law—and when in court ask liberty to go out and make a settlement. *They settle by agreement.* And the court allows it to be done. Now they cannot go back of that settlement and say what is on the books: for they agreed to settle, and did settle satisfactorily: and AS HONEST MEN THEY MUST ABIDE BY THE SETTLEMENT. Just let all parties now be still. Honesty seems to me to demand that no trouble be made any further. Surely enough was done; and Mr. Conover, I judge, had ill advisers when he was moved to ask for the testimony in the case, to show that he had satisfied Presbytery that his charges were all true. But I must not write more, as I am in haste,

"Yours as ever."

"P. S. You will not regard me as writing officially; but I do say as a member of that Presbytery if called to the decision judicially on the testimony before us, I should have been constrained to regard the charges as not proved, and in sifting and putting the testimony given in its true light, it would have been shown to have been far from what was needful in order to make out a case—and I am not alone in my views about it. I think Mr. Conover should be still; and the stiller the better: and I should say so to him if I could see him."

I prefer to state in the language of this excellent scholar and divine, the nature of this withdrawal on the part of the prosecution, that the reader may see by the explanation of the Moderator himself, the view which the Presbytery entertained of the procedure. It may not be out of place here also to request the reader to notice the phraseology in the P. S. as well as through the letter in respect to the testimony offered by the prosecution; and the statement that if Presbytery had judicially decided on the evidence already before them (*though the evidence for the defence had as yet been but partially elicited*), the prosecution could not have been sustained.

The reader may well suppose that having gone through such soul-harrowing scenes for nearly a week, and witnessing the conduct of Mr. Barnes, and the distress of my family, and the injury which had been occasioned to religion; that I was pretty well prostrated: and I was so truly. On Thursday I became quite ill with dysentery; and on Friday and Saturday could scarcely sit up. And yet, I must, even without counsel, through the procedure of Mr. Barnes, still continue to go through the terrible ordeal. I asked twice to be favored with counsel, but as the number of brethren present was so small, I finally relinquished my right in the matter: while the prosecution were favored with both Mr. Hunt and his son. My procedure in this matter was wrong. I trusted too much to the goodness of my cause (when assailed by a set of the most malignant beings that ever combined to destroy a man), and set too light a value upon those means of defence which I ought to have employed.

At Mr. Barnes' instance, an interlocutory meeting of the Presbytery was called at the school-house, professedly to arrange this business of the withdrawal. Mr. Hunt was first conferred with, and then, by this same instance, I was desired to express myself in reference to the truth or falseness of the charges. This procedure I regarded as grossly unconstitutional. I, however, went over the charges one by one, and reiterated my denial of their truth, gave what explanations were necessary, but declined to answer a question or two suggested by Mr. Barnes, the obvious aim of which was to lead me to inculpate my accuser, whose childish familiarities with me I never suspected to be of an evil design; nor would I descend to the baseness of even seeming to wish, in return, by accusing her to free myself from her imputations. My plea of not guilty and my reiterated denial were sufficient, and I scorned, by submitting to such an unconstitutional procedure, to furnish a precedent for the like oppression of others.* Mr. Barnes then at once began to write the decision of Presbytery in the case, *though as yet no committee had been appointed in the business of preparing a minute.* If there could be such a thing as ludicrous atrocity, this certainly is an example. *This minute is entirely the work of Mr. Barnes, and was prepared by him alone before he had been nominated for the work or any committee appointed.* Having brought the matter into this shape, he seized, with greediness, upon the opportunity which was now afforded of finishing it, as he obviously at first designed. When a man, influenced as he was, offers himself as judge, he is certain to shape facts so as to suit his inclinations. As he had written the minute, some one nominated him, and others were added *pro forma.* This minute will be given in the next chapter.

As Mr. Hunt had made a declaration, confessing his guilt in the business, and the prosecution had been withdrawn, Mr. Barnes now reminded me of my acknowledged willingness to own wherein I felt that I had erred. Though exceedingly ill, I cheerfully complied with this suggestion, as furnishing occasion to Presbytery to caution or reprove me, (that so the promised peace might be restored,) and, with the aid of Brother Thompson, prepared a statement to read before Presbytery and

* It is scarcely credible that a Protestant clergyman in this land, should, on any pretence whatever, dare even to suggest such a procedure. Its iniquity cannot, perhaps, be better expressed than in the words of Henry on 1 Tim. 5 : 19—"*Against an elder receive not an accusation, but before* (εκτος ει μη επι, *unless it is offered to be proved by*) *two or three witnesses.* Here is the Scripture method of proceeding against an elder when accused of any crime. Observe, 1st. There must be an accusation; it must not be a flying, uncertain report; but an accusation, containing a certain charge, must be drawn up. Further, *He is not to be proceeded against by way of inquiry; this is according to the modern practice of the Inquisition, which draws up articles for men to purge themselves of such crimes or else to accuse themselves;* but, according to the advice of St. Paul, there must be an accusation brought against an elder. 2d. *This accusation is not to be received, unless supported by two or three credible witnesses;* and the accusation must be received *before them;* that is, the accused must have the accuser face to face, because the reputation of a minister is, in a particular manner, a tender thing; *and, therefore, before anything be done in the least to blemish that reputation, great care must be taken that the thing alleged against him be well proved, that he be not reproached upon an uncertain surmise.*"

Nothing can evince the nature of that influence which Mr. Barnes then exerted over the brethren of the Presbytery, so strikingly as the fact that he induced them silently to acquiesce in such palpable violations of gospel order and right principle. And when we compare the foregoing rules with his conduct at the very outset, in first receiving Mr. Hunt's letter and retaining it; circulating and supporting its statements, and shaping his whole course according to them, *before I had any trial, or the least opportunity of being heard,* the upright mind must not only be inexpressibly shocked at the comparison, but, as it seems to me, can be left in no doubt whatever as to the nature of those motives which have actuated him in this whole procedure.

the people, when the interlocutory meeting should cease. The expressions used were not precisely such as I should have preferred; but I was in too much pain and suffering, from my sickness, to think much about phrases and verbal criticism. I have reason to believe that Mr. Barnes dictated the part of the paper which Mr. Thompson wrote for me (without suspecting the least harm however), and if I am wrong herein, that brother can easily set the matter right.

At length Mr. Barnes' minute was finished. He says that it was read to Mr. Hunt and myself, and perhaps it was read in my hearing. At all events I could have made no objection to it then. Mr. Hunt, however, did hear it, and so soon as he became aware of the fact that Presbytery had not even censured his conduct towards me, he professed to regard it as a justification of his proceedings, and went amongst his friends exulting greatly. But the interlocutory meeting was now closed, and Presbytery proceeded to the church, and after Mr. Hunt, junior, had formally, and on behalf of the prosecution, withdrawn the charges, I arose and formally acceded to this proposal of the prosecution, and stated, moreover, that I felt bound in that connection to repeat, in the most solemn manner, my denial of the truth of the accusations, or of ever having indulged even the least lascivious desire or feeling towards my accuser. I candidly admitted that I had been imprudent, and that I had unwittingly laid myself open to misconception and misrepresentation—for which I desired the forgiveness of all who had been thereby offended. And, in conclusion, I read my paper, which will be found, in connection with the minute, in the next chapter.

Presbytery then called upon Mr. Hunt, senr., to arise and repeat the statement which he had made to Mr. Barnes. But, instead of doing this, he attempted to take advantage of these, my admissions. At this shameful procedure, Brother Thompson called out twice, with great indignation, "*Brother Landis has been caught in a trap!*" Mr. Barnes, however, whose manœuvring had brought the matter to this crisis, *said not one syllable.* But now a loud and indignant call was made by all the other members of Presbytery for another interlocutory, and all straightway removed again to the school-house. But the history of this interview must be reserved for another chapter, for it is now in place to introduce this minute of Mr. Barnes.

CHAPTER IX.

THE MINUTE PRESENTED BY MR. BARNES.

Though it will necessarily somewhat anticipate some of the facts of this history, I shall here present the whole record of the proceedings of Presbytery in the case, including my own paper, an improved version of Mr. Hunt's remarks to Mr. Barnes, and also the minute prepared by Mr. Barnes, as aforesaid. The first of the two interlocutory meetings referred to in this record is the one described above, and the second will come up for consideration in our next chapter. The record is as follows:

"Presbytery agreed to have an interlocutory meeting in the school-house;

about an hour was spent in this meeting, when the interlocutory was closed, and the Presbytery proceeded to the church and resumed the unfinished business. Mr. Hunt, Jr., expressed a desire that the cause should here be arrested, and the parties stated that they were willing to submit the cause to the Presbytery, without hearing further testimony or commenting on it. Mr. Landis waived his right to adduce further testimony which he deemed important to his cause, and agreed that additional witnesses should be examined by the prosecution to establish the character of Ann Seal, a witness in the case, whose character for veracity had been impeached.

"(The witnesses referred to having been examined,)

"Mr. Landis at this stage of the proceedings read the following paper, viz: 'I have been greatly misrepresented in the affidavits that have been taken against me in the case of Mrs. Vanderbelt. I freely admit that my intercourse with the ladies of my congregation has been faulty and indiscreet, as I fully and willingly asserted on Sept. 4th; that I have been free and familiar, and have indulged in such liberties, as, if not morally wrong, are at least perilous to ministerial character and usefulness. In respect to the young woman who has accused me, I am free to admit the same, which I have always admitted. I have been free and familiar with her (having been intimate with her father's family since she was a child), but with no criminal intent, and in no such way as to affect her chastity; but yet may have given occasion to Mr. Vanderbelt for jealousy without any intention or criminal feeling on my part. I think myself to have been hardly dealt with by my aged predecessor, but I have never had any hard or unkind feelings toward him, and I am willing to unite with him in bringing this matter before Presbytery, and let them judge whether the (accusation in his) letter to Presbytery ought not to be as formally withdrawn as it was made.'

"After a few remarks by Mr. H. W. Hunt, Jr., and Mr. Landis, the whole case was submitted to Presbytery.

"Rev. Messrs. A. Barnes, Thomas Brainerd, and Rev. E. W. Gilbert, D.D., and Messrs. Jos. Montgomery and Thos. P. Sparhawk, were appointed to prepare a minute expressive of the views of Presbytery in the case.*

"The Presbytery agreed to hold an interlocutory meeting in the school-house; and continued in this meeting some considerable time. The interlocutory was closed, and the Presbytery met in the church and resumed business.

"The committee to prepare the minute expressive of the views of Presbytery in the case, presented the following, which the chairman of the committee said he had submitted to Rev. H. W. Hunt, Senr., and Rev. R. W. Landis, and that they had expressed themselves satisfied with it.† Before reading the report of the committee, Mr. Barnes, the chairman, made the following statement of a conversation which Mr. Hunt had had with him in the morning, and which Mr. Hunt had desired he would repeat before Presbytery: viz.

"'After I had risen in the morning, Mr. Hunt called to me, and requested me to come down, saying that he wished to have some private conversation with me.‡ As soon as I had dressed, I went down into the parlor, and found him alone. He appeared exceedingly tender, and was either weeping or had the appearance

* The reader will bear in mind that during the first interlocutory, Mr. Barnes was thus appointed, and prepared the minute: the committee as above-named was afterwards appointed, *pro forma*, in the church.

† How heartless is this expression, so cunningly wrought into the minute! Had I made a will at this time, I doubt whether Mr. Barnes would have been willing to swear that I was in a state fit to make testamentary bequests. The phrase does not express the truth, moreover; for I never was "satisfied" with the paper as *here presented*. Mr. Hunt's speech, moreover, has been utterly changed (as will be shown) from what Mr. Barnes made for him to me in the morning. And while I was now too ill to put the words of this paper together, or to criticise them, the "satisfaction," if I expressed any, was only in reference to the settlement as proposed by the prosecution. I do not, however, recollect its being read to me.

‡ Would that we might know what passed between him and Mr. Barnes *on the evening previous.*

of having been weeping. He told me that he had passed the night in watching and prayer; that he had thought much of Mr. Landis and his case; that Mr. Landis was poor and dependent, and that it seemed hard at this season of the year to send him away:* that Mrs. Hunt had talked with him, that she had always been friendly towards Mr. Landis; "you know," said he, "how it is with women, how much they are attached to their ministers:"† and that she thought the matter might have been quashed without this difficulty. Mr. Hunt then said that he felt that from his age, and the fact that he had been so long a pastor among this people, he ought to be a peace-maker; and that he felt some relentings in regard to the course that had been taken; that he felt that the matter had been carried far enough; that David sinned and was forgiven, that Peter denied his Lord and was forgiven, and that there ought to be a kind and forgiving spirit.‡

"'He proposed that there should be a cessation of arms, "an armistice;" that the matter should be arrested here, and left to the disposal of Presbytery; that if the parties should go on to plead, their pride would be incited: and that Mr. Landis should remain and go on preaching for three or six months, on a sort of trial: and that if he preached the gospel, and there were no more imprudences, he hoped that the whole matter would die away: that he had not been able to attend church much for some weeks past; but that he would drop in, and hoped that those who acted with him would also drop in; and that harmony would thus be restored; matters would become smooth again, and all this difficulty be done away: that perhaps there should be an admonition from the Presbytery to Mr. Landis to be cautious on the subject; and the ultimate disposal should be left to the Presbytery.

"'He then stated that he had felt his family pride offended because Mr. Landis had not noticed him: that when he came there, and for some time after, he had been consulted and treated with respect: but that recently he had been neglected; and that there had not been that notice taken of him which he thought was due to him as the old pastor of the congregation.§

"'He proposed that I should see the brethren of the Presbytery before the meeting (this morning) and confer with them on the subject; and that I should also see Mr. Landis and see if there was the same conciliatory spirit on his part; and if there was, he was willing to propose to the Presbytery that the whole matter should be arrested here and submitted to them. In the course of the ride to the church, and speaking on some subject respecting the change which a man's mind may undergo, he said, "You see what a change has been produced in a single night in my own mind."

"The report of the committee of Presbytery was then read and adopted, and is as follows, viz.

"'The Presbytery having fully considered the charge alleged against the Rev. Robert W. Landis, and the evidence adduced in the case, and having received from the Rev. Robert W. Landis the foregoing paper, *in view of all the evidence before them*, adopt the following as expressive of their judgment.

"'1. That in their judgment, while the Rev. Mr. Landis has not been guilty of any such offence as to make proper his deposition from the ministry, or suspension from this office, the charge has been sustained in part, so far as refers to improper familiarity with the daughter of the accuser, in a manner perilous to the

* This idea was not in the remotest manner alluded to by Mr. Barnes in his repetition to me of Mr. Hunt's asserted conversation: and I am very confident he never intimated such a thing in repeating that conversation in the church. The object of Mr. Barnes in placing it upon this record, is to give a different coloring to the withdrawal of the prosecution. The matter will be referred to again hereafter.

† Another politic stroke of these two men; and designed to neutralize the force of that striking fact, that all the ladies of my large church and congregation still nobly adhered to their persecuted pastor.

‡ Another politic stroke, as aforesaid.

§ Another stroke of cunning, by which to neutralize the effect of Mr. Hunt's admission in evidence, of a long-standing conspiracy to remove me from Bethlehem.

character of a minister, and highly improper in one who has charge of a Christian congregation.

"'2. That while the Presbytery still have confidence in the purity of Mr. Landis, and a belief that in this matter he has not intended to give indulgence to lascivious passions, and while in view of his expression of regret, they do not regard him disqualified to be a minister of the gospel, they are of opinion that his conduct has been such as to deserve the censure of his brethren, and that he should be admonished of his error.

"'3. That the Rev. Robert W. Landis be earnestly exhorted and admonished to exercise a special circumspection in regard to his conduct in future; that he give himself to earnest prayer; and set a special watch upon his conduct to preserve himself from the very appearance of evil.

"'4. That in the judgment of this Presbytery it is to be deeply regretted that those who thought themselves aggrieved and injured had not sought an interview with Mr. Landis, and stated their feelings to him, instead of resorting to a method adapted to inflame popular feeling; and, as the Presbytery think, contrary to the spirit enjoined in the New Testament, and in the constitution of the Presbyterian Church.

"'5. That in view of this judgment of the Presbytery, and of the statement of Mr. Landis, the portion of the church and congregation of Bethlehem, which has been dissatisfied and alienated from him,* be earnestly exhorted to again receive him as their pastor, as one who is truly penitent, and one whose public labors have been faithful and much blessed in years that are passed: and that the whole congregation, with deep humiliation that these events have occurred among them, lay aside all causes of difficulty and contention; and unite in their endeavors to promote their mutual edification and the cause of the Redeemer.'

"After the adoption of the foregoing minute, Mr. Hunt, Senr., made some solemn and impressive remarks to the congregation, expressive of his desire that peace and harmony might prevail: and he and Mr. Landis in the presence of the congregation shook hands and professed reconciliation. Mr. Landis and Mr. Conover and Mr. Vanderbelt also shook hands, and Mr. Conover expressed forgiveness of Mr. Landis. The Presbytery then expressed thanks to God, Rev. A. Barnes leading in prayer; and united in singing a hymn.

"The following minute was adopted at the adjourned meeting of Presbytery, held in Missionary Rooms, Philadelphia, December 14th, 1847:

"'The stated clerk informed Presbytery that application had been [made] to him by Mr. Conover, one of the parties in the late trial, for a copy of all the testimony in the case, together with the minute containing the decision of Presbytery, and asked advice in the premises: whereupon, he was directed to furnish the parties with copies of the entire minute in relation to the case of *Garret Conover* vs. *Robert W. Landis.* The consideration of the case of Mr. Garret Conover for a copy of the testimony in the case was postponed until the next stated meeting of Presbytery, that an opportunity may be given to the parties for calm reflection, before anything be done to mar the happy settlement of the matter which was made at Bethlehem.'

"The foregoing is a true copy of the minutes of the fourth Presbytery in the case of *Garret Conover* vs. *Robert W. Landis.*

"ROBERT ADAIR, *Stated Clerk.*

"*Philadelphia, Dec.* 21*st*, 1847."

I frankly confess that the greatest difficulty which I have ever experienced in controlling my spirit (which is by nature none of the mildest) has been when considering the foregoing report, and the manner in

* Mr. Barnes knew that none of my people had been "alienated from" me in consequence of a belief of these silly charges. Why, then, does he here throw out an intimation of the contrary? Was it that the record might countenance any future efforts which he might see proper to make by means of my enemies to have me removed from Bethlehem? The reader will be able to determine this point hereafter.

which it was drawn up and pushed through Presbytery by Mr. Barnes. That he, with the feelings towards me which he had uniformly displayed through this whole matter, and which are briefly delineated in the foregoing descriptions, feelings of whose existence he could not but be conscious, should not only have consented, but actually volunteered, unbidden and uncalled, to act thus in a case which involved more than life itself to any honorable mind, and to write and place in a permanent form what must stand as long as this book of records exists, and pass upon the world as *the deliberate judgment* of Presbytery, argues so utter an absence of all upright principle and conscientiousness, that human language fails in the effort to give it a name! At the time when the great Presbyterian Church case was about to be brought up for adjudication before the Court of *Nisi Prius* in Philadelphia, the accomplished Judge Sargeant was one of the judges before whom it was expected to come; he was, moreover, a member of Mr. Barnes' congregation. The interests of that congregation were in no way specifically concerned in the matter to be tried, but so just were Judge Sargeant's conceptions of equity, that simply on the ground that his pastor had been concerned in the religious controversies which ultimated in the civil suit about to be decided, he at once, and peremptorily, refused to sit upon the judicial bench while the case was pending, and avowed his determination to resign his office as judge of the court, rather than comply with any such requisition. This conduct created no surprise, for it commended itself to the heart of every good and honest man. But in a case involving infinitely more to a fellow-being than all that was then in litigation, the pastor and religious instructor of this very judge, and while under the influence of the most disreputable feelings that the human breast can indulge, not only suffers himself to be appointed as a judge of that brother, but volunteers so to act, and does act, and takes the opportunity thus afforded of striking that brother to the earth, beyond all reasonable hopes of recovery. The guilt or innocence of the accused brother is not a question which enters into this matter; were he as guilty as David himself, that fact could furnish no exculpation for Mr. Barnes. I say nothing here of the numerous similar acts of this gentleman, as stated in the preceding chapters of this work; either of them is sufficiently revolting, but if the reader has ever, among Protestants, met with a case parallel to this, he has met with what has never come to my knowledge.

But admitting, for the sake of illustration, that I had perpetrated everything that malice, combined with cupidity, had imputed to me, and in what aspect must a minister of Christ appear, who thus evinces a disposition to mount foremost on the back of such a rumor, and attempts to ride his offending brother to death? This is bad enough, though such scenes have been witnessed. But oh, how ineffably worse is it, when in order to gratify a preconceived prejudice, or spirit of jealousy, or rivalry, a clergyman will come forth as the first in such a crusade, and endeavor in every possible way to make the impression that a falsely accused brother is guilty, coolly placing the matter in such a shape, by virtue of his own elevated position in the church, as must render it utterly impossible, without the special assistance of God, for that brother ever to recover from the odious imputation, so as to return to usefulness while living in this censorious world! Is it too much to say of such a crime, that it excels in turpitude anything that has been for a century past charged against a professed minister of Christ, and excels it as far as a crime of cool malignity can in guilt excel any crime induced by a sudden inroad of temptation?

My judgment in the matter may be, imperceptibly to myself, too much influenced by the cruel wrongs which I have thus been made to suffer; but as the case appears to me, such a course is not only revolting to religion, but abhorrent from all the dictates of humanity, and is deemed to be in keeping with the characters of the worst of mankind. If Mr. Barnes can free himself from the imputations which are suggested by a calm and candid consideration of these facts, in the name of God and of religion, and of humanity, let him do it; I shall rejoice. What is an assassination by fire or sword, or poison, or the cutting up and concealing of a murdered body, compared with such an assassination of character, and of the happiness of one's self and family, and of all life's dearest hopes? And from what could it have arisen in the breast of that man? Why should he treat me so? "Vanity, in a small degree," says Burke, "and conversant in little things, is of little moment; when full grown, it is the worst of vices, and the occasional mimic of them all; *it makes the whole man false;* it leaves nothing sincere or trustworthy about him; his best qualities are poisoned and perverted by it, and operate exactly as the worst." Well did Mr. Barnes in the first edition of his "Notes on the Gospels," quote from Shakspeare:

"Who steals my purse steals trash—'tis something, nothing;
'Twas mine, 'tis his, and has been slave to thousands;
But he that filches from me my good name,
Robs me of that which not enriches him,
And makes me poor indeed."

Why he has omitted it (as I believe he has), in all his later editions, he can probably explain.

Now, reader, turn to the first three paragraphs of the foregoing report, which Mr. Barnes, in such a frame of mind, suffered himself to draw up, in order to hand down to future ages the character of his Clitus. What think you of them? Look at the following words and ideas repeated and dwelt upon, as though the mind of the writer luxuriated therein: "Improper familiarity"—"perilous to the character of a minister"—"highly improper in one who has the charge of a *Christian* congregation"—"not intended to give indulgence to lascivious feelings"—"*in view of his expression of regret*, they do not regard him as disqualified to be a minister of the Gospel"—"his conduct has been such as to deserve censure"—"should be admonished of his error"—"that he be earnestly exhorted and admonished to exercise a special circumspection in regard to his conduct in future"—"that he give himself to earnest prayer," "and set a special watch upon his conduct," &c. To think of all this emanating from the Rev. Albert Barnes! and under such circumstances!

But the subject has still another bearing, and a very serious one. What is the first and spontaneous impression of your soul in reading this document? Is it not this: That Presbytery believed me guilty, and on account of my "expression of regret" were endeavoring, with as good a grace as possible, to save me from punishment? No one who understands its language, and is unacquainted with the circumstances which resulted in its production, can possibly peruse it without being impressed with this idea, and that a person accustomed as Mr. Barnes is, to writing and weighing the force and import of expressions, and acting too, from a settled and defined plan, should have used language which thus infallibly conveys such an idea, and yet did not design to convey it, I hold to be actually impossible. It is what I can neither comprehend, nor, at least as yet, believe. The point, however, has further and ultimate bearings. I will here specify a few particulars, and others will come up hereafter.

Now, let the reader, with the whole of the foregoing record in his mind's eye, take notice:

1. How utterly impossible it is to avoid a total misapprehension of the case, if nothing further is known of it than is here communicated. The proposal to withdraw the prosecution came altogether and solely from the prosecutor and his friends, and this proposal came from them while I was in the course of examining witnesses for the defence. The prosecutor, through his counsel, proposed to take the case out of the hands of Presbytery, for settlement between ourselves, and it was then agreed to by us, to refer the whole matter to Presbytery for advice in the premises. How perfectly this is lost sight of in the paper of Mr. Barnes! And then, further, in his written version of Mr. Hunt's conversation with him, there is the most cruel injustice done me, as will be more particularly pointed out in another chapter. Mr. Barnes, for a long time, and for obvious reasons, refused to furnish a written copy of the language therein attributed to Mr. Hunt, and in fact did not furnish it until several weeks after his return to Philadelphia, upon which it was, as above given, incorporated in the record.

2. Mr. Barnes' paper does me flagrant injustice, also, by conveying the impression, that the "dissatisfied members" of Bethlehem church had become dissatisfied with me in consequence of this charge; when the fact that they were dissatisfied on other grounds, and before this charge was made, Mr. Barnes heard fully and expressly stated by Mr. Hunt, when giving in his testimony. Fuller and most satisfactory evidence will be presented of this hereafter, when we come to speak of the subsequent action of the congregation. Mr. Barnes, however, knew the fact; and yet in the face of such knowledge, has conveyed an impression exactly the reverse.

3. The impression is also here made, that those members who were "satisfied" with me, and had confidence in me, were those who believed me to have been guilty of this charge, and to have repented. Now there was *not one member of the church or congregation* who took this ground, or who gave any evidence of entertaining such views. This, also, will be fully proved hereafter. That I felt and expressed the deepest sorrow of heart for having been in any way the occasion of injury to the cause of our blessed Redeemer, I readily own; and such sorrow as will, I trust, by the grace of God, effectually preserve me from giving any such occasion hereafter: but that I was penitent for what I never did, or attempted, or designed, or desired, to do, is an idea which Mr. Barnes

ought not to have sought to convey—for such an assertion is as inconsistent with religion and morality, as the fact itself is impossible on his own avowed principles of theology.

4. In respect to the admission of testimony to help the character of the poor creature who had been suborned to tell what no one, even, of my enemies could believe, it was consented to by me, after the prosecution had thus come forward and requested leave of me to withdraw the case from Presbytery, to prevent their judicial action thereon—promising, also, to withdraw the civil suit on condition that I would assent to this proposal. It was then that the counsel asked of me the privilege to allow any one who "felt that they could say something in her favor, to do so—as she was a poor girl, and might be destroyed utterly in public estimation, and thus rendered helpless, if this were not done." Mr. Barnes heard this, and knew that for this reason alone, I permitted the witnesses to be introduced. But where is this matter stated? The very opposite impression is conveyed by his language.

5. Mr. Barnes knew, also, that it was in view of said offer of my enemies to withdraw the suit, so as to be amicably settled by the parties, that I waived the introduction of other witnesses, and of other documentary evidence: witnesses and testimony, too, of more actual importance to the case than had as yet been elicited. But where is this idea suggested by that gentleman? His language conveys an impression the very reverse.

So much for what Mr. Barnes introduced into the paper. But there are other things which are not in it, and which it is impossible he could have forgotten, and the omission of which is in perfect keeping with all the facts connected with his whole procedure in the case. When some of the more prominent members of Presbytery (after the adjournment) came to consider that paper deliberately, they perceived grievous oversights, and mentioned them to Mr. Barnes. The plea, however, that the matter could not then be remedied without a vote of reconsideration, and thus throwing the whole subject out at sea again, was deemed sufficient to require that it be left where it was. A single one of these oversights is all that I can here dwell upon: others will be specified hereafter.

The reader has noticed the course pursued by Mr. Hunt, as described in Part I., and also as acknowledged by himself, under the sanction of an oath. I need not dwell upon it here further than to say, that he owned himself guilty of what ought, under the circumstances of the case, to have brought upon him the heaviest censure, if not deposition from the ministry. Mr. Barnes heard his confession, and was perfectly acquainted with his worldliness, and opposition to everything evangelical: and also knew of his deep-seated and deadly hostility to me, and also how studiously he labored to circumvent everything that I endeavored to do for the glory of God, or the good of man. He knew, too, that, if Mr. Hunt did not originate this plan of attack, he yet did concentrate the efforts against me; and obtained an extra-judicial oath, so as to prevent the poor young woman from retracting what she had said: and that he had written one of the most scandalous and libellous letters against me that malignity itself could suggest: and yet in this minute, Mr. Barnes suffers him to pass without one word of either expressed, or even of implied censure, save by a far-fetched and almost impracticable construction—thus sanctioning his lawless procedures, and leaving it to be inferred that as he was right in what he did, so I was sufficiently guilty to deserve it all. Left him, too, to ravage still with all his fury, the precious fold of Christ; still to distract, and divide, and harass it—as though Presbytery approved of all he did. When they came to think of it afterwards, bitterly did those brethren of Presbytery regret this exculpation. But it was then too late. I hold Mr. Barnes responsible before God for the dreadful consequences which have resulted to the church from this omission. Mr. Hunt could have been restrained, and his wickedness, in its power to do injury, effectually prevented by the stringent disapproval of Presbytery. Mr. Barnes had it fully in his power to apply it, and his brethren, and the church, and community, would have rejoiced to have had it done. But he was obviously prevented by the fear of doing anything which might be construed favorably in regard to myself. Thus he suffered Mr. Hunt to escape; and sad has my own heart been, as I have called to mind the history in 1 Kings 20 : 38–43, in view of this matter. I cannot but believe that all the injury which this mischief-making, worldly-minded old man has since effected, will be required at the hands of Mr. Barnes.

There are other things in this minute which bear still harder against that gentleman; but their proper place will be in a future chapter.

I have remarked above, that no one who is unacquainted with this case, can read the minute of Mr. Barnes, and not feel that Presbytery was therein trying to put a good face upon their effort to save me from merited infamy and destruction. In closing this chapter, I will mention a single instance illustrating this statement; and by means thereof, the reader may obtain a "bird's-eye view" of a part of what it has already effected in this manner. My prosecutor, of course, had a copy of the document sent to him;* and my enemies, seeing at once the impression which a perusal of it could not fail to make, copied and circulated it through the whole country. During my trial at the civil court, it was artfully laid before the judge who had jurisdiction in the case. And, in consequence thereof, he, in the course of the trial, and from the bench, twice reflected on the Presbytery in a severe manner (and allowed the foul-mouthed counsel to call them "*monks*"), for giving such a decision, *and strongly evinced his own determination to set the matter right.* His mind became so blinded by this paper of Mr. Barnes, from the conviction that it was a weak and miserable attempt to screen the guilty from justice, (and how, in the name of sense, could his clear and scrutinizing mind derive any other impression from it?) that he never appeared to notice that the witnesses deposed to an actual physical impossibility; and did not appear to see the constant Free Mason intercourse between my accuser and her father, as narrated in a preceding page. So I was cast in consequence. A wretched pettifogger in Trenton was hired to publish in a paper an account of the trial, and he filled it with the most ridiculous and grossest falsehoods, as I have learned from a person who saw

* The stated clerk was directed to send a copy to him, and another to Mr. Hunt, *before mine was sent to me;* and this, of course, occupied a good deal of his time. So that, by the time that my copy had arrived, the constitutional term for entering a protest had so nearly expired, that before I could draw it up, though I wrote rapidly, it had quite expired. Mr. Barnes, in directing the clerk to send the other two copies first, had, *of course*, not the least idea of debarring me from this right and privilege.

it. The news reached my aged mother. She had always been proud of the son who, in childhood (with two of his brothers), had gone out to work by the week, and then had given her his hard earnings, to assist her, and to cheer her desolate and widowed heart; and who then, by incessant toil, had acquired an education for the holy function, to the exercise of which he felt that God had called him. The news reached her. She immediately wrote to me, stating that she knew the accusation must be untrue; and urged me, (as only a mother could urge,) not to fear to trust still in a good God, who had hitherto been my portion and protector: assuring me that, while she lived, she would rejoice to share with me her last crust of bread. But the matter preyed upon her spirits (how could it be otherwise!); and she soon after received a stroke of paralysis which speedily brought her to the grave! "Cursed be their anger, for it was fierce: and their wrath, for it was cruel! Oh, my soul, come not thou into their secret; unto their assembly, mine honor, be not thou united."

CHAPTER X.

THE NARRATIVE CONTINUED.

"Things ill begun, strengthen themselves by ill."

"*The first step*," says the proverb, "*is the only difficult one.*" This truth is the basis of those impressive exhortations in the word of God against indulging towards another any feeling of prejudice or malevolence: for if even no opportunity is afforded of consummating such emotions by overt action, it is still true, that "he who hateth his brother is a murderer." And then, when once prejudice obtains an ascendency in the soul, it is as impossible to tell, as it would be idle to inquire, to what extremes it may proceed. Its limits will be bounded only by its power to accomplish its desires.

A late writer, on an important branch of moral philosophy, employs these words: "Such is the prevailing tendency, in society, to prey on the reputation of others (especially of those who are at all *distinguished* either in public or private life); such the propensity to impute *bad motives* to *good actions;* so common the fiend-like pleasure of finding or imagining blemishes in beings, on whom even a *motive-judging world*, in general, gazes with respectful admiration, and bestows the sacred tribute of well-earned praise;—that I am convinced there are many persons, worn both in mind and body by the consciousness of being the objects of calumnies and suspicions, which they have it not in their power to combat, who steal broken-hearted to their graves, thankful for the summons of death, and hoping to find a refuge from the injustice of their fellow-creatures, in the bosom of their God and Saviour."* Calumny conquers the most excellent, says the old adage (*νικᾶ γὰρ αἰεὶ διαβολὴ τὰ κρείττονα*), as birds pluck the ripest fruit first. Through Christ I have learned that any degree of calumny may be borne (though nothing is more intolerable than to suffer from it, *ὀυδὲν διαβολῆς εστὶν ἐπιπινώτερον*), still, I must say, that I have keenly felt how true are the foregoing remarks of Mrs. Opiè: and how striking their application

* Opiè's Illustrations of Lying, Chap. VIII. pp. 106–7.

to myself, so far as this attempt to destroy my character is concerned. Often did I resolve to carry my burden in silence to the grave; and I should have done so, had my reputation been the only sufferer. But the honor and interests of my blessed Redeemer's kingdom, in this world, are dearer to me than character or comfort; and an imperious sense of duty forbade me to be silent, and sternly required this effort at my hand. I shall, probably, not live to be essentially benefited by it; but I trust that no short interval will elapse before another man will presume to tread in the footsteps of Mr. Barnes.

At the period of the history now under review, I neither did, nor could, believe, that Mr. Barnes was coolly and deliberately aiming to accomplish the terrible results described in this work: for the facts did not then loom up before my mind with the fullness with which they did when the concealed was discovered, and the plot, in all its serial steps and ramifications, was brought to light. But even at this late day, I am not unwilling to suppose that Mr. Barnes may be able to furnish some such key to the actions and conduct, which produced those results, as may, in a measure, relieve him from the otherwise inevitable consequences, that cannot but accrue to him from a course like this. But if he cannot extenuate or justify what he has done, and still refuses to make what reparation may yet be in his power, to the suffering cause of Christ, let him be given up, to furnish to this age a much-needed example, to illustrate the consequences which may be expected to result from the indulgence of such dispositions as are here exposed. Such an example will be salutary to coming ages, and cannot but operate so as to deter the tempted from a perpetration of similar deeds. But let not this penalty be inflicted by anger, resentment, rivalry, or from any other base and cowardly motive: but from a proper regard to the interests of the church of God. Let it be seen and felt, that though an individual, by prostituting to sinister purposes his influence and position in society, may so far succeed in the accomplishment of his purposes, as to defy detection by any established conventional process, he yet cannot secure impunity. The avenging cobbler of Messina may not arise to make the hardened oppressors tremble; but there still is a tribunal, even in this world, to which the injured may appeal, with confidence that his cause will there be impartially adjudicated, and sooner or later a just decision assigned.

But to return to the history. No sooner had Mr. Hunt perceived, from the foregoing report of Mr. Barnes, that I had consented to the withdrawal of the prosecution, than he at once "burst out of the traces," ceased shedding tears, and attempted to make the impression upon the people, who were standing about in the grove, that the case had been *judicially decided by bringing me in guilty*. The arrangement made by Presbytery for introducing the report of the committee was as follows: The prosecution was to renew their overture to withdraw their charges; then I was to assent to this, and read my paper, and offer what remarks I deemed proper: Mr. Hunt was then to reaffirm what he had said to Mr. Barnes in the morning; after which, the committee was to report. But when Presbytery had reassembled in the church, and called upon Mr. Hunt to speak, he arose, and retracted all that he had said to Mr. Barnes; and one might have supposed, in fact, that no such conversation had taken place between them. In a word, he behaved so perfectly outrageous, and betrayed such a total disregard for his pledged word, that (as before remarked) one member of Presbytery indignantly called out twice, " Brother Landis has been caught in a trap." I need offer no comments upon a procedure like this. Mr. Hunt's aim had been to stay the investigation, and so prevent a judicial decision ; and then to take just such an advantage of it if possible; not supposing that at this stage of the proceedings, a vote of reconsideration could be introduced. It were folly to attempt to describe the indignation of Presbytery at this display of treachery. A motion was instantly made and carried, to hold a second interlocutory at the school-house. And thereupon, the Moderator, (his voice trembling under the effort to repress the feelings which almost overpowered his soul,) said to Mr. Hunt, " What are we to understand, sir, by this conduct of yours?" He answered, (*and the Rev. Albert Barnes was present*,) that after consulting with some of *his friends*, his mind was different from what it was in the morning ; and that he and they thought that I had better go away immediately. He added some other insulting language, the impression of which I retain, though I have forgotten the words.

Reader, if you possess any pure and high-minded principles of honor and veracity, imagine for yourself what effect such conduct must have produced upon the honorable-minded men who composed the majority of our Presbytery. I had said nothing on the subject, except to ask Mr. Barnes, *whether this were the contemplated method of carrying out the design of the committee?* I was so astounded, and sick withal, that in the simplicity of my heart, I did not notice the far-reaching import of this question, and should not have thought of it perhaps, had not the singular expression of Mr. Barnes' eyes, as he glanced into mine, compelled me to call it up afterwards. He however answered the question in these three monosyllables, "I think not ;" and this was all that he said on the subject.* This occurred just before the motion for the interlocutory, and after our arrival at the school-house, I made no remarks, except to brethren who came to converse with me. But when the Moderator put the aforesaid question to Mr. Hunt, and Mr. Hunt was replying thereto, I looked at Mr. Barnes. He was calmly surveying the scene, as an unconcerned spectator, though it was *solely* through his agency, that Mr. Hunt had been enabled thus to outrage the feelings of the Presbytery, and of the church, and of myself. The other members of Presbytery, however, could not control their feelings. The Moderator, so soon as Mr. Hunt had finished his reply, came down upon him in a storm of burning, eloquent indignation, such as a scene like this was alone capable of producing. It had little effect upon Mr. Hunt, however, for he was obviously waiting to hear another voice, before he should resolve whether to persevere or repent. All the Presbytery, also, waited now to hear the burning reproof of the man, who had, through Mr. Hunt, succeeded in bringing the matter into this state. Not a syllable, however, escaped his lips. Another brother, (Mr. Adair) then took up the subject, and seemed to skin the very soul of the old sinner ; he was followed by another, and still another; till, finding that Presbytery was about to reconsider their decision, granting

* A less equivocal answer to that question is still a desideratum.

to the prosecution permission to withdraw the case; he began to cry again, and came to me, his eyes dropping tears, and said, "Brother Landis, will you forgive me?" He also repeated the question with a request to be forgiven. I told him that I forgave him. His subsequent deportment will be described hereafter.

In this last or concluding act of the drama, Mr. Barnes' course was consistent with what it had been throughout. He who should have been first to scorch the soul of Mr. Hunt with the burning words of truth for so shameless a violation of his pledge, said not a syllable. Had he spoken but one stern word of rebuke, the old sinner, whatever had been their previous conversation, would have cowered before it like a truant child. But no such rebuke was given; and hence, and for other reasons, Mr. Hunt concluded justly that he who was not against him was for him.

The intended object of Presbytery in having Mr. Hunt make a speech, as above-stated, was to offer him, by way of introduction to Mr. Barnes' minute, an opportunity to confess the wrongs of which he had been guilty, and formally to reiterate the pledge given by himself and Mr. Conover to withdraw the civil prosecution by entering a *nolle prosequi.* This pledge, moreover, the brethren insisted on having in writing, but Mr. Barnes was not willing to accede to such a requisition. Hence this reiteration was demanded. Now, however, when Mr. Hunt seemed to be deeply humbled on account of his treachery; and had repeatedly begged my forgiveness for treating me as he had done; and there was danger of his confessing more guilt and expressing more sorrow than my enemies deemed politic; and danger too perhaps of letting slip something respecting his previous intercourse with Mr. Barnes, what expedient, reader, do you imagine was adopted to meet this crisis? Will you, *can* you credit the assertion when I tell you that *the Rev. Albert Barnes undertook to make his speech for him, and actually did make it, under the assumed pretence that Mr. Hunt might a second time disappoint the expectations of Presbytery!* The English language itself, or my knowledge of its power of expression is here at fault, for I can find no terms by which adequately to describe conduct like this. The simple fact therefore is all that can be stated. It must speak for itself. Mr. Barnes made for him what ought to have been the last dying-speech of the ministerial life of this old transgressor, and thus the matter was carefully and effectually guarded so as to preclude the possibility of my deriving any advantage from the penitence expressed by Mr. Hunt, either in respect to his late treachery, or his previous conduct. I have in a former chapter presented this speech as it was stated to me by Mr. Barnes on the morning of this day. The repetition by him now differed *toto cœlo* from that, and also from the one which he subsequently incorporated with the minute presented in our preceding chapter.* At the close of the speech which Mr. Barnes now made for Mr. Hunt, (and greatly and manifestly to his relief, for he was at no loss to appreciate the kind interference of his patron,) the old man penitently said "That *is* so. It *is true*, every word of it!" The minute was then read and adopted. Mr. Hunt then came, and reached out his hand to me

* This will be fully demonstrated in another chapter.

saying "God *bless** you, my son Landis!" And he shed many tears. He asked me also again, "Do you forgive me?" I, of course, assured him of my forgiveness. Messrs. Conover and Vanderbelt then came up, and we exchanged professions of forgiveness; and the Presbytery adjourned.

In the evening, during a conversation on the whole subject, with some brethren of the Presbytery who went home with me, I remarked that a brother had asked me whether I did not regard the decision as just; and that I had answered to this effect, that "I considered it unjust as being virtually judicial, when properly it could have been only advisory; and as being based on accusations which were false." To this one of the brethren remarked to me, "Well, you must take what is unjust in this, and set it over against your other sins." This, though said in a playful and pleasant manner, conveyed one impressive truth, which has kept me from murmuring amid all the unjust and cruelly false imputations under which I have suffered. I had not been faithful to my God and Redeemer, and to the souls of my fellow-men, and in view of this consideration, I even "restored that which I took not away."

I was however very much struck with the anxiety which two brethren, (Thompson and Sparhawk, who though greatly under the influence of Mr. Barnes, were in no wise partakers of his spirit towards me,) evinced in endeavoring to induce me to admit that the censure upon me in Mr. Barnes' paper was just. Brother Thompson (to whom I refer in the above paragraph) came to me again on Sabbath evening, and repeated the same query. Brother Sparhawk took equal interest in the matter. No other member of Presbytery did anything of the kind; and these brethren, (both of them good and excellent men,) had no personal interest in doing so, more than the others had; and I am certain that of themselves they would not have exhibited any such anxiety in the matter. From this extreme readiness to oblige Mr. Barnes in other things, I doubt not (and they can correct me if wrong) that it was in compliance with his wishes that they did this; and if so, the reason for his anxiety may be found in the words of a writer quoted in the margin, who remarking on the conduct of some "who pass for good men," observes that they evince a disposition to degrade a rival "if possible through self-degradation," and "to force you to becoming a consenting party to that humiliation."† The quotation is well worthy of serious considera-

* There was present at the trial a shrewd Yankee, (a descendant of Miles Standish, though by no means the heir of all the virtues and piety of that great Puritan,) thoroughly acquainted with the character of Mr. Hunt, who on witnessing the above-described *penitential* scene, said to an acquaintance, that "If instead of the word *bless*, Mr. Hunt had used the term which expresses exactly its opposite, (and beginning with a *d*.) he would have uttered his *real* feelings." Subsequent facts proved the truth of this observation. And his treatment of me calls to mind the remark of one of Le Sage's heroes, who, describing the manner in which his father treated him, says, "At these words he embraced me *very affectionately*, and turned me out of doors."

† An able writer in Blackwood for July, 1845, thus speaks: "Too much even in later life, I have perceived in men that pass for good men, a disposition to degrade (and if possible to degrade through self degradation,) those in whom unwillingly they feel any weight of oppression to themselves by commanding qualities of intellect or character. They respect you: they are compelled to do so: and they hate to do so. *Next, therefore, they seek to throw off the sense of this oppression, and to take vengeance for it, by co-operating with any unhappy accidents in your life, to inflict a sense of humiliation upon you, and (if possible) to force you to becoming a consenting party to that humiliation.*

tion in view of the facts of this history. Napoleon communicated with the imprisoned Pope by *verbal* messages, though the messengers to and from his Holiness were never the wiser. So too, unless I err, the aforesaid brethren performed their mission without being aware of either its import or design.

Thus ended the business with the week; and, as there was no returning to Philadelphia on Saturday evening, the members of Presbytery (except Mr. Barnes and Dr. Brainerd) remained at Bethlehem over the Sabbath. Late as it was, however, Mr. Barnes insisted on proceeding to Flemington, where (as he had ascertained) Mr. Wurts resided — the counsel whom I had engaged to defend me in the civil suit. As Dr. Brainerd had accompanied Mr. Barnes on horseback from Philadelphia, and they were the only members of Presbytery who thus travelled, he of course accompanied him on his return. But so incredibly horrible was the zeal of Mr. Barnes to destroy me utterly, *that, though not personally acquainted with Mr. Wurts, he had an interview, and held a long conversation with him respecting my case!* His conduct needed but this climax to render it complete. Can anything equal it? After having accomplished against me all that he had done, why under heaven should *he* now go and endeavor to sap the confidence which my excellent counsel entertained of the goodness of my cause? Whatever you may *think* of such iniquity, reader, I cannot trust myself to speak of it. The effect of the interview was apparent in a short time, for in a day or two Mr. Wurts *stopped at my residence and urged me to take measures to have the civil suit withdrawn!* I was justly surprised at this; which Mr. Wurts perceiving, he said that Mr. Barnes had called upon him and stated that I had been acquitted of crime, but wished *me* to write to Mr. Conover *and request him to enter a nolle prosequi.* "And if you will do so, Mr. Landis," says Mr. Wurts to me, "Mr. Reading (the State's attorney) will gladly do it; I assure you he will gladly do it." To this I replied as follows: "Mr. Conover has pledged himself to myself and to the Presbytery, that if I would permit him to withdraw the prosecution from Presbytery, he would withdraw it from the civil court. This was his own offer, and I acceded to it. If he is disposed to violate his pledge, my request could not alter his determination; though such a request coming from myself might, and doubtless would, be construed to my disadvantage. I shall therefore make no such request; and would not, though my every interest and hope on earth were involved therein, and should be forfeited by this refusal. The charge upon which I have been indicted is false and malicious, and I shall leave the whole matter with God." "But, my dear sir," says Mr. Wurts with deep and visible emotion, "you have no chance at all in such a case. You have no witnesses that can meet the point, and you must be left entirely at the mercy of theirs. You know what lawyers they have secured,* and

Oh, wherefore is it, that those who presume to call themselves the 'friends' of this man or that woman, are so often those above all others, whom in the hour of death that man or woman is most likely to salute with the valediction—Would God I had never seen your face!" The sentence in *italics* will be seriously pondered by more than one person who witnessed Mr. Barnes' procedure throughout my trial. See also Prov. 10 : 18.

*I had not then engaged Clark for my counsel, or I might have felt this remark to be rather severe. But I did know what *kind* of lawyers my enemies had en-how much the vicious and profligate love to see a clergyman assailed. Indeed, Mr. Landis, you have no chance left you, if the case go to court!" Mr. Wurts would doubtless at once have gone for me to Conover on this business, if I had said the word; but I merely replied that I should not consent in any way or manner to make such a request, and here ended the interview.

I have remarked that my counsel was the best that could be found upon the circuit. Mr. Barnes knew this; and that his main design, in going to Flemington so late on Saturday evening, instead of remaining with his brethren at Bethlehem, *was to have an interview with him*, will be neither questioned nor denied. There may have been subordinate ends, such as a wish to be eight miles on his journey by Monday, &c., which were sufficient to cover his real intention; but to see Mr. Wurts was the great inducement. His *object* in wishing to see him is also clearly apparent from the preceding paragraph. Ponder it, reader; for, viewed in connection with Mr. Barnes' previous efforts to effect my destruction, it transcends any act of cold-blooded cruelty that ever came to my knowledge. What an instance is this of wishing to degrade a rival by means of self-degradation, and of forcing him to becoming a consenting party to the deed!

There is still another matter connected with this. Notwithstanding the declaration made to me by Mr. Barnes on Saturday morning, and repeated by him to the Presbytery, that the prosecution would withdraw the civil suit, I am assured that he did not really believe that they would do so. I do not say that he intended that they should violate their pledge; though we have seen that he refused to have them reduce it to writing and signed by them. But I do say that he did not *believe* that they would keep it. In fact that he *thought* they would not is certain; for we find him a few hours afterwards calling on Mr. Wurts, and urging him *to induce me to request Conover to keep that pledge.* This is satisfactory.* Now if, after he left Bethlehem, some misgivings had entered his mind, that Conover might violate this pledge, why did not he sit down and write to him, instead of wishing to induce *me* to do it? And what is the conclusion from this fact, taken in connection with the fact that he refused to have Conover and Hunt pledge themselves in *black on white*, as the brethren desired they should do? Did he then design, by the course he pursued, and when he found that the Presbytery would infallibly acquit me of the charges, — did he design to deprive me of such judicial decision of that body, pointedly given in my favor, (and which must have had a powerful effect upon the court and public,) and then to let the case go before the court in that wretchedly mutilated and mangled state to which he had reduced it, that so my condemnation might be certain? *Did the Rev. Albert Barnes deliberately design to perpetrate such a deed?* The facts which seem irresistibly to involve this conclusion are before you. If they can bear any other explanation, let him

gaged; and others may know it too when I mention that their names were Hamilton and Halsted, (I forget their surnames,) a couple of hungry hounds, the former of whose portraits, if I mistake not, may be found in Dickens' *Quilp*, and the latter in Fielding's *Murphy;* whose useful *end* may be likewise profitably considered by such individuals.

* Other reasons, substantiating the same truth abundantly, will be found in the next chapter.

have full opportunity to give it, that the reader of these paragraphs may not be compelled to blush at the thought that he himself is a man.

I wish not to awaken within the mind of the reader emotions which might incapacitate him to judge coolly and calmly on this subject; and I only wish to ask him how it happened, as Mr. Barnes had assumed the control of this business in Presbytery; and as he was at least doubtful whether the prosecution would observe their pledge; how did it happen that he was thus willing to place me entirely at their mercy, and in a position so utterly ruinous? Why did he not exact of them a written declaration that they would keep their pledge, on the condition that I would permit them to withdraw the charges?—*a condition stipulated by themselves.* His brethren wished him to do this; and why was it not done, seeing that he was doubtful whether they would keep it, unless they were thus bound? And if there was any necessity for applying to Conover, why did not he, who had taken the control of the business, apply to him, instead of endeavoring to induce me to do it? If these points are not cleared up, there is but one conclusion that can be drawn, and that is stated above. The man who would knowingly and deliberately thus treat even an enemy, would be regarded as having forfeited every shadow of a claim to honor or magnanimity.

A day or two after the brethren returned home, and when I had somewhat recovered from my illness, I furnished one of them with a statement showing how much I had been wronged by this paper of Mr. Barnes; and mentioned likewise the injurious reports which Mr. Hunt and his servant girl had begun to circulate respecting the conversation had with his guests in relation to myself. These matters however have a future bearing. But it is in place to remark here that Mr. Hunt now greatly boasted publicly, that "*He and Mr. Barnes had done up the business*:" a declaration of no trivial importance in this connection.

CHAPTER XI.

RESULTS.

THE members of Presbytery had no sooner gone from Bethlehem, than Mr. Hunt and my other enemies circulated a number of rumors, based upon the most preposterous falsehoods, and proceeding from the same desire to effect my removal, which had prompted their efforts in the first instance; for those persons well knew that while my people sustained me, little could be done with effect, either abroad or at home, to destroy my reputation and thus break me down. These falsehoods were soon traced up, however, and fastened directly upon Mr. Hunt and his servant girl; and this renewed effort of my enemies had no effect, save upon those who had been all along prominent in their opposition to me; they desired an excuse for violating their promise to return to the church again, and Mr. Hunt thus readily furnished one to their hand.

Presbytery was obliged to convene twice in Philadelphia, (in December,) before Mr. Barnes could be satisfied with the *record* of the aforesaid proceedings, or would be prevailed upon to furnish in writing the speech which he had made for Mr. Hunt: for even as made by him, with the phraseology guarded by the most consummate cunning, it contained many admissions of Mr. Hunt, both expressed and implied, which were of the utmost importance to me. And this I am afraid was the great reason why Mr. Barnes refused at once to furnish it. In these two meetings the most kind and sympathizing spirit was manifested towards me, by all the members who had been at Bethlehem, except Mr. Barnes. His heart, and God knows why, was still steeled against all tender emotions, though in full view of his whole course as heretofore described. What human being would not have thought, that knowing as Mr. Barnes did, how much I had always had to struggle with at Bethlehem, and that I was now, either by oversight or design on his part, left to struggle onward with all these superadded burdens, his heart would have relented? That seeing a brother who had always stood by him in his difficulties, now almost crushed to earth by his management; and, unsupported except by Heaven, against all the adverse influences which the old man with his power unimpaired by any censure, was now again endeavoring to concentrate against me; asserting too that his course herein was sustained by the absence of disapproval in the paper of Mr. Barnes; who would not have thought that in consideration of all these matters, in connection with a perfect knowledge of how the vile rumor was got up against me, he would have been induced at last to step forward and return a little of the kindness which I had so freely, and at so high a cost, extended to him in the day of his trial: or, if he were incapable of this, that he at least would not have endeavored in every way possible to chill the sympathies and kind feelings of my brethren, which they were so ready and so desirous to extend to me? Why did he not thus step forward? And why, instead of this, did he still continue to do all in his power to discourage the growth of their affectionate sympathies, which were now peculiarly active in view of these considerations? Mr. Barnes knows why this was done; and God knows it likewise. If such conduct be right in a clergyman and professed follower of Christ, Mr. Barnes will be sustained therein; but if otherwise, he may rely upon it that every such blow struck at his brother will, with a fearfully increased force, rebound against its author. See Is. 51 : 21-23.

As above remarked, the brethren were very desirous to have the statement and pledge of Mr. Hunt and the prosecution written down and given to me: they urged it upon Mr. Barnes; but their reasons for wishing it seemed to be the very reasons why he refused; so that he declined for a long time even to write the speech of Mr. Hunt; until the phraseology which he employed had full time to vanish from the recollection of those who had heard it. In illustration of this, his refusal, I must here insert a single brief letter from a member of Presbytery, written soon after his return home. I give the whole letter; and it may speak for itself.

"PHILADELPHIA, Nov. 25, 1847.

"MY DEAR BROTHER LANDIS: From what Bro. Barnes said on Monday at Bristol, I fear that he will *not* write out Father Hunt's statement, which he authorized Bro. Barnes to repeat. If he do not send it to you, do not, I beg of you, read your written statement. *The Resolutions of the Presbytery alone should be read.* I urged Bro. B. to send the statement to you; but whether he will or not I cannot say. Bro. Gilbert said he would urge him to do it. I hope he will.

"We reached home on Tuesday morning at 2 o'clock, having been delayed by a fog in the river from 7 to 12 o'clock."

The writer of this will not disown it; though, as no necessity requires my doing so, I shall not disclose his name. But what was the design of Mr. Barnes in this strange refusal? It is a matter worthy of inquiry in this connection. He volunteered to deliver the speech for Mr. Hunt, and did deliver it: and although he had carefully guarded many of the expressions, and utterly changed the tone and argument of the speech from that which he repeated to me in the morning, (as I shall show presently,) he could not but discover that its repetition before the congregation, even in this mutilated state, was attended with great and good effect. But inasmuch as he thus undertook so willingly to *deliver* this speech for Mr. Hunt, why, in the name of candor, should he now refuse to *write it*, though requested again and again by the members of Presbytery to do so? This refusal was given immediately after he had delivered it for Mr. Hunt; and when Mr. Hunt would not only have consented to its being written, but would have willingly *signed* it. Yet Mr. Barnes *then* refused, though urged by his brethren to consent to it, and he *continued* to refuse for some weeks afterwards. Now why was this? If his reasons for refusal were just and sufficient, why should they not have still continued to operate so as to induce him to withhold it altogether? instead of merely inducing him to withhold it only until sufficient time had elapsed to permit the form and force of the expressions to be varied without the liability of detection? These are questions which demand a direct answer.

But let us now to the speech itself. In Chapter X. I have given it as amended and written out to be handed down to posterity by this ecclesiastic: *with the tone of the statements attributed to Mr. Hunt altogether changed from what it was when he said over the thing to me in the morning, and to the congregation in the evening.* I feel an unconquerable disgust at the task of exposing such duplicity, but will specify a few particulars.

1. The reader will remember that at Mr. Barnes' own request, I had an interview with him in the morning of the last day of the trial, and that in this interview he purported to detail to me the remarks of Mr. Hunt *as an inducement* for me to consent to stay proceedings, and to permit the prosecution to be withdrawn. *This was his sole avowed purpose, and everything said by him to me on that occasion was designed to secure this end!* Mr. Hunt had been weeping, &c., and said that he relented for his treatment of me; that Mr. Barnes should see me, and learn whether I had a conciliatory spirit towards him. Such were *the arguments* to induce me to comply with the request. Then *an apology* is offered for this his treatment,—he thought that I had slighted him. Here, then, is the object of the interview. *And it was in view of all this*, as even a child can see, that I refrained from going on with the defence, examining witnesses, &c. I acceded, therefore, to the request of Mr. Hunt, because of this his penitential confession that he relented or repented of his cruel iniquity towards me. I had asked no favor; I intended to ask none: and all the Presbytery and people knew it. Such are the facts: plain to the apprehension of all. But now in the whole of this *written* speech, where is this idea developed? Where can the least vestige of it be found? It is excluded by Mr. Barnes, and the whole tone and argument are utterly changed! To comment upon such a deed would be an insult to the reader.

2. The written speech also represents Mr. Hunt as proposing, and me as acceding to the proposal, to submit the case to Presbytery for their advice. And hence Mr. Barnes, though against the expressed convictions of the other members, brings in (as he doubtless intended to do from the first) a *judicial* decision, under the pretence that it is advisory. Now, reader, look calmly at this whole matter as it stands upon record. That I should have thus consented to a *judicial* decision, before the most important part of my testimony was elicited, none but a fool could suppose for a moment. And that such *was not* the intention either of Mr. Hunt, or the Presbytery, or myself, is placed beyond all doubt (if any doubt could exist on such a subject) by the letter of Dr. Fairchild, in Chapter VIII. above. The prosecution was withdrawn, because Mr. Hunt, acting for and on behalf of Mr. Conover, relented for having treated me as he had done. This being a clear confession that he had led on Mr. Conover and his daughter, and made tools of them; and an acknowledgment of my innocence; I, of course, had no further demand for witnesses: for here was the admission that the whole accusation was, either through malice or misapprehension, a miserably got-up affair to do me an injury which I did not deserve. We therefore submitted the case to Presbytery *for advice* simply, and nothing more; for in the nature of things it could be for nothing more. But now this ecclesiastical self-appointed judge hurries a *judicial decision* through Presbytery: a judicial decision, also, which, while it inflicts *censure* on me, *justifies in effect the very course of conduct which Mr. Hunt had confessed to be wrong, and of which he had professed truly and deeply to repent!* Words fail me here! There is something about this blundering, high-handed, and unparalleled iniquity, which almost approximates the sublime.

3. In this whole interview, Mr. Barnes said not one syllable to me of any such thing as the written speech contains on the subject of my being "*poor and dependent:*" but now he introduces it with a gusto, as though he was saying something which surely must inflict a sense of degradation upon me, and lessen me in the eyes of others.* He represents

* I had, by my writings in defence of this ecclesiastic, relieved him from the imputations of fundamental error, and restored him to the confidence of multitudes who viewed his productions with suspicion and distrust. Thus had I assisted him in establishing a reputation which secured the ready sale of his publications, and by which he has been enabled to lay up perhaps $50,000. And now, because I have chosen another course, and, as I pass on through life, prefer to distribute the means which God bestows upon me, he thus arrogates to himself superiority, and twits me with being "*poor and dependent.*" How truly has Burke remarked, (when referring to the characters of men,) that "It is in the relaxation of security, it is in the expansion of prosperity, it is in the hour of dilatation of the heart, and of its softening into festivity and pleasure, that the real character of men is discerned. If there is any good in them, it appears then or never. Even wolves and tigers, when gorged with their prey, are safe and gentle. It is at such times that noble minds give all the reins to their good nature. They indulge their genius even to intemperance, in kindness to the afflicted, in generosity to the conquered; forbearing insults, forgiving injuries, overpaying benefits. Full of dignity themselves, they respect dignity in all, but they feel it sacred in the unhappy. But it is then, and basking in the sunshine of unmerited fortune, that low, sordid, ungenerous, and reptile souls swell with their hoarded poisons; it is then that they display their odious splendor, and shine out in the full lustre of their native villainy and baseness. It is in that season that no man of sense or honor can be mistaken for one of them."

Mr. Hunt as *compassionating* me, and endeavors to impart this idea to the whole speech, whereas his true and only attitude as represented to me in the morning by Mr. Barnes, was that of *a penitent supplicating a favor at my hands:* and this was the attitude taken by the prosecution so soon as they discovered from the evidence which I was adducing, what their fate must inevitably be at the hands of Presbytery. How, then, durst the Rev. Albert Barnes thus venture to change the whole aspect of a paper like this? How durst he trifle with human character in this way?

But further: In this paper he represents Mr. Hunt as giving a *reason* for this *mercy* towards me, to wit, "that it was wrong to turn me away at this season of the year," because "I was poor and dependent:" hence he "had *some* relentings." It is difficult to speak with temper of such shameless iniquity. Now, Mr. Barnes, though purporting to detail the whole, or, at least, the substance, of his conversation with Mr. Hunt, said *not one syllable* of all this to me; and he knows that if he had, I should have been very prompt with both message and messenger. I am quite confident, too, that he never gave any such *reason* in his detail of the conversation before the congregation: though he may have done so, for I was very unwell at the time, and may not have noticed it. At all events, he never breathed such an idea to me: and his object in placing it upon record is *to give a different coloring to the withdrawal of the prosecution.* But did Mr. Hunt use this language to Mr. Barnes? Admit that he did, and that the foregoing were his reasons for wishing me to consent to the withdrawal of the prosecution: and what right had Mr. Barnes to withhold them utterly from me, and then to introduce them in this manner into a record? But a darker shade still is cast over the transaction, by the fact (referred to in a former chapter), that before he delivered this speech for Mr. Hunt, he heard him expressly deny any such *merciful* disposition towards me. Mr. Barnes, I repeat it, was present, and heard Mr. Hunt express this denial, and affirm that he wished me to leave my pastoral charge immediately. If, therefore, he had told Mr. Barnes this wretched rigmarole in the morning, and given it as a reason why he "relented," why did not Mr. Barnes now remind him of it? There was a plain and pointed issue between them, with a superaddition of all possible motives calling on Mr. Barnes to speak in reproof of the wretched old man. Why, then, was he silent?

4. Further: In Mr. Barnes' interview with me in the morning, and in his repetition of the remarks of Mr. Hunt before Presbytery and the congregation in the evening, he distinctly and emphatically stated that Mr. Hunt had said that "he *relented* on account of the course which he had pursued against me, and that he appeared to have been weeping on account of it; *for Mr. Landis is greatly beloved by the congregation;*" [further, that Mr. Hunt could not sleep during the night in consequence of thinking of his conduct towards Mr. Landis; that he was up early in the morning, and came into Mr. Barnes' room before he was dressed, to talk with him on the subject; and that his wife had urged him (Mr. Hunt) to stop in his course; and that he wept like a child and said he *relented* (or repented) that he had gone so far against Mr. Landis. It was urged at Presbytery that Mr. Hunt's statements (through Mr. Barnes) should be written down and signed by Mr. Hunt; but Mr. Barnes refused again and

again to write his verbal statement down at that time.]* and more of the same kind. All this, I say, Mr. Barnes mentioned to me in the morning, and to Presbytery in the evening, *as furnishing a reason why the prosecution should be withdrawn ; and yet there is not one word of the whole to be found in the written speech !* Everything is omitted except the word "*relent*," and that is employed in the most carefully qualified and guarded manner. At the meeting of Presbytery, Mr. Barnes said that "*Mr. Hunt wept like a child, and said* that he *relented* on account of the course which he had pursued." In the written speech, this most important statement is changed into "he had *some* relentings." Oh, can anything exceed such conduct in baseness and cruelty ! Whatever others may think, I have no hesitation in saying that rather than thus trifle with the character of a servant of Christ, and with the interests of religion, and the souls of men, I would beyond all comparison, (if I must choose,) incur the guilt of Dr. Dodd and take his doom. Perhaps I am incapable of calmly weighing a matter that has so deeply affected and injured me: but this is really what I feel, in view of this utter changing of the tone and argument of this speech. The bald impression (so far as Mr. Barnes can effect it) is thus to be made on the minds of all who peruse these records, that Mr. Hunt was, in this matter, actuated by kindness and pity towards myself; and not by his own justly excited fears and sense of criminality ! And this false impression must be conveyed by Mr. Barnes in the very face of Mr. Hunt's counter statements ; and against all the above-stated facts !

5. In Mr. Barnes' interview with me in the morning, he said not one word on the subject of my being "on a sort of trial for three or six months." If Mr. Hunt stated anything of this kind to Mr. Barnes, and if it were worthy of being mentioned publicly, and in the written speech, surely it should have been mentioned to me. Why then was it omitted ? But Mr. Barnes knows, as well as every Presbyterian, that such an idea, under such circumstances, is the sheerest nonsense ! and why, then, was it brought forward in public at all ? *Was it to make the impression that Mr. Hunt had gained the prosecution, at the same time that he had anxiously requested permission to withdraw it ?* Mr. Barnes certainly knew that, according to our constitution, the very idea of such "a sort of trial" is preposterous ! but so desirous is he to let no opportunity pass of striking his unoffending brother, that he thus travels entirely out of his way in order to find an occasion for doing so.

6. The same remarks apply with equal force to the clause, "David sinned and was forgiven," &c., which was inserted with the manifest design of changing the tone and argument of the speech as aforesaid. But the remark in that clause was in no way hinted to me in the morning, or anything like it. Mr. Barnes came to me professedly to solicit a favor for Mr. Hunt—and that favor was permission to withdraw the charges on which he and Mr. Conover had prosecuted me, and which they had been endeavoring to establish against me ; *and Mr. Barnes knows, in his own soul, that, if they could have proved those charges, the*

* The passage included in brackets was added to this point in the narrative by a member of Presbytery, a clergyman, who was present at the trial, and who has read this work in manuscript. Mr. Barnes, in delivering the speech, notwithstanding all his care in guarding it, was obliged to utter all this for Mr. Hunt, and Mr. Hunt endorsed it all by saying, "*That is true, every word of it.*"

prosecution never would have been withdrawn. Now the fatuity of attempting to reconcile this with the reference to David's and Peter's sins (unless the reference was really to Mr. Hunt himself, and not to me), baffles description. It would be equivalent to saying: "Mr. Landis, David sinned and was forgiven—and so did Peter; and Mr. Hunt, believing you to be guilty of the charges brought against you, thinks that you ought to be forgiven, though he does not know whether you are penitent or not. He therefore begs that you will not refuse him the privilege of withdrawing his charges against you. Don't go on to prove your innocence, for he has wept like a child, and was not able to sleep all night, because he has thus accused you." Had Mr. Barnes made such a speech as this, can any one suppose that I would have stayed the investigation, ceased to examine witnesses, &c., when my most important testimony was still unheard? Well might Mr. Thompson exclaim: "Brother Landis has been caught in a trap!" There is something awfully dark hanging over Mr. Barnes' agency in this business, but which I am persuaded that God will sooner or later dissipate, and expose the whole matter to the noon-day light of heaven.

7. Another instance of cruel injustice to me may be found in the fact that, though Mr. Barnes here repeats all these statements, asserted to have been made to him in a conversation with Mr. Hunt—and although he states, likewise, that he had seen and conversed with me on the subject, he yet never, in any way, even refers to those counter statements which I made to him on the occasion, and which we have given in Chapter VIII. above. Now why was the impression thus left by him upon the mind of the reader that I had acquiesced in all the nonsense and falsehood of Mr. Hunt's asserted declarations, and that therefore the truth of his representations is undeniable? The reason is too plain to be mistaken. Had my remarks been repeated, or only summarily given in the written speech, or before the congregation, Mr. Barnes could not successfully have played the game he was playing. My reply would have shown what his own remarks to me must have been.

8. Another instance (more striking if possible), evincing the disposition of Mr. Barnes to ruin me, utterly, is the following: Mr. Hunt, as the reader has seen, had, in his testimony before the Presbytery, entirely neutralized the force of all his malignant slanders against me, even though he seemed to have adopted the Satanic maxim, *Fortiter calumniari, aliquid adhærebit*, for he had deposed that "*all the women are in favor of Landis.*" This was a strong fact, and could not but make a powerful impression in my favor; for thus all that instinctive abhorrence of vice, and that peculiar discernment and power to discriminate a vicious character, under whatever guise he may assume, which are so justly attributed to pious and intelligent females, was at once, and by the prosecution itself, brought in to exculpate me from his accusations of immorality. The impolicy of this step, after it was too late to retrace it, was apparent to all who were aiming at my overthrow. Greatly did my brethren of Presbytery (with the one exception) rejoice over this admission of Mr. Hunt, and they were not backward in giving expression to their joy, for they felt towards their accused brother as Christ would have them feel. In his conversation with me in the morning, Mr. Barnes brought out this fact substantially by telling me that Mr. Hunt said

"I was greatly beloved by the congregation." But now, reader, suppose there was a human being capable of wishing to neutralize this strong fact, in the most effectual manner, by destroying its force, and how do you suppose that he would seek to accomplish it? I really cannot think of any course so effectual for the purpose as that which Messrs. Barnes and Hunt adopted on this occasion; for, take notice, if you please, with what cunning there is incorporated with this speech the little clause: "*You know how strong the attachment of women is to their ministers!*" But cunning as is this stroke of policy, however, it can afford no relief to these gentlemen—for however strong the attachment of intelligent, virtuous women may be to *their ministers if virtuous*, nothing can exceed their just detestation of them *if vicious;* and none could discern such a character sooner than they, if the vice were of the kind thus charged upon me by Mr. Hunt and his friends. The fact therefore that both before and after the prosecution, the female members of this very large church and congregation stood my firm friends and supporters, is, of itself, with every reflecting and candid mind, sufficient to expose to scorn such attempts as these men had made to injure me. And what can exceed, in meanness, the effort made in this paper to deprive me of the support derivable from this consideration?

There are many other things in this speech, and connected with it, which call for remark, some of which, however, will occur to the mind of the reader. But I must dismiss the subject with a reference to one or two other points.

9. Mr. Barnes here represents Mr. Hunt as saying to him that, "*perhaps* there ought to be an *admonition* from the Presbytery to Mr. Landis *to be cautious* on the subject;" "and that he should *remain and preach* three or six months on a sort of trial." *And all this is represented to have been said before Mr. Hunt knew "whether there was the same conciliatory spirit in Mr. Landis;"* and it all was based, not upon Mr. Hunt's belief of the charges, but upon my having "frankly admitted that I was sorry for having given any occasion for reproach;" *which clause Mr. Barnes has, however, omitted in his written speech, though he employed it as a part of the speech to me in the morning.* (See Chapter VIII. above.) And now, reader, you may here obtain a glimpse of the game which this man was, through Mr. Hunt, playing against me; and also see an exemplification of the truth, that, however cunningly crime may be perpetrated, it never can sufficiently guard all the avenues of detection. Just compare these declarations of Mr. Hunt with the representations which he had made in his letter to Mr. Barnes (which is given in Part II. Chapter II. above,) and especially with the following deliberate assertion of his: "*It is out of my power not to believe this affidavit to be true.*" Here are the facts; and now what is the inference from them? Is it that Mr. Hunt believed that crimes of so grave and heinous a nature as those which the affidavit charged upon me deserved "*perhaps* an *admonition*" to the criminal "*to be cautious on the subject;*" at the same time that "he should remain and preach three or six months," *though it was unknown whether he was penitent or not?* No one in their senses can believe this. The only other possible inference therefore, is, that Mr. Hunt felt, and knew, and acknowledged, that the charges themselves were as false as they are scandalous, and got up to serve only a sinister

purpose; and that he, therefore wished me to allow to him the privilege to withdraw them. So that here we have a fair and full withdrawal of the charges by Mr. Hunt, and a retraction of his belief of their truth; and of course, a clear acknowledgment, that his object in sending Mr. Barnes to me was to get me to consent to his withdrawing them, as false and unsustained; and consequently, that it was on this ground, and this only, that I consented to their withdrawal, and complied with the expressed wishes of Mr. Hunt, that "the proceedings might be HERE stayed." And now, reader, oblige me by calmly considering whether these things be so, for the facts and documents are before you. If these things are so, then under what category are we to rank a deed, coolly and deliberately perpetrated, that would, (in a case too where character, and the honor of religion are concerned,) exclude all these considerations, and substitute contrary ones in their place! Is there an event in the history of literature or morals that, all the circumstances being considered, can compare with this?

10. I must not omit to notice also "*the change*" here attributed to Mr. Hunt; and which, at the close of the speech, is presented by Mr. Barnes in the light of an illustration from Mr. Hunt himself: "You see *what a change* has been wrought in my mind since yesterday." This expression was employed in the delivery of the speech, at Bethlehem, and is substantially incorporated with it, as written by Mr. Barnes. It had great effect at Presbytery upon the congregation; for as Mr. Barnes there repeated it, this clause had direct reference to the fasting, and praying, and weeping, and relenting of Mr. Hunt, on account of the course pursued by him, in persecuting me; and pretending to believe the affidavit, and what not. But the effect is really ludicrous, if you look into the amended and written speech, for the reasons of this relenting and change of mind. The statement of the fact of such a change, Mr. Barnes could not omit in the new version, for all the brethren of Presbytery noticed and remembered the expression. What was it then, about which this *change* took place? and in respect to what did these "*relentings*" occur? Though the concluding sentence makes this change to have been very considerable, the amended and written speech makes Mr. Hunt *relent in no practicable or available sense whatever*. Did he, therefore, thus relent and change, because "Mr. Landis was poor and dependent"? And did Mr. Barnes thus sanction such a contemptible reason, as sufficient to justify the arrest of a prosecution on charges so grave and scandalous? Weak as Mr. Hunt is, he never pretended to do such a thing; and Mr. Barnes never would have sanctioned it, if he had. His disposition towards myself would have prevented it, if nothing else. Why then did Mr. Hunt thus weep and relent? Was it because "Mrs. Hunt loved her pastor?" Was this the cause of so great a change? and a sufficient reason to stay such a prosecution? The man must be an idiot who would believe it. Why then did Mr. Hunt thus relent? Was it because he had endeavored (either formally or informally) to remove a base and wicked man (as he had represented me to be) from the pastorate of the church? And did Mr. Barnes approve of relenting on such ground? Did he sanction it? and this too before he knew whether that pastor was penitent for the crimes laid to his charge? I ask again, therefore, what was the reason of this great change in Mr. Hunt—

this fasting, and praying, and sleepless night, and relenting, and weeping like a child, &c.? There is but one other reason—omitted, however, by Mr. Barnes, in the speech itself, to wit: *Mr. Hunt thus repented because of his iniquitous treatment of me in relation to the charges and prosecution; and of course this was the reason why he wished the proceedings then and there stayed, and the prosecution and charges withdrawn.* To attempt to add one word of comment on such a fact, were a reflection on the reader.

In a word, then, the whole paper, so far as the speech and Mr. Barnes' minute are concerned, is just such a production as is, in the best and most artful manner, calculated to bleed a brother to death in the public estimation, without his being able in any way to help himself, or obtain redress. And though the subject is fruitful of reflections and remarks, a single one or two must suffice. I ask, then, why did Mr. Barnes act thus in the matter? Why did he thus reverse the whole tone and argument of this speech? Why did he endeavor, in unison with Mr. Hunt, to save him from the difficulties in which his crimes had involved him; and also from their just punishment? And why did he also, in this most incredibly heartless manner, labor to prevent my deriving any advantage from all those circumstances, so favorable to me, which had been elicited throughout the trial? If forgetfulness be pleaded, how happens it that he refused to write and give to me the statement of Mr. Hunt, when the brethren first desired him to do so; and when there was a fair prospect of its being really useful to me? And how happens it too, that this *forgetfulness* extends only to those things which had made, and must continue to make, a strong impression in my favor? Why should they alone be forgotten and omitted, and everything else be remembered and retained?—to say nothing of the additions aforesaid. These questions must be answered. "*Personal enmity*," says Horne Tooke, "*is a motive fit only for the devil.*"

As I now dismiss this paper, I desire the reader once more to turn to it, and note, that it is a concentration of all that my enemies, with all their efforts, and wealth, and influence, together with the deepest malignity, (in the person of Mr. Hunt,) seated at the helm and guiding those efforts, have, even with the cruel agency and self-appointed secretaryship of the Rev. Albert Barnes, succeeded in laying to my charge. As it stands, it is sufficiently bad, to be sure. But take it even as it is, without any of the overwhelming statements to which I have referred, and what is there in it to justify the relentless manner in which Mr. Barnes (in person and by representatives,) has ever since been following me up with untiring efforts, to impair my influence and ruin my character? Efforts, alas! which have fearfully succeeded, for a time; (for they have wounded religion, and hurried a mother and a wife, broken-hearted, to the grave!)—but which have brought as fearful guilt upon their projectors! Prejudice, and personal animosity may, and in this world, doubtless, often do, array themselves in the costume of Justice and Retribution; but it is not often, even in this world, that the mask can be supported against ultimate exposure. God grant that so it may ever be.

What a lesson too is here taught those brethren in New York and elsewhere, who, without troubling themselves with any proper inquiry into the case, have adopted the representations emanating from Mr.

Barnes as unbiassed and impartial? Not one of them wrote to me on the subject, to learn what I could say in relation to it; and when I have met them they made no inquiries, but even passed me without recognition. They were satisfied with merely assuming that Mr. Barnes could have had no sinister design in what he said and did, and that therefore his representations must be according to truth and righteousness: and hence they have treated me and spoken of me as guilty of I know not what; but at all events, as sufficiently so to justify such treatment on their part. What remedy can a man have when accused and treated thus? Had they been treated and accused as I have been, they could have seen, and would have felt that it was all wrong; and why could they not perceive it to be so in the case of their brother? Had they treated me otherwise, I should have had the opportunity which I have been anxiously wishing and praying for, to set this matter right, without the terrible exposures of this narrative; and perhaps so as to have rescued and saved from its consequences, my poor erring brother Barnes. Those excellent brethren, who know that I have ever treated them with the most affectionate and respectful consideration, could have learned also from the minutes of our General Assembly, and from the dismission and recommendation of the Presbytery that tried me, that I stand as fair in the church as they do. And what right had they thus without inquiry to assume against me that Mr. Barnes' representations were just and impartial? Perhaps it is scarcely possible for poor frail humanity to avoid yielding somewhat to so strong an influence brought thus artfully to bear upon it: but in all such matters at least, it is much safer to abide rigidly by the precepts of Christ than to trust our own feelings and inferences. Quaint old Quarles expressed the truth when he said "Be not censorious, for thou knowest not whom thou judgest: it is a more dexterous error to speak well of an evil man, than ill of a good man. And safer for thy judgment to be misled by simple charity, than uncharitable wisdom. He may tax others with a privilege, who hath not in himself what others may tax." The right of these brethren to treat a brother as they have treated me, may well be reconsidered by them; for by such a procedure they have unwittingly associated their efforts with those of Mr. Barnes. My own work in this world will soon be finished; the deep anguish of spirit occasioned by the necessity which required the preparation and publication of this narrative, and also the consequences which will thence result to me in the present state of things, (for I am not so sanguine as to expect that this narrative will bring my persecutors at once to repentance,) cannot but hasten the period of my departure; and then this whole matter, if not previously righted, must meet them at the tribunal of Him who has taught his followers that such proceedings can never receive his sanction.

CHAPTER XII.

ACTION OF THE LADIES.

The trial at the church was attended by a mass of human beings, who could not be accommodated within the house of worship, large as it is: But after the testimony on behalf of the prosecution had been heard, many returned home, declaring that it was all they needed to hear on the subject, in order to assure them that I had been falsely accused. My enemies with great industry had asserted and circulated many things against me; but now when their boasted strength and resources were tasked to the utmost for the production of appropriate results, a real *parturiunt montes, nascitur ridiculus mus*, was witnessed:—forth came this poor, contemptible, self-contradictory tale. The story of the prosecution itself forever settled the matter with that portion of the community who were previously unacquainted with the facts. So absorbing, however, was the interest felt in the trial by the church and congregation itself, that it attended *en masse* throughout. Hence the strange proceedings of the Rev. Albert Barnes attracted much attention, and excited not a little remark. His name had always been an honored one there, and though I had known of his idiosyncrasies, as they were charitably termed, no one, either of my family or congregation, knew of them through me; and his acts which I had noticed both previous to the trial and during it, were kept locked up within my own bosom, save where they had attracted the observation of others, who spoke of them to me. So that Mr. Barnes is indebted solely to himself for the just appreciation of his character and conduct entertained since then by the people of Bethlehem.* If men will thus trifle with, and prostitute their influence and position in society, they must take the consequences.

At the close of the meeting of Presbytery, however, the ladies of the church and congregation resolved amongst themselves to have a meeting, as soon as possible, for the purpose of expressing their views and feelings; and Thursday, the 25th inst., (being the day of annual thanksgiving,) was finally fixed on for this purpose. When I heard that this was their intention, I earnestly advised and besought them to desist from the undertaking. Nothing was replied to this entreaty, however, and so I gave up the point. And so soon as the religious services closed, and the benediction was pronounced, on the day aforesaid, notice was given that "*when* the gentlemen had retired, the ladies would hold a meeting." They did so, and the following preamble and resolutions are the result, and were unanimously adopted:

"*Whereas*, The females of the Bethlehem Congregation, feeling themselves grossly insulted by the insinuations of the Rev. H. W. Hunt, Sen., during the late meeting of Presbytery, held in the church on the third week of the present month, [they] have met and adopted the following resolutions, embodying their views and sentiments in relation to this matter:

"*Resolved*, That we feel ourselves deeply aggrieved, that one who is bound by the most sacred obligations to protect the reputation of the daughters of the church, should by his invidious assertions, expose them to the jests and sneers of a promiscuous assembly, by denouncing their pastor as a man of impure morals, dangerous to the community, corrupting and taking improper liberties with females, adding that 'the women all go for Landis;' making it appear by induction, that the 'women' were equally corrupt in advocating and supporting a minister whom he (Mr. Hunt) had publicly denounced as 'the likeness of Bishop Onderdonk.'

"Therefore, *Resolved*, That the highly offensive clause in the paper, read by

* With the mass of that people, Mr. Barnes has ever since stood in the rank in which he then placed himself: that is, with Mr. Hunt and his associates. And since then, his name and influence at Bethlehem are of no more account than the name and influence of Mr. Hunt himself.

Mr. Barnes,* and dictated by Mr. Hunt, on Saturday last, alluding to this subject, shall be erased from the paper, and not suffered to be read from the pulpit on next Sabbath.

"*Resolved*, That the clause be also erased in which Mr. Hunt says, 'Mr. Landis shall preach three months on trial.' The matter was submitted to the decision of Presbytery, and we cannot acknowledge Mr. Hunt's right to dictate on this subject.

"*Resolved*, That we do not consider this a proper subject for jesting. The late deep wound inflicted on the Church of Christ bears a most impressive moral to be held up to all churches, to both pastor and people—that while the former should avoid even the 'appearance of evil,' the latter should be deeply sensibleof the sacred nature of a minister's character.

"*Resolved*, That we do not believe that any female of truth or purity of character, has ever accused Mr. Landis of taking improper liberties; and that the base slanders circulated to ruin and destroy him, originated with the 'father of lies;†' who, like other great inventors, has lost much of his reputation by the very ingenious improvements recently made upon him.

"*Resolved*, That as the insults were publicly given by Mr. Hunt, we feel it due to our wounded feelings that an apology equally public be made to the daughters of the church, as we are resolved to be 'first pure, then peaceable.'

"*Resolved*, That a copy of these Resolutions be sent to Mr. Hunt, and that Mr. Landis shall not be made acquainted with them until carried into effect."

"*November* 25, 1847."

Such were the feelings and sentiments of the ladies of my charge in view of these efforts to impair my usefulness; and how cruel and relentless must that heart be that could, in view of such facts, deliberately set to work still to crush a suffering and injured brother, who, if only left to himself, and without the countenance and support of Mr. Barnes, could have outridden the storm in triumph; and have saved his congregation from disunion and distraction. Yet such a disposition did Mr. Barnes exhibit. He knew that the multitude do not often trouble themselves to inquire into the circumstances of a case, but are satisfied with bare results; and feeling assured that I could never be seriously prostrated while my people thus adhered to me, he had the alternative either to abandon the aim which he had thus steadily been pursuing, or to follow it up still further, until, by the dissolution of the pastoral relation between myself and a people whose welfare was dearer to me than life itself, the public mind should be led to the conclusion, that my congregation deemed me guilty of the charges which had been preferred against me.

I leave the foregoing resolutions of the ladies to speak for themselves, adding only a single remark in explanation of the phrase which speaks of the parts of the paper of Mr. Barnes, which "shall not be read from the pulpit *on next Sabbath*." At the adjournment of Presbytery it was expected that the clerk of Presbytery would send to me before the Sabbath referred to, the report of Mr. Barnes. Through delays however, which were mainly attributable to him, and for what reason the reader

* The ladies supposed that Mr. Barnes *read* the statements made by him for Mr. Hunt, because he looked on a paper which he held in his hand while repeating them. Many others made the same mistake. Mr. Barnes may have had a few phrases or "catch-words" noted down; but the paper he was looking on, was that which contained his report aforesaid, and which was not large enough to hold both the speech and the report.

† Mr. Hunt foolishly took great umbrage at this expression, professing to think that he himself, and not Satan, was here alluded to.

must judge, the report did not reach me until about a month afterwards. I had informed my people that I should read it to them, and hence the reference to its being read in the resolves of the ladies.

CHAPTER XIII.

VIEWS OF THE CASE ENTERTAINED BY MY BRETHREN OF PRESBYTERY.

The views and feelings entertained towards me by my brethren of the Presbytery (always excepting Mr. Barnes and a satellite or two, not present at the trial,) after the trial was over, ought, perhaps, to be referred to here. I received a great many letters from them and from others expressing the warmest sympathy on my behalf; and though private, I do not think it improper to quote from some of them, as Mr. Barnes has endeavored with Mr. Hunt to disseminate a thousand vague suspicions and rumors unfavorable to me, and in allusion to the trial, and I cannot, perhaps, as the case stands, meet these more effectually than by showing what were the views and feelings of my brethren in relation to the whole matter. It is not often that a case occurs whose necessity is such as to justify a procedure of this kind, except where reputation or character is involved, but where such is really the fact, it constitutes, as I take it, a claim, whose just demands are paramount to all the conceded obligations of secresy.

In a previous chapter I remarked that immediately after the adjournment of Presbytery, Mr. Hunt and his servant girl circulated a report that I had acknowledged myself guilty of the accusations against me. On tracing this matter up, I ascertained that the confession was said to have been at the school-house, during the interlocutory, and that Mr. Sparhawk, elder of Mr. Barnes, had so stated. Not being personally intimate with Mr. S., and unable to tell how a letter could most directly reach him, I mentioned the circumstance in a letter to Mr. Brainerd, and he took my letter at once to Mr. S. Upon this he wrote to me as follows under date of Dec. 3d, 1847:

"My dear Sir: I am not a little surprised to learn from a perusal of your letter to Mr. Brainerd, for the first time to-day, that a member of Mr. Hunt's family has reported upon my authority, that you had admitted the truth of the charges against you. I think there must be some mistake in this; and you do me justice in saying that you do not believe it. If such a statement has been made, I have been misrepresented.

"I remember being asked in the presence of the elder Mr. Hunt and young Dr. Hunt, what statement you had made to the Presbytery, and my reply was, to the best of my recollection as follows: 'That you had admitted being imprudent, perhaps I said indiscreet, but that you had been *misrepresented* in the affidavit, that a *different coloring* had been given to the matter by its statement than the truth would warrant, that you had no criminal intentions, and that if Mr. Conover and Mr. Vanderbelt had consulted you, you could have satisfied them that you had none.' This, sir, I believe, is the very language I used, certainly they are the ideas I meant to convey, and my recollection is very clear in regard to the matter. *They are substantially the same statements you made in public, and such as I have understood you have always been willing to acknowledge.* You can judge for yourself what foundation there is for such a report. I regret that such a one should have gained currency, as I should be extremely sorry to rest under such an imputation. Will you please acknowledge the receipt of this.

"You have, my dear sir, my sincere sympathies, and best wishes for your restored health and new usefulness. That you may have in your time of trail richly and bountifully the consolations of that gospel which you have so often presented to others, and that our Father in Heaven may sanctify every dispensation of his Providence to you, and add to you his abundant blessing.

"Yours very respectfully,

"THOS. P. SPARHAWK."

Notwithstanding all the adverse influences under which this excellent young man had been brought at Mr. Hunt's, and though he might have known, to some slight extent at least, the feelings of his own pastor towards me, here stands his solemn protest against all those efforts which since that time, his pastor has been making, for the purpose of utterly destroying public confidence in me. The statements of this letter will haunt Mr. Barnes in a dying hour, and he must meet them also at the bar of God.

The next letter is from Mr. Brainerd, under date of Nov. 26:

"DEAR BROTHER LANDIS: I received your letter this morning, and though tired out with sermon-writing to-day, must send you a line in reply. You are too much excited. Try to dismiss, for the present, recent events, and go right to work as if nothing had happened. The general impression we have made at Flemington, Ringoes, Pennington, and Philadelphia is, that you have been *acquitted of crime.* So the impression will stand abroad generally. We settled a thousand rumors by your trial. The imagination of the envious and malicious can no longer picture crimes and attach them to you. We were placed in circumstances where we had to judge you under the eye of the world. In our private opinions, as we know human nature, and estimate your temptation, we have lost no confidence in your piety or worth, and time and our representations will protect you from final injury."

"What I am now about to say, you may, if you please, read or repeat to your judicious friends. *In acquitting you of crime, and enjoining your opposers to be at peace with you, we designed to leave among your people a full impression that the Presbytery regard you as a pious, honest, and faithful minister of the gospel, worthy of a confidence and love in no manner diminished by recent events.* This is our feeling, and with this assurance, I must close this letter.

"Yours, as ever, THOMAS BRAINERD.

"P.S.—We design to send you a general epistle signed by all the brethren, to show that we all regard you, as in '*auld lang syne.*' If necessary, show it to others. We were rigid in investigating truth; we design to be *just and paternal now in sustaining your character*, and we are able to do it. T. B."*

The above letter speaks for itself, and needs no comment. Such were the views of Dr. Brainerd, and of the rest of the brethren who attended the trial, excepting Mr. Barnes.

The next letter is dated December 7th, and is from the Rev. Robert Adair.

"MY DEAR BROTHER: I received yours of the 6th instant, this P.M., and hasten to reply in a few words. I sympathize with you in the terrible affliction through which you have just passed, and pray that you may be sustained, and carried through it without any permanent detriment to your health. I think it will be a blessing; but it is a terrible ordeal to pass through, to obtain a blessing. I had often noticed your familiarity with females, but never thought, for a moment, that you had any improper feeling at the time; but I feared that at some time, this familiarity might be construed to your damage, by your enemies, or those who did not know your warm and affectionate manners; and when I heard

* This promised epistle was never sent to me, as I believe it would have been, had Mr. Barnes been favorable to the design.

of the case of Mrs. Vanderbelt, I feared your innocent freedom with females might redound to your disadvantage then. You may say, 'Why, then, my brother, did you not frankly tell me your mind about my indiscretions?' I acknowledge I ought to have done so, but I felt as if you might think me too scrupulous about such matters, or would not fully appreciate my motives in performing such an office. In the sad case which has so oppressed you, I have felt, and the brethren too, that you had no evil design, and we are prepared to sustain you by our fraternal counsel and sympathy. We know our own liability to err, and to be indiscreet; if not in the particular referred to, in others no less displeasing to our Master, though not, perhaps, so injurious to our characters, in the eye of men. The brethren, while they wish to deal honestly in the matter brought before them by Mr. Conover, are no less anxious to do all they can to put you in an honorable position before your people, and the church at large. I can assure you they have a fellow-feeling for you, and will leave nothing undone, to protect you from the malice of your accusers, as you will learn in the sequel.* It grieved them to do what they have done, and yet in doing that, they have taken care to express their unabating confidence in you as a man of piety, worthy of the continued affection and confidence of your people as their pastor."

I may here remark, once for all, that I should never have troubled the public with any comment upon this minute of Mr. Barnes, had he only contented himself with inflicting that stroke, and those which he had struck before it. Dreadfully wicked as I regard his course in the whole matter, I should have kept silence (for it could not seriously have injured me, or religion through me, supported as I was by the sympathy of the rest of my brethren), and should have left his punishment with God, and the exposure of his guilt to that Providence which will not suffer such deeds to slumber forever in secrecy, but, as will be seen hereafter, he was not yet content, he must follow me up still, until I had no alternative left me but to make this appeal.

The next letter is from the Rev. C. S. Conkling, my successor in the other branch of my charge, who, with a large number of his people, attended the trial at Presbytery. The letter is of no consequence in itself, except as showing what the feelings of this part of my former charge were towards me. It is an invitation to attend a Sabbath-school anniversary.

"*Mt. Pleasant*, 15*th Dec.*, 1847.

"Rev. R. W. Landis: Very dear brother, we (*i.e.*, wife and myself) have had *three days* fixed on, on the which to visit the Bishop of Bethlehem, but rain and mud have prevented. Now, I can't come till after the forthcoming *anniversary*. Now, this is to say, *we hope confidently to see you and company* (*i.e.*, Mrs. L.) *at the anniversary on Tuesday* next, 21st, evening. Come early. *Don't fail.*

"In the best of bonds, as ever."

As my name, along with that of the Rev. Mr. Junkin, and a Methodist brother, was, without my knowledge, put upon the printed programme for the services, I attended, and took part. So little was the confidence of the community, who knew the facts of the case, impaired in me by all the efforts of my enemies to destroy me. And I may remark, also, that this confidence was never really impaired, except so far as to lead them to think that, on account of the perpetual harassings which I received from my enemies, it would be better for me to leave

* This kind-hearted and Christian design also failed, simply out of deference to the determined opposition of the man who sought my ruin.

the ground. The nature, and moving cause of these harassings, will be pointed out in the next chapter.

The next letter is from Dr. Converse, editor of the *Christian Observer*, and dated December 30th, 1847.

"REV. AND DEAR BROTHER: For more than a month, I had been intending to write to you every day; for daily have your recent trials been upon my mind. I rejoice that your character was vindicated by the testimony brought before Presbytery, and that you have the confidence of your people, your brethren, and what is better than all, the favor and supporting hand of God. I was detained from Presbytery by the ten thousand labors of my office, and the circumstances of my family. * * * * But God has mercifully spared us all, and our sufferings are not worthy to be named. Since suffering in some form must be a part of our discipline, the wonder is that we suffer *so little*. Your trials are a part of that discipline, and you, no doubt, bear it in mind, that we are *made* to *suffer*. When *God* became *man*, it was *to suffer*, by having his name cast out as *evil*, as well as physically. The statement respecting myself and family, is the reason for my silence.

"I have no doubt that you have your support in the review of the scenes through which you have been passing, and though *many* have risen up against you, and some of your brethren in the ministry may have evinced *less* confidence in your integrity than you had reason to expect,* yet God has sustained you, and will, I trust, sustain you against all who would wrong you, and make these very trials a means of increasing your influence and usefulness in the cause of truth and holiness. Your most useful days, and your most important services, I hope, are yet to come. Turn then, from the past, to some portions of truth, which you may elucidate with your pen, and when other duties permit, send some of your best thoughts to your old friend and brother."

The next two letters will speak for themselves, and were written on the same sheet enclosing the note referred to therein. The first is from Dr. Fairchild, and is dated January 3d, 1848.

"MY DEAR BROTHER: An application is now in the hands of Rev. Dr. Converse, for a clergyman of suitable qualifications, to take charge of the Presbyterian church in Shelbyville, Tennessee, and to have charge of the academy there also. It requires a man of experience and learning to occupy that post. The town has ten or fifteen hundred people in it, as I understand the case, and the Presbyterian interests there are in the ascendency, or have the control of things generally. They can make, to the man who will take charge of their affairs, a salary of about $1200 a year.

"Now, *you* have *the learning*, and *you* have *the experience;* and in the WEST, your writings have preceded you (if you choose to go), I think Dr. Converse will include in this sheet a note from that church, &c., which you will peruse, and from which you will learn more than I can tell you. And as *your notions of slavery, I presume*, are SUCH as would *not* lead you to hold (withhold) the gospel *from* sinners, I conceive you can go there, if you desire, without any detriment or misgiving, and when once on the ground, and having formed an acquaintance with the people generally, and obtained their confidence, may do good to all complexions, and more aid *the slave* than a thousand men at the north can do, who do *not understand* the matter *well*.

"Now, my dear brother, it may seem like a great thing for you 'to pull up stakes' and pitch your tent elsewhere. So it is a great thing; but if you can do more good by putting your influence with your brethren at the west, in moulding public opinion, than another man, ought you not to take it into serious consideration?

* These brethren were Messrs. Hunt and Barnes; and Parker, who did not attend the trial.

"I know you have many people about you, and attending upon your ministry. But are they a literary people? Are you now doing as much for the world and church as you could do if you had charge also of a seminary? But I must cease to write, and give way to Rev. Dr. Converse."

Dr. Converse's letter is as follows:

"PHILADELPHIA, Jan. 8th, 1847—(1848.)

"MY DEAR BROTHER LANDIS: Brother Fairchild has kindly presented the subject of this note, in the preceding letter. I have time only to say 1st. The opening is an important one. 2d, There are reasons why it may be desirable for you to have a call from Providence and withdraw from all associations and influences connected with those who may have sought your overthrow. Without great independence and very strong confidence in God, some things about you may impair your peace of mind and usefulness. You ought not to *run* away from them; but if Providence *call*, ought you not to obey the call? 3d. I am acquainted with some of the brethren in S. They are intelligent, affable, and apparently devoted brethren. *I would* cheerfully go there to live and labor were I at liberty; and I think the place is one where your learning and labors will be more justly appreciated and more useful than at Bethlehem. I shall write to Mr. Cowan to-day, and say to him that you are the man for the place. If you decide that you cannot go, please enclose his letter which I send to you, and forward it to me at an early day."

The sum of $1200, stated by Dr. Fairchild, was the minimum of what the enclosed note assured me I might expect: and this was double of that which I was receiving at Bethlehem.

The next letter is from Dr. Brainerd, under date of Jan. 25, 1848. It is lengthy, but the following extracts will speak for themselves. As I wish Mr. Barnes to experience no injustice at my hands, I shall give him the benefit of the passages in which he is named.

"MY DEAR BROTHER LANDIS: You know I hate letter writing, when sermon-making *uses up* what of nerves are yet left me. * * * * Neither Barnes nor myself said a word to *Wurts* that was not in your favor.* So he will tell you. We honestly designed to leave an impression favorable to you on every mind, and I think we did. None asked us for particulars, and we gave none, except that we had acquitted you of designing crime, and censured you for imprudence which laid you open to misconception. Just so far as the facts would admit, I aimed, at the trial and at all times and places elsewhere, to represent you as a brother innocent, and worthy of all confidence. * * * * From your account, I think matters are all shaping themselves kindly in your congregation. There is no intrinsic reason why you should not labor long and usefully where you are. Time will heal every wound, and efface every scar, if you leave its silent power unobstructed. If I were in your place I would show no uneasiness, nor special sensitiveness about reputation. It is enough for your official course, and confidence that your brethren have entrusted to you after a full hearing their confidence and the continued office of the ministry. For the present, be satisfied and hold on in your work, and reputation will follow you; but no attempts to create it or repair it at present will avail anything. I admire the course you are pursuing. Assume that all will follow the advice of Presbytery. Plant yourself on our decision; and if you cannot make enemies friends, you will draw their teeth. The affections of your friends, and the force of your talents, and, I may

* This is undoubtedly so. But Dr. Brainerd had not the remotest idea of the design of Mr. Barnes in conversing with my counsel. Mr. Barnes wished to induce my counsel to get me to apply to Conover to enter a *nolle prosequi*, which would have been a tacit confession of guilt on my part. But if Mr. B. really wished this done, why did he not urge upon Conover himself to do it? And how durst he take the liberty thus to call upon my lawyer, and by urging the matter upon him as above stated, weaken his confidence in the goodness of his client's cause?

add, your real piety and worth, will batter down all effectual opposition: and your trials will be amongst the events that *were*. Can you do this?

"You know perhaps that I opposed Conover's getting a copy of the testimony until after the next meeting of Presbytery. He shall not have it then, if I think he means to do mischief with it. He has no right to it *as the matter was compromised and settled, and accepted by him.*

"As to the *trial*, keep out of it if possible. It hinders the subject from dying. It creates bad associations around your name and acts. It will hush no malice, whatever be the decision. It will make a public scandal, injurious to religion. All this you have doubtless thought of. If you can get any influence to draw off Conover, do so. If you think a letter from some [of] us representing the injury it will do his daughter will be effective, write us on the subject.* We may be able to recall his reason.

"But if you must go to trial, meet it, and do your best in it. You stand an even chance of an entire acquittal on the facts; and a still better chance on your present position, as one who has abided by a settlement made by your brethren. It will be regarded now as persecution for no good end. The effort to punish you by law, will divest them of all sympathy. So if you are dragged to court, I would 'care not for it;' while at the same time prudence would dictate to you to escape it if you can.

"As to leaving, I would act entirely independent of these late affairs. They are 'a nine-day's wonder,' and of no great consequence, the whole of life being considered. I think with the full credentials to which you are entitled,† you would find no bad result anywhere; and hence do just as wisdom suggests.

"All the brethren here regard you with continued confidence, and affection. Even Brother Barnes, concerning whom, I perceive you have misgivings, is kind in his feelings [professions?], and I doubt not prepared to regard you as a 'brother beloved.' Don't increase your troubles by doubting your friends, who are what they have ever been—disposed to show you their fraternal regard. I am sorry to have delayed [my answer] so long, and at last to have written so crudely. But it is all I can do."

This excellent brother, in two months' time, and without seeming to be aware of it, had become considerably influenced by Mr. Barnes, with whom he was in the habit of constant intercourse. Upon this however, it is unnecessary here to dilate, and I shall instead of adding other letters from the mass of similar ones which I received from other brethren during this affliction, conclude the series with the following (also from Dr. Brainerd), written soon after the civil suit had been decided.

PHILADELPHIA, June 6, 1848.

"DEAR BROTHER: I have been moving and crowded with labor, and hence could not reply to your letter as I could desire; and to-day must put you off with a mere scratch. I was surprised and grieved at the verdict; and deplore its moral impression so far as it injures your peace and usefulness. But, Landis, your brethren are all of age, and have common sense; and hence know that *no fact has been changed by a Jersey jury. We mean to stand by our verdict, not theirs; and hence you may count still on our love, confidence and efforts to do you good.* A state of things may arise to make it desirable for you to leave Bethlehem; but *for the present be quiet.* If you can now stand a *few* months, you may

* I made no attempt in any way to influence Mr. Conover, knowing him to be the mere tool of Mr. Hunt and Dr. Sicarius. I however did write (in reply to the above) to Dr. Brainerd stating that if Mr. Barnes would write to Conover, or to the party, advising them to desist, it would no doubt be done. But that clergyman, who was *so desirous* to enlist my lawyer in the matter, did no more to accomplish the end aforesaid, than what is advised in the second chapter of Jude, or the tenth of James.

† Even *these* Mr. Barnes wished to prevent my obtaining, when I subsequently applied for them.

for years. If your circumstances are intolerable, we may do you some good, by another meeting of Presbytery in your church."

Such, then, were the sentiments and feelings of my brethren, in respect to me, in full view of all the efforts of my enemies, and of all which had been laid to my charge. And nothing can more strikingly show the cunning with which Mr. Barnes was operating against me, than the fact that he so perfectly succeeded in concealing his real aims and motives from his intimate friends. But many a reader will be utterly amazed as he views even the decision itself along with these letters, and contrasts them with the impressions which Mr. Barnes, both in person and by representative, has been endeavoring to make against me. Look at the dreadful effects which have already resulted from this heartlessness and cruelty! and will not God visit for these things? nay, is not His terrible visitation already begun? Consider but for a moment what has been the condition of constitutional Presbyterianism, in and about Philadelphia, *ever since the period when this cruel iniquity began!* Revivals have utterly ceased there; churches have been broken up, and scattered, and lost; and the retrograde movement has been so marked that it has been noticed abroad, and word has gone forth that this branch of the church is dying in that vicinity. Who has not noticed these things? who has not been puzzled to account for them? and who has not been struck with the vain attempt to do away with such an impression, by the erection of a large and expensive house of worship in the city? But it will not do. This matter must be set right before the favor of God can be expected to return. For "He whose hatred is covered by deceit, his wickedness shall be showed before the whole congregation. Whoso diggeth a pit shall fall therein; and he that rolleth a stone, it will return upon him." Prov. 26: 26, 27.

CHAPTER XIV.

MOVEMENTS OF THE OPPOSITION.

SCARCELY had Presbytery reached Philadelphia ere Mr. Conover, by the advice of old Mr. Hunt and Dr. Sicarius, wrote to the stated clerk for a copy of the testimony taken on the trial; though, as before remarked, he knew that the most important testimony on the defence had not been taken, in consequence of his withdrawal of the prosecution and charges. This procedure looked, on the one hand, very much like the anxiety of a criminal to escape from investigation; and, on the other hand, evinced a disposition to take an unprincipled advantage of the favor which I had, at his solicitation, granted him, to stay the proceedings; for his purpose was (which he did not scruple to own), to represent the testimony as equally complete on both sides. And through the influence of Mr. Barnes this unheard-of application, instead of being indignantly thrown out of the house, was received and debated.

Immediately after my enemies had received their copies of Mr. Barnes' minute in my case, they formally renewed their efforts to accomplish my removal from Bethlehem, though in total violation of the pledge they had given at Presbytery; and first, that paper was circulated through the whole community. The effect of this was not great, however, amongst those who were acquainted with the facts; but those who were not, received from it the impression that a poor abortive attempt had been made by Presbytery to screen me from justice; and, my enemies calculating upon this, determined to make the most of it. Accordingly, on Jan. 15th, 1848, a meeting was held at the residence of a disaffected elder, who, some months before, had violated his temperance pledge by engaging in the sale of intoxicating liquors. The persons who attended and took part in this meeting, took the precaution to style themselves "The friends of Bethlehem Church," being aware that, without this, no one would even suspect the most of them of being such. The leading man was Mr. Hunt's son (styled *Doctor*), a member of an Old School church, who was also appointed chairman of the committee to draw up the resolutions, which were adopted by the meeting. The aforesaid Peter Case was also there; and distillers, topers, liquor-sellers, Sabbath-breakers, and profane-swearers (the counterfeiters were not, I believe, permitted to attend), all figured here as "the friends of the Bethlehem Church." Along with these characters was a number of well-meaning men, whom they had inveigled into the matter, for the purpose of giving character to their meeting and proceedings, but who had no conception of their real design. The following is the report:

"The committee retired, agreed, and reported the following:

"1st. *Resolved*, That the recent investigation, in the case of the Rev. R. W. Landis, at the Bethlehem Church, has not resulted, as the Presbytery supposed, in our re-union, but the breach is widening; and, therefore, we think that something ought to be done, or action taken, to save the congregation from destruction.

"2d. *Resolved*, That a committee of five be appointed to wait on the Rev. R. W. Landis, and, in a kind and corteous (courteous?) manner, request his consent to apply to the next stated meeting of Presbytery for a dismission from his pastoral relation with the Bethlehem Church. (Here follow the names of the committee.)

"3d. *Resolved*, On his refusal to accede to this our desire, based, as we belive, (believe?) on the peace and prosperity of this part of Zion, to use every lawful and Christian effort for the accomplishment of this object.

"4th. *Resolved*, That the committee be desired to request an answer from the Rev. R. W. Landis in writing."

Several days after date the committee referred to called at my house and laid before me a copy of this paper unsigned. The spokesman (Mr. Jas. P. Huffman) was a gentleman for whom I have ever entertained a high regard, and he still continues to be a warm friend of mine, and has always treated with contempt the very idea of believing the story of my accuser. He honestly believed that the parties might come together again if I were to leave, while he deplored that things were in such a state as to seem to render it necessary. I knew by what peculiar influence he had been brought to this conclusion, and had a long conversation with him, the rest of the committee saying little or nothing. I pointed out to them the phraseology of the 3d of their resolutions, and stated that such an alternative was therein presented to me as would not permit me to listen to their proposal; but that yet I would call a meeting of the congregation and church, and promise to abide by their decision. That, at that very time, I had before me an invitation to an excellent situation in the West, and should at once conclude to leave Bethlehem if I believed that its real interests could be thereby promoted. That it was the interest of the church, and not my own, that would influence my determination. Mr. Huffman, and several others of the committee, seemed perfectly surprised at the obvious import of the resolution referred to, and wondered that it had escaped them, and assured me that I might rely upon it that it was not their intention to sanction any such idea as that which appeared to be conveyed by the phraseology; and that such, too, was certainly the idea of others who attended that meeting. I told them that I thought it had better be re-considered; and, had the matter rested with them, it would, beyond doubt, have been done. But the Hunt family, who had drawn it up, had well weighed its import, and were unwilling that it should be modified. I dismissed the committee with the assurance that I would call together the church and congregation, at as early a date as possible, and immediately thereafter transmit to them my answer in writing. This meeting convened again, in a few days afterwards, but the majority refused to consent to any modification of the meaning or phraseology referred to.

According to due notice from the pulpit, the congregation convened on the 27th inst. The meeting was a very large one, and, on motion, a committee, consisting of Asher S. Housel, Esq., John A. Young, and Wm. S. Wyckoff, and others, was appointed to draft resolutions expressive of the sense of the meeting. After due deliberation they returned to the meeting, and reported the following preamble and resolutions, which were unanimously adopted:

"Whereas, a series of resolutions, adopted at a meeting of a number of persons, held at the residence of Daniel Carhart, on the evening of the 15th inst., have been laid before this meeting by our pastor, to whom they were submitted by the committee therein named, be it

"*Resolved*, As the sense of this congregation,

"1st. That we regret that any portion of the members of Bethlehem congregation should take a step thus calculated to promote disunion in the congregation, by refusing to submit to the decision and recommendation of Presbytery. The individuals who were dissatisfied with our pastor, and who sought his overthrow in the recent trial in the church, and who had three months to collect and mature all the charges which they could procure against him, did, after the prosecution had been heard and the defence entered upon, come forward, of their own accord, and volunteer to withdraw the prosecution, assured that their accusations could not be sustained; and professed a willingness to acquiesce in the recommendation of Presbytery in the case, their chief witness freely and fully exculpating him from any harmful intentions. And now they seek to accomplish, in the manner aforesaid, what they endeavored to do by the prosecution itself, and aim to induce him, by implied threats, to resign his pastoral charge—and all this, without having made any attempt to comply with the recommendation of Presbytery. And we hold this conduct to be a breach of good faith, so far as the leaders of this procedure are concerned.

"2d. *Resolved*, That, as we understand those resolutions, an intimation is therein given, of the intention of these persons to resort to law to gain their ends; therefore, we do hereby mutually pledge ourselves, to each other and to our Pastor, to sustain him throughout any legal proceedings which they may see proper to institute for such purpose. And that, if they resort to law, he is entitled to proceed with his prosecution of those who have been guilty of slandering him.

"3d. *Resolved*, That as they also (as we understand it,) intimate their intention to seek their ends by inducing Presbytery to reconsider their action,* we do

* This was a silly report started by my enemies, for the sake of "*helping to scare.*" It ought not to have been noticed at all.

hereby declare, that any statements which would make the impression that this church and congregation would consent to the removal of its Pastor under such circumstances as the present, is a false representation; and should Presbytery entertain any such idea, we desire him to take such action as the circumstances may require, and assure him that we will sustain him in such action.*

"4th. *Resolved*, That as two or three of the enemies and persecutors of our Pastor have been riding through the congregation, and even stating that many of us were favorable to his removal, we respectfully request all the friends of Bethlehem church and congregation to be upon their guard, so as to afford no advantage to designing men,—some of whom are not members of this church, or even of any other, but who are endeavoring to divide the church, and to involve them in the same guilt in this matter as they are involved in themselves.

"5th. *Resolved*, That as Mr. Hunt, Sen., declared on oath before Presbytery, that when the report was charged against our Pastor, he recommended Mr. Conover to go and convene the prominent opponents of Mr. Landis, to take action on the subject, so it is true that the origin of the dissatisfaction of these men with our Pastor, lies far back of the report which originated the recent trial. A number of these leaders were bitter enemies to him years ago, and objected to him on the grounds that he preached temperance, and the divinity of Christ; was in favor of the cause of benevolence, admitting agents into the pulpit; and because he introduced the Confession of Faith, and was opposed to slavery. Some opposed him for one of these reasons; some for another. The origin of this dissatisfaction may, therefore, be traced, as we firmly believe, to the course which he has taken in endeavoring to discharge his duty faithfully among us. Had he been willing to be controlled in these matters, it is our full belief that this opposition would never have been made. Some, through the erroneous statements of these men, have become involved with them, who do not participate in their prejudices; but we feel assured that, upon further reflection, they will not take part with those who, from sinister motives, have long been, and still are, endeavoring to promote dissatisfaction.

"6th. *Resolved*, That we believe our Pastor, by his meekness and conciliatory spirit, has thus far met the recommendation of Presbytery to the letter, and that while he has been the subject of repeated and new attacks† since that time, has still evinced a conciliatory spirit, and a disposition to promote the welfare and happiness of the church, more than his own comfort.

"7th. *Resolved*, That, as this controversy is a controversy of principle, as above stated, we cannot see how it can be settled by a change of Pastors. The points in dispute between us and the leaders of the opposition, cannot be thus avoided. Under any other Pastor, those points must come up again and again, and must be settled before there can be peace and harmony in the church. And it is our unanimous conviction, that they had better be settled now, rather than after a long and protracted dispute for years to come.

"8th. *Resolved*, That, by proposing to our Pastor such terms, and giving him the choice, either to leave voluntarily, or be driven away, they have put it out of his power to entertain any proposition from such a source, until there is a full and formal withdrawal of these resolutions. But few of the members of Bethlehem church who were present at that meeting, would have consented to such a resolution as the 3d, if its true meaning had been presented to their view; and as some have disclaimed it, we are assured that others will acknowledge the same, when they come to reflect upon it.

"9th. *Resolved*, That, as the meeting at Mr. Carhart's has arrogated to itself the appellation of 'a meeting of the friends of Bethlehem church,' we hereby declare our firm belief that only such are true friends to Bethlehem church as evince a disposition friendly to her peace and unity. Nor can we regard any one as friendly to the church, who endeavors to stir up contention and dissatisfaction in her midst; or who, after virtually promising to adhere to the recommenda-

* My people already began to see the designs of Mr. Barnes.

† Referring to the falsehoods refuted in the preceding letter of Mr. Sparhawk.

tions of Presbytery, have, neither by word nor action, since evinced any disposition to do so.

"10th. *Resolved,* That this church and congregation have undiminished confidence in its Pastor, as a Christian and faithful minister of Jesus Christ. We regret that he has been unguarded, as he has frankly and with deep sorrow admitted; but the combined efforts of all who oppose him have not succeeded in proving that he has been guilty of anything to forfeit the esteem and confidence of this congregation and church, for whose spiritual and temporal welfare he has labored with untiring zeal and great success. Our Saviour said to Peter, 'If thy brother offend thee, and turn and say, I repent, thou shalt forgive him.'

"11th. *Resolved,* That our Pastor be respectfully requested to return as an answer to the resolutions aforesaid, the following statement, as the unanimous sense of this meeting, to wit: That we recommend him to continue, as he has heretofore done, to abide by the late decision of Presbytery; and that we purpose to do so ourselves; and hereby pledge ourselves to sustain him in so doing. And that we earnestly recommend to every member of the church and congregation to abide by it likewise, assured that, in the end, this will be the best for all concerned.

"12th. *Resolved,* That the proceedings of the meeting at Mr. Daniel Carhart's, and also the proceedings of this meeting, be read to the congregation by the President of the Trustees, on the first Sabbath in February next.

(*Signed,*)

"JACOB S. JOHNSON, *Chairman.*

"WM. EMERY, *Secretary.*"

Immediately after this meeting, I obtained from the Secretary a transcript of the 11th resolution, and sent it to Mr. Huffman and the committee, with a note, stating that it expressed my answer to their proposition. Soon after, a formal intimation was given, that my enemies designed to make an effort to break me down, by prosecuting me at court on the charge of assault and battery. My brethren in Philadelphia, as well as my people, were much grieved at such an atrocious breach of faith; and Dr. Fairchild did what he could to induce the Presbytery to hold Mr. Hunt responsible for it. Had this been effected, the prosecution would have never been attempted: and I am perfectly sure that had Mr. Barnes been favorable to the measure, it would have been accomplished.

When asked by Dr. Brainerd, in one of the preceding letters, whether the brethren of Presbytery could do anything to prevent this prosecution, I replied that I believed a letter from Mr. Barnes would prove effectual in the matter. Why I selected him will be easily understood; but why he did not write, when he had mainly contributed to bring things to such a pass, while he professed to be so anxious to have my lawyer induce *me* to apply to Conover, I cannot explain on any just or equitable principle. A word from him to Mr. Hunt would, I am assured, have stayed the matter. He was urged to do it. He may have deemed it useless to write: but, admitting this to be so, why did he not attempt it, or, at least, put forth an indignant remonstrance, and so have placed it in my power to say that he disapproved of such a course; and that he had no idea the prosecution would thus violate their pledge? And further, would he not, had such been his desire, have inserted, either before or after the trial, on the records of Presbytery, a censure of this gross breach of faith? He, and he only, was the man to have these things performed, for the reasons already stated. The breach of faith at the church in Lower Providence (mentioned above in Chapter I.), in which he felt that he might suffer by implication, was thus indignantly noticed even on the records of Presbytery; and why was not this likewise noticed? *Reader, it is folly to try to escape from the only legitimate conclusion.* Mr. Barnes, by his management with Mr. Hunt, having brought me into all these disadvantages, was willing that I should remain under them. And this is a further comment on his expressed wish that "no spot might remain upon the character of Brother Landis."

I have already, in Part I., described the effort made by my enemies at the court in February, to induce me to leave my church, and the result of that effort. On March 1, the congregation held its annual meeting to elect trustees. The opposition all appeared on the ground, but by an overwhelming majority every measure they proposed was voted down. In consequence of this, a number of them gave up their seats; but other applicants for the "sittings" immediately took most of them; so that no real detriment resulted to the prosperity of the church and congregation from this measure: and we soon after elected four new elders.

The prosperity of the church and congregation had not been impaired ut really promoted by what had thus far transpired: for we had got id of a set of worldly-minded, troublesome men, who had for years been a curse to the cause of Christ. Mr. Patton visited the church, as an agent for the Education Society, and took up a handsome collection. He was delighted with our prosperity, and remarked that he had never seen a finer congregation, nor one where the members so generally contributed, as the subscription papers were presented to them. He expressed himself peculiarly delighted with the number and fine appearance of the youth.

Soon after this, the civil suit came on, as I have described in Part I. I met it as a man and a Christian should do. The blow did not affect me very seriously, however; for the community uttered one burst of indignation against the treachery by which such a result had been obtained. And though the feelings of my family and church were much distressed at the boasting of my enemies, and particularly of Mr. Hunt, *the trial and its result changed not the mind of one of my people, in respect to my innocence.* It injured me abroad, where the facts were unknown or misrepresented, but not at home among my people. And such a result can only be ascribed to the goodness of a faithful and covenant-keeping God.

Thus supported by my people, and by the favor and blessing of God, how easy had it been for me to weather the storm in security, without detriment to the cause of Christ. But the man who had set out at first to prostrate me, saw that nothing had really as yet been gained to that effect, if I remained at Bethlehem. And he now, therefore, began to move in the matter again, endeavoring to sap the confidence which my people still had in me; and to strengthen the hands of those who had now actually ceased from their efforts to get me away. The consideration of these matters must, however, be reserved for another chapter.

CHAPTER XV.

NEW MOVEMENTS OF THE ENEMY. GLIMPSES AT MR. BARNES.

During the week which succeeded the civil prosecution, my people called much upon me and my family to express their sympathy; and to show that their kindness and confidence were unabated and unimpaired. The language they employed when speaking of the subject to others, was to this effect: "We now love our pastor more than ever, and shall take still higher ground against his enemies." The effect of the trial soon died away: but as I now began fully to realize how inveterate was the disposition with which I was on every occasion pursued by Mr. Barnes; and how ceaselessly he sought to influence my brethren of the Presbytery to sympathize with him in his prejudices; and I had now stood forth boldly and met everything that my enemies had laid to my charge, I concluded within my own mind, that at farthest by the end of the pastoral year (March 1, 1849,) I should select some other location for labor, where I and my family might not be so mercilessly harassed, and through the *odium theologicum* of a rival, be in a measure deprived of the sympathy and co-operation of my fellow-presbyters in doing the work of the Lord. I, however, kept this determination to myself.

Soon after the trial at court (May, 1848,) and when the congregation was settling down in peace and quietness, and my enemies in Jersey had, in despair and perhaps also from remorse, abandoned their efforts to remove me, Mr. Barnes took a journey to the town of Belvidere (about 25 or 30 miles north of me,) to visit a church member of his who had formerly been a pupil of Mr. Hunt. His name is Dr. J. Marshall Paul; and being in good circumstances, Mr. Barnes was in the habit (if I err not) of paying him a visit once a year, during the latter part of the sultry month of August. He, however, *now* took the journey in the early part of the season; and doubtless for reasons which furnished him a sufficient inducement to do so: probably concluding that the latter part of August would not be so sultry as it usually is. But what strange coincidences sometimes occur! He had scarcely returned home again, before renewed trouble began in the Bethlehem congregation. But in order to present the case fully, I must go somewhat into particulars.

The Rev. Mr. Allen, (a relative of the aforesaid pettifogger who laid Mr. Barnes' minute before the judge,) who had been living awhile at Belvidere without charge, and under the patronage of Dr. J. M. Paul,* came into my congregation, and after visiting and counselling with a "special opponent" of mine, called at my house, and evincing a disposition to spend some time with me, his horse and carriage were disposed of, and he himself invited to dinner. I had no acquaintance with Mr.

* I need scarcely say that it is extremely painful to my feelings to be compelled even *to appear* to implicate worthy and excellent brethren, by bringing them forward in such connections. Justice to myself and to the suffering cause of Christ, however, requires that it be done. I believe that Dr. Paul, and Mr. Allen, and some others thus brought forward, are truly good men, desirous to do what is right, and to glorify and serve God: and that they were not aware of the real design of the man who induced them to play the part they have in these affairs. My duty, however, I repeat it, is clear in the matter. The part they did play is an essential feature of the whole drama, and demands its place in the narrative. I state simply the facts, and it remains for such brethren to do what they deem proper in the premises. They are found in the connections herein stated: and the *why* and the *wherefore* is for them to explain. If persons will "judge," and take action in a "cause before they hear it," the responsibility of doing so is with them, and there it must remain. Prov. 18: 13.

Allen, and had never before even seen him. After introducing himself, he said, "I have heard, Brother Landis, that it is your intention soon to leave Bethlehem; and it will be gratifying to me if you will secure to me a hearing by your people, in view of my being your successor, and employ your influence in my favor." I thought this was cool, and felt disposed to smile: but soon finding him to be a frank, companionable man, and one who seemed truly to love the kingdom of Christ and the promotion of his glory, my surprise and amusement at his manner of self-presentation gave place to far higher and better feelings: and I doubted not there was an unexplained something in the back ground, which, when developed, would, in a great measure, relieve the brother from the apparent imputation of an unwarrantable intermeddling in the affairs of myself and my congregation. He obviously felt that he was acting on sufficient information, and *cum permissu ac approbatione superiorum:* and therefore in conversation with another member of my family, was also particular to inquire in relation to the expenses of living in that region; the price of property, &c. He, moreover, came, fully expecting to preach for me on the morrow; but as I had assigned that day to the presentation of the claims of the American Bible Society, I could not gratify him, and he accordingly returned home. I, however, invited him to return at his convenience and spend a Sabbath with me.

This good and worthy brother (of whom I mean not in the slightest degree to speak disparagingly; for, upon further acquaintance, I cannot but regard him as a faithful and devoted servant of God) was in no way particularly embarrassed, though he seemed at first to feel the awkwardness of his position, for he had brought no letter of introduction; and the "opponent" of mine, a Mr. Exten, who brought him to the door, did not wait to present him to me. In the course of our conversation he stated that the brethren in Philadelphia had given him to understand, (in some way that he mentioned not, and I asked no questions,) that they would be pleased to have him succeed me when I should leave my charge. With the same frankness, and in the course of conversation on some other topic, he stated also that he was unacquainted with any of the brethren referred to, and knew none of them—except the Rev. Albert Barnes! * Him he had lately seen at Belvidere.

On the following day the Agent of the Bible Society (a Mr. Stratton) laid the claims of that Institution before my people, and took up a collection of $44, an amount greater than had been contributed altogether to all the benevolent societies of the day during the whole forty years of my predecessor's ministry. This fact may in a measure serve to evince how little the attendance and real prosperity of the church had been impaired by the cruel efforts made to destroy me; and if compared with the collections made by agents since I have been compelled, through Mr. Barnes, to resign my charge, a glimpse may be obtained of one train of the unhappy consequences to the cause of Christ which have resulted from the fatal course of procedure adopted by that individual.

About this time some two or three of the elders were seen holding caucus-meetings near the church on Sabbath mornings, and whispering to

* He was acquainted with Dr. Fairchild also, but he had ere this left Philadelphia for Montgomery, N. Y.

some members of the congregation. Word had somehow arrived that Mr. Barnes now professed to believe that I was guilty of the charges which had been brought against me; and it was also said, that if I only would leave the church, Mr. Allen would come at once and supply my place. Such caucuses and whisperings were well calculated to distress my people, and the rumor was artfully employed by Mr. Hunt and his family so as to keep open the wounds that had been rapidly healing. In the course of two or three weeks after the aforesaid proceedings, these elders called upon me, and said that they had no sympathy with my enemies, but believed that the charges brought against me were utterly false: yet that the state of things now existing in the congregation, with which (said they) "we have a much better opportunity than you have of becoming acquainted, is such as to render it necessary that you should retire from the church. We are sorry to have you go; but we have been consulting with them, and feel sure that unless you do so at once great confusion will arise. A large number of pew-holders intend to give up their pews on the first of September if you continue till then. The congregation will freely make up your salary for the whole year if you will now resign." Such was in substance their communication. I was taken by surprise, for I had not the remotest idea that any such state of things as this existed. I have however often since regretted that I consented to hold any intercourse with them on such a communication thus presented. These things had no doubt been so artfully told to them by some of Mr. Hunt's friends, that they in their unsuspecting simplicity felt that they might even assert them to be true. But seeing from their manner that some controlling influence was at work back of these men, (for they were not only very tender about descending to particulars, but often prodigiously puzzled to explain how they had arrived at their conclusions,) I told them that if such were the facts, I of course had no idea of standing in the way of the prosperity of the church. What can a pastor do at best, (much less in such circumstances as mine,) with an eldership divided, and the majority taking such ground as this? My enemies, knowing the predicament to which I should thus be reduced, had spared no pains to gain over these men. I told them moreover that I should willingly join with them and the congregation in endeavoring to procure a successor in whom they might be united; for that I had had no idea that any portion of them was dissatisfied with me; and that so soon as they could fix upon a man who could probably labor amongst them with advantage and success, I should resign the charge to make way for him. As they said nothing about the resolutions adopted by the people in January, (and given in Chapter XIV. above,) I did not care to mention it; but told them that they might procure the promised salary as soon as possible, as I should need means to enable me to visit some other field of labor. They promised to do so, and this was the last that I heard from them for a number of weeks.

Meanwhile the first of September arrived, and the congregation met to pay the semi-annual instalments for the pews. Not the least excitement or want of harmony, nor coolness towards myself, appeared in any way. Every one, not excepting these elders themselves, treated me with the same affectionate regard as usual, *and not a pew was given up.* One or two single sittings were, but this was as common an occurrence as that of renting new sittings at the end of each half-year. Before the congregation dismissed, however, the aforesaid conduct of the elders transpired, and this at once aroused the people to a perfect tempest of indignation against them; and the declaration that Mr. Barnes had said as above stated was treated with ineffable contempt. These elders, however, though thus left unsupported, were not disheartened by such a demonstration, for they felt sustained by considerations which they cared not to make known; nor were they at all abashed, though it now fully appeared (nor did they attempt to deny the fact) that, instead of having really consulted with the congregation on the subject, they had been consulting with the emissaries of the Hunt family; nor could they mention, though called upon to do so, a single member of the church or congregation with whom they had advised as to the step which they had taken. Some of my enemies, hoping to be able to accomplish my removal by means of this movement of the elders, (though at the same time, and with a most ludicrous strangeness, the same party denounced the proceeding as base and treacherous,) had renewed the overture to advance me my salary if I would resign. The statement that Mr. Barnes desired my removal came from Mr. Hunt and his friends; and the idea of pleasing so famou.. a man, together with the hope that perhaps a change might be beneficial, had been sufficient to lead these elders into the adoption of such a course. Thus the matter rested for the present.

Mr. Hunt now went out on another crusade. He first called on Mr. Sigler, the distiller, and had a long conversation with him. In speaking of this interview, a short time afterwards, Mr. Sigler mentioned to Mr. Stryker, that "Mr. Hunt had called on him, and stated that Mr. Barnes thought that Mr. Landis ought to leave Bethlehem; and that, if it were necessary, in order to make him leave, to bring the matter before Presbytery, he (Mr. Barnes) had promised to be his (Mr. Landis') prosecutor. And now, Judge, (says Mr. Hunt to Mr. Sigler,) do you go round and get up a paper, with signers, and this will be soon done." The idea that Mr. Barnes would become my prosecutor, was much talked about, and used against me by my enemies. I cannot persuade myself, however, that he made a promise involving such a preposterous absurdity; and the story, whatever it may have originated from, doubtless *lost* nothing in its transmission. He knows how much, or whether any part of it is founded in truth. Still, the evidence in support of the statement is far stronger than any brought forward to sustain the charges against myself; and upon the strength of which he was constantly employing his influence to undermine me in the confidence of my fellow-men.

Mr. Sigler, however, promptly refused to undertake any such procedure against me. He had always been my friend, until my efforts in the temperance cause had exasperated him; but after the trial in court, he had expressed his determination to do nothing further against me. Upon his refusal, therefore, Mr. Hunt went to Mr. Bird, one of the new elders, and spent part of the day with him. Up to this time, Mr. Bird had stood firmly my friend, and had in no way consented to the aforesaid action of the elders. His whole course of conduct now, however, underwent a marked change. He professed to have no confidence in Mr. Hunt's integrity, and never did believe the charges which were made against me. But in a frank conversation which I had with him, a short time after this his interview with Mr. Hunt, he told me that Mr. Barnes approved of their efforts to get me away. He said that there were others who thought that I ought to leave; but Mr. Barnes' name was the only one which he mentioned. Who can meet such a course of procedure, when an enemy, occuping the commanding position of Mr. Barnes, is so destitute of principle as to resort to it? Who can defend himself against one who is thus willing to prostitute every attribute of manhood and humanity, in order to take advantage of a brother circumstanced as I was; and with the cruel wounds too, inflicted mainly by his own management, not yet healed? My people, however, with a few exceptions, (which had been thus influenced,) still adhered to me; when, all unlooked for, I received the following epistle, in the handwriting of the Rev. Albert Barnes:

"PHILADELPHIA, October, 1848.

"REV. ROBERT W. LANDIS:

"Dear Brother,—We hope and believe that you will not regard it as improper for us, as brethren, to drop you a line, in regard to what we understand, from various sources, to be the state of things in the Bethlehem Church. We are not insensible, indeed, to the fact, that, at this distance, we may not be as well qualified to judge as to the existing facts, as if we were on the ground; and we feel that it is possible that we may have been misinformed as to some things: but we have received such an impression, in regard to the condition of the congregation, and have such apprehensions from your remaining there, as to the future prosperity of the church, that we venture to take the liberty, which we think faithful brethren ought to take, in expressing our fears. We ought to say here, that our impressions are not derived from your enemies in the congregation, but that the subject has been so brought before us, from other quarters, and from those who wish well to you and to the congregation, that we can not doubt as to what seems to us to be desirable. When the trial before the Presbytery closed, we *feared* that there was such a state of feeling in the community, that you could not labor there in peace; though we were not without *hope* that your continuing there *might* allay the feeling, and that harmony might be restored. But if our impressions are now correct, we cannot but regard the prospect as hopeless. There are too many influences there at work, we apprehend, to make that view practicable or possible; and the opposition is so much strengthened and consolidated, that we fear that the most unhappy results would follow to the church and congregation.

"We need not assure you that we are your friends; that we desired that you might wholly free yourself from the charges against you; that we endeavored to save you from this result if we could.* Nor need we assure you of our united conviction, that you are a good man—a sincere Christian, and that you are, in an eminent degree, desirous of doing good. We are truly thankful for the *great* good which you have been the means of doing in that church, in the early part of your ministry there; and we feel that you have had great obstacles to contend with in your efforts to do good. Nor do we doubt that the present opposition to you, in no inconsiderable degree, has been originated and strengthened by your fidelity. But it seems to us, and you will allow us to express the conviction, that, under all the circumstances of the case, it is not to be hoped that you can breast the torrent, and that your own ultimate peace and usefulness, as well as the peace of the congregation, would be promoted by a dissolution of the pastoral relation.

"In any way in our power we shall be ready to stand by you as brethren, and to render you any aid that we can; and shall ever pray for your welfare, and rejoice in your success. Permit us to say, that at your time of life, and with your talents and attainments, and real love for the cause of the Master, we cannot doubt, that in some other part of the great field, you may have many years of eminent usefulness and happiness. And for that, we, as your brethren, shall ever fervently pray.†

(Signed) ALBERT BARNES. THOMAS BRAINERD.
E. W. GILBERT. DAVID MALIN."

* The writer of this letter is Mr. Barnes, and I doubt whether a more striking illustration of that fearful power of self-deception, which exists in the human heart, was ever furnished, than that which is contained in this sentence: A man, if he wishes to do so, may conceal, even from himself, the motives which his actions develop to the view of all other persons.

† I must here request all those brethren, without exception, who have received unfavorable

This letter was postmarked November first, and was received by me on the third: that is, almost one year after the trial before Presbytery. Nothing can be kinder, or more fraternal than the spirit which it displays, whatever may be thought of the policy of such a procedure under the *real* circumstances of the case. The sole aim that Mr. Barnes sought to accomplish by means of it, was my removal; knowing that the multitude judge only from *results*, and seldom trouble themselves to inquire how those results were accomplished. Hence, while this result is sought, there is full room granted for a full expression of the real feelings and sympathy of my brethren towards me. Mr. Barnes well knew, that whatever might be the feelings which were thus expressed, and however truly they mirrored the hearts of my brethren, I could not, while his influence over them remained, reap any advantage therefrom, when once separated from my charge. The letter is of use, however, to show his own avowed impressions concerning me at the time referred to.

On the same day that this letter reached me, I returned a lengthy reply, which was however, as I remarked, to the Rev. Mr. Adair, a few days afterwards, not designed for Mr. Barnes, so much as for the other brethren who signed his letter; for had his signature alone been attached to it, he would have received a very different epistle. I answered it therefore according to what I knew to be *their understanding of it*, and this was all I could do. The following passages are taken from my reply, and need no comment:

"To give anything like a detail of the reasons upon which the following statements are based, would render my reply tedious to you, and require more leisure than I can just now command. But I doubt not you will believe me, when I say that it was only after weeks and months of as sincere prayer for heavenly direction, as it is possible for my soul to utter; and as entire a willingness to be directed as I think the human heart can feel, that I, (after the meeting of Presbytery here,) arrived at the conclusion that duty required of me to remain here, at least for a season. How long, I knew not, but only that it should be, till in some way Providence should open a door for my removal. I read your letter with pleasure because it seems to indicate that Providence is preparing the way for a change in the scene of my labors. I judge, however, that you feel and justly, that my not being able to remain here, after all that I have been called to suffer, is calculated to make an impression unfavorable to me abroad; and further, that you suppose this may influence me to wish to continue. *I do not think it does.* True; it may increase my burden in my up-hill course in life's warfare, but I am not influenced thereby, and would leave on to-morrow could I see any indication of Providence that called for it, no matter where my steps might be directed.

"As to the state of the church, my own views are widely different from those which you express. Still, as I am assured that you could not, without very sufficient reasons, arrive at the conclusions which your letter announces, I am entirely willing to believe that my own views of the matter are erroneous; and as a consequence, have no hesitation to fall in with what you express as the result of your own deliberations.

"The case in brief stands thus: In January last I received through Brethren Converse and Fairchild, an invitation to Shelbyville, (Tenn.,) offering me $1200 per annum. It came not, however, until my opposers here had had a meeting, and had passed some resolutions offering me the choice of leaving my charge, or of undergoing a civil prosecution on the same accusation which they promised Presbytery to take out of court on condition that I would allow them to withdraw their prosecution of me before the Presbytery. The Congregation, thereupon, had a large meeting, and unanimously adopted a series of resolutions urging me to remain; and also advising me to pay no attention to the threat aforesaid. I stated to them that I would prefer

impressions concerning me, through the influence of Mr. Barnes, to ponder this last paragraph at least. Such is the character which even Mr. Barnes himself could not deny to me, after everything had been done both at Presbytery and at the civil court to destroy me utterly. Lord, what is man!

to leave, so far as I was personally concerned, and that I had then a field open before me. They therefore passed a resolution, stating that they considered the welfare of the church involved in the matter as it then stood, and that if I left, the interests of religion would be prostrated in their midst. So the matter stood. The civil prosecution came on. Its result gave my opponents ground for triumph, but it had not much effect upon my friends. The manner in which the Lord enabled me to bear it only endeared me the more to many of them. The effect, however, had died away, and my congregation was a large and good one, and my meetings out of the church also well attended; and there was a great mellowing down of the feelings of the community towards me, when a man who had been playing false all along in the matter (unknown to us however) began to stir in it again.* This was in the latter part of summer. He soon enlisted several others, and they bent their energies to compel me to leave. This could not do otherwise than produce a strong feeling of sympathy for me. And a late careful estimate by the President of the Board of Trustees, and several others, evinces, that of our 106 pew-holders, we can calculate with certainty on all but 30, even counting all the doubtful with the opposition. Now these are the men who have ever given character to the church as a church. They comprise its vitality, piety, efficiency, liberality, and intelligence in chief.† They passed a resolution to abide by the decision and recommendation of Presbytery in November last, and also to stand by me while I should adhere to it. And they have expressed it as their unwavering determination, (which I have not countenanced however,) that if I am compelled to resign my charge on account of these perpetual harassings by my foes, they will not remain with them in church fellowship, but say to them as Abraham said to Lot, 'Let there be no strife,' &c.

"In the mean time I have been as still as a man could be under the circumstances; and have been watching and waiting for Providential direction. My way hitherto has appeared to be plain. God (without whose support I should have often sunk) has supported me marvellously. And though my continuance here would point to me a prospect of suffering and annoyance for months to come, from which my soul shrinks; yet it is my conviction that with the countenance and united co-operation of my brethren in Presbytery the tide *can* be breasted. I feel quite sure that there never can be a re-union between Mr. Hunt's friends, and the congregation, (that is a permanent and vital union;) I feel sure that the real prosperity of the church, while it may be greatly hazarded by my removal, yet would be truly promoted by my being thus sustained. I believe that it will be difficult to find a brother who would come here, in whom the congregation would be so fully united as in myself, and for whom there would be so large a salary raised. Such have been the settled convictions which have induced my course as above-mentioned. The reasons on which they are based (and which may be fallacious) it is impossible here to state. Your communication, as you will have seen, *is calculated essentially to modify them*, (for without the concurrence of Presbytery they must be in a great degree rendered nugatory,) *and it has done so.*"

"I thank you much for your kind proffer of aid. It is very opportune. You can see that a resignation of my charge, without (my) entering upon another field of labor somehow or somewhere, must put upon the face of the matter the aspect of my being forced away by my opposers; (and rather than give up the church to the inevitable consequences of such an impression, it would be beyond all comparison better that I should remain at all hazards.) (Hence) it is important that I should have some field of labor. I have none in view.—My acquaintance abroad is not extensive.—Be kind enough then, dear brethren, to use your influence to do this much for the church and for me. Let it be done as soon as you conveniently can, and the sooner the better now on many accounts; and I can easily keep my people from coming into the threatened collision for several weeks longer. I am indifferent as to the *where;* but if my own *most decided* preferences are consulted, let it be some charge where I shall not have, as here, three times as much labor as any human pastor can be reasonably expected to perform. Let it be a little out-of-the-way place; (I never had any ambition to be prominent in the church,) where I can, a little longer, get bread for myself and my family. More than this I *never* asked; and more *I do not desire.* Give me, if you can, a retired field, in which to work a little longer for God; and in which I

* This was intended for Mr. Barnes' benefit; and I apprehend he understood it. The man referred to had been compelled awhile before, as I am informed, to give a libel to a neighboring gentleman to save himself from a prosecution for slander. He was the chief tool pitched upon by Mr. Barnes in this last movement.

† In Bethlehem, as in other churches, there were many pious individuals who did not hold pews. They were with me *en masse.*

shall not be called so much to be in the noise and uproar of the world; and it is all I want on this side heaven."

Such was this correspondence; and it ended as it begun. Mr. Barnes did not design to procure me another field of labor. His sole aim was to secure my removal from Bethlehem; for while I continued there, little was the danger but that I could easily recover myself from his efforts to prostrate me. I immediately put his promises to the test, and they resulted as I supposed they would. *He took no further notice of them.* The other brethren, whom he sought to involve with him, took the requisite means to do what they had promised to do, and sought to obtain for me another field. But this man would acquiesce in nothing that promised such a result, but discouraged every movement of the kind. Nor could he have acted differently toward me, if his thoughts had been as follows: "I have truly brought him now pretty well down: but there seems to be something about the man that won't die. He must quit the ministry, or go into another denomination. If I let him be in peace where he is, he'll soon rise up above all that has been done. If we get him a place in the west, he'll soon return a member of the General Assembly. So let him even sink into forgetfulness." I do not say that these were Mr. Barnes' thoughts; but I do say, that he could not have treated me differently if they had been. The facts are undeniable: Let him explain them.

I soon afterwards ascertained who were those *friends* of mine, mentioned in Mr. Barnes' letter. They *called themselves* my friends, and said that they believed the charges against me were false: hence Mr. Barnes made the other signers of the letter believe that they were really my friends; though in his own soul he must have known that they were not truly so, and that they were entirely under his influence and direction.

This letter from Mr. Barnes, and my correspondence with him, I kept a secret from every one—even from my family. And what think you, reader? A very short time after I had received the letter, one of my bitterest and most unprincipled enemies told through the congregation that "*Mr. Barnes had written to Mr. Landis, advising him to resign his charge.*" The man's name is Race; and with this man Mr. Barnes, either directly or indirectly, had held a correspondence of some kind, and enabled him to use against me the fact, that I had received the letter aforesaid; and this, I doubt not, was one object which Mr. Barnes had in view in writing that letter. It gave my enemies strength, and weakened the hands of some of my friends. Reader, have you the feelings of a man? What think you of this, after all that had already transpired. Is this a coincidence, or is it a further manifestation of that vampire disposition, which (as preceding facts evince) would not be satisfied with anything short of my life's blood?

But suppose there had been (though there was not) such a state of things in the congregation as required the interference of Presbytery? and on what principle is it that Mr. Barnes was so forward to redress it? In his whole life, he can show no single instance, of all the cases that have ever invited the attention of Presbytery, in which he displayed such readiness to counsel, advise, suggest and lead, as he exhibited here, and in the case of the church at Lower Providence (Pa.), before referred to. Have not such acts a language? What do they, and innumerable other facts mean, in this connection? Am I, and my beloved charge at Bethlehem (to say nothing of my family), to be thus sacrificed to a disposition which all good men execrate; and which is as disgraceful to humanity as to religion? But not only is it true that Mr. Barnes displayed throughout the whole of my case, this readiness to enable my enemies to strike me with most effect, but it is true that he is (excepting old Mr. Hunt) the only member of Presbytery who evinced a disposition to lead in this crusade. Let him undertake to show *that any other member, who knew the facts in the case, was thus active against me*, without encouragement from himself, and I will demonstrate that no such member can be found.

In every considerable body of men, there are always some to be found who aspire to occupy the elevated position of "*toad-eaters*" to any one whose favor and patronage they are desirous to secure. So it was in the Fourth Presbytery. Two individuals in Philadelphia, (neither of whom attended Presbytery at Bethlehem), and another who had settled over that part of my charge, in Jersey, which I had in 1844 resigned, and who was under great personal obligations to me, were pre-eminently of this character. They regarded it as a peculiar honor to be employed in any service whatever by Mr. Barnes.* Nor were they kept long in waiting, for he now found full scope for their activity, and brought them forward into co-operation with my enemies on this occasion.

In pursuance of the encouragement thus afforded, the Ingrate above referred to (Rev. C. S. Conkling), without in any way either apprising or consulting me, actually came into my congregation, and, by previous appointment, met the disaffected members, and formally organized them, so as to act against me with the most efficiency. He knew that if the matter should come before Presbytery, his course would receive the countenance and support of the man for whom he was acting, and therefore adopted a procedure disapproved of by his own congregation, and so flagrantly contrary to all etiquette, propriety, and decency. He advised them to call a meeting of the congregation, and drew up for them a form of application to myself to that effect, and which was to be read from the pulpit to the people. No censure can be severe enough for conduct like this. Yet what could I have accomplished, by bringing him up before the Presbytery? Little or nothing. So I suffered it to pass, with a private expression of my disapprobation.

The weather of the two following Sabbaths being too stormy to permit the congregation to assemble, the notice could not be given. Another was then prepared; but neither it nor the previous one mentioned the *object* of the meeting. I suggested this to the elders when they presented it to me, and remarked to them that no formal business could be transacted by the congregation, on the ground of such a notice; but they replied that they preferred not to specify the object. In fact they feared to specify it, lest the congregation should thereby be aroused to turn out largely. The note simply requested me "to give notice from the pulpit, that there will be a meeting of the parish, held on Wednesday, the 6th

* "A GREAT MAN," says Fielding, "ought to do his business by others; to employ hands to his purposes, and keep himself as much behind the curtain as possible. Though, to confess a melancholy truth, it is a circumstance much to be lamented, that there is no absolute dependence on the friendship of *great men*."

day of December next, at the church, at 11 o'clock, A. M." I mentioned to several gentlemen of the congregation the fact, that such a strange notice had been handed me; and they immediately appended to it the following additional item: "Mr. Landis is requested to give notice, that at the meeting of the congregation and church on the 6th of December, the subject will come up for Consideration, respecting the recent efforts made by the eldership to induce the Pastor to resign his charge; and that order will be taken thereon, agreeably to the Constitution." The object of this last notice was, that the people might not be called together without being able to act in the premises, as they must necessarily have been, had the first notice only been given; our constitution requiring that the notice for such a meeting should specify the object for which it is called.

At the specified time the meeting convened, and the following is from a copy of the record thereof, which I received from the Secretary:

"Mr. Charles Carhart was appointed Chairman, and Mr. William Emery, Secretary. The meeting was opened with prayer.

"The signers of the notice first read, were requested to state their object in calling the meeting: whereupon they affirmed their object to be, to carry out the following resolutions. 1st.—*Resolved*, That this church and congregation respectfully request our pastor, the Rev. R. W. Landis, to unite with us in asking an immediate dissolution of the relation now subsisting between us. 2d.—*Resolved*, That in case the Rev. Mr. Landis does not see fit to comply with our request, that we appoint five commissioners to represent the state of the case to Presbytery, as soon as possible. Whereupon, the first call was not acted upon, as no notice had been previously given to that effect.

"The object of the meeting then being stated, by the Chairman's having the second notice read again, the reading of the resolutions passed in January last, was called for. Whereupon the following preamble and resolutions were proposed, and after considerable discussion, adopted—to wit:

"Whereas, we pledged ourselves in a public meeting, at the beginning of the year, to sustain our pastor, if he would remain with us: and, whereas, the elders, on their own responsibility, and without consulting the congregation, have been trying to induce him to remove; therefore,

"*Resolved*, That they had no right, or authority, for any such proceedings whatever.

"The following resolution and preamble were then adopted.

"*Whereas*, it has been declared here to-day, as the purpose of some of those who have called this meeting, to call a meeting of Presbytery, to try to accomplish their ends; therefore,

"*Resolved*, That Messrs. L. N. Boeman, Asher S. Housel, Esq., and Charles Carhart be, and (they) hereby are, appointed to represent the state of the case before Presbytery, should they thus call a meeting thereof.

"On motion, the meeting then adjourned."

Such were the merciless harassings that I and my congregation, and family were compelled to endure, and without remedy, at the hands of an ecclesiastic: and all to enable him to accomplish a sinister purpose—the very mention of which is sufficient to make humanity blush. For such an end, must the peace of the flock of Christ be sacrificed, and the hands of its worst enemies strengthened. I did all that a human being could do, to save this large and flourishing church from the impending ruin which that man was thus, through the agency of others, bringing upon it, by the effort to alienate the affections of a devoted and sympathizing people from its persecuted pastor: and at the door of the Rev.

Albert Barnes must the guilt lie, of all the consequences which have resulted from these dark deeds and hideous wrongs.

The individuals who were, by an overwhelming majority of the congregation, so severely censured in the foregoing resolution, had scoured the country over, in order to assemble on the appointed day all those persons who had been brought to sympathize with them in this last effort to effect my removal; and not only this, but they brought quite a number of persons to vote (and who did vote) who had no right to do so. We suffered it to pass without notice, however; for, with all their efforts, they had but a miserably small minority.

Immediately after the meeting, they went again to the aforesaid satellite of Mr. Barnes, for counsel; and that Ingrate advised them to call *another meeting* of the congregation, and after that to convene the minority, and through them, call a meeting of Presbytery; for the object was obviously (and even acknowledged by several) to weary out my people, until they should be compelled to yield. Another meeting was accordingly called, on Dec. 27, and the *object* as specified in the notice was to effect my removal. The day was very stormy, but my enemies were all in their places; though many of the friends of the church, who felt deeply interested in my remaining, and who had a long distance to come, did not attend; supposing, from the violence of the storm, that the meeting would not take place. It did, however, and was organized, by appointing Asher S. Housel, Esq., to the Chair, and Mr. Wm. S. Wyckoff, Secretary. The following resolution was offered by Wm. Butler:* "*Resolved*, That we request the Presbytery immediately to dissolve the pastoral relation between the Rev. R. W. Landis and this church." This resolution was also drawn up for them, as they openly admitted, by the same Rev. C. S. Conkling (whose mental and moral insignificance alone saves him from a more particular notice), who had for some time been almost daily in communication with them; and upon its being seconded, the question was raised as to who were the electors of the congregation? which was at once decided agreeably to the Constitution,—that pew-holders, or contributors to the maintenance of the ordinances of religion, were alone such. The question came up then upon the resolution of Mr. Butler; and the vote stood thus. In favor, 13; against it, 31.

This vote, and under such circumstances, seemed to have quite a penitential effect upon most of the opposition; and a motion was thereupon made, the object of which was to reconsider, in order to rescind the censure passed upon the elders at the former meeting. I supported the motion by stating to the congregation that as the censure had in a measure accomplished its design by making known the views of the people, no great harm could result from indulging the wishes of the applicants. This speech was a foolish one as I saw afterwards, but I was prompted to make it, from a feeling of pity for the men, and from the assurance that they were only the tools of Mr. Barnes; a reason, which it was, of

* How trivial are the motives which not unfrequently influence human conduct, in the most momentous affairs! This good brother became the exception in a family which was affectionately devoted to me, because in compliance with Dr. Converse's repeated request, I had twice urged him to pay his subscription to the *Observer*, which had accumulated to a very large sum. It displeased him exceedingly. However, almost immediately after I resigned my charge, he united with the Methodist church, as I am informed.

course, out of the question for me to state under the circumstances. After considerable debating, the motion however was put, and the decision of censure was re-affirmed with crushing effect.

At the close of the proceedings, a meeting of the minority was called, by Mr. Conkling's advice, to take place during the following week. The day appointed for the purpose was clear and unclouded, but after all their efforts in electioneering, and beating up recruits, there were but TEN solitary individuals who could be induced to attend it, so perfectly were they paralyzed by the indignant voice of the congregation and community (for most of my former opposers did not hesitate to denounce their conduct as unprincipled and treacherous), and so well assured were they that they could not destroy the confidence of my people in me. But these poor men supposed that because such a famous man as Mr. Barnes wished me away, that therefore I ought to be removed. These ten men, however, appointed delegates to Presbytery, and, without at all apprising me, a meeting of that judicatory was thus called; Mr. Conkling, and at that season of the year, going all the way down to Philadelphia with them. His reception *from some of the brethren*, however, as I have been informed, was not of the kind which is best calculated to flatter a man's vanity; and he returned home with his organ of self-approbativeness in a state of not the most marvellous prosperity, and doubtless reflecting too on his disappointed expectations of gratitude and patronage. Great men of *a certain class*, are not apt to be overstocked with generosity, even to those who serve them most faithfully, thinking, no doubt, that the *honor* of being thus employed is a sufficient recompense; and Mr. Barnes had now no further use for Mr. C. S. Conkling. The final step had been taken, and thus, through Mr. Barnes' influence, a meeting of Presbytery was called in order to carry out the wishes of TEN *disturbers of the peace of a large and flourishing church and congregation!* The Providence of God, in some matters, seems still to proceed upon the principle of the *lex talionis;* but may the infinite mercy of Heaven interpose to prevent in this instance such a catastrophe!

And now let the reader pause and reflect upon the facts here presented. They show that about the time when Mr. Hunt went to Mr. Sigler the distiller to induce him, as it is said, to get up a paper with signers, and so to commence a new crusade against me, and assuring him that when the matter came before Presbytery, Mr. Barnes would take it in hand and secure my removal, this new opposition in my church commenced to carry out that idea in the most reckless manner, and without any apparent or openly assigned reason. What then could have been the motives of Mr. Conkling and of these men for such conduct? Both parties (my friends and my former enemies, as above remarked) opposed their course, and they had knowingly forfeited the esteem or regard of both by pursuing it. We cannot presume that they thus acted, and so zealously in the matter from *no motive;* for this would be to suppose them natural idiots. And to suppose that they were so absurd as even to hope to secure the confidence of either party, or both, by pursuing a course which both regarded as unprincipled and treacherous, would be a no less foolish supposition. Whence then arose this sudden and remarkable zeal? They all continued to profess to be my friends, and to disbelieve the stories of my former persecutors; and they all cordially despised Mr. Hunt and avowed that they were not acting through his primary instigation. There was no influence operating against me in Presbytery, except what Mr. Barnes' proceedings had favored and developed. And now, reader, draw your own inference. Can you avoid the conclusion that Mr. Bird told the truth when he inadvertently slipped out in conversation with me that they were acting under the encouragement of Mr. Barnes? I may not be a competent judge in the case, but I cannot avoid this conclusion. Mr. Conkling can, however, if he will, explain many things in this connection; and I hope that before he goes to his final account, he will see it to be his duty to disclose fully the influences which prompted at least his own cruel agency in this affair.

I ought to have remarked that at the meeting on the 27th inst., and after the censure of the elders had been reiterated, I gave notice of my determination to resign my charge at the end of the pastoral year (March 1), even though every member of the church should insist upon my remaining. I found my own health and that of my family breaking down under these perpetual harassings, which already had broken a mother's heart and hurried her to the grave. This notice I gave formally and publicly; and took occasion to call upon the opposition to come forward and labor now for the peace and harmony of the church whose interests they professed to love. But Messrs. Butler and Bird both then declared that their object was *not to allow me to go without the censure of Presbytery.* They spoke honestly and openly; but the fatuity and impolicy of such an avowal in such a connection, it must be admitted, baffles all efforts at description; and can be accounted for only by referring it to that merciful Providence, whose invincible determination is to uncover all iniquity. They were in this only expressing the wishes of the member of Presbytery, who had promoted their opposition to me, as will be seen in the next chapter. And though I have, as Mr. Barnes must know, unfolded but a part of his cruel proceedings against me, I cannot even dwell upon what has been presented, lest this protracted narrative should be swollen to an undue bulk. I therefore hasten to the catastrophe.

CHAPTER XVI.

THE CATASTROPHE.

"My footsteps rove not where they roved,
My home is changed; and, one by one,
The once familiar forms I loved
Are faded from my path and gone."

Agreeably to the wishes of these ten agitators, Presbytery was called together, and the following notice was sent to me by the Moderator:

"Darby, Jan. 8th, 1849.

"Brother Landis:

"Pursuant to constitutional request, I give notice of a *pro-re-nata* meeting of the Fourth Presbytery at Philadelphia, to inquire into certain alleged difficulties in the First Presyterian Church in Bethlehem, N. J., and to do what may seem desirable to promote the interests of the congregation; said meeting to be held in the Lecture Room of the Third Presbyterian Church, Philadelphia, on Tuesday, the 23d inst., at 3 o'clock, P. M.

"Yours in the best of bonds,

"MARCUS E. CROSS, Moderator."

This letter was post-marked "Jan. 12th," and *was addressed to me at "Bethlehem, New Jersey,"* instead of "*Sidney*." It consequently arrived at a post-office some eight or ten miles distant, where, after lying a week, it was forwarded by the postmaster (who did not know my proper address) to another office nearly four miles off; and where it remained, without my having an opportunity to procure it, until after the meeting of Presbytery. The Moderator, who is an excellent man and able minister of Christ, had previously corresponded with me, and always addressed his letters to *Sidney*, my proper address, as marked in the published Minutes of the General Assembly: and why in this instance it was not mailed until *four* days after it was written, and then directed to me by a wrong address, I cannot tell; unless some one had taken the responsibility of having it thus delayed and directed, fearing that, if I had received timely notice, I should have been prepared, with the appointed representatives of the congregation, to be present at the meeting, and thus frustrate the design that was subsequently carried out by Mr. Barnes. A fact like this, however trivial in itself, derives at least some importance from being found in such a connection, and perhaps the subsequent disclosures of this history may throw some light upon it. At all events, however, I am assured that Brother Cross is innocent of designing to do wrong in the matter, and incapable of doing willful injustice to any man.

The following letter to Dr. Brainerd, touching this subject, is in place here, and will speak for itself without any introduction:

"SIDNEY, N. J., Jan. 21, 1849.

"MY DEAR BROTHER:

"Last night, at ten o'clock, I received from a ministering brother* a letter, stating that some elders of my church, and the Rev. Mr. Conkling, had gone to Philadelphia for the purpose of calling a meeting of Presbytery. This was the first notice I received that such a matter had been undertaken; and to-day at church, finding that by undefined rumors many of the congregation were much distressed, I adverted to the subject when giving my notices, and stated that they might rely upon it that Presbytery would do them no injury willingly—that there was no occasion for anxiety, &c. After service I asked one of the elders whether a meeting of the Presbytery had been called. He said there had been, and that it would take place on Tuesday next, at 3 (o'clock) P.M. Of the *object* of the meeting he stated nothing; and on that subject I am left to conjecture, and wholly in the dark. No notice has reached me, though I heard for the first time to-day, that a letter had been lying in a post-office three and a half miles distant from here for two or three days, which is thought to be said notice.

"Now, my dear brother, I should like to meet with you; but, under existing circumstances, even were it certain that it is important for me to be present, it is very doubtful whether I could be down at the time referred to. Mrs. Landis also is quite too ill with influenza to allow of my leaving home to-morrow for an absence of several days. Then by the time I could get the letter to-morrow, and (on the supposition that the meeting concerns me) also notify the committee appointed by the congregation to attend Presbytery in case any such meeting

* This was the Rev. Mr. Allen of Belvidere, referred to above.

was called, it would be too late to get down by any private conveyance, and the stage itself leaves between 9 and 10 o'clock, A.M.

"If anything therefore should be introduced at said meeting, which is important to the interests either of myself or the congregation; and should the matter be deemed worthy of consideration; I have only to request that Presbytery will take such order in the premises (by adjourning to meet either here or elsewhere, or by the appointment of a commission to investigate the facts in the case) as will secure to myself and people the opportunity of being heard in relation thereto.

"Truly yours in the best of bonds.

"P. S. If Brother Brainerd would lay before the brethren what portion of the above he deems necessary in order to make known my request and reason for absence, he will confer a favor upon me for which I shall be grateful."

Dr. Brainerd courteously did as above requested. In this meeting Mr. Barnes took the lead in the business, and, in a speech of considerable length and point, spoke of "*the interests and rights of Brother Landis*" in such a manner as to lead the brethren to hope that he had my interests and those of my people truly at heart; so that whatever misgivings had been previously felt by any of them on the subject, were now quietly laid asleep. He advised also that Presbytery should not meet at Bethlehem (as Dr. Brainerd had proposed to me), but that a commission, with advisory powers, be sent up instead. This motion was carried, and he, being most willing to act in that capacity, was appointed, along with Messrs. Parker and David Malin, ministers, and Mr. Joseph Montgomery (one of the best and most simple-hearted men under heaven), and Dr. J. Marshall Paul (a pupil of Mr. Hunt*), elders. Dr. Brainerd and Mr. Farr were likewise named, but I shall speak of this hereafter. Such was the commission that attended, and of which Mr. Barnes was the sole animating spirit. But before I advert to their doings, I must turn back for a month, in order to bring up another item of this history.

The reader has seen that on Dec. 27, at a meeting of the congregation, I gave public notice that on March 1st I should resign my charge. I had come to the conclusion to do so for the reasons already stated. I myself fixed upon this time, so that the opposing party could not boast that they had compelled me to leave, and thus make the breach irreparable between the minority and majority of the church.

When I had thus arrived at the conclusion to take this step, I soon perceived that another and a most important step was also necessary; and it was in relation to the course which Mr. Barnes had pursued throughout, and in every aspect of my case as it came up before Presbytery, or in conversation with any of my Christian brethren. I long dreaded to think of that step; and sought the direction of God, in most

*I did not know that this brother had been a pupil of Mr. Hunt until he, as a member of this commission, publicly announced it to my people as justifying the great interest which he took in their business. He felt that his course herein needed to be justified, for both before and after this he certainly did take a most wonderful interest in the affairs of the congregation—coming amongst them, making speeches to them, &c. I refer to the fact of this his pupilage, therefore, merely to announce what is his justification. I can hardly, however, suppose, that if Dr. Paul learned and recited to Mr. Hunt his "*Ecclesiastical and Historical Catechism*" aforesaid, (See Part I., Chapter I., *supra*,) he still entertains all the ideas therein inculcated; though from the apparent pride and satisfaction with which he brought forward the fact on this occasion, and the effect which he obviously hoped to produce by its announcement, one might reasonably be led to infer *that he continues to go for the Catechism.*

earnest and repeated supplication, as to the course which duty required at my hand. I could not believe that God designed that, under these circumstances, I should, to the detriment of religion and of my usefulness, remain, under the false and odious imputations of my enemies, and which Mr. Barnes had so perseveringly and unreasonably favored; I felt it to be impossible to get the matter righted by formal ecclesiastical adjudication; and that as now his efforts had in effect resulted in separating me from my people, which laid my conduct open to the most injurious constructions, nothing remained for me but to prepare and lay before the public this history of the whole matter. Mr. Barnes, in an underhand manner, had injured me with the public, and in a way which never brought himself and myself at a fair issue, and thus there was left to me no alternative but to make an appeal to that tribunal whose decision he had sought in this heartless manner to procure against me. I would not willingly come into conflict with the civil jurisprudence of my country, except when duty to God and to myself demanded it. But as I had been thus assailed, I felt that I had the right thus to defend myself, and to relieve the cause of my Redeemer from the odium which the aforesaid falsehoods and misrepresentations concerning myself had occasioned, even should the truths, which were necessary to be stated in order to accomplish this, bear hard upon the guilty. I believe, too, that the civil law will sustain a man in such a procedure (See 5 C. and P. 543, *Cockayne* vs. *Hodkinson*, and 8 C. and P. 88, *Todd* vs. *Hawkins*); and even if it did not, that there is a higher law by which I shall be justified, (See it as implied in Ex. 20 : 16, and illustrated in Matt. 23 : 4–33, and Matt. 28 : 11–15). Hence after I had concluded to make this appeal, and had arranged the materials and written a considerable part of it, I sent to Mr. Barnes the following note, which needs no explanation:

"Rev. A. Barnes: "Sidney, N. J., Dec. 26, 1848.

"Brother Barnes,—It has at length become necessary (though, till late, I fondly hoped it never would be) that I should appear before the public with an exposition of my case; and you are aware that I never have been heard in relation to it.* While I could remain at my present post or, at the undoubted call of Providence, leave it for another field of prospective usefulness, I felt, that without this step, I might in duty refer the whole matter to the good Providence of God; and that, without any direct agency of mine, He would bring about such an adjustment as would, while it redounded to his glory, sustain me in my labors to do good, and free me from the cruel and unjust aspersions under which I had been so long suffering. That this will eventually be done, I am assured, and fully; but that my agency is now required for the attainment of such a result, is also clear to my own mind.

"In the performance of this duty, it will be necessary to take into consideration the course which you have throughout seen proper to pursue in relation to me; and as I shall do this plainly and pointedly, I feel it to be but proper and fair that you should not be taken entirely by surprise, but be made aware of the fact before the appearance of the publication.

"I have given notice to my people,† that I shall resign my charge; and as this step, under such circumstances as have transpired, irrevocably determines the performance of the duty aforesaid, you will understand that this note is not designed to open a correspondence (which would be useless, as no possible alternative remains for me), but to avoid the imputation of wishing to take any advantage of a brother in a matter wherein, before being called to act, he may desire a little time for serious consideration: in saying which, however, I have neither the disposition nor intention to assume that you do not feel prepared at once to meet all the facts in the case. Fraternally yours," &c.

* Mr. Barnes understood this, for it was he who prevented my being heard: see *ut supra*.

† I had given the notice privately and informally, and on the next day repeated it formally and publicly.

To this letter Mr. Barnes replied as follows:

"PHILADELPHIA, Dec. 29, 1848.

"MY DEAR BROTHER,—I received your letter to-night, and I confess what you say rather surprised me. I have done nothing in reference to you which I am not willing that all the world should know. I shall make no objection to your publishing it, if you think that it is necessary for your vindication, or if it will in any way do you any service. I have no idea whatever that you would publish anything which you would not regard as in the strictest sense true; but it is *possible*, that in such a publication, there might be some misapprehension, or something that I could explain; and if so, it would be better that the explanation should be given *before* the publication, than afterwards. What I wish to suggest then to your brotherly feeling is, whether it would not be better, and quite in accordance with what you would wish should be done to you in similar circumstances, that you should read over to me what you have written about me; that together we might make it perfectly correct, if there should be anything which I might desire to explain? I do not exactly claim this; but as you speak of dealing with me '*plainly* and *pointedly*,' and as I never should think of replying *after* the publication is made, and as you would desire to have all things according to truth between brethren, it seems to me that the request is not an improper one.

"I am sincerely and truly yours."

Such was the reply of Mr. Barnes to my letter, and I must own that its apparent frankness and candor led me to doubt whether his real designs previously had not been misapprehended. I therefore, on the same day that his letter arrived, wrote to him as follows:

"You misapprehend the design of my book. It is not a *defence* of myself, nor a tractate *against* yourself; but a statement of my case. The course things have taken has thrown over me a huge cloud of unjust suspicion, by which religion is needlessly made to suffer through me; and I am cut off even from the prospect of usefulness, as my brethren all stand aloof.* I do not *complain* at all of their doing so; for I am satisfied to be just in those circumstances where God would have me to be, when I shall have conscientiously discharged my duty. A frank and free statement of the case will dissipate this cloud, and prepare the way for my return to usefulness. I shall not therein spare myself at all, nor attempt to justify anything wrong which I have really done: and with the same frankness I shall speak of any one of whom it is really necessary to speak.—I know that the Christian public will hear me, and hear me kindly, great as are my relative and *prima facie* disadvantages in the matter: though until I am heard, the course which events have taken must still operate to crush me."***"And when I have frankly made known the grounds upon which this treatment is based, I am sure that the Christian public will extend to me that practical sympathy, which could have been so easily, and without any sacrifice, extended to me by my brethren; but which they have seen proper to withhold.

"As to your request to see the MS. I shall cheerfully accede to it; and the reasons which you give are sufficient to prove that you have the right to ask it, according to the principles of the gospel, which we both profess to receive. As for copying it however, and sending it down to you, that is impossible. The first draught is not yet complete; and as the book will not be less than three hundred pages, and perhaps exceed it, I cannot copy it. I calculate that the work will be of use to the Church and Christian ministry for a long time to come.

"As to the concern which my Brother Barnes has in the matter, it is only so far as his course has operated to produce results whose effect is and must be to crush me entirely. Until I can be heard, I have nothing to say of his motives. It is enough for me that God searches both our hearts.

"I like the tone and spirit of your letter: but in the compass of a sheet, I cannot say half that I wish to say in reply. But as the MS. will not be completed for some weeks, and as I cannot now write so fully as I could wish (for to-morrow is our congregational *visitation*,† and the next day the mail goes too early to allow me to write fully), let me at once offer a suggestion.

* The reader will understand the design of this; and Mr. Barnes, who had, by the course he pursued, influenced them to act thus, evidently understood it too.

† In the Eastern States this is known by the name of the "*donation visit.*" At the time referred to above, the large house in which I resided was too small to accommodate the throngs of my people, who attended the "visitation;" and we were obliged to set apart two more days, at intervals of about a week, in order to accommodate all who wished to express their good-will to me and my family.

"I believe you have, and without any sufficient reason, injured me beyond the power of human reparation. I have long believed this; and God only knows how often and how earnestly I have desired the opportunity to lay the matter before you. To volunteer to do this, while my case was *in transitu*, would subject my motives to misapprehension and could in no way operate to change your feelings towards me, on the supposition that they were not what they ought to be; a supposition which I felt it right to make. And yet *you* are the only human being to whom I have yet mentioned the matter. Had I felt a sense of injury *rankling* in my breast, and kindling my resentment, I should have set aside every other consideration and should have told you the whole matter at once. But as I felt nothing of the kind, except a little anger sometimes, which I could and did overcome with perfect ease, I permitted the matter to rest for the reasons above given, assured that God would bring it all right at last.

"If then you will calmly hear me, and are willing to accord to me kindness of intention, I will, at my first convenience, write to you, and, in a more direct and less formal manner than is required in a publication (for *aliud est epistolam, aliud historiam: aliud amico, aliud omnibus, scribere*) and tell you frankly wherein I feel that your course has been thus oppressive. You will use the same frankness to me in reply. A frank statement on my part, and explanation on yours, may, as you say, do much to correct misapprehension where it is found to exist. And while neither of us would descend to offer or accept a compromise, where reputation is concerned, or character; you may fully believe me, when I assure you, that it would greatly abridge both my labor and my sorrow to ascertain that there exists no reason why I should attempt to right myself at the expense of my Brother Barnes.

"Sincerely and truly yours.

"P. S. When I say above, that you are the only human being to whom I have said that I believe you have so greatly injured me, you will understand me literally. I never have sought sympathy by prating about my sufferings: and as I still hoped there would be no necessity for my coming before the public, I kept these things to myself; and even, when persons have remarked to me (as many have done) upon a specific action or two of yours which they had observed, I have remarked only on that action. So you will understand that the matters which I propose to mention to you, I have as yet laid before no one but God. Though I think proper to mention this, I take no credit to myself for it. The honor of Christ is connected with that of his people, and for this reason I was determined to do nothing which might injure you, unless circumstances left me no alternative."

Such was my offer, putting Mr. Barnes' professions at once to the test, and containing plain and sober statements in reference to the injuries which he had done me; which if they had been made in reference to myself by any human being, and I felt as Mr. Barnes here professes to feel—*innocent of the charge,*—I should never have rested until I had in the fullest manner investigated the subject, and done whatever duty and the circumstances of the case might require. But how did Mr. Barnes proceed? Whether he felt that "a rotten case abides no handling"* the reader must judge for himself; but at all events he first wrote me the following letter, and then proceeded to act as shall be described hereafter:

"PHILADELPHIA, Jan. 8, 1849.

"MY DEAR BROTHER: I received your letter to-day, and sit down to acknowledge it. I did not wish that you should *transcribe* what you have written in regard to me; but my idea was, that it would be brotherly, and might save misapprehension, if you would *read* it to me, or let me read it before it was published. I think it would be better, if convenient, that you should *read* it to me, as I could then make all the explanations, if any are to be made, without the trouble of writing.

"For the same reason, I would suggest, that instead of *writing* to me, and stating your grounds of complaint, that we should have an opportunity to *talk*

* "*Mowb.*—Well, by my will, we shall admit no parley.
West.—That argues but the shame of your offence.
A rotten case abides no handling."—*Shakspeare*, Henry IV. Part II. Act IV.

the matter over. *Manet litera scripta*—and I have a great reluctance to going into a written correspondence about differences between brethren. An hour's conversation, I am persuaded, would be more satisfactory than a ream of correspondence. Of one thing I am certain, that I have never designed to injure a hair of your head. I am very liable to err, as all men are, but I have intended to do justice* to all parties in the affair referred to as far as I knew how. Perhaps on the points to which you refer, altogether unknown to me, and of which I cannot form a conjecture, I might state things which would relieve your mind, as I certainly should desire to if in my power.

"I am sincerely and truly yours."

I need not say how seriously disappointed I was by this letter. I however replied in a brief note, stating my entire willingness that he should peruse the MS. before publication. The reader will notice that the above letter of Mr. Barnes *was dated on the same day with that of the Moderator's call aforesaid* for a meeting of the Presbytery, and whether my letters to Mr. Barnes had any influence in shaping the course which he now resolved to pursue, the reader must judge for himself. At all events, so devoid of true delicacy and of all the proprieties of life was he, that though conscious of his "liability to err," he now actually, *with this correspondence in full view*, undertook to come again to Bethlehem and conduct the business of my enemies to its consummation. This fact speaks volumes, and needs no comment.

In fact he did not wish to see my MS., but simply to cripple me beyond the power of issuing it from the press. Hence he exhibited my correspondence, and made it an excuse for representing me as seeking vengeance against him; and thus succeeded to some extent in alienating from me the feelings of my brethren in Philadelphia. Some of them proposed to come up and visit me, and inquire into the matter; and had he felt as he professes in his letters to me, he would have at once assented to the proposition, but he opposed it, and then went to work with his committee to strike a last blow which will be described in the sequel.

I had, in the above letters, apprised him of my determination to leave my people, and they too were now assured that such would be the fact. But as my resigning my charge thus, would give it the aspect of having been done by me voluntarily, Mr. Barnes was unwilling to permit this, but by his system of wire-pulling, the Ingrate before referred to was induced to take the aforesaid measures to call a meeting of Presbytery, for the ostensible purpose of rectifying the difficulties between me and my people, at the very time in which, by my own arrangement, we were to be separated. Shallow as this pretence and the procedure based upon it were, it was all that yet remained to Mr. Barnes, as affording him a pretext to inflict a further, and, if possible, a fatal injury upon me; and hence he adopted it as aforesaid. But as the Presbytery had been called, and a commission appointed, my people determined to make use of the occasion for the removal of those elders who had so shamefully betrayed the interests of the congregation.

* Admit this declaration for argument's sake. But why, with this conscious liability to err, did Mr. Barnes take the lead in this whole business, (for it was not forced upon him.) and volunteer to act as my judge, as in the cases referred to already? And why should he again, at the very moment of writing this letter, as the reader will see, voluntarily assume the same office?

On the 6th of February (1849), the above named commission met; and the reader must judge whether the manœuvres of their leader were not equal to any exhibited by him in the whole case previously. He would not (after the reception of my letters) so utterly set at naught all appearance of decency as to act as chairman; and accordingly Dr. Parker consented to occupy that office. To save appearances, Dr. Brainerd (though it was known that in consequence of a severe cold, he could not attend,) and his elder, Mr. Farr, were nominated. Neither of these men could be easily influenced to do me injustice willingly, and had they been there, they would have insisted upon fair play. They were not wanted however, and no *very* strenuous efforts were made to prevail upon them to attend. Dr. Brainerd advised the committee as to what his views in the matter were, and what he wished them to do; but his wishes were unnoticed in the whole procedure; and as he could not attend, Mr. Farr deemed it unnecessary on his part to do so. But let us now proceed to the doings of the commission.

They at the outset refused to meet the congregation at the church, that the matter might be publicly heard and adjudicated, but insisted on meeting their representatives only, and in some private place. Mr. Barnes was the sole author of this procedure; and let the reader consider whether its cunning and iniquity, in the circumstances, can be easily paralleled. *Ten* disturbers of the peace of the church had by this man's ecclesiastical wire-pulling, called a meeting of Presbytery, not to effect my removal, but to carry out some sinister purpose by attempting to give to my voluntary resignation the aspect of having been effected by compulsion in consequence of my people's belief of the false charges which had been brought against me. How then was this object to be brought about? I and my people courted and challenged public scrutiny, and Mr. Barnes knew it. He knew also that these men shrunk from it. How then was their end to be accomplished? Why, instead of meeting at the church (at which the congregation at this very time met daily under the hope that this might be done, but the time was there spent in religious exercises), it was insisted on by this candid ecclesiastical Judge, who is so conscious of his "liability to err," that a private house was the most appropriate place; and Gen. Hope's Hotel at Clinton was accordingly selected. Such was the first step, though every one knows that an attempt to settle any such alleged public difficulty privately is sheer nonsense, and never can succeed. But in order to enable these agitators to gain their point, the rest of the commission must be made tools of, and the business upon which they met must be transacted wholly in the dark. *O pudor! O pietas!*

The next step was that no one save the commission themselves should be present at the hearing of the parties concerned, and each party was heard separately! Such was the resolution of these brethren, led on by this most honorable-minded personage, who was so conscious of his liability to err, and so anxious that no spot might remain upon the character of Brother Landis! But, reader, I am tired of exposing this series of iniquitous and complicated wrongs. And it is a comfort that the facts of this part of the history will require no comment. A plain straight-forward narration is all that is needed; and you can make your own comments. This man *thus* constituted himself a judge of affairs most intimately connected with my welfare, and that of my family and people; and thus shut out the possibility of its being known whether his decision was according to facts or prejudice! The parties were thus heard: I *first*, my "friends" (so named, but properly my congregation), *second*, and my enemies *third*. Then of course came the *advisory judgment*.

In my interview with these gentlemen, I laid before them the state of the case in full. Directed their attention to the settlement made in November, 1847, and to the fact that I and my people had fulfilled it to the very letter. Exhibited to them also the manner in which that agreement had been violated by my enemies, and the course which the congregation had taken in view of their conduct. And the fact that at court in February, 1848, the prosecutors came forward and offered to withdraw the prosecution, and to allow me to remain unmolested a year or eighteen months, and to pay me a year's salary in advance if I would only fix upon a time, were it even two years distant, in which I would resign my charge. But that as this offer was made to me upon an assumed right on their part to perpetrate a flagitious injury by violating their own voluntary engagement with myself and the Presbytery, I refused to entertain it upon any terms. I also stated (and in support of these statements the fullest documentary evidence was laid before the commission) that a strenuous effort had been made to carry their point on March 1st, at the election of trustees, which failed by an overwhelming majority; and that nearly all the "sittings" which they hereupon threw up were immediately taken by the people. That on March 29th, we elected our elders, and ordained them on April 7th. I showed them also that our collections for benevolent operations had not at all diminished, for that the piety of the church still adhered to me. And that from March 1st, until the trial at court on May 10th, the congregation was at perfect peace; and in confirmation of the statement respecting its prosperity, referred them to Mr. Patton's account of it as already given.

I directed their attention to the fact also that the trial, notwithstanding its occasion for triumph to my foes, produced only a momentary effect; and that from that time till July or August the congregation steadily increased in numbers; and that our collection for the Bible Society was larger (I believe) than had ever before been given by us to that institution. I showed also that not a soul had left the congregation from March 1st; and that many who had been wrought upon by my enemies, and who had stayed away for a few weeks previous to and after March 1st, began to attend regularly again.

The manner in which the peace of the congregation then became disturbed (as referred to in the preceding chapter, and which need not therefore be repeated here) was then gone into. Though I felt an unconquerable disgust at being obliged to strike the poor men whom Mr. Barnes had placed between himself and me, hoping that they would be mistaken for chief actors in the scene. So I let them pass rather easily, knowing that they had already destroyed themselves utterly with the congregation. The documentary evidence which I had adduced, I left with the commission, until the business should be concluded.

During my statement, Mr. Hunt's former pupil, Dr. Paul, walked deliberately out of the room, and began conversation with several of the persons collected at the hotel, by the ten agitators. This rudeness I did not resent as perhaps I should have done. He was however promptly recalled and mildly, though properly, rebuked by Mr. Barnes, but attempted no apology; and I resumed my statements. Whether this act of Dr. Paul's was designed to indicate on his part a foregone conclusion, he can probably tell. It may, however, evince that he felt no very pressing need of being thoroughly informed as to the facts of the case in order to give a decision.

The church and congregation were next heard by their delegates. These gentlemen not only confirmed the truth of everything that I had offered, but brought forward many important facts in relation to the trial, state of the church, &c., which I did not feel at liberty to adduce. They were closely questioned by the commission, who attempted to induce them to allow the elders to remain in office; telling them (the delegates) that the censure aforesaid of the congregation was very severe, &c., &c. They however refused to yield the point on any terms; and would accept of no settlement with any portion of my enemies unless it was stipulated therein that the elders should resign their eldership. This point, therefore, though reluctantly, the commission were obliged to concede. These poor men had been faithful tools of Mr. Barnes, and it perhaps made him feel badly to see them thus punished for doing only what he had encouraged them to do; but there was no other alternative—out they must go.

The representations of my people made a strong impression upon the commission itself; for these gentlemen were compelled to respect the facts which were brought before them; and the congregation, when it was known that these facts had been laid before the commission, were very sanguine that their cruel wrongs at the hands of my enemies were at length in a fair way of being redressed. How then was this impression to be neutralized? for its existence was found to be sadly incompatible with the result to which Mr. Barnes obviously wished to arrive. There was one way practicable, and but one, and that was adopted. It had been so well provided for by the aforesaid arrangements for secrecy, that one can hardly resist the impression that the emergency had really been foreseen by Mr. Barnes. A member of the commission, the Rev. David Malin, who has ever evinced the utmost readiness to do the bidding of that gentleman, was now selected to accomplish this neutralizing process, though I do not for a single moment suppose that he fully contemplated the purpose which a more cunning head sought to accomplish by means of him. This may be an extenuation, but no conscientious man will regard it as an exculpation; for Mr. Malin ought to have known that nothing could justify his listening to any such proposal: and the mere suggestion of such an act under the circumstances, ought to have aroused every manly feeling and principle of the soul against the tempter, whoever he might be, that would dare to wish to induce him to be guilty of its perpetration. Well, this man was at our evening meeting for public worship, sent into the pulpit to introduce the services by prayer (for I surrendered the pulpit, for the time being, entirely into the hands of these gentlemen), and while performing that solemn part of worship he uttered the isolated sentence (for it had no obvious connection whatever with anything that either preceded or succeeded it),

"*O Lord, grant unto the Pastor of this church* CONTRITION!" What relief has a man thus assailed? How can he parry a blow like this, without affording the enemy, who was base enough to attempt it, occasion to repeat the insult? Even Mr. Barnes' aforesaid paper had declared that I was "truly penitent;" and in my intercourse with the commission I had exhibited no disposition which could have justified the offering of such a petition. But it is folly to dwell upon an enormity like this. When the perpetrator of this deed descended from the pulpit, he (to some extent, at least), conscious of the iniquity of which he had been guilty, glanced at me; and no doubt saw what I thought of an action so indescribably base. Had I listened but an instant to the promptings of my heart, I should have insisted on his immediately leaving the house, or offering an apology. I calmed my feelings however, for with a moment's reflection, I understood the object of the insult, and saw that I had no alternative but to suffer it in silence. But the effect upon many of my people was instantaneous; for taken in connection with a statement made just before by Dr. Parker through Mr. Bird (which will be mentioned presently), they supposed that some unknown and dreadful thing had transpired in the secret conclave of the commission, that had suggested and would justify such an indecency. My poor dear wife, who had participated in the exhilarating hopes aforesaid, was struck to the heart by this poisoned arrow; and in the greatest distress asked me what it meant. This act will, it *must* be, called up for Mr. Malin's consideration by an awakened conscience in a dying hour; and how it will then be viewed, is, perhaps, not difficult to determine. He must, at all events, however, meet it, along with his injured brother, at the bar of God.

The next day the dissatisfied elders came with as perfect a Falstaff's regiment (who were now persuaded to act with them) as ever could be drawn out of a Christian community. They were men who had totally disregarded and trampled under foot the decision and recommendation of Presbytery (of November, 1847), and who in violation of their pledge, had refused to enter the *nolle prosequi*, all of which was known to Mr. Barnes, through whose influence they were now brought forward to complain of *grievances*, and were regarded without the remotest dissatisfaction. There, for example, was Mr. Hunt's son, W. A. A. Hunt, called *Doctor*, by courtesy. He was an Old School man, and neither a member nor pew-holder of the church. He appeared and took the lead in this business with the perfect approbation of Mr. Barnes. There had not been in Jersey so inveterate and malignant an enemy of mine. The history of his connection, too, with the church which he had joined two or three miles north of him, would be in point here as illustrating the disposition of the man to make difficulty in churches; but it would lead us from the point now before us. His son-in-law (pastor of that church) can however tell a story of personal violence which might rank the perpetrator with the ancient *Sicarii*. There too was the son of this man (the overgrown child before referred to), who was joyfully recognized by Mr. Barnes and Dr. Paul, as having rights in the case, though he neither was nor ever had been either a pew-holder or member of the church. There too, and as active as any, was *Judge* Sigler, the distiller, who was neither a pew-holder nor member, and yet was welcomed as a "brother beloved." There too was the individual who, several years before, had been compelled to refund the money of the church and the part of my salary aforesaid; since which time he had not been tolerated in the Society of Bethlehem. He too appeared as one who suffered "grievances," and was, of course, received. These persons and several more were now admitted by Mr. Barnes as the representatives of a *third* party, who had *rights* in the matter, and were by his management and influence thus placed upon an equality with the self-denying and devoted friends of the Redeemer. And why? Oh! reader, why? Was it not all done to gain a final opportunity to strike, with apparent reason, an unoffending brother to the earth, beyond the hope of recovery? Decide for yourself. In this interview with these men, as they themselves admitted, and as is evident also from the report of the commission, not one word was spoken disapproving of their treatment of the recommendation and decision of Presbytery; not a syllable disapproving of their horrid breach of faith with Presbytery and myself; but by the treatment they now received, they were encouraged to believe that they would be sustained in their opposition to temperance, benevolence, &c., &c., and in trampling under foot their own solemn pledge aforesaid. And thus these individuals who had no right nor title to aught but the severest censure, were received and treated in this unprecedented manner, in order to give the appearance that the state of the church and congregation demanded my removal. In this manner he led these enemies of all righteousness to triumph in their conflict with the cause of the Redeemer, simply because they were *my enemies.*

After I had built, and in a manner re-created these once poor, prostrated, languishing congregations, and was just training them onward in religious knowledge, for active service in the kingdom of Christ, Mr. Barnes thus comes in—takes the part of the enemies of that kingdom—destroys, so far as he is able, my character—and breaks up my family, and the church. And why was all this? and wherefore? Oh, can it be, that a professed disciple of Jesus would thus—without any assignable reason, in which either his own, or my welfare, or the welfare of the church of God, or the honor of religion, bears a part—should, from the mere indulgence of that "spirit in man, which lusteth to envy," (James 4 : 5,) THUS seek to crush down, and utterly destroy a brother who had never intentionally given him the least provocation, or the semblance of a justifiable occasion; but who, on the contrary, had stood by him, shoulder to shoulder, amid all his trials and difficulties, and joyfully took part in all his sorrows! Can it be, that such a one should seek to undermine every foothold of kindly earth which I had succeeded in gaining, in the wearying ascent of life, and thus hurl me down again; remorselessly disregarding my church, and my family, and all life's dearest interests and hopes! Can it be, that in order to strike me down, he should thus again and again, sheathe his sword in the very vitals of the blood-bought church of Christ, and obdurately trample her groaning and expiring life in the dust? Haman, immediately after issuing his bloody decree for the utter extirpation of the people of God, could sit down with the king, to eat and drink, amid all the consternation which it produced; but does not the course above described, furnish an equally forcible illustration of the truth, that jealousy or revenge, when intent on its own gratification, is insensible to everything else?

Thus it was that this unhappy man pursued me; and though from the first, he prejudged me and my cause, and sought to make out the worst possible case, (instead of the fair and honorable construction which a generous Christ-like brother would put upon the actions of another;) yet, all that he has dared to allege against me, after taking the entire control of the matter, was, that on one occasion, I had been, not criminal, but imprudent, or indiscreet. But he was resolved thus to follow up his supposed advantage, to its fullest results, until an affectionate and devoted people should be, if possible, entirely alienated from me. *And for what? This question must meet Mr. Barnes not only here, but at that tribunal which is soon to determine, forever, his destiny and mine.* Let him, however, here enjoy the fullest opportunity to explain himself. He has already been heard against me; but let him be fully heard in favor of himself; (for I solicit no unjust judgment against him,) and for the honor of the profession, I shall rejoice to find that the explanation itself is not even worse than the accusation. If Mr. Barnes knows not the import of this intimation, (though he scarcely can help knowing it,) I shall make it perfectly legible, and easily understood, if from any attempted false issue, or further injustice on his part, I should be called upon to resume the pen. But to return.

When matters had proceeded thus far, and the aforesaid indescribable coterie had been heard through their chief spokesman, *Doctor* Hunt, Mr. Barnes, with a view to prepare the congregation for the reception of the Report of the Commission, preached a sermon; and what the Rev. David Malin had done with his above-mentioned prayer, this man now did with his sermon—made it a vehicle for the accomplishment of a sinister aim. By way of fostering the impression which the *prayer* had made, he took occasion to say many things which I could not take hold of, for the purpose of calling him to account, without furnishing apparent reason for him to repeat the insult; and yet they were things which my enemies could employ against me. For example, he introduced the case of Zaleucus, the Locrian law-giver, and with peculiar gusto, expatiated on the story of his son's adultery. (See Valerius Maximus, Lib. X., Sec. 3.) After which, he brought forward the case of Dr. Dodd, of England, and eulogized him as a man of *unblemished reputation*, (which every child knows to be incorrect,) "*until* he perpetrated the one act of forgery, for which he was forever after branded as a criminal, and executed as such, notwithstanding the unparalleled efforts made to save him.* This was the style of the sermon

* Men who have long practiced deceit or cunning, acquire at length, a fatal power of deceiving themselves; and finally indulge that very belief of their own merit, ability, honesty, &c., into which they had endeavored to lead others. How else can we account for this most unfortunate reference to Dr. Dodd! What can surpass the cold-hearted cruelty of introducing this case, as Mr. Barnes did? But as it is thus brought up for review, it may be proper to add a remark in relation to it.

Dr. Johnson says of Dr. Dodd, and referring to other matters besides the forgery: "His moral character is very bad;" yet " he was a very popular preacher, an encourager of charitable institutions, and author of a variety of works, chiefly theological." "He was at first what he endeavored to make others; but the world broke down his resolution, and he, in time, ceased to exemplify his own instructions." Yet this *character* must now be eulogized, in order that Mr. Barnes might strike me a blow.

Dr. Dodd, referring to the years in which he was pursuing a worldly policy, and at the sacrifice of all moral and religious principle, following up a heartless ambition, to be regarded as the *first man* in the church—and even offering a bribe of $15,000 to Lady throughout; and at the conclusion of the services my people inquired of me "what all this meant?" for they could not understand its design, though they saw the use which could be made of it by my enemies. No reader who has the feelings of humanity, can be at any loss to know how to regard such unsurpassable enormity.

The commission now prepared their report. The Rev. Albert Barnes, who was so conscious of his liability to err, and in full view of the aforesaid letters which I had recently written to him, *drew up every line of that report, and then from his paper, dictated it to Dr. Parker, the chairman, who copied it verbatim in his own hand!* This last *coup de main* was perhaps charitably designed by him to be the *coup de grace;* but I have survived even it, and by the grace of God shall continue to do so. This report was read to the congregation, in the evening, and as I was now to leave them in a few days, I did all in my power to produce a kind state of feeling between my friends and those whom the more recent movements had led to conclude that I ought to resign the charge. The most of the congregation, however, would not express their assent to the report, much to the perplexity of Dr. Parker, but sat weeping; for they regarded the commission as having abandoned the ground-plan of settlement recommended by Presbytery in November, 1847, and as sacrificing their interests to men who, in the most unprincipled manner, had violated their pledge, and trampled the dearest interests of the church and its pastor under foot. I wept at this state of things—how could I help it?—but left its responsibility with the men who had brought it about.

As the time for the meeting of the congregation to grant me my dismission had been fixed upon for the Tuesday of the following week, I, fearing that the intervening Sabbath might prove rainy, did, in the hearing of the congregation, request Dr. Parker (after he had finished reading the report*) to give notice that at the time appointed, the church and congregation would meet for this purpose. He did so. Here ended the matter, and on the following day the commission returned home.

As the meeting closed, and the people were separating, Mrs. Landis, who had been weeping, said to me, "I wish to see Dr. Parker." He

Apsley, to induce her to secure to him the Rectory of St. George, in Hanover Square—says of himself: "Nor was I idle during this period; as my *Commentary on the Bible*, *my Sermons to Young Men*, and several other publications, prove."

The poor man, calculating upon his position in the church, thought that by his "Commentary on the Bible," and his "Sermons to Young Men," and other writings, he might counterbalance in the public mind the infamy of the iniquitous worldly policy and management, which he was pursuing. But how vain must such expectations ever be! I have never seen his "Sermons to Young Men;" but his "Commentary on the Bible," (republished subsequently, and with an unaccountable want of conscientiousness, by Dr. Coke, *as his own*,) was, in many respects, the best in the English language; and is as much superior to the "Commentary" of Mr. Barnes, as the elaborate production of the ripe and thorough scholar is to the crude efforts of the rustic freshman. And yet the spirit of the gospel shrinks with abhorrence from all contact with such an advocacy; and every sincere Christian cannot but say, *non tali auxilio, nec defensoribus istis, tempus eget.* Bunyan has some striking thoughts in this connection, in his characters and conversation of Talkative, By-Ends, and old Mr. Hold-the-world.

* I wrote to Dr. Parker requesting him to furnish me with a copy of this report; he did not do it, however, and I have not yet been able to procure it; for I should like to lay it before the public.

was just passing out of the door, and I stepped to him, and announced Mrs. Landis' request, upon which, with his characteristic politeness, he returned, and addressing her in the kindest manner, said, "Mrs. Landis, do you wish to speak to me?" In order that the nature of this interview may be understood, I must here remark, that when it was ascertained that nothing could alienate from me the confidence and affections of my people, a final effort was resolved on in view of the meeting of this commission, and the blow was to be struck just before they should come to Bethlehem, so as to allow me no time either to parry it, or recover from its effects. Accordingly, when Mr. Bird, one of the delegates from the minority of *ten*, returned from Philadelphia, he said, that during the meeting of Presbytery, Dr. Parker had taken him into his study, and told him that at my interview with Mrs. Vanderbelt, I had really *desired* to have illicit intercourse with her. This horrible story Mr. Bird immediately circulated through the whole congregation, and asserted that Dr. Parker had said that I confessed it in the school-house during the interlocutory meeting aforesaid. Now, Dr. Parker did not attend the meeting of Presbytery referred to; and upon a little reflection, my people perceived the falseness of this report, for they remembered that immediately upon the close of the interlocutory at the school-house, I entered the church, and in the course of my aforesaid remarks *to the whole congregation and Presbytery*, "affirmed that I never had had the least desire of the kind towards the woman, much less had I done what she said," a statement which Presbytery would not have allowed me to make if I had just before in the school-house confessed to them any such thing as Mr. Bird now reported on the authority of Dr. Parker. My people providentially remembered this; so this cruel effort failed of its intended effect. Upon the assembling of the members of the commission at Bethlehem, I saw Dr. Parker, and asked him whether he had asserted any such thing? He denied it in the most solemn manner. Mr. Bird was then immediately seen, and he re-affirmed his assertion, and declared that he was willing to depose upon oath that Dr. Parker had told him so. Mr. Bird has the character amongst those who are intimate with him, of being candid and truth-loving, and Dr. Parker ought not to have suffered the matter to rest here, for the deliberate assertion of such a man as Mr. Bird, in relation to a matter of fact like this, is not to be sneered down. There is also other evidence in favor of Mr. Bird, which to my own mind, and to others, is of an overwhelming character, *and which can leave no doubt that Mr. Bird told the truth, unless Dr. Parker has something more to offer than a bare denial.* Mrs. Landis had, however, heard the horrible rumor thus raised. Her heart was already very much crushed, and she now, after referring to the story, and mentioning the language attributed to him, said, "Dr. Parker, did you say this of my husband?" He answered, "*No, Mrs. Landis, I did not!*" "But why," continued she, "at such a time did you speak at all to Mr. Bird against Mr. Landis, when you knew that he was doing all that he could to injure him?" To this, Dr. Parker attempted to give no answer, and bowing respectfully, he retired. He has since had occasion to think of this interview, with feelings which no one could envy.

On the following Tuesday, a congregation assembled according to the notice aforesaid, and the following is the full record of their proceed ings. I transmitted them to Presbytery, and requested that the resolutions therein incorporated might be entered upon the *records*, instead of being merely placed upon file; but whether it was done or not, I have not ascertained. The following is an attested copy of the whole proceedings, though I ought to remark, that not one of my friends who had, as aforesaid, refused to assent to the action of the commission, attended this meeting. They all stayed away, and nothing could induce them to consent to my removal, or to vote for it in any way, and as their opposition could now be of no use, they resolved to have no hand in the matter of my removal.

"*Bethlehem, N. J., Feb.* 14*th*, 1849.

"The church and congregation of Bethlehem met this afternoon, agreeably to previous notice from the pulpit, to consider and act on the application of our pastor, the Rev. Robert W. Landis, to resign his charge as pastor. Elder Jacob S. Johnson was appointed chairman, and John R. Emery secretary. After the meeting was opened with prayer, our pastor made a statement expressing his wish to resign, and his hope that no one would object to it: whereupon a committee of five was appointed to prepare a statement on the subject, to be forwarded to Presbytery. The committee retired, and after about an hour or upwards, returned and reported, which report, after considerable interchange of views and feelings by the congregation, was amended, and (with the exception of one vote, or two at most,) was unanimously approved and adopted, and is as follows:

"The committee appointed to prepare a statement expressive of the sense of the church and congregation of Bethlehem, in view of our pastor's proposed resignation of his charge, would hereby report;

"1st. That our pastor has labored earnestly to compose our unhappy differences, but being unable to effect it, announced his intention some time ago to resign his charge, that some other servant of God might have the opportunity to heal them. At this stage, in the good providence of God, a reference was made of the whole subject to Presbytery. A committee of that body was appointed, who came to us with the sincerest wishes to do us all good.* They had an interview with all our representatives, and with our pastor, and having approved of the step he had taken,† proposed a plan upon which we have been able to meet harmoniously once more. Our pastor set us the example of approving of this plan,‡ and we, having considered it ourselves, have also agreed to it, and at his own earnest request that no one should object to his removal, we would hereby unite with him in his application to Presbytery for a dissolution of the pastoral relation which he sustains to us.

"2d. That the feelings of our hearts upon being brought now to realize that we are so soon to see his face no more, are too strong for utterance. God has brought it about, and we therefore consent to his removal. But when we call to mind that he has devoted to our welfare, seven years of unceasing toil, and of the best portion of man's life; and that in that period the most of us and of our families have been brought to renounce the world, and to indulge a blessed hope in our Saviour; we feel a desolation of spirit which words cannot express, at the thought of hearing the counsels, entreaties, invitations and admonitions of that

* I never exposed to my people the disposition of Mr. Barnes towards me, for it could do them no good. They, therefore, were left to suppose that his aims might be pure, and that he was simply laboring under a mistake of facts. They had seen much in him that they disliked, and had all the people been now present, perhaps he might have heard of it.

† That is, after Mr. Barnes' unparalleled cruelty had driven me to it.

‡ The plan simply affected me by my removal, and this, as the reader sees, I had previously resolved upon. Of course, therefore, I acceded to it.

voice no more. We cannot look upon our children and dearest earthly friends, without being reminded that his faithful and untiring labors have, by the divine blessing, brought many of them to Christ; and many too, who have already passed away from us to heaven. Oh that God would be with us, and send us an under-shepherd, whose labors shall likewise be blessed to the salvation of ourselves, our families, and the community!

"3d. Our pastor has assured us that our interests, both as a church and individuals, shall always be dear to him. This we most cordially and sincerely reciprocate. And we feel sure that that God who has sustained him amidst his sorrows and afflictions here, will still be with him, and bless his labors in whatever part of the vineyard of the Saviour he may be called.

"4th. He has assured us of a remembrance in his prayers. We feel sure that he will often plead at the throne of mercy for his beloved flock; and we assure him that we shall often remember him in like manner while we remain on earth.

"5th. As we thus at his own earnest request, and for the sake of peace in the church, consent to our pastor's removal, whom we so fondly hoped God would continue to us through life; we hope and pray that all of us shall now study the things that make for peace and harmony; and that God's blessing may return to us as in the day when he so abundantly poured out his Spirit upon this our beloved Zion.

"6th. That while we thus consent to a separation from our pastor, we feel impelled by a sense of duty, to declare that nothing which has transpired in relation to his difficulties amongst us has shaken our confidence in his integrity as a Christian and Christian minister; and that the meekness with which he has endured his severe afflictions has only increased our affection for him. And that nothing should induce us to consent to this separation from us, except the consideration of the difficulties above referred to, and the hope of his being more extensively useful elsewhere. And with all the affection of our hearts we recommend him to the confidence of any community where, in the providence of God, his lot may be cast to labor as a minister of Christ."

"Immediately on the report of the committee, the pastor begged leave to retire, in order to afford an opportunity for a full interchange of views on the subject. Then after its adoption, Elder William Emery was unanimously chosen as our delegate, to lay this our action before the Presbytery at its next meeting. And further: that in case Mr. Emery should not be able to be present at said meeting, our pastor be requested in the mean time, to inclose to the Moderator of Presbytery a certified copy of the same. The meeting then adjourned.

"The within (*i. e.* the above,) is a true copy of the report, adopted by the church and congregation of Bethlehem, Feb. 14, 1849; and also a true account of the action in relation thereto.

(Signed,) "JOHN R. EMERY."

These records need no comment; though in view of them it may be in place to quote a remark of the venerable Dr. Green, in his memoirs of the Rev. Joseph Eastburn. It is as follows: "The best evidence of a man's real character is derived from the public sentiment in the place of his stated residence, and where, of course, he is most fully known." On Sabbath, Feb. 25, I bade my people farewell; and if I am somewhat particular in this part of the narrative, the reader will, perhaps, pardon the tedium of the detail. The text of my sermon was 1 Cor. 2: 1–5; and soon after its delivery I received the following application, signed by sixteen members of the church and congregation:

"Rev. and dear Sir: It is the earnest wish of the Bethlehem church and congregation, on whose behalf we address you, to have your farewell discourse to them published, as they would wish to preserve it in a permanent form; and we would respectfully ask that you would gratify them in this matter,

and furnish us with a copy of the same for publication. We are very respectfully your affectionate friends and brethren, L. N. BOEMAN.
W. S. WYCKOFF," &c.

Before I had it half written out, however, my own heart was too much stricken to permit me to finish it, so it was never fully written. The following abstract will not be out of place :

I. *The design of preaching the gospel.*

II. *The proper method of its exhibition.*

I. Its design is simply to make known Christ crucified, as the only way of salvation. Let us consider

1. His doctrines.
2. His precepts.
3. His examples.

That only is the gospel which brings these out plainly and fully to view. All other preaching is but a delusion and a lie.

II. The proper method of its exhibition.

1. Not with ambitious excellency of speech. Such were the teachings of the philosophers. See v. 2, 4.

2. But with plainness and simplicity. God has taught his truths plainly, and we must exhibit them so, if we would secure his blessing.

3. With a proper sense of our responsibility. This will lead us to guard against attempts to compromise God's truth, or to make it more suited to carnal reason. The Spirit will accompany such teaching. v. 4.

Thus, for seven years, and not sparing myself, have I endeavored to labor amongst you. I omit all mention of the difficulties with which I have had to contend. The success with which God rewarded my efforts may properly be referred to. (Revivals in both churches.)

This success was through the plain preaching of God's truth. Cleave then to the doctrines which I have taught you in his name. Cleave also to his precepts, and never compromise either.

I came determining not to know anything amongst you, but Jesus Christ and him crucified; and so by God's grace have I continued. And as I now retire from your midst, I say again, remember these truths, and treasure them up. I have not shunned to declare to you all the counsel of God; and my next meeting with some of you will be at the Judgment-Seat of Christ. Hear me then once more.

1. Ye careless and impenitent souls. Hear me.

2. Ye professed followers of Christ. Your profession will be of little account in the day of trial, if you have nothing else to depend on. Remember that God knoweth your hearts.

And now *adieu*, a final adieu to you.

1. Ye kind and faithful friends. Ye have been true and faithful to the unworthy servant of God, who has so long been privileged to minister to you in holy things. You have not considered me your enemy, because I told you the truth. You have aided me by your prayers and counsel, and influences; and that God whose I am, has remembered it all.

2. Farewell ye who have thought proper to oppose me. You thought it evil, but God meant it for good. A death-bed will afford an occasion of tender retrospection of the scenes through which you and I have passed. When that solemn hour arrives, remember that your pastor has from his heart forgiven everything unkind that you have done to him; and has earnestly prayed, and will continue to pray that God too may forgive you. Farewell, may we meet where sin and misunderstanding exist no more.

3. Farewell, brethren and sisters of the church.

4. Farewell, dear youth and children.

The discourse was then closed by reading Acts 20 : 17-35.

Such is a very brief outline of my adieu to this beloved charge.

Through Mr. Barnes' influence, the efforts made by my brethren to procure me another situation failed to accomplish any thing. On this point, I could say much, but, like many other topics, it can only be thus glanced at, though like them, of great importance, as illustrating the unparalleled selfishness of this strange man.

I now began to prepare for my removal. And as my income was thus entirely cut off, and I had never accumulated any property, I could not, of course, continue the establishment, which required the greater part of my salary to maintain. So on March 27th, the auctioneer's hammer struck off all the little comforts and conveniences which I and my dear wife had been for many years gathering around us. Her feelings and mine may be imagined, but not described; though she strove to appear cheerful and even gay, and to conceal from me her tears. As I stood by her on the day of sale, and saw surrendered up "to the highest bidder," many an article of household furniture which we now could not keep, but which were endeared to her by many a fond and tender association, and called to mind whose heartless malignity it was that had produced this crisis, how could I help but think what an illustration was here furnished of the truth that jealousy is more insatiable than the grave. Where my cruellest persecutors had refrained, and were overwhelmed with remorse at the success of their falsehoods, Mr. Barnes stepped in and took the matter up, and followed me on and on, until my living was now taken from me, and finally my home broken up and all its comforts gone. Such was its result upon myself and family; to say nothing of the heart-bursting agony of my beloved church.

We now took a set of rooms in the house of one of our people, and engaged board with the family until, on a small scale, we could recommence housekeeping: and then left home on a visit to some relatives and friends in New York city and its environs, hoping that the change of scene would be beneficial to us both. On April 17th we returned, and found that in our absence our kind friends had not been unmindful of the comforts of our little home. Early on the morning of the 18th, however, Mrs. Landis was suddenly seized with the pleurisy, the dreadful anguish of which utterly baffled the learning and skill and experience of our best physicians to allay. But I need not narrate the days and nights of intense anxiety which I endured while witnessing her sufferings! After one week of unspeakable anguish, I was alone in the world, and her long and heart-breaking sorrows were forever healed! She sweetly fell asleep in Jesus. My mother was gone, and the endeared home of my childhood broken up; and now before my lacerated heart-strings could heal, this last and heaviest stroke was inflicted: but I repine not. The God who doeth all things well has taken them to himself; and blessed be his name! the sorrows which hastened their removal can now afflict them no more.

During the illness of my dear wife, the ladies of the congregation attended in throngs, anxious to minister to her comfort and relief: to whom she stated that her only wish to live was, to see me through my present sorrows and difficulties. All who were acquainted with her, know that had she entertained a doubt as to whether the accusation against me were true, nothing on earth would have prevented her from acting accordingly. And had she *believed* the story, she would have preferred to die in an alms-house rather than to remain another hour under my roof. A day or two before she died, I received a letter from the Rev. G. N. Judd, D.D., of Catskill, N. Y., inviting me to take charge of a vacancy in the bounds of Columbia Presbytery. The letter required an immediate answer. I read it to her, and asked her what reply I should make? She answered, "Tell Brother Judd how ill I am; and that in a few days there will be a change one way or the other, which will enable you to give a definite answer." On the morning of the 25th (the day of her death,) she calmly made arrangements for her funeral, requesting that Dr. Kirkpatrick, of Ringoes, N. J., might officiate on the occasion. And during a few moments that I was absent from her room, she said to two ladies who were in attendance (Mrs. Sarah C. Hoyt and Miss Hannah Chandler), "Say to Mr. Landis' enemies that with my dying breath I affirm my full belief that every one of their evil reports against him is false." And soon after, waking, as it were, from death's incipient sleep, she repeated, "Say, that with my dying breath I affirm my full belief that the evil reports which they have raised against him are wholly false."

Awhile after the conclusion of the aforesaid correspondence between Mr. Barnes and myself, and after I found that he was not disposed to repent of his wickedness towards me, I made Mrs. Landis fully acquainted with the course which he had pursued. She was surprised, greatly, for it furnished the only solution of the strange acts of that man, which she and the rest of the congregation had noticed and remarked upon. She then advised me to prosecute this history with vigor, and I did so; submitting to her perusal the chapters as they were completed. Little did she or I then suppose that it was to have such a termination. On the morning before she died, she said to me amongst other things, "I told Mrs. Hoyt, I think it was, that I had no hard feelings towards any one of them (my persecutors). They have acted wrong; but I forgive them."

On the 30th, we took her remains to Philadelphia, to be deposited in their last resting place. A large number of the brethren of the Third and Fourth Presbyteries of Philadelphia met us there,* and after some deeply impressive services in which Messrs. Ramsey and Grant, and Dr. E. S. Ely took part, the cold tomb received the last object which had bound my heart to earth. And on May 4th, I started for Hillsdale, N. Y., (to which I had been previously invited by Dr. Judd,) in which place God has continued to bless my poor labors as heretofore, in the upbuilding of his church.

Shortly after the death of my wife, the Rev. Wm. Ramsey, of Philadelphia, transmitted to me the following letter of hers, in relation to the trial before Presbytery in November, 1847, and written immediately after the adjournment of that body. It speaks for itself, and with it I shall conclude this already protracted chapter.

"SIDNEY, Nov. 23, 1847.

"REV. MR. RAMSEY:

"Dear Sir—I take the liberty of writing you some of my feelings relative to the late painful trial. I am writing without my husband's knowledge, and sure

* Mr. Barnes was not amongst them, but Dr. Parker was; who evinced toward me much kind feeling and sympathy.

I am without his approbation; but I think a sense of duty to him is my sole object. If I understood Mr. Barnes rightly, he said the charges against Mr. Landis were *in part sustained.* The crime, I think, charged, was *lascivious conduct.* Am I right? If so, I dissent from the decision with all due respect. The members of Presbytery are all aware that Mr. Hunt had every advantage in the prosecution; and that Mr. L. gave up many rights guaranteed by the Constitution. Many others he gave up out of respect to the feelings of his brethren, they being so long in session; and many others he gave up from his unwillingness to expose the character of his accuser, but which for his own sake ought to have been done. I regret that the members of Presbytery did not publicly make their views known; and that Mr. L. did not make a defence. It was certainly evident to all that each of the statements on the principal charge greatly disagreed." (Mrs. L.'s remarks on the evidence I omit.) "I greatly regret that more witnesses were not brought by the accused. He could have had them in abundance to testify what his *general conduct* was among his people. Few settled pastors have ever labored more, in season and out of season, for the salvation of his people: and yet he is represented by Mr. Hunt as a dangerous man! No father has ever guarded the chastity of his child more faithfully than has Mr. Landis all that he associated with. He may be charged with *indiscretion;* and that is only to be charged to *constitutional infirmity,* and not to a *corrupt heart.* From the infant of a month old, to the matron of four-score and fifteen, all (both male and female) share alike his *affection* and his *confidence.* Since he has been my husband,* I can truly say, I do not believe he has ever had *one thought* inconsistent with moral purity towards any female. Clerical dignity, if nothing else, however, requires he should be more guarded in future. It is the opinion of more than myself that had Presbytery continued in session on Monday, the members, on mature reflection, would have acted differently. There was too much haste at the close. My husband was not in a state either of mind or body to pursue things further at that time; and the feelings of Mr. Barnes and some others† sympathized too much with Mr. Hunt. True, it was affecting to see an old man of four-score in tears, and telling of his watching and his prayers; professing penitence, and willing to recall what he had done (after doing *all* he could do). But we, as a people, have not forgotten, (for our wounds are not yet healed,) we, sir, have not forgotten—the anguish of a single night?—no! in our remembrance is the anguish of many long, long, wearisome nights, with its watchings, and its prayers; of days of fasting and weeping; of the entire neglect of family duties; the thousands of tears which were shed, compared with (which) Mr. H.'s were but as a drop in the bucket: and this not only in the church, but in the community. And why was all this? Was Mr. Landis regarded as a guilty man? No! because he was regarded as a *slandered, persecuted man.* And all this could have been spared, had Mr. Hunt done his duty as a Christian. Though no member of Presbytery *witnessed* our agony, it was no less *real.* And could it have been embodied and laid before your Honorable Body, it would have appeared a mountain compared to a mole-heap. And yet Mr. Hunt receives no *censure!* Think you we are satisfied? I answer, No! If *honestly* the charge of *lascivious conduct* can be "partly sustained," so let it be; but if *indiscretion,* only, why use the phraseology that is used?‡ I think it was not well considered; otherwise it would not have been as it is. Can you not *review* this? Cannot some other term less offensive be used, that would meet the case? We do think the words used are too *severe.* I admit he may have been imprudent; but are there not many of his brethren (with the same materials as Mr. L. has had in his church), who are now considered blameless, who, if passed through the same ordeal, must have shared the same unhappy fate? I again repeat it, Mr.

* We were married April 29th, 1835.

† Referring to those who, not knowing the deep hypocrisy of old Mr. Hunt, believed him truly penitent because he wept, and thought he ought to be forgiven: though all but Mr. Barnes, I believe, thought he deserved censure.

‡ *A question that Mr. Barnes must meet at the Bar of God!*

L. knows nothing of this; I write by stealth. If you can make any good use of this, as a Christian and gentleman I believe you will do so. As a wife I feel for his situation. He is much *depressed:* and if, hereafter, he becomes acquainted with what I now do, though he may blame the *act*, I know he will honor the *motive;* therefore I do not fear his knowledge. May the Lord guide and direct (you) in the way that is most for his honor and glory, is the sincere prayer of

"Your sister in Christ,

"ELIZABETH LANDIS."

CHAPTER XVII.

SEQUEL TO THE CATASTROPHE.

WHEN the last scene of this tragedy had been acted, I proceeded to the place in which I now am laboring, and where I at once took charge of a Presbyterian church which was in no flourishing condition. God, however, left me not without his blessing; but of this I need not speak; and yet so embittered still were the factions which sought my ruin, that scarcely had I arrived at this place and begun to labor, ere Mr. Hunt's grandson, the aforesaid Thomas Hunt, came here, and, during an interval of my absence, told against me the story of my accuser, with enormous additions and improvements, after which he returned to Jersey and boasted that he had utterly destroyed my character in Hillsdale. Through the goodness and mercy of a covenant-keeping God, however, this malice failed of effecting anything of moment. I was subjected, it is true, to all the disadvantages of being a stranger; but the community, without my intervention, looked into the matter candidly and impartially, and came to the conclusion, which they extensively announced, that *Thomas Hunt was an unprincipled scoundrel, whose scurrility could be harmful only in the intention.* I must do his grandfather the justice to say, however, that he expressed the strongest disapprobation of his conduct in this matter. Upon my leaving Bethlehem the heart of the poor old man had mellowed down, as he called to mind my inexpressible sorrows, and the part he had taken in their infliction. This effort, therefore, at Hillsdale, to injure me, did not amount to much, even though a bigoted clergyman of another denomination (who had even announced from the pulpit, before I went to Hillsdale, that the Presbyterian church there was dying) sought to make capital of it; but there was no heartless rival amongst my brethren of the Presbytery here to favor the evil surmise and create odium against me, otherwise this little branch of the Redeemer's Zion might have perished beyond recovery, for most of its friends had given it up to die.

About a year, if I recollect rightly, after I came to this place, the wretched Ann Seal, upon whose testimony alone I was cast at court, was expelled from the Methodist Church for the crimes aforesaid; and what an admirable opportunity did this event furnish for a pure-minded man to come forward in behalf of a persecuted and calumniated brother! So soon, however, as the word reached Philadelphia, a common friend of mine and Mr. Barnes, and one who had mourned over the fact that he professed to believe me guilty, joyfully hastened to him and announced the intelligence, supposing that his mind must at least be greatly relieved by it, and that he would at once rejoice to embrace the opportunity thus afforded of relieving the character of a Christian brother and minister of Christ from dishonorable and scandalizing imputations. Would not this have been done, if he had had the honor of religion at heart?—who can doubt it? But how did Mr. Barnes treat the intelligence when thus communicated? Why, instead of evincing joy, he seemed displeased that my friend should evince such anxiety on the subject, and said, "At any rate, there *must be something wrong* in Mr. Landis' conduct according to his own *confession*," or *concession*, for I am not certain which term he used; and thus for some length of time he even closed up against me the warm-hearted sympathies of one of the kindest and best of earthly friends! "*Something wrong*"! what think you of this?—and this "something wrong" must be *so wrong* as to justify Mr. Barnes' whole course of unparalleled cruelty towards me and my family and church; though at the same time that wrong is consistent with all the aforesaid facts, and favorable statements of his own, (in his letters, minute, &c.,) and of my brethren; and with the continued and unimpaired confidence of my people. Yes, in view of all this, and of the fact that I utterly denied the tale of this wretched woman, and challenged my enemies to do their best, this man would thus darkly insinuate suspicions against me; and when Providence also is appearing on my behalf by exposing to open view, and beyond the possibility of doubt, the character of my accusers, and, by consequence, the obvious aim of their efforts against me; this unhappy man must array himself against the proceedings of Providence, in order to gratify his feelings towards me, and to secure impunity to himself by preventing my full restoration to public confidence. To think of the Rev. Albert Barnes thus referring to a "something wrong" in my conduct, as an abiding reason why the public should continue to withhold from me their confidence, when he ought to know that any one of the hundred acts which he has perpetrated against me and my church evince more of deep-seated depravity than would be exhibited by the perpetration of everything which my enemies so falsely charged against me. He from the first had the heart to wish me guilty rather than saved, and his whole course since has been in accordance therewith. His success, however, has insured the promised recompense: Justice may linger, but she is sure;* and let him remember that

> "He who but once hath acted infamy,
> Does nothing more in this world."

Ever since the part he took in my affairs his hands have been utterly paralysed to everything that is good. Not a revival, nor even the appearance of religious interest, has arisen amongst his people since the fatal year in which he thus first put forth his hand to strike me. The most appalling events have likewise broken down the influence of New Schoolism in and about Philadelphia. Since the time referred to he has also refused to unite with his brethren in their efforts to promote the revival of religion, and declared that he could not attend even the weekly evening prayer-meetings, (in which the city pastors met to pray for a

* Raro antecedentem scelestem
Deseruit pede pœna claudo.

revival,) because he must finish his Commentary. He was then writing on Daniel. The work has long been finished; and though a publisher has been *incidentally* sought through the papers, none I believe can be found who are willing to risk the issue of a work which is of so much more importance to the Church than a revival of religion. But the effects of this sin have extended farther, and, as in the case of Achan, it has brought guilt and punishment upon the whole army of our Israel. Who has not seen and noticed and deplored the fact above-mentioned, that, since 1847, the progress of New Schoolism at and about Philadelphia has been arrested, and that throughout our country our accessions since that time have been as nothing, compared with those of the years which preceded? Our army has stood still, or turned its back upon the enemy. Guilt exists somewhere; greater guilt than that of merely coveting a wedge of gold and a Babylonian garment: and, before it be too late, let us examine and ascertain what is necessary on our part to turn away the wrath of God from our beloved Israel, lest our Zion soon be numbered with the things that were.

After the final arrangement had been made for my leaving the Bethlehem church, I, not knowing where my lot should be appointed, or what would become of me and my family in this world, committed a little work to the press which had long been the companion of my hours of leisure from the more important duties of my profession. It was a poem on my country's achievement of her Independence. It had cost me sixteen years of severe study, and though not so perfect as I wished to make it, I preferred to publish it, in order to secure the copy against accident in my thenceforth uncertain state of life. Perhaps I was too partial to this cherished offspring of my brain, but I never wrote a work under a higher sense of duty both to God and man; and I have never doubted that it will have a bright day of its own in years to come. At all events it could do no harm; and if read, must do good. Not a few have read and re-read it with a delight which, in my most sanguine moments, I dared not anticipate, and which has already recompensed me for all my toil in its production. Well, this poor little unsupported, though favorite, child of its author, made its appearance a few months after my removal to Hillsdale; and immediately all the influence which had been following me up as above described, was concentrated to strangle it to death. The subject is not sufficiently important to require a particular detail; but two booksellers, who had advertised the work for sale in Philadelphia, were thereupon directly influenced against it to that degree that they would not keep it on hand, though it was repeatedly called for. In process of time, too, a scurrilous notice of it appeared in New York, in a paper which, in the religious world, occupies a position and sustains a character analogous to that which the "*Herald*" (published in the same city) does in the political world;* and that low scurrilous notice

* Far-seeing editors, aware of the nature of their position, and also of the consequences which may result to their establishment, from their mistakes and infirmity, sometimes associate with them in the editorship an individual, with the design that he shall occupy the place of a "scape-goat;" and whose mental character being sufficiently well known, the public will spontaneously attribute thereto all the disgraceful littlenesses which, in unguarded moments, may proceed from the excited pen of the senior. The individual thus engaged, is however, of course, not aware of his position, but deems himself "as good a man as the best of them;" and hence you will see a

(written, too, by one who confessed that he had never read the work) was, by virtue of the same influence aforesaid, (which I doubt not also led to its production,) taken to the "ministers' meeting" on Monday, and read to all who were there assembled. This was a very small business, but it was resorted to for reasons too obvious to require to be specified. And the idea that a meeting, founded by the Rev. James Patterson for prayer and religious exercises, should be desecrated in a manner and for a purpose like this, would be ludicrous, were it not too closely allied to something else to admit of the indulgence of such a sensation.

About the middle of July I wrote to the Moderator of the Fourth Presbytery (Dr. Gilbert) requesting, that at as early a day as convenient, my certificate of membership and dismission from the Fourth Presbytery might be forwarded to me; though not desiring that a special meeting should be called for the purpose. This fact was immediately seized upon by my aforesaid enemies, and it was rumored over the city that such papers would be refused to me. In the mean time, Mr. Grant's case had been tried, and was also to come before Synod by appeal. I, of course, while a member of the Fourth Presbytery, was a member of that Synod. Mr. Barnes has always evinced a nervous excitability at the thought of my being heard in my defence; and, as in the course of Mr. Grant's trial, one of Mr. Barnes' satellites (P. F. Smith, Esq. of Westchester, Pa.) went out of his way to speak unkindly of me, there was reason to apprehend that if I attended Synod, some unpleasant disclosures might be made, when the aforesaid appeal was brought forward: for, as a member of that body, I should have demanded the right of repelling, in the same connection, the "toad-eating" of the above-named individual; at all events, the kind-hearted sympathies of my brethren of the Presbytery, in this instance, met with no serious opposition. And at their meeting in October, the *first thing* done (if I recollect rightly) was to attend to my request; and the following dismission, kind and handsome beyond that request, was granted me:

swelling in his inane lucrubations, which evinces not only his desire to equal the stately ox in size, but also the conceit that he has done so, because he has perhaps even exceeded him in noise. Something however is necessary besides noise and vituperation to constitute a real "*Independent*." Joseph not only did not read my work, but he possesses not a tythe of the literature requisite to form any just opinion in relation to it. I should not have asked him to write *my* biography, for, with a far better subject, as all can see, such a biographer places a man under the *invincible necessity* of dying twice, without the privilege of living more than once. It is unfortunate for the reader when those who have anything to do with the press, do not understand the true nature of their position.

I have been informed that another editor of the same paper wrote the criticism which appeared in the *Tribune* against my book. I have some knowledge of the man, and must say that there seems to me to be some mistake in regard to that matter. The criticism is unworthy of such an intellect and heart as I know he possesses. And if he did write it, I can only say—

"Then ****** essay'd; scarce vanish'd out of sight,
He buoys up instant, and returns to light:
He bears no token of the sabler streams,
And mounts far off among the swans of Thames."

In the Dunciad (B. II.) *as well as here*, he comes next after *Smedley*.

"PHILADELPHIA, Oct. 3d, 1849.

"Meeting of the Fourth Presbytery of Philadelphia.

"The Rev. Robert W. Landis, a member of this Presbytery, applied for letters of dismission and recommendation to the Presbytery of Columbia.

"On motion, the request of Mr. Landis was granted, and he is hereby affectionately recommended to the fellowship of the Presbytery of Columbia."

"*Extracted from the Minutes.*

"CHARLES BROWN, Stated Clerk."

As I had, however, received no answer to my application for dismission, and being apprised of the fact that an enemy or two would, in all probability, attempt to prevent my obtaining "clean papers," I proceeded to Philadelphia; and as I walked into the place of meeting, saw Mr. Barnes, and Mr. Hunt's pupil, Dr. J. M. Paul, in close conclave with the pastor-elect of Bethlehem Church, and one or two of its members. He wished still to supervise the interests of that people; and I did not envy his feelings when he saw me eyeing himself and his conclave. No other member of Presbytery sat near them. As I looked at him and his Belvidere elder, I could not but think of the words which referred to a matter to which my own case seemed to me to be strikingly analogous: "Hast thou killed, and also taken possession?" 1 Kings 21: 15–19. A little incident however occurred, a few moments after, which ought, perhaps, to be referred to as illustrative of several points of interest which have been brought out to view in the course of this history.

The Bethlehem church and congregation had sent delegates for the young man above-referred to, to become its pastor. Messrs. Joseph Boss and Jacob M. Johnson were thus appointed. It was, however, the wish of the people that Presbytery should send a committee to instal him; and while this request was under consideration, and a committee, consisting of Rev. Messrs. Ramsey and Adair, and Elder Forbes, appointed to consider and report thereon, Messrs. Johnson and Boss (both of whom had acted with the dissatisfied elders against me) came privately and requested me to employ my influence with Presbytery, in order to secure for the purpose aforesaid, the appointment of several individuals whom they named. But they did not wish Mr. Barnes on that committee—he, whose attendance had always previously been solicited by the churches of our Presbytery on such occasions. I did as I was requested by the delegates; but as I was obliged to leave Presbytery before the business could be finished, I presented them to the above-named committee; and after stating their request as to the individuals whom the congregation wished to attend, I remarked that it was highly desirable that the wishes of the congregation should be regarded in the matter. The committee promptly acquiesced in the suggestion, and I left. But so desirous was Mr. Barnes to attend to the matter, and so anxious that there should be no meeting of the brethren there, unless he were present, though he just before (as stated above) had advised a commission to meet there in my case, he actually, in a speech or two, urged, that the *Presbytery itself* should adjourn to meet at Bethlehem; though he must have known that there was not the least hope of the brethren leaving their charges and taking a long and expensive journey in order to attend to a matter which in no way required them to do so. The brethren, however, whom (at the request of Messrs. Boss and Johnson) I had named to go up, did go, and I believe no others, *except Mr. Barnes.* His self-sacrificing spirit was so superior to that possessed by the others, that he would not descend even to think of such things as toil, expense, or *even time*, though his commentary on Daniel was yet upon the anvil. *He actually went up and took part in the business*, though I suppose there was scarcely a soul in Bethlehem who wished to see him there. He of course took the lead in the proceedings: and was, moreover, *very expeditious.* He did not deem it desirable to have the brethren scatter through the congregation, but preferred keeping them together and bringing them down with him: and hence, as I am informed, the business was finished, and the brethren brought back some distance from Bethlehem, all in one day. What a pity it is that he never felt such a yearning interest for any congregation but mine! His care over mine was so great, that from September, 1847, until this time, he could not trust any one to transact their business without his dictation. But, *il n'y a que moi, qui a toujours raison.*

God continued greatly to prosper my poor labors at Hillsdale. Successful efforts also have been made to rebuild, in a most beautiful style, our house of worship, which was in a very dilapidated state when I went there. During my intervals of leisure, I have been completing this history, for the impulse kindled within my soul to do it, was like a fire in my bones, and allowed me no rest, until it was done. As Mr. Barnes had, however, by his conduct, cut himself off from all right to receive any attention in this matter from me, and as I did not care to proceed to my final action in the case, without permitting him to have a clear idea of the leading points, on which it would be necessary for him to explain or defend his conduct, a letter was written to a clergyman of Philadelphia, (with the design that it should be laid before Mr. Barnes, without his being able to ascertain who had been its recipient from me) containing an analysis of the work; but which our limits will not permit us to introduce.

CHAPTER XVIII.

REMARKS ON THE CASE.

Such is the tragedy from its prologue to its catastrophe; and the mass of material all tending to illustrate and confirm the truth of the foregoing representations, but which for want of room I am compelled to omit, is very great. I believe, however, that the preceding facts will be found sufficient; yet, if there be any occasion for me to resume the pen, I shall ask attention to the remainder.

That God has, by his wise and kind Providence, shaped all the aforesaid diversified interests, &c., so as to bring about the results which have been, and still remain to be secured, I rejoice to believe; and they have brought me into that condition which is best for me; and all have happened, so far as I am personally interested, as the just desert of my sins. Innocent as I am of the crimes charged upon me, (as already remarked,) yet I am not innocent of sin: and I fully believe that any sin, however trivial in the view of man, deserves, and would lead to eternal ruin, did not the infinite goodness of God interpose.

13

That the result, however, is yet final, I do not, and never did, believe. Its ulterior purposes have not yet been developed; but they will be. My name shall not always remain under the reproach thus brought upon it: and just so sure as there was horrid crime, and lying, and perjury, and enmity, and literary jealousy, &c. enlisted, to secure this result, as respects myself, just so sure will every blow struck against me from these and other improper motives, rebound with seven-fold force upon its author. God's promised protection and interference are on the side of his children, who are thus assailed; and that promise has never yet, in any such case, failed of fulfillment, and it never can fail. He has said to me, as he says to all such: "Be still, and know that I am God." The relation of these ulterior results to Mr. Barnes and others will be referred to in another chapter.

Many will read with surprise and astonishment, the facts narrated in the preceding pages. Through the efforts of Mr. Barnes to take every possible advantage of the false position into which I had been brought by Mr. Hunt and my other enemies, a hundred vague impressions of most injurious tendency had been made against me, while my friends at a distance from Bethlehem were awed to silence. Mr. Barnes being frequently requested to state "the truth of the matter," and being aware that the position to which we had exalted him before the public would exempt him from a suspicion of being actuated by sinister motives, made good use of the occasions thus afforded—little dreaming that he was thus digging a pit, in whose foul and loathsome damps he himself might be suffocated; for when once this whole matter is fully understood, the Christian public will not be slow to award to me its best recompense, for having treated me as it has done, on the assumed, but fallacious ground, that no man could be found sufficiently dishonorable to take such advantages as Mr. Barnes has done. I never have, knowingly, courted either popular favor, or sympathy; and surely I shall not begin to do so now. A decision pronounced against a man, on such grounds as the aforesaid, ought not, perhaps, to be laid much at heart. The time of recompense, even in this world, will come. Its arrival will probably find me in the grave: but Justice will embalm my memory; and her fearful retributions to those who have "joined hand in hand" to accomplish the ruin of a minister of Christ will prevent a reiteration of such deeds, for centuries to come. If Mr. Barnes has, designedly, pursued the definite result, to which his whole course in this affair has so directly tended, he deserves to be held up as an awful beacon, until the end of time; but if, on the contrary, he has acted thus without designing such results, let him make it appear. The *facts* are before the reader.

The efforts of Mr. Barnes, by insinuations, as well as by direct attempts, to influence my friends and brethren against me, and which have induced a portion of the public to prejudge my case, are of a character scarcely to be paralleled; and all perpetrated too with that peculiar cunning, which aims to leave its victim defenceless, and destitute even of the power to parry the thrusts, without seeming to acknowledge that the insinuations are just. A patient endurance of wrong will, however, generally succeed in baffling such expectations, and will enable the victim in some way to obtain redress. The injury done him may have been perpetrated with such refinement of littleness, as to baffle all attempts to detect and expose it, by any or all of the technicalities of legal or ecclesiastical jurisprudence—but still there is a remedy. Public sentiment, however much abused by attempts to pre-occupy it against a fellow-citizen, is, nevertheless, a tribunal of ultimate and safe appeal in such cases; and is ever ready to rectify and reverse a judgment, by which, on insufficient grounds, it has inflicted such an injury. And while I appeal to this tribunal, I am willing, also, to abide its judgment on the question, whether any other resort is left in such circumstances as mine.

I must now ask the reader's attention to a few considerations which I could not present in the preceding historical development, without too great a deviation from the strict analysis which we have therein attempted. Let him bear in mind then how atrociously I have been calumniated, even to the loss, in a considerable degree, of public confidence in me as a minister of Christ; and also how Mr. Barnes and his satellites have even favored those rumors against me. And now, in view of all, I ask attention to the fact that this whole story at first originated, as above stated, amongst a herd of counterfeiters, distillers and liquor-sellers, sabbath-breakers, profane swearers, and other enemies of all righteousness. Just such persons as have ever made it a point to assail the characters of all who have labored faithfully in the gospel of Christ; and whose assaults good men have ever regarded as *prima facie* evidence, not only of the innocence, but of the faithfulness and fidelity of the accused. How fiendishly was Bunyan assailed in this manner! He may tell the story in his own language: "But when Satan perceived that his thus tempting and assaulting me would not answer his design, to wit, to overthrow my ministry, and make it ineffectual as to the ends thereof; then he tried another way, which was to stir up the minds of the ignorant and malicious to load me with slanders and reproaches; now, therefore, I may say, that what the devil could devise and his instruments invent, was whirled up and down the country against me, thinking, as I said, that by that means they should make my ministry to be abandoned. It began, therefore, to be rumored up and down among the people that I was a witch, a jesuit, a highwayman, and the like. To all which, I shall only say, God knows that I am innocent." * * "But that which was reported with the boldest confidence, was that I had my misses, my whores, my bastards, yea, two wives at once, and the like. Now these slanders, with the others, I glory in, because but slanders, foolish or knavish lies, and falsehoods cast upon me by the devil and his seed. And should I not be dealt with thus wickedly by the world, I should want one sign of a saint, and a child of God. Matt. 5 : 11, 12. These things, therefore, on my own account troubled me not; no, though they were twenty times more than they are. I have a good conscience," &c. &c.*

But suppose that some wicked old covetous man had sympathized with these malevolent traducers, and had daily watched for an opportunity to get up some plausible story against Bunyan; he could have found many ready to swear to the truth of either of the reports alleged. He then takes an affidavit, and sends it to another Mr. Barnes (whose soul was jealous of the success which God had given to the labors of Bunyan); who at once resolves to make the utmost out of it for the purpose

* See Bunyan's Works, p. 40, Philadelphia edition, 1832.

of prostrating the accused. Bunyan would doubtless have been crippled for awhile; but, overwhelming ruin from God would sooner or later overtake these unhappy men. Striking indeed, and in accordance with the word of God, is the remark of Homer:

> 'οπποτ' ἀνηρ ἐθελη προς δαιμονα φωτι μαχεσθαι
> 'ον κε θεος τιμᾳ, ταχα οἱ μεγα πημα κυλισθη.
>
> He who assails the man whom God protects
> And honors, wars with God; and vengeance shall
> With hideous ruin sudden him o'erwhelm.

So too in the case of the devoted Nettleton. His successful labors in the cause of Christ roused up enemies wherever he went, so that when he visited Virginia, some of his brethren there doubted the propriety of inviting him to preach. At length Dr. Rice wrote to the north in order to learn how Dr. Nettleton's character stood in the place where he was best known. The letter was answered by Drs. Day, Taylor, Fitch, Beecher, Goodrich, Spring, M'Auley and others; and the vile rumors were thus set at rest. But suppose for example, that Dr. Taylor had yielded to feelings of envy and rivalry, and had replied to the letter in an ambiguous manner, and had taken pains to go among his brethren, and insinuate that they had better not be too forward in identifying themselves with Nettleton, &c. Had Dr. Taylor been capable of such baseness, it is hardly probable that he could have extensively influenced his brethren aforesaid; but if he had thus succeeded, Dr. Nettleton would have been thoroughly crippled in every succeeding effort to advance the Redeemer's kingdom. But where, oh where, would have rested the guilt?

But take another case; it is that of the seraphic Payson. A wicked woman once brought against him an accusation, under circumstances which seemed to render it impossible that he should escape. She was in the same packet, in which, many months before, he had gone to Boston. For a time it seemed almost certain that his character would be ruined. He was cut off from all resource, except the throne of grace. He felt that his only hope was in God; and to him he addressed his fervent prayer. He was heard by the Defender of the innocent. A "compunctious visiting" induced the wretched woman to confess that the whole was a malicious slander.* But suppose that before this compunctious visiting came, some old enemy had secured her statements by such a course as was pursued in my case by Mr. Hunt, and thus left her only the alternative of imprisonment for perjury should she retract her statement. God would doubtless have interfered, as I know he will do in my case; but then how easily might Payson have been pursued almost to ruin by some jealous rival, under these circumstances. My accuser did everything she could do (without subjecting herself to the aforesaid penalty) in order to relieve me from this wicked charge; and it would have relieved me, had it not been for the course pursued by Mr. Barnes.

In view of this attempt to destroy Payson, his biographer remarks as follows: "There are in the lives of eminently faithful ministers, events which it is painful to narrate, and yet which ought not to be passed in

* Payson's Works, I. pp. 352, 353.

silence. The hostility which they sometimes experience illustrates the depravity of mankind, and confirms the authority of scripture by evincing the truth of the declaration—'If any man will live godly in Christ Jesus, he shall suffer persecution.' We need not be surprised, therefore, if Dr. Payson should have been wickedly assailed in his character, as a preacher of a kindred spirit was assailed before him. It is related of Richard Baxter, that when he was shaking the strongholds of error and iniquity at Kidderminster, a drunken slanderer reported concerning him, that he had been seen under a tree with a profligate woman; and thus he was made 'the song of the drunkards.'" This accusation turned out to be a silly falsehood on the defamer's own acknowledgment.

In every way were efforts made to destroy this man of God. On one occasion, says Baxter, "a Mr. Dyet, son to old Sir Richard Dyet, Chief Justice in the North, and brother to a deceased dear friend of mine; the wife of an old dear friend, said openly that I had killed a man with my own hands; that it was a tinker, at my door, who, because he beat his kettle and disturbed me in my studies, I went down and pistoled him. Mr. Dyet told Mr. Peters that a hundred witnesses would testify it was true, and that I was tried for my life at Worcester for it." The wretch however ultimately came to Mr. Baxter, and asked his forgiveness for the falsehood.

At Langport too a report, says Mr. Orme,* "was for a long time privately circulated to the great prejudice of Baxter's character. Will the reader believe that he was actually charged with killing a man in cold blood with his own hand! At last it was publicly laid to his charge by Major Jennings himself, *in the form of an affidavit*, and published by Vernon in his life of Dr. Heylin." (Here follows a copy of the affidavit, and also of Baxter's utter denial of the truth of the charge, after which the biographer continues:) "Such is Baxter's full and satisfactory explanation of one of the most improbable and wicked calumnies that ever was propagated against a man of God. It is a curious illustration of the state of the times, that such a base story could find reporters and believers, *not only among the ignorant and the profligate, but even among the respectable part of the clergy*." And, I may add, what would have become of this man of God, had either of those rival clergymen for the time being, possessed the power and influence to enable them to follow him up by such relentless and merciless persecution as the Rev. Albert Barnes has followed up myself? But God *then* protected his servant from their malice and rendered it utterly impotent; and in like manner he *now* will sooner or later evince his faithfulness by protecting me.

And now, in the light of these and a thousand similar cases, let the reader look back upon the origin of the wicked slanders with which I have been assailed, and of which Mr. Barnes has endeavored at my expense to make such capital: and let him say whether anything can be more merciless and heartless than to seek to pursue a laborious minister of Christ to destruction on grounds like these, even though circumstances should not have been so strongly in his favor as they were in mine! In such a case to follow on a brother with every refinement of cruelty, by seeking to alienate from him his friends and brethren, would

* See Baxter's Works, by Orme, vol. I. p. 55, London, 1830.

be a crime of no small magnitude. But what must it be then in such a case as mine, when not only my accuser freed me from the charge of doing or even of intending wrong, but when Mr. Barnes himself is compelled to admit that I am "a good man, a sincere Christian, and eminently desirous of doing good; and one whose labors have been greatly blessed." The reader must decide this question, while I proceed, as above stated, to present a brief view of the points upon which I could not dwell in their historical detail.

Take then the paper of Mr. Barnes, which he drew up at the close of my trial, and in which he has studiously presented my case in its worst possible aspect, and its worst features really amount to nothing, if compared to the actual impression which he has since that time constantly endeavored to make against me. I justly hold him responsible for all the real and actual injury which has been done to me in this whole matter: and which he has labored to do in the very face of his declaration that I had been guilty of nothing which deserved deposition or suspension from the ministry, or which was incompatible with my continuing to be the pastor of my people; and that I was still worthy of their confidence and support. Even Mr. Hunt relented of his iniquitous course against me; and no other member of Presbytery besides Mr. Barnes felt sufficiently interested to secure my ruin, to lead them by any and every means in their power to endeavor to prejudice the public mind against me. He therefore and he alone is responsible for all the evil and injury under which I and my pastoral charge, and my family and friends, have suffered in this affair. I have proved this declaration to be true; let him, if he can, show any solid reasons for dissenting from the conclusion.

The next point is the resolutions adopted unanimously by the ladies of my congregation; and whose unanimity in sustaining me and believing me to be innocent of this accusation is also attested by Mr. Hunt himself. They avow their full belief that no woman of truth or moral purity has ever accused their pastor of taking improper liberties with her; and also that the attempt to injure me originated with Satan himself. Had I been guilty of any such conduct as Mr. Barnes would fain have the public believe, it is impossible that the ladies of my charge should not have in some way discovered it; for their sagacity could not have been baffled in such a matter. Yet instead of welcoming this strong fact, and allowing it to have its proper and full effect, as every truly good man would have wished to do, Mr. Barnes coolly and deliberately sets to work to destroy its influence. The reader, however, will, I am persuaded, do full justice in estimating it.

Let the declarations also of my brethren of the Presbytery be contrasted with the impressions which Mr. Barnes has endeavored to convey and encourage concerning me since the trial. Some of them (as for instance, several of the expressions in the letters of Dr. Brainerd) I might have justly omitted; as they were made under the perverse influence of Mr. Barnes; for Dr. Brainerd will not dispute the fact, that in the whole business of my trial he was somewhat considerably under the influence of that man; but I scorn to suppress them. Let them go for what they are worth. I could satisfactorily explain them, but it would be at my Brother Brainerd's expense (for in my trial he committed two errors, chiefly, if not entirely, through the influence of Mr. Barnes); so let the matter go, and let the reader in view of all the plain and pointed declarations of my brethren (in these letters), and in view of the fact that no one since the trial has dared to lay anything else to my charge; consider what the real state of the case must have been: and also how dreadful must be the malignity that would coolly endeavor to make the public believe me a guilty man, and undeserving of its confidence, in a matter concerning which these brethren would thus utter forth their sentiments and feelings.

Let the reader next consider the resolutions already given of the congregation, and unanimously adopted by them at one of the largest meetings that ever there assembled for business. Not a soul of them believed me guilty; and they say so boldly and openly, declaring that their confidence in their pastor's integrity and piety is undiminished: explaining too the true origin of the effort to impair my influence. Consider too their terrible and withering censure of those elders who, at Mr. Barnes' instigation, endeavored to induce me to resign my charge; and the reiteration of their declarations of unimpaired confidence in me. This censure of the elders, and reiteration of their sentiments concerning me, was given more than a year after the trial, and nearly a year after the passing of the resolutions above referred to; and long after my trial at court: and herein, therefore, are declared not only the fullest conviction of my people that the charges against me were false and malicious, but, by the clearest implication, the fact that nothing else had been laid to my charge since the trial. Why was I not then, in view of all these strong facts, taken by the hand and encouraged and sustained by my brethren of the Presbytery? This would have saved me from injury; and my people from distraction and division. It could have been easily done; and why, therefore, was it not done? Reader, *it would have been done had not the agency of the Rev. Albert Barnes prevented.* The facts are before you; and to your judgment in the matter, I appeal. And let Mr. Barnes remember also that he must soon meet myself, and this declaration, and these facts, at the bar of God. Let him not therefore attempt to evade these facts, and if my life is spared, no such evasion will profit him even here. For it is not my purpose to allow this matter to evaporate in a silly personal controversy, or in false issues, or vapid declamation, or dull argumentation; whatever be the tribunal to which he may resort.

Let the reader next consider (and compare with these efforts to destroy public confidence in me) the letter written to me by Mr. Barnes, to induce me to resign my charge. I need not quote it again, though I request that particular attention be paid to its phraseology. And let it be remembered, too, that the man to whom and of whom Mr. Barnes uses this language in a private letter, is the same man against whom he has countenanced the circulation of the most malignant insinuations, and whom he sought, in every possible way, even to deprive of the pastoral office. What think you, reader, of the declarations of this letter, as contrasted with such conduct? Yet there it is before you.

Let your mind revert, also, to the manly and kind, yet dignified and most affectionate, dismission, which I received from my beloved charge, when, through the incessant harassings of this man, I was compelled to leave them for the sake of their own peace and that of myself and family. No pastor has ever obtained a nobler testimony to his own faithfulness, and of the unimpaired confidence and good will of his people; and, in the light of this fact, let these efforts to destroy me be again subjected to a rigid scrutiny.

The correspondence which passed between Mr. Barnes and me in reference to the present publication, ought not to be here overlooked. If I were as unworthy of confidence as he has since (as well as previously) endeavored to represent me, why did he not say to me, as I should have said to him, or to any other man in similar circumstances: "Sir, you are by me believed to be a guilty man; what I have done in your case, I am prepared to sustain; take your own course, therefore." This would have been manly and right. Bnt, instead of this upright course, we have a wretched snivelling about "differences between brethren," &c., &c., though at the same time engaged, in a covert manner, in endeavoring to deprive me of all the rights and privileges of brotherhood. Why did he not meet my proposal to lay the matter before him? and say, as a man ought to say, "Tell me your grievances, and, if I have wronged you, I will do my best to make reparation." But you find none of this; and why? Simply because Mr. Barnes' conscience (I apprehend) had become his own accuser in the matter. If there is any other legitimate conclusion, let it be deduced; for I cannot even imagine what it could be.

Call up too, reader, the deeply impressive statement of my dying wife. She knew everything that had been said against me. And yet, when about to appear before the Almighty and Eternal Judge, she declared, in view of that fact, her firm and utter disbelief of the truth of everything that my enemies had said, with the view of impairing confidence in my moral character. Look, too, at the statements of her letter to Mr. Ramsey! No one that knew that lady will entertain the least doubt of the truth of these statements; and they, like all the preceding facts, are wholly inconsistent with the existence of any supposed facts upon which Mr. Barnes should so pertinaciously endeavor to crush me down. But whatever his reasons for such conduct have been, he now has the opportunity of making them fully known.

I shall, in another chapter, offer a few remarks on the subject of the relation which Mr. Barnes sustains to this case; but there are aspects of it which relate, also, to others. Many have taken the representations which he has made of it, and assuming that he must be candid therein, and even friendly towards me, on account of the manifest obligations which I have conferred upon him, have given his view of it as the only true one. Even clergymen, whom I could name, have taken apparent pleasure in circulating those vile slanders amongst their brethren and others, without any apparent definite aim or object, in which my own good or that of religion is concerned; and have thus evinced a high disregard of some of the most important features of the gospel which they preach. One case I ought not to pass entirely over; and I shall refer to it briefly. Should my attention, however, be called to it again by the person referred to, I shall be more particular, in order to administer a timely and wholesome caution to individuals of this class.

In Part I. I have remarked that persons, whose characters were most exceptionable, took the most active part against me in this business. There was not a counterfeiter, nor distiller, nor drunkard, nor adulterer, in the whole region, whose *sense of propriety* did not seem to be outraged, and who did not unite with Mr. Hunt in his efforts to put me down by destroying my character; for the old maxim is not yet obsolete that, in proportion as a man is wicked himself, he will suspect wickedness in others.* I could name also a clergyman, who, without any personal knowledge of the matter, took remarkable pains to circulate evil suspicions and rumors against me amongst my brethren. He did not seem at all aware that, by thus believing too easily, "a reproach against his neighbor," he was unconsciously laying bare the secrets of his own heart and character. I do not conceive myself to be travelling at all out of the line of my duty to administer a little wholesome counsel to such an individual; especially if he be one who, out of a regard to his own reputation, ought to have been silent in respect to mine. I presume that no one will question the propriety of my course, if I say that any such individual who (whether out of mere compliance with the wishes of Mr. Barnes, or from the fountain of his own corrupt heart) has sought most assiduously to prejudice the public against me, ought to be handled without ceremony, if he be one whose life and actions have laid him open to exposure. If he be one, for example, who, having first endorsed high anti-slavery views at the north, did, upon a removal for a short season to the south, become, in the most offensive sense, pro-slavery—and who, by the course he pursued, hastened the crisis of the devoted Lovejoy's fate—and whose flagrant violations of the Sabbath were heralded through the whole country, and palsied the hands of those who were laboring to promote a correct observance of that day—and whose treatment of a pious and devoted anti-slavery elder of his church cannot be known without being detested —and who has publicly boasted of his power to put several young ladies asleep, and to render them entirely subservient to his will, to say nothing of matters of still more serious import: if he be a man of such a character, who has industriously sought to extend evil surmises against a Christian minister, ought he not to be handled without mercy? I think so. I have, however, no disposition to pursue him, even to the appearance of resentment; though, for the sake of truth and righteousness, I must briefly, in this connection, refer to his causeless attempts to do me injury.

Now I know a clergyman whose character is as much open to exposure as the foregoing representation might intimate, who, without knowing anything of the facts in my case, and who was not even present at my trial, favored all the aforesaid rumors against me. In fact, so soon as the first rumor respecting Mrs. Vanderbelt reached Philadelphia, he went to a highly respectable gentleman who was friendly to me, and succeeded in inducing him to go to a family with whose intimacy I had been honored all my life, and narrate to them the foul story (and subsequently employed a member of his own family on the same mission also); and soon afterwards meeting with a youthful member of that family at a wedding, he stated to him that there could be no doubt that all which was reported against me was true. He subsequently narrated the same

* If this be rightly considered, we may understand the saying of the poet, that *God gives short horns to the mischievous ox;* or that of Plutarch: *The physician of others, while he himself teems with ulcers.*

to a weak-minded officer of my church, and thus put him upon a course of evil-doing which resulted in sacrificing the poor man in the community, and added many a pang to the already lacerated heart of my church and family. In Boston, New York, and in other places, he has also spoken of me in the same style, and thus has injured me greatly, so far as he had the power.* He knew that the fairer and brighter side of the picture was infinitely the most probable, as well as the most creditable to the cause of religion and truth; and yet has preferred the part of a calumniator.

There is another case or two, though not so flagrant as this, which I omit to dwell upon, as they are not needed for illustration; and the individuals referred to were, morever, only acting out the wishes of Mr. Barnes, and the feelings which he had not the courage openly to avow. He seems to delight in taking a position which will enable him to strike a blow without incurring the responsibility; and my indignation cannot be so justly excited against those who merely acted out his inclinations: for the actions of the subalterns should be set over to the account of the principal.

But why is it, let me here ask, for the fact is as well known as it is disgraceful—why is it that, of all classes of men (physicians, perhaps, excepted), there are none amongst whom there is so utter and practical a disregard for the principles of the gospel in this matter, as amongst clergymen? The majority, I know, are not so; but the very reverse. But how few are there, even of them, who act towards others in this thing, as they would have others act towards them? The wide-sweeping censure of the Roman satirist would have a fearfully pungent application to not a few who are acquainted with, and who profess to be governed by, as well as to proclaim, the higher principles of a gospel of which the satirist never even heard.† One would suppose, judging from their zeal in the art of defamation, that they regarded the gospel as teaching nothing else but how to treat a brother as a heathen man and a publican. It is certainly time that this matter was looked into.

In order, however, to get at the precise point to which I desire to call attention, in relation to the matter before us, I will admit the accusation so far as regards imprudence, to be true. Now, it is known that God, in a very remarkable manner, has blessed my labors as a preacher of the gospel; it is known that my pen, and whatever abilities God has

* Henry, in his annotations on Psalm 7:16, remarks that the statement there made "is often remarkably true of those who contrive mischief against the people of God, or against their neighbors; by the righteous hand of God it is made to *return upon their own heads;* what they designed for the shame and destruction of others proves to be their own confusion.

'Nec lex est justior ulla,
Quam, Necis artifices arte perire suâ.'

There is not a juster law than, That the author of a murderous contrivance should perish by it. Some apply it to Saul, who fell upon his sword." It may not be out of place also, to quote in this connection, the following well-known passage:

"Crimina qui cernunt aliorum, non sua cernunt:
Hi sapiunt aliis, desipiuntque sibi."

† ———Absentem qui rodit amicum,
Qui non defendit, alio culpante; solutos
Qui captat risus hominum, famamque dicacis:
Fingere qui non visa potest: commissa tacere
Qui nequit: hic niger est: hunc tu, Romane, caveto.

bestowed upon me, have always been employed on the side of virtue and religion. On the supposition, therefore, that I had gone further and perpetrated the crime, and had become "truly penitent," how ought the case to have been regarded and treated by Christians and Christian ministers? That is, how does Christ require that it should be regarded? I leave Mr. Barnes and his immediate coadjutors all out of the question.

"Why," says one, in answer to the question, "the honor of religion requires that we should have nothing more to do with you." But is this so? And are we in danger of compromising the honor of religion by a strict adherence to the teachings of Christ? Where is such a principle inculcated? *Not in the word of God!* And if the state of society requires it, the state of society is so far wrong, and ought to be resisted by all who are followers of Christ. How would Christ himself treat such an one, were he on earth? His actions while here have already decided the question. Take the case of Peter for an illustration. And that he designs his example herein to be imitated by his people, no one will question. See Gal. 6 : 1–3.

But further, if the charges and rumors are not true, and yet, without any sufficient examination, are made the basis of treating a Christian brother as I have been treated, can it be the legitimate operation of the principles of Christ's gospel that leads to such results? You have heard thus and so; you suppose it to be true, and so believe it, and act upon that belief. You have thus inferred it to be true, when it is false. Are you innocent therefore? And is not this the dreadful crime of "taking up a reproach against your neighbor," which must exclude the soul from heaven? Ps. 15 : 3.

But to continue the aforesaid reflections. Suppose the rumors to be both true and believed, what does the gospel require should be the treatment of the offending brother? Is it not this, that every effort should be made that kindness could prompt, to restore him? While the utmost abhorrence is expressed of his guilt and crime, he should, if penitent, be taken by the hand, and encouraged to look upward; and soothed with the hope of forgiveness through a Saviour's blood, and with the hope of prospective usefulness even here, when the evidences of his repentance and reformation should be sufficient and satisfactory. He should thus, by the sympathies of his brethren, be shielded from the merciless and soul-crushing treatment of a world that is estranged from God; and find in their sympathies, and in the hope of forgiveness, that support which a crushed and broken spirit needs when, to all the other ills of life, the superadded burden of conscious guilt presses it down. "A little force," says the poet, "is sufficient to break that which was cracked before." But let not that little force be added, but let the poor guilty, but penitent culprit, thus find in that charity which hideth a multitude of sins, the relief which alone can save him from despair. What heart that has ever felt the burden of its own sins, and has been touched with a Saviour's love, will not say that, in such cases, this is the course of duty prescribed by the Son of God?

Such is truly the course: but oh, how differently have some of my brethren acted towards me! The story has been briefly unfolded in this volume, and therefore need not be here repeated. But let me now inquire what did Mr. Barnes and Dr. Parker hope to accomplish by the course which they have seen proper to pursue in relation to myself? What were proceedings like theirs calculated to effect? Was it my reformation, on the supposition that they regarded me as guilty? Why, a child could see that the very idea of such a thing is folly. Was it, then, the good of the church, or the glory of God, that they sought? And were their efforts calculated to promote these? No; in no single instance: for they were efforts which set wholly at naught the principles of the gospel of Christ,—and were calculated, if not designed, to effect my utter destruction, and that only. But why should this be effected on such grounds, and by such means? or on any ground whatever? What could they hope to gain, either to the cause of God or of truth, by thus breaking me down? And what motives, therefore, could have induced their course? These questions they *must* answer.

Then further; what is the *design* of the institution of discipline? Is it to destroy or to save those who are subjects of it? *Now let these two men show, in their entire proceedings, a single act which was calculated to effect anything but my prostration and destruction?* I refer to acts deliberately resolved upon, and performed; and I know of none. They must, therefore, settle their own account with the public and posterity.

As respects myself, I felt, while enduring these accumulated wrongs and indignities, that the time had not yet come for me to be heard; I suffered Patience to have her perfect work, assured, that in the good providence of God, such a time must arrive. I said little or nothing, but went on with my work in the Master's vineyard, and silently observed the course of events; and especially was I struck, by observing the conduct and feelings of many of the professed followers of Christ, towards me; for I knew on what grounds they treated me as they did. I did not repine, however, for I hoped that through these, my sufferings, when the attention of the people of God should thus be called to the matter, other sorrow-freighted hearts may hereafter be saved from many a cruel pang. I could write a volume on this single point; but let it suffice to say, that of all my honored and beloved brethren (and those too who had known me), where Mr. Barnes' influence bore sway, scarce a hand was held forth to me. Men whom I had obliged, seemed to take pleasure in endeavoring to destroy my character—others utterly slighted me; and none of them to whom I thus refer, had even investigated the question, as to whether I was guilty or not. They took it upon trust, simply because they had heard evil surmises against me. One clergyman, whom I had known intimately from childhood, and who had possession of all my heart—a man of deservedly high rank in the church—met me in the aisle of the Tremont Chapel, Boston (in 1848), and though there were scarcely any others present, passed me without even a nod of recognition. Another, who had known me as well, saw me there, and to avoid meeting me, went out of his way, in order to pass through another door. These may serve as instances. The whole of this in these instances may, it is true, be attributed to the management of Mr. Barnes, and his coadjutor aforesaid; but does even this free such conduct from the imputation of guilt, when viewed in the light of Christ's precepts and example?

Through the culpable neglect of my brethren, therefore, to inquire into the matter, before they received it as true, I have been allowed the alternative of still suffering quietly under the vile imputations which were producing such results, and of seeing the cause of religion continue to suffer through me, or of coming forward with this brief narrative of the facts of the case; and perhaps, on that account, of suffering still more from the power which my enemies may yet possess to harass me, by any appliances which they may find available. As I have, however, done what I believed to be right in the matter, I shall shrink from no consequences, resulting therefrom; being assured that the ultimate judgment of mankind will be what I desire it to be—impartial and just. No one in this world will ever know the anguish of spirit which it cost me to adopt this alternative; but God knows it, and I am satisfied to leave it with him.

Of nothing do I feel more certain, than that God will, in his own time and manner, fully rescue my name from all these indignities, and not permit religion to suffer through me; and perhaps afford me the privilege of being far more useful than ever in his kingdom on earth. I base these hopes, not upon any expected aid of my brethren, for they have suffered me to stand very much alone in this severe and soul-crushing conflict. I base them not upon any power or ability of my own to contend successfully with my foes; but I base them upon the glorious promises of God, taken in connection with the fact, that the malignity which has assailed me arose from my efforts to be faithful to the interests of his truth and kingdom; for in the discharge of my duties herein, I have neither feared nor flattered any man. I base them upon the fact, that many who have joined together to injure me, and who seemed to think it desirable to put me out of the way, have taken advantage of grievous falsehoods and misrepresentations; that many have condemned me upon the merest presumption; that others have so treated me in violation of all the courtesies of life, from statements wholly *ex parte*, and unexamined, and have evinced an *à priori* willingness to do so; that they have not extended to me the sympathy which Christ recommends to be shown to an erring brother, and which they should have extended, even on the supposition that the charges against me were true, and had been shown to be so: and finally, I base them upon the fact, that God, who sees the heart and knows our inmost thoughts, knows that it has been my incessant prayer, and unwavering aim, to be wholly consecrated to his service and glory; and that to this end, even the cup of affliction itself, which he in his kind providence has presented, has been willingly drained by me to its most loathsome dregs. He knows my foolishness, and my sins are ever before him, and that I lay no claim to be other than a miserable and lost sinner—guilty, helpless, and polluted by nature and practice; but he knows too, that for more than a quarter of a century, he has enabled me to hate sin, and to make it my study and most earnest prayer, to be able to avoid offending him. He knows that I have been falsely and maliciously accused in this matter, and that perjured witnesses have arisen, who have laid to my charge things that I knew not. Hence I have been encouraged, when I have heard him say: "They shall not be ashamed that wait for me." "Who is among you that feareth the Lord, that obeyeth the voice of his servant, that walketh in darkness, and hath no light? Let him trust in the name of the Lord, and stay upon his God." "Therefore, hear now this, thou afflicted, and drunken, but not with wine: Thus saith thy Lord the Jehovah, and thy God that pleadeth the cause of his people, Behold, I have taken out of thine hand the cup of trembling, even the dregs of the cup of my fury; thou shalt no more drink it again: but I will put it into the hand of them that afflict thee; which have said to thy soul, Bow down, that we may go over; and thou hast laid thy body as the ground, and as the street, to them that went over." Is. 49 : 23, and 50 : 10, and 51 : 21–23.

CHAPTER XIX.

REMARKS ON MR. BARNES' CONNECTION WITH THE CASE.—CONCLUSION.

"*Num negare audes? Quid taces? Convincam si negas.*"

I HAVE therefore been in no haste to appear before the public. Time is the great discoverer of truth; and after what I had suffered I had but little difficulty to sit still and wait until the plot should ripen, and the fruits, bursting as they fell, display that loathsome corruption, which a fair exterior had concealed, but to which they must infallibly be brought, under the wise arrangements of the providence of God.

It is human nature, says Tacitus, to hate those whom we have injured.* The remark is as true as its truth is humiliating; and perhaps no fact more conclusively and strikingly displays the dreadful nature of that depravity, which, in the word of God, is predicated of the unregenerate heart. How forcible is the illustration of this truth furnished in Matt. 27 : 22, 23: "Pilate saith unto them, What shall I do with Jesus, which is called Christ? They all say unto him, let him be crucified. And the governor said, Why! what evil hath he done? *But they cried out the more, saying, Let him be crucified!*" They had grievously and falsely accused him. The inquiry of Pilate was both reasonable and proper; but it only exasperated the prejudiced multitude the more, because they were unable to answer it; and in proportion to the clearness with which Jesus was exculpated from the charges they had brought; and in proportion to their inability to sustain them, was their determination to destroy him. Hence their deep and determined utterances now more loudly than ever demanded, "Let him be crucified!" It was not *truth* they sought, but his destruction; consequently their hatred was only inflamed in proportion as his innocence appeared; for where envy (see ver. 18) or malignity is bent on destroying the innocent, the absence of proof against the accused will only exasperate the accuser, and induce a more deadly determination to carry the point. Such is human nature when under the guidance of that "*spirit in man which lusteth to envy,*" Jas. 4 : 5.

All men have their weaknesses. And one of the most prominent in the character of Mr. Barnes is his inability to tolerate a competitor in any favorite pursuit. He knew that I had devoted myself to the study of sacred literature; and being conscious of his own superficial attainments in this department, and evincing also a desire to avail himself through his "Notes," of the pecuniary advantages which an ephemeral popularity had secured to him, he felt uneasy at the bare idea of any co-presbyter coming into competition; and could not resist the temptation of adopting any course which promised with impunity to secure him against the probability of such an event. Hence the sound scholarship

* "Proprium humani ingenii est, odisse quem læseris." *Agricola*, Cap. XLII. Seneca likewise, in his *De Ira*, *Lib.* II. Cap. 33, has the same idea. "Hoc habent pessimum animi magna fortuna insolentes, quos læserunt, et oderunt."

and signal ability of Dr. Duffield annoyed him; and nothing could induce him to lend the little aid which would have enabled that excellent brother to remain in Philadelphia. And neither could he give his influence to secure to his most devoted and self-sacrificing friend, the Rev. Dr. Peters, an appointment which we all desired he should have, and which we all felt assured could thus be easily obtained. Hence too my essays in the Repository (though written in his defence), which secured the plaudits of many of the most eminent scholars, annoyed him; for his attainments were thus shown to be inferior to mine. The little works on Campbellism and on the Resurrection, containing a good deal of scripture criticism, increased the annoyance; and hence he began to improve every little advantage that his position furnished, to disparage me and my writings. Instance upon instance could be named, evincing this disposition in the earlier stages of its development; until the time when it finally assumed the terrible form which has been delineated in the foregoing pages.

The case, as developed by the facts already presented, might safely be committed without argument, yet a few remarks may not be out of place.

For the sake of illustration let us suppose that in an unguarded moment I had even done the silly and indecent thing attributed to me; yet with the fact before the mind of Mr. Barnes, that my accuser did not believe that I intended her any harm, either then or at any other time; and the fact also that she stated in an indignant manner in reply to one of the members of Presbytery that I never had in any way intimated a desire to perpetrate crime with her; and with the evidence too before him that I had been the object of the most relentless opposition and persecution on account of my fidelity as a preacher of the gospel of Christ; what is the course which a Christian was bound to pursue in relation to me? I place out of the question the obligations which I had laid Mr. Barnes under by defending him when he was unable to defend himself; and base the inquiry simply upon Christian principles. What course ought any man who feared God, to have pursued in such a case? Was it to be the first to condemn?—to volunteer to lead the crusade to crush me down?—or to volunteer unbidden to draw up the cruel minute presented by Mr. Barnes to Presbytery? Or to harass me in the innumerable methods referred to above? Will any one pretend that such should have been the conduct of a Christian minister under such circumstances? Oh, if there was in the breast of this man no regard for me, or my suffering family and friends, ought there not to have been for the precious cause for which I had been toiling and contending?—the suffering interests of the blood-bought church of Christ; for the souls of perishing men; for a commencing revival, and the awakened, inquiring souls in my congregation?

How different was his conduct, from the noble and magnanimous deportment of Prof. Bush! The public voice, and his own frank acknowledgment, had alike awarded to me a victory over the Professor in his favorite branch of study. A little mind, thus circumstanced, would have found cause for malignant satisfaction at the idea of my suffering in my reputation. But the Professor, so soon as he had been informed of these calumnies against me, took his pen, and, from the promptings of his own noble nature, assured me he did not believe the accusation, and that I should bear up under it. That I had perhaps been guilty of some indiscretion or imprudence upon which my enemies had founded their assault; but that God would set it all right and appear for me at last. He gave me also the warmest and fullest assurance that I suffered not in his esteem or regard. And the Professor's conduct since has magnanimously evinced the reality of the feelings he thus expressed.

Compare this generous conduct with the littleness displayed by Mr. Barnes in this whole case; and from the commencement to the conclusion of the matter, you look in vain for any exemplification of Christian principle, or even of manliness.

But let us return to the supposition aforesaid, and for the sake of the argument admit the whole charge to be true. And flagrant as it is, would it furnish any reason for following up in the way above narrated, a poor unfortunate soul, who, from their own account, must have been overcome in a moment of temptation? Is such withdrawal of sympathy, and such relentless persecution as Mr. Barnes has been guilty of, in accordance with the direction of the Spirit of God? Let us see: "Brethren, if (ἐὰν καὶ, *although*,) a man be overtaken in a fault, ye which are spiritual restore such an one in the spirit of meekness; considering thyself, lest thou also be tempted. Bear ye one another's burdens, and so fulfill the law of Christ," Gal. 6 : 1, 2. See also Matt. 18 : 10–14, Luke 22 : 31, 32, Heb. 12 : 13, &c. How then does such conduct as the aforesaid, comport with these and kindred declarations, even on the supposition of my actual guilt? Can any one hesitate to decide? And how also do they comport with the examples set us by our fathers in the best and purest ages of the church? A single illustration will suffice to show.

The Rev. Robert Cross, in the early part of his ministry, was guilty of violating the seventh commandment, under circumstances of peculiar aggravation. With great humility and evidences of sincere penitence, he acknowledged his guilt, and was accordingly suspended from the ministry. Then, at a time which was deemed suitable, Presbytery restored him; and, as the generality of his congregation desired his continuance as their pastor, he was re-instated over them. There was no old clergyman to concentrate and lead onward the efforts of the enemies of religion, and no jealous unkind brother to take advantage of his sorrows; but his brethren having expressed, and by deeds manifested, their high disapprobation of his crime, stood by him, and comforted him with the hope of Heaven's forgiveness, and cheered his crushed and broken heart. They might have stood aloof from his sore, and let him sink and die, but they had not so learned Christ. They treated him as a sinning though penitent brother; and, in consequence, he subsequently became one of the most efficient ministers, as well as one of the finest scholars in the American Church, and his fame was known in other lands. He also accepted of a call to become pastor of the First Presbyterian Church in Philadelphia, and died in charge *anno* 1766, after serving that church for nearly thirty years. He descended to the grave beloved and revered by all the American Church. Such were the happy consequences resulting from following the precepts of Christ in relation to the guilty though penitent man.

But now a pastor of that same First Presbyterian Church finds a brother cruelly calumniated—and how does he act? He has the heart to believe and to express his belief, that the slander is well founded, before the case is at all investigated, and he even seeks to induce others to believe it. He has the heart to welcome, and to con, over and over again, an infamous libel upon that brother, got up and sent by an old worldling, whom he knew to be that brother's bitterest enemy, and whom he had denounced as dishonest and as the most worldly-minded man he ever knew. Then, after using his influence and bringing to bear all his powers of contrivance to put this calumniated brother to every possible disadvantage, and his case into the worst possible shape, he, of his own accord, draws up, under the pretence that it is advisory, a judicial decision against him, of the character described in the foregoing pages, and sanctions the whole of the iniquitous course pursued by the old enemy aforesaid. Then, when he afterwards finds, that in consequence of the violation of the pledge which the prosecution had given (and which, through his contrivance, was not written) there is breaking in upon this brother sorrow and calamity, with breach upon breach, he by his silence encourages the violation of said pledge; and not only does not extend a hand to assist his brother, but discourages and frowns upon every effort to afford him relief. Then, while his ears are thus closed to the groans of this calumniated man, they are eagerly attentive to the renewed clamors of his foes, through whom he continues still to operate, until he has accomplished the separation of this brother from an affectionate and beloved people, who had nobly stood by him throughout all his afflictions, and, by this step, he secures the false impression abroad, that this brother's people believe him guilty, and have, therefore, abandoned him.

Now, reader, look at the contrast! In the aforesaid paper, drawn up by Mr. Barnes, he acquits me of crime, both in act and intention; and, in his letter to me in October, 1848, he speaks handsomely of me as a good man and one eminently desirous of doing good. But, in the case of Mr. Cross, there *was crime*—the perpetration of a heinous iniquity. Mr. Cross was penitent; Mr. Barnes' paper asserts that I was "truly penitent." And yet Mr. Cross, thus guilty, is sustained and treated by his brethren according to Gal. 6: 1, 2; and I, though innocent (yet charged with being "penitent"), am treated by the Rev. Mr. Barnes, in every possible way, as deserving of utter ruin and prostration. Further: The generality of Mr. Cross' congregation wished him to continue in charge as their pastor, and, by the aid of his brethren, he did so. The great majority of my people believed me innocent, and refused even to listen to a proposal for me to leave them; and yet, as above described, by the manœuvring of Mr. Barnes, my removal was at last effected.

This comparison and contrast needs no remarks from me to suggest some very impressive reflections.

But why should Mr. Barnes be so exclusive and so desirous of preeminence? What has *he* done, or what is he now doing for the cause of those who, at so great a sacrifice, sustained him when his aberrations from the received theology of the church brought the aforesaid censure upon him? Has he been at the call of the suffering interests of that branch of the church to whose protection he owes his present position before the public? Has he endeavored to make at least some return by evincing a willingness to be at her call, when opportunity was afforded him, to promote her best interests? or has he sought his own emolument by taking pecuniary advantage of a temporary notoriety to manufacture and bring into market his mis-shapen wares, half burnt and rough—his unturned cakes, and his half-finished merchandise? He has thus greatly profited by the excitement, and by favoring it with issue upon issue during its continuance; but where is the profit to the church in return for all that she has sacrificed to save him from prostration? Had he been out and active at the great crisis of her interests, he could have done more real good than by ten thousand books like his "*Notes on Romans*," or on anything else. He has compiled a few volumes filled with inconsistencies and contradictions, and which can live no longer than the ephemeral necessity that called them into being; and which *he*, at all events, was not required to supply; while, in consequence of waiting upon his expected movements, his brethren have lost that "tide in the affairs of men," which can now return to them no more.*

Further: Was it then superior zeal in the cause of religion and moral purity, which induced Mr. Barnes to pursue the course he did in relation to me? There must have been some cause for it—some strong motive, for he certainly left all other members of Presbytery (except his "Father Hunt") greatly in the distance. True, it would not be very modest to arrogate to himself such a claim, in such a body of men as in general composed that Presbytery; but even this plea would not stand were he to adopt it, for in the case of the lamented Harris, he was as far behind his brethren in zeal, as he was before them in my case. But I return to the question: Why should the Rev. Albert Barnes, of all the members of Presbytery, be *the* man thus to fall in at once with the efforts of the aforesaid enemies of religion to destroy my influence? Why should he, in the manner above narrated, encourage the wicked efforts of counterfeiters, drunkards, liquor-sellers, distillers, Sabbath-breakers, and profane swearers, to ruin me? Is Mr. Barnes the only man in Presbytery, who has the welfare of Christ's cause at Bethlehem at heart? Or is it that he is the only one who sought both directly and indirectly to accomplish some sinister purpose against me? I frankly say, that I cannot explain his conduct on any principle consistent with vital piety. Others may prove more successful, in ascertaining the figure in which the supposed ellipsis, the parabola, and the hyperbola may unite, but I cannot find it. One thing, however, is certain, that had it not been for the course pursued by Mr. Barnes, the whole thing would have been dead, buried and forgotten long ago. And neither would my church have been distracted and reduced to its present deplorable condition. The

* Mr. Barnes seems conscious that his usefulness has ceased since the part he took in my affairs; and it is as ludicrous as it is humiliating, to see the manner in which he endeavors to keep the public eye directed to his former achievements—*e.g.* to his "*Notes.*" Even the *Bibliotheca Sacra* must be laid under contribution, to tell how many copies of "*Cobdin's edition*" of this puerile performance have been sold in England; and the newspapers must also inform us that some of them are to be *even translated into Welsh*, and that he has written "*Notes*" on Daniel, which *are not published*, (a modest way of begging some bookseller to engage in the hopeless task,) and that he *may* write on the Psalms, &c. &c. All these things have a language which I need not interpret. It is time that such matters ceased, and that Mr. Barnes should be led to regard these abortions of annotation in their true light. Their only utility has been to show the need which exists for some thorough works in this department, and so to call attention to the fact. I can never contemplate their intrinsic value as contrasted with their sale, without being reminded of the words of *Gellert*, *Friz bedarf nichts, er kommt in der Welt durch seine Dummheit fort.*

position assumed by him is therefore one of a most fearful nature. But having thus voluntarily assumed it, nothing now remains but for him to prepare to sustain its tremendous responsibilities.

My own duty in this most painful matter has been plain, and gladly would I have spared Mr. Barnes, and myself also, the labor and anguish of laying this work before the public; but responsibility to a higher than any earthly power left me no alternative as to the course to be pursued. And as to one or two other individuals connected with him in this matter, and whose conduct perhaps deserves a more specific notice than that which I have briefly given, they were not primary, but secondary actors in the tragedy, and therefore, unless they see proper to attract particular attention to themselves, they may pass without further notice. But if the reader discovers in this work anything unnecessarily severe, or anything false or unfounded, let it be treated without mercy ; and let Mr. Barnes have the full benefit of such discovery. In a full and free history like this, referring to dates and circumstances, and stating a vast number of facts, nothing is easier than to detect the element of falsehood, if it be lurking therein; and if a malevolent spirit has actuated the writer, nothing is more certain than that evidences of it have escaped him in so long a narrative, and that they can be detected. In such narratives, no feigned feelings, nor hypocritical garb, can long endure the scrutiny of the public.

As to Mr. Barnes' duty, it likewise is plain, but it is not for me to say much on that subject.

He has declared beforehand that he will not reply to me. Whether this is because he deems that his case will not admit of handling, or whether he wished by this announcement to prepare the way for representing me as taking advantage of such an impression, I know not; but I do know, that this is neither the age nor country, in which a man may act as he has done, and then refuse an explanation. This refusal on his part is not based on want of time, for he is now at leisure; his "Notes" on the New Testament being, if I mistake not, completed. He is accustomed to the use of the pen; has the reputation of a learned man, and is in full possession of his physical and mental powers. His influential and noble-hearted congregation can and will sustain and protect him from any injustice, so long as he proves himself worthy of their protection. It is right that they should hope all things of the man whom they have chosen to minister to them; nor would it be unreasonable, if this regard for him should, at the first blush of this disclosure, dispose them to think hard of me; for how can they without inexpressible anguish, admit for a moment the truth of the declarations herein brought forth boldly to view? I shall, however, submit to all this willingly, until they have taken time for due reflection; knowing that in the end they will decide aright, both as respects Mr. Barnes and myself. God will give them wisdom herein and guide them in the path of duty. Mr. Barnes, therefore, occupies a position possessed of all these advantages, and let him now come forth and explain himself. He cannot be sustained in a refusal to do so. I must and will hold him to the points on which the subject turns, and no attempt to evade them shall profit him. Let him explain why, at the very outset, he took the lead against me as aforesaid? and why he has followed me up so relentlessly ever since? Was it to promote my welfare, or that of my family, or of the church, or of the public? And if so, let us have the matter explained, as to how either could have been promoted by such a course,—by taking decided ground against me, and in favor of my enemies before the trial: and by such conduct as he pursued during the trial, and subsequent thereto, in respect to myself and my congregation. Let us have the explanation; for if none be given, there is but one inference which can be drawn from deeds like these.

Before concluding this painful and protracted narrative, there are several things which require to be adverted to; and *first*, the delay which has occurred before publishing the work.

I have not been and neither have I designed to be hasty in the matter. As I sought simply the glory of God and the good of his church, I felt that delay, while it could do no real injury,* might, by God's blessing, so operate as to lead to repentance the chief actors in the aforesaid drama. This would have promoted the glory of God, relieved religion and my own character from odious imputations, and rendered the work unnecessary. The voice of Providence likewise seemed to favor this view: for the pecuniary losses which I suffered in consequence of this persecution exhausted my resources so much that I could not put the work to press with any reasonable prospect of paying for it; and a large sum of money also which was due me, was taken possession of by a villain, in the hope of being able to hold it, because my character was so much injured by the aforesaid efforts of my enemies, that he supposed I would rather resign the sum, than by contesting the matter with him in court encounter the abuse which his lawyers might cast upon me.† Then the breaking up of my family, the death of my wife, the duties of a new pastoral charge, and much severe sickness which I have suffered, have all tended greatly to retard its completion. And lastly, the assurance that God had me and this matter all in his holy keeping, and would guide me in every step of the way, operated to produce patience, and to still my anguish and anxiety on account of such slanders resting upon my name. Henry, on Psalm 38: 12–22, has expressed the idea as follows: "It is a good reason why we should bear reproach and calumny with silence and patience, because God is a witness to all the wrong that is done us, and, in due time, will be a witness for us, and against those that do us wrong; therefore, let us be silent, because if we be, then we may expect that God will appear for us, for this is an evidence that we trust in him; but if we undertake to manage for ourselves, we take God's work out of his hands and forfeit the benefit of his appearing for us. Our Lord Jesus, when he suffered, *therefore*, threatened not, because *he committed himself to him that judges righteously*, and we shall lose nothing at last by doing so."

No one can peruse this narrative, and have confidence in the author, without feeling that the subject possesses an intrinsic interest and importance in its relations to religion and to the good of society, which is far beyond its mere local relation to Mr. Barnes and myself. God's

* A forcible writer remarks, that "Inexperienced persons think when great plans only stand still, they must be going backwards. The truth is, however, that wise men are never in a hurry to force events. They know that patience works more wonders than activity."

† The court and jury have since awarded it to me; but the funds are not yet available, owing to those unavoidable delays, which the observance of legal forms not unfrequently renders necessary.

ways are not as ours; and we cannot pretend to scan his designs, or to fathom his purposes: but we may rest assured that his hand is in this matter, and that one aim which he intends to accomplish hereby, and in his own best way, is the good of his church, and the sanctification of his people.

Some of the results which my enemies have accomplished in this effort against me, have already been mentioned, and it is proper here to remind them also of a few others: for the contemplation thereof may prove to be salutary.

How sad is the effect upon poor Mrs. Vanderbelt and her husband! They could have been brought back to God, and led in the way of life: but now, unless the infinite goodness of God prevent, they will perish forever. Poor old Mrs. Stiger, also, has gone to her account, with that affidavit and asserted revelation unrepented of, so far as I can learn. Poor old Mr. Hunt, who is now upwards of eighty years of age, and, of course, cannot be far from the judgment, has been thus, through Mr. Barnes' conduct, hardened in his impenitence, and will probably go to the grave in his sin. He might have been made to feel his guilt, and repent of it, so as to be saved. Those, too, who acted with him in this business have, by the same agency, been led to persist in and even to attempt to justify their course, while they are passing away to a dread eternity! A rising revival in Bethlehem Church was likewise thus wholly destroyed. Impenitent sinners, though once awakened, have, in like manner, been induced to neglect their salvation. The effect upon religion abroad has likewise been very sad; for persons who are governed by their feelings and desires, rarely consider the folly of supposing that at a distance, they could form a more accurate judgment of the case, than a large and intelligent congregation and community on the spot; and thus religion has been injured. The present deplorable condition of that once efficient church is to be attributed to the same agency. The cause of benevolence, too, has suffered, for the contributions of that church are as nothing now, compared to what they were when I was pastor. My own pecuniary resources have also been so utterly absorbed, that I have scarcely at all been able to help the poor and needy.

Such are *some* of the awful consequences of indulging that "spirit in man which lusteth to envy;" and of thus "taking up a reproach against a neighbor." Ponder then, reader! and then call to mind, also, the crushed spirit of him who now addresses you: and who, as he looks back solitary over the vale of life which you and he have been traversing, sees rising in the distance the graves of a beloved but heart-broken mother and wife, associated too with these sad scenes! Think upon them; and under their impressive influence, resolve to discountenance sternly and forever, *the common but diabolical practice of slander*. Never in any way become a partaker of the crime. Its guilt is as deep as hell, and its results are far-reaching and extend beyond the vision of earth's scenes.

That the exposure of injury and wrong-doing which is presented in these pages is calculated to awaken the sympathy of every generous and manly bosom on behalf of the sufferer, and its indignation against the authors and abettors of such cruel oppressions, is plain; and that this must fall heavily upon Mr. Barnes, unless he exculpate himself by fairly meeting the facts, is perhaps too clear to be doubted. Yet no one but a singularly thoughtless or vicious heart, and no professor of religion but a hypocrite, would wish to see this brother unnecessarily prostrated, as I have been. His heart at present is too dark, and selfish, and obdured, to appreciate my feelings on his behalf; but I feel assured that he will hereafter appreciate them fully. His only proper course, as a man and a Christian, is to acknowledge his guilt, and to do what he can to repair the injury which he has done to religion, to the souls of men, and to myself. This will be an appeal to the Christian feelings and sympathies of his brethren, the force of which all will acknowledge, who are in truth partakers of the spirit of Christ. The course of his brethren is likewise plain. Too many of them, alas! have sinned with him. But let all who love the Gospel plant themselves on the broad basis of Gal. 6 : 1, 2, and never forsake him, if he be penitent. Thus will he become weaned from himself, and, by the blessing of God, do more real good in his latter days than in all his life before. See Job 11 : 13–20, and 22 : 21–30, and 33 : 19–33.

Here ends my statement and appeal. For nearly three years I have been called to endure all the anguish that a broken spirit and blighted hopes can awaken within the soul. I had truly, with all the sincerity of my heart, sought to devote my whole life and powers to promote the glory of God, and the good of my fellow-men. But blighting winds have swept over the fair blossoms of hope, and, as they wither, I feel that I too am passing away, soon to find the repose I never sought on earth. After toiling and studying as I have done, to qualify myself for usefulness in my blessed Master's vineyard, it seems hard, in the very midst of life and manhood, to go to the grave, thus crushed and broken in heart, and hope, and reputation; but yet it is best—or my Faithful and Covenant God would never have permitted his poor, confiding child to be thus afflicted! But to the operation of his own kind and ever-watchful providence, I cheerfully commit my character and name, and the honor of his cause.

SUPPLEMENTAL.

More than a year has now (September, 1851) elapsed since this work was finished and submitted to some of my brethren, in manuscript, and I feel that I may with propriety here add a word or two, expressive of my present views and feelings. By unavoidable delays I have been disappointed of receiving money which is due me; and, as I could not, with the pen, multipy copies of so large a work, it became necessary to print, or publish it, so as to enable all who are personally interested, to consider the facts. God in his providence also supplied, at the very time they were thus needed, the means necessary to defray the expense of printing: for upon its being known in Bethlehem, that I had not yet received my money aforesaid, and that I wished without further delay to print the book, several of my people there volunteered to advance the funds necessary for the purpose. They have my thanks for this instance of kindness, as well as for all others which that beloved people have ever extended to me and mine.

In my late visit to Bethlehem, my heart was deeply pained to witness the condition of that once flourishing and efficient church. I cannot here speak particularly of this matter however. There are many praying souls there, and let them not fear still to trust in a faithful God. He never has failed of his promise, nor disappointed the souls that trusted in his name. He has the best interests of his people at heart, and will bring out everything right at last.

There are also, many there who once were my enemies, and who, on the preceding pages are referred to as such: but who now think and speak of me very differently. Some of them will feel pained in view of some things which I have mentioned; but they are aware that I could not omit those matters in justice to the case: and let them with true magnanimity consider the whole subject, and they will not blame me for being, even at their expense, faithful to the cause of God and truth.

Others of my enemies, both there and in Philadelphia, are still malignant and somewhat powerful; but the work I have in hand I purpose to accomplish! and we shall see whether, at this age of the world, God is not as faithful to his promises as formerly; or whether his purposes shall not stand, because some men have purposed the contrary. See Jer. 44:28. They may take whatever course they please. I am prepared still to act or to suffer, as circumstances may require; and I know that God will, in his own best way, protect me from all ultimate injury. In the attainment of just ends, I deem present inconveniences and sufferings as of but little moment, however great they may be; and I am willing to concede to my foes the HODIE TIBI; for it is not in their power to withhold the CRAS MIHI. Every effort to inflict further injustice upon me will only furnish renewed occasion for God to display the faithfulness of his ever-enduring promise. I have hitherto with the Hebrew Psalmist sang, and still expect to be able to sing, "By this I know that thou favorest me, because mine enemy doth not triumph over me. In the shadow of thy wings will I make my refuge, until these calamities be overpast. Thou which hast showed me great and sore troubles, shalt quicken me again, and shalt bring me up again from the depths of the earth. Thou shalt multiply my deliverances, and comfort me on every side. I will cry unto God Most High; unto God that performeth all things for me. Be thou exalted, O God, above the heavens; and let thy glory fill the whole earth."

Mr. Barnes is still, though feebly, represented in Jersey. But it is not wonderful that many there, who once were my enemies, or spoke disparagingly of me, should have experienced a great change, both in their feelings and views. The hand of God is still upon the main actors of the tragedy; and the condition to which poor Vanderbelt and his wife are reduced, is such, that even enmity itself could not wish to add another pang to what they have suffered. Another malignant foe, who did all in his power to injure me, has had rather a narrow escape from the penitentiary, on the charge of stealing a gold watch. The matter was however compromised. Conover and his brother have had a dispute also respecting Vanderbelt's goods; in the course of which, some strange disclosures were elicited. I must also state, that on making inquiry respecting Ann (the wretched creature who was suborned against me, and on whose testimony I was cast at court), I at length learned that she had, during the latter part of August, given birth to an illegitimate child; attributed to a vagabond Irishman, who had been laboring on the railroad. But surely enough has been said respecting such matters.

I must add a single word in respect to Mr. Barnes, and his connection with this whole business. My conviction of his unutterable guilt remains the same, and is only deepened the more I am led to reflect upon the subject. But yet, I ask not the reader to take the expression of my poor erring judgment as infallibly correct in a matter of such interest. I have endeavored to be just and conscientious in what I have written, but perhaps it is not in human nature to look calmly and in an unbiassed manner at the matter, when suffering such injuries and provocations as I have endured. It requires a degree of divine grace to which I can scarcely hope to have attained, although to attain it has been my earnest and continued prayer. Let not the reader therefore suppose that I shall be pleased to have him implicitly endorse my views of the matter without due consideration; or that any partaker of the spirit of Jesus will thank him for a rash, hasty, and merciless judgment against Mr. Barnes. If I sought the hopeless ruin of that brother, I might, perhaps, wish this; but I know that hell has no such control over my heart as to be able to kindle within it a desire like this. I seek his real happiness, through the accomplishment of that which is still dearer to me—the welfare of the blood-bought Church of God. Let the matter therefore be impartially considered and decided; nor let sympathy, on either hand, blind the mind to the demands of duty. The Spirit of God has said, that "*charity rejoices not in iniquity*;" and immediately thereafter adds, that "she rejoices *in the truth*:" that is, in equity and righteous dealing, for this is the antithesis of the word *iniquity*, as here employed. I ask nothing but what is right, and what the suffering interests of religion demand: BUT THIS I DO ASK AND INSIST UPON. In the mean time, however, let Mr. Barnes have the full benefit of whatever abatements ought to be made on account of the writer's human infirmity (for, if rightly understood, these words of Publius Syrus contain a deep truth, "*ad tristem partem strenua est suspicio*"); the deceitfulness of the human heart; unconscious latent prejudice or passion; or anything else which may justly be attributed to human nature when suffering the most appalling wrongs and injuries at the hands of a professed brother and friend. Mr. Barnes and I, and the reader likewise, will soon be beyond the possibility of rectifying the wrongs we may here have done, and the errors into which we may have fallen.

THE END.

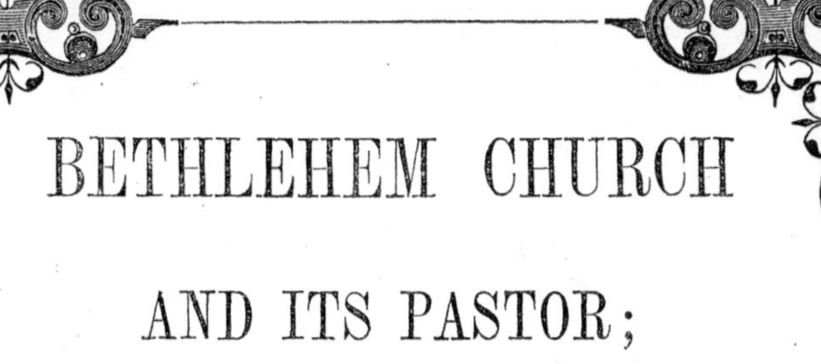

BETHLEHEM CHURCH

AND ITS PASTOR;

OR, A NARRATIVE OF THE

INJURIOUS PROCEEDINGS

OF THE

REV. MESSRS. ALBERT BARNES AND H. W. HUNT, Senr.,

IN RELATION TO THE PASTOR OF THE

PRESBYTERIAN CHURCH, BETHLEHEM, NEW JERSEY.

BY ROBERT W. LANDIS.

Hath God forgotten to be gracious? Hath he in anger shut up his tender mercies? And I said this in my infirmity: but I will remember the years of the right hand of the most High.—*Psalm* lxxvii. 9, 10.

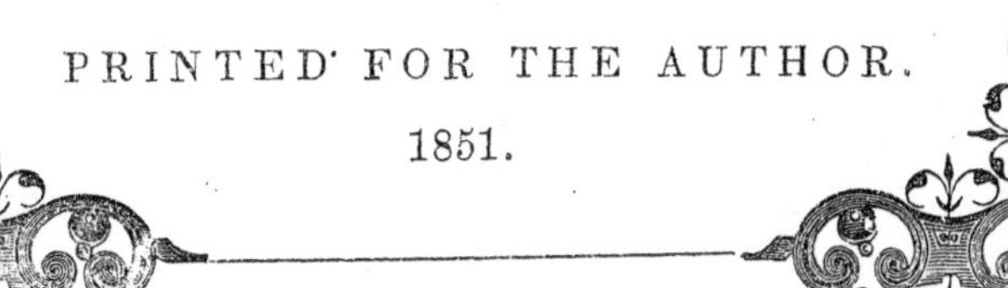

PRINTED FOR THE AUTHOR.

1851.

www.ingramcontent.com/pod-product-compliance
Lightning Source LLC
LaVergne TN
LVHW011202110826
845150LV00006B/1294

* 9 7 8 1 4 2 5 5 1 8 9 5 0 *